Microsoft Blazor

Building Web Applications in .NET 6 and Beyond

Third Edition

Peter Himschoot

Apress®

Microsoft Blazor: Building Web Applications in .NET 6 and Beyond

Peter Himschoot
Melle, Belgium

ISBN-13 (pbk): 978-1-4842-7844-4   ISBN-13 (electronic): 978-1-4842-7845-1
https://doi.org/10.1007/978-1-4842-7845-1

Managing Director, Apress Media LLC: Welmoed Spahr
Acquisitions Editor: Jonathan Gennick
Development Editor: Laura Berendson
Coordinating Editor: Jill Balzano

Cover designed by eStudioCalamar

Cover image designed by Freepik (www.freepik.com)

Distributed to the book trade worldwide by Springer Science+Business Media New York, 1 New York Plaza, Suite 4600, New York, NY 10004-1562, USA. Phone 1-800-SPRINGER, fax (201) 348-4505, e-mail orders-ny@springer-sbm.com, or visit www.springeronline.com. Apress Media, LLC is a California LLC and the sole member (owner) is Springer Science + Business Media Finance Inc (SSBM Finance Inc). SSBM Finance Inc is a **Delaware** corporation.

For information on translations, please e-mail booktranslations@springernature.com; for reprint, paperback, or audio rights, please e-mail bookpermissions@springernature.com.

Apress titles may be purchased in bulk for academic, corporate, or promotional use. eBook versions and licenses are also available for most titles. For more information, reference our Print and eBook Bulk Sales web page at http://www.apress.com/bulk-sales.

Any source code or other supplementary material referenced by the author in this book is available to readers on GitHub via the book's product page, located at www.apress.com/978-1-4842-7844-4. For more detailed information, please visit http://www.apress.com/source-code.

Printed on acid-free paper

Table of Contents

About the Author xvii

About the Technical Reviewer xix

Acknowledgments xxi

Introduction xxiii

Chapter 1: Introduction to WebAssembly and Blazor 1

A Tale of Two Wars 1

The First Browser War 2

The Second Browser War 3

Introducing WebAssembly 4

Which Browsers Support WebAssembly? 6

WebAssembly and Mono 7

Interacting with the Browser with Blazor 8

How Does It Work? 8

Blazor Server 10

Pros and Cons of the Blazor Server 11

Your First Blazor Project 12

Installing Blazor Prerequisites 13

Using Visual Studio 13

Using Visual Studio Code 15

Understanding the Blazor Templates for VS/Code 16

Generating the Project with Dotnet CLI 17

Generating Your Project with Visual Studio 18

Running Blazor with Visual Studio Code 20

Running the Generated Project 20

Examining the Project's Parts 23

The Server Project 24

Using a Shared Project 27

Understanding the Client Blazor Project 28

Layout Components 30

Debugging Client-Side Blazor 31

Debugging with Visual Studio 32

Debugging with Visual Studio Code 34

Developing with Hot Reload 36

Hot Reload with .NET CLI 36

Hot Reload with Visual Studio 37

The Blazor WASM Bootstrap Process 37

The Blazor Server Bootstrap Process 41

Nullable Reference Types 43

An Apology 43

Using Null in C# 43

Using References 46

The Null-Forgiving Operator 47

Nullable Reference Types and .NET Libraries 49

Summary 49

Chapter 2: Data Binding 51

A Quick Look at Razor 51

One-Way Data Binding 53

One-Way Data Binding Syntax 53

Attribute Binding 55

Conditional Attributes 56

Event Handling and Data Binding 57

Event Binding Syntax 57

Event Arguments 57

Using C# Lambda Functions 58

Two-Way Data Binding 59

Two-Way Data Binding Syntax...59

Binding to Other Events: @bind:{event}..61

Preventing Default Actions 62

Stopping Event Propagation 63

Formatting Dates...66

Change Detection...66

The PizzaPlace Single-Page Application 69

Creating the PizzaPlace Project..69

Adding Shared Classes to Represent the Data 70

Building the UI to Show the Menu 75

Converting Values..78

Adding Pizzas to the Shopping Basket..79

Displaying the Shopping Basket..81

Entering the Customer Information 86

Debugging Tip..88

Blazor Validation 90

Letting Entities Validate Themselves 90

Using FormField and InputText to Enable Validation...91

Showing Validation Errors 92

Customizing the Validation Feedback..95

Summary..97

Chapter 3: Components and Structure for Blazor Applications.....................99

What Is a Blazor Component?...99

Examining the SurveyPrompt Component...100

Building a Simple Alert Component with Razor..101

Separating View and View Model...105

Creating a DismissibleAlert Component...105

Understanding Parent-Child Communication...107

Adding a Timer Component 107

Using Two-Way Data Binding Between Components..110

Using EventCallback<T> 114

Referring to a Child Component 117

Communicating with Cascading Parameters 119

    Using the CascadingValue Component 120

    Resolving Ambiguities 122

Component Life Cycle Hooks 123

    Life Cycle Overview 123

    SetParametersAsync 128

    OnInitialized and OnInitializedAsync 129

    OnParametersSet and OnParametersSetAsync 130

    ShouldRender 131

    OnAfterRender and OnAfterRenderAsync 132

    IDisposable 133

    A Word on Asynchronous Methods 133

Refactoring PizzaPlace into Components 134

    Creating a Component to Display a List of Pizzas 134

    Showing the ShoppingBasket Component 138

    Adding the CustomerEntry Component 142

    Using Cascading Properties 145

    Disabling the Submit Button 148

Summary 151

Chapter 4: Advanced Components 153

Using Templated Components 153

    Creating the Grid Templated Component 153

    Using the Grid Templated Component 155

    Specifying the Type Parameter's Type Explicitly 159

    Using Generic Type Constraints 159

Razor Templates 160

    Wig-Pig Syntax 162

Using Blazor Error Boundaries 165

Building a Component Library 168

Creating the Component Library Project 168

Adding Components to the Library 169

Referring to the Library from Your Project 170

Using the Library Components 170

Static Resources in a Component Library 172

Virtualization 173

Displaying a Large Number of Rows 173

Using the Virtualize Component 177

Adding Paging 178

Dynamic Components 182

Component Reuse and PizzaPlace 191

Summary 194

Chapter 5: Services and Dependency Injection 197

What Is Dependency Inversion? 197

Understanding Dependency Inversion 198

Using the Dependency Inversion Principle 199

Adding Dependency Injection 201

Using an Inversion-of-Control Container 202

Constructor Dependency Injection 202

Property Dependency Injection 203

Configuring Dependency Injection 204

Singleton Dependencies 206

Transient Dependencies 207

Scoped Dependencies 208

Understanding Blazor Dependency Lifetime 209

Blazor WebAssembly Experiment 211

Blazor Server Experiment 213

Using OwningComponentBase 215

The Result of the Experiment 217

Building Pizza Services.. 218

Adding the MenuService and IMenuService Abstraction................................. 219

Ordering Pizzas with a Service.. 223

Summary... 225

Chapter 6: Data Storage and Microservices 227

What Is REST?.. 227

Understanding HTTP 227

Universal Resource Identifiers and Methods... 228

HTTP Status Codes 229

Invoking Server Functionality Using REST 229

HTTP Headers 230

JavaScript Object Notation 230

Some Examples of REST Calls.. 231

Building a Simple Microservice Using ASP.NET Core 233

Services and Single Responsibility... 233

The Pizza Service 234

What Is Entity Framework Core?... 238

Using the Code-First Approach.. 239

Preparing Your Project for Code-First Migrations 242

Finding Your Database Server's Connection String 244

Creating Your First Code-First Migration 246

Generating the Database 250

Enhancing the Pizza Microservice 253

Testing Your Microservice Using Postman... 256

Summary... 260

Chapter 7: Communication with Microservices 261

Using the HttpClient Class... 261

Examining the Server Project... 261

Using a Shared Project. Why? 263

Looking at the Client Project 264

Emulating a Slow Network in Chrome.. 266

Understanding the HttpClient Class 269

    The HttpClientJsonExtensions Methods 270

    Customizing Serialization with JsonSerializerOptions 273

Retrieving Data from the Server 273

    Implementing the MenuService 275

    Showing a Loading UI 278

Storing Changes 280

    Updating the Database with Orders 280

    Building the Order Microservice 284

    Talking to the Order Microservice 286

Summary 288

Chapter 8: Unit Testing 289

Where Can We Find Bugs? 289

    Requirements 290

    Coding 290

    Integration 291

    Beta Testing 291

    Post-release 292

Why Should We Use Unit Tests? 292

    What Makes a Good Unit Test? 292

Unit Testing Blazor Components 293

    Adding a Unit Test Project 293

    Adding bUnit to the Test Project 294

Write Your First Unit Test 295

    Writing Good Unit Test Methods 295

    Running Your Tests 296

    Making Your Test Pass 299

    Using Facts and Theories 300

    Checking Your Sanity 301

Write a bUnit Tests with C# 303

    Understanding bUnit? 303

    Testing Component Interaction 308

    Passing Parameters to Our Component 311

    Testing Two-Way Data Binding and Events 315

    Testing Components that Use RenderFragment 317

    Using Cascading Parameters 325

Using MOQ to Create Fake Implementations 327

    Injecting Dependencies with bUnit 328

    Replacing Dependencies with Fake Objects 330

    Using Stubs 331

    Using Mocks 333

    Implementing Stubs and Mocks with MOQ 336

Writing bUnit Tests in Razor 339

    The First Razor Test 339

Handling Asynchronous Re-renders 343

Configuring Semantic Comparison 345

    Why Do We Need Semantic Comparison? 346

    Customizing Semantic Comparison 346

Summary 349

Chapter 9: Single-Page Applications and Routing 351

What Is a Single-Page Application? 351

    Single-Page Applications 352

Layout Components 352

    Using Blazor Layout Components 352

    Configuring the Default Layout Component 355

    Selecting a Layout Component 357

    Nesting Layouts 359

Blazor Routing 360

    Installing the Router 360

    The NavMenu Component 361

Setting the Route Template 364

Redirecting to Other Pages... 366

Understanding the Base Tag 368

Lazy Loading with Routing... 369

Lazy Loading Component Libraries 369

Marking an Assembly for Lazy Loading... 371

Dynamically Loading an Assembly 372

Lazy Loading and Dependencies 374

Adding Another Page to PizzaPlace 377

Summary.. 386

Chapter 10: JavaScript Interoperability 389

Calling JavaScript from C#... 389

Providing a Glue Function... 389

Using IJSRuntime to Call the Glue Function 390

Storing Data in the Browser with Interop 390

Passing a Reference to JavaScript... 393

Calling .NET Methods from JavaScript... 395

Adding a Glue Function Taking a .NET Instance 396

Using Services for Interop.. 398

Building the LocalStorage Service 398

Dynamically Loading JavaScript with Modules.............................. 403

Using JavaScript Modules 403

Loading the Module into a Blazor Service...................................... 404

Adding a Map to PizzaPlace... 406

Choosing the Map JavaScript Library... 406

Adding the Leaflet Library 407

Building the Leaflet Map Razor Library 408

Registering with the Map Provider 409

Creating the Map Component.. 409

Consuming the Map Component 411

Adding Markers to the Map 413

Summary.. 419

Chapter 11: Blazor State Management 421

Examining Component State.. 421

What Not to Store 422

Local Storage.. 422

The Server 426

URL 432

Using Protected Browser Storage 433

The Redux Pattern... 434

The Big Picture 434

The Application Store 435

Actions.. 435

Reducers 436

Views 436

Using Fluxor 436

Creating the Store 437

Using the Store in Our Blazor Application.. 438

Adding an Action.. 441

Implementing the Reducer 441

Redux Effects 443

Adding the First Action 444

Adding the Second Action and Effect 446

Summary.. 448

Chapter 12: Building Real-Time Applications with Blazor and SignalR............... 449

What Is SignalR?.. 449

How Does SignalR Work? 449

Building a WhiteBoard Application 450

Creating the WhiteBoard Solution.. 450

Implementing the Mouse Handling Logic 453

Painting the Segments on the Board.. 455

Adding a SignalR Hub on the Server.. 458

Implementing the BoardHub Class 458

Configuring the Server 459

Implementing the SignalR Client.. 461

Making the SignalR Hub Connection 461

Notifying the Hub from the Client.. 462

Cleaning Up the Hub Connection 463

Summary... 464

Chapter 13: Efficient Communication with gRPC 465

What Is gRPC?... 465

Pros and Cons of RPC.. 465

Understanding gRPC.. 466

Protocol Buffers... 466

Describing Your Network Interchange with Proto Files.. 467

Installing the gRPC Tooling 467

Adding the Service Contract... 469

Implementing gRPC on the Server 471

Implementing the Service 472

Adding gRPC 473

Building a gRPC Client in Blazor 475

Creating the ForecastGrpcService... 475

Enabling gRPC on the Client 477

Updating the FetchData Component.. 478

Comparing REST with gRPC.. 479

Summary... 482

Chapter 14: Supporting Multiple Languages in Your Blazor Application.............. 483

Understanding Internationalization, Globalization, and Localization........................ 483

Representing the User's Locale 484

CurrentCulture vs. CurrentUICulture... 486

Enabling Multiple Languages... 486

Using Request Localization 486

Internationalizing Your App 492

Localizing Your App 494

    Adding Your First Resource File 494

    Localizing SurveyPrompt 496

    Understanding Resource Lookup 498

Adding a Language Picker in Blazor Server 499

Making PizzaPlace International 506

    Enabling Globalization Data 506

    Globalizing Your Components 507

    Adding a Language Picker in Blazor WebAssembly 512

Using Global Resources 518

Summary 519

Chapter 15: Deploying Your Blazor Application 521

Deploying Standalone Blazor WebAssembly 521

    Hosting on GitHub 521

    Creating a Simple Website 523

    Deploying a Simple Site in GitHub 524

    Deploying a Blazor WASM Project 525

    Fix the Base Tag 531

    Disabling Jekyll 533

    Fixing GitHub 404s 534

    Alternatives for GitHub 535

Deploying Your Site As WebAssembly 535

Deploying Hosted Applications 536

    Understanding the Deployment Models 536

    Deploying to Microsoft Azure 537

    Creating the Publishing Profile 537

    Selecting Publishing Options 543

    Publishing the Application 545

Summary 546

Chapter 16: Security with OpenId Connect...**547**

Representing the User 547

Using Claims-Based Security 547

Understanding Token Serialization 549

Representing Claims in .NET 550

OpenId Connect...551

Understanding OpenId Connect Hybrid Flow 551

Identity Providers 553

Implementing the Identity Provider with IdentityServer4....................553

Adding the Login UI to Our Identity Provider.......................................558

Understanding User Consent 561

Protecting a Blazor Server Application with Hybrid Flow............................562

Adding OpenId Connect to Blazor Server...563

Implementing Authorization in Blazor Server 564

Using AuthorizeView...572

Adding and Removing Claims..577

Enabling Role-Based Security 580

Accessing a Secured API...583

Using an Access Token 584

Registering the API Project with the Identity Provider.........................587

Adding JWT Bearer Token Middleware...589

Enabling the Bearer Token in the Client..591

Using Policy-Based Access Control 595

Summary..603

Chapter 17: Securing Blazor WebAssembly **605**

Authorization Code Flow with PKCE...605

Understanding PKCE..606

Registering the WASM Client Application..607

Creating and Examining the Application..607

Registering the Client Application 610

Implementing Authentication 611

Customizing the Login Experience 614

Accessing a Protected API 615

Fetching Data from the WeatherService API.. 615

Using the AuthorizationMessageHandler.. 618

Adding Client-Side Authorization... 620

Using Role-Based Security.. 621

Creating the Claims Component.. 621

Enabling RBAC... 624

Promoting the Role Claim.. 626

Using Policy-Based Access Control... 628

Updating Scopes... 628

Adding Policies 629

Summary... 631

Index... 633

About the Author

Peter Himschoot works as a lead trainer, architect, and strategist at U2U. He has a wide interest in software development that includes applications for the Web, Windows, and mobile devices. He has trained thousands of developers, is a regular speaker at international conferences, and has been involved in many web and mobile development projects as a software architect. He has been a Microsoft Regional Director (from 2003 to 2019) and co-founded the Belgian Visual Studio User Group (VISUG) in 2006, which is a group of trusted advisors to developer and IT professional audiences and to Microsoft.

About the Technical Reviewer

Gerald Versluis (@jfversluis) is a software engineer at Microsoft from the Netherlands. With years of experience working with Azure, ASP.NET, Xamarin (now .NET MAUI), and other .NET technologies, he has been involved in numerous projects and has been building several real-world apps and solutions.

Not only does he like to code, but he is also passionate about spreading his knowledge – as well as gaining some in the bargain. Gerald involves himself in speaking, providing training sessions, writing blogs or articles, recording videos for his YouTube channel, and contributing to open source projects in his spare time.

Twitter: @jfversluis

Website: https://jfversluis.dev

Acknowledgments

When Jonathan Gennick from Apress asked me if I would be interested in writing a book on Blazor, I felt honored and of course I agreed that Blazor deserves a book. Writing a book is a group effort, so I thank Jonathan Gennick and Jill Balzano for giving me tips on styling and writing this book, and I thank Gerald Versluis for doing the technical review and pointing out sections that needed a bit more explaining. I also thank Magda Thielman and Lieven Iliano from U2U, my employer, for encouraging me to write this book.

I thoroughly enjoyed writing this book, and I hope you will enjoy reading and learning from it.

Second Edition

As the first edition of *Blazor Revealed* was published (using pre-release software), the Blazor team had made a bunch of changes to the razor syntax, stopping my examples in the first edition of *Blazor Revealed* from working. Now that Blazor has been released and is completely official (YEAH!!!!), the time has come to publish an updated version of *Blazor Revealed*, now renamed as *Microsoft Blazor*.

Should you get stuck with an example, I invite you to consult the accompanying code samples for comparison purposes.

Third Edition

I wrote the third edition of *Microsoft Blazor* using the previews of .NET 6 to get this book in your hands right after the official release of .NET 6. This of course means that the last-minute changes made in October 2021 could not make it to this book. However, I have set up a repository in GitHub where you can find last-minute additions and errata at `https://github.com/PeterHimschoot/microsoft-blazor-book-3`, including every sample and exercise using the latest version of .NET.

Introduction

Full Stack Web Development with C#

Building modern Single-Page Application websites today typically means writing JavaScript on the client and C# on the server when you are using the Microsoft development stack. But with Blazor, you can build everything using C# and reuse the knowledge and experience you gained with .NET. Porting existing C# applications like WinForms to the Web does not involve translating some of your logic to JavaScript; you can again reuse most of this code, resulting in less testing and bugs.

Is This Book for You?

This book assumes you know C#, and you have some experience writing applications with it. Since this is also about web development, basic knowledge about HTML, CSS, and JavaScript is also required. Completing this book will allow you to build professional applications with Blazor, including mastery of some harder topics like authentication. You will see learning Blazor is fun!

Practical Development

I wrote this book with practice in mind, so sit down next to your computer and follow along with the examples; the best way to learn is to just do things with Blazor. I did my best to make the code samples easy to read, but this means breaking lines of code to fit nicely on the page. When in doubt, you can always consult the included code, which you can download from the book's product page, located at `www.apress.com/{{ISBN}}`. You can find last-minute additions and errata at `https://github.com/PeterHimschoot/ microsoft-blazor-book-3`, including every sample and exercise using the latest version of .NET.

CHAPTER 1

Introduction to WebAssembly and Blazor

I was attending the Microsoft Most Valued Professional and Regional Directors summit 2018 where we were introduced to Blazor for the first time by Steve Sanderson and Daniel Roth. And I must admit I was super excited about Blazor! Blazor is a framework that allows you to build Single-Page Applications (SPAs) using C# and allows you to run any standard .NET library in the browser. Before Blazor, your options for building a SPA were Angular, React, Vue.js (and others) using JavaScript, or one of the other higher-level languages like TypeScript (which gets compiled into JavaScript anyway). In this introduction, we will look at how browsers are now capable of running .NET assemblies in the browser using WebAssembly and Blazor.

A Tale of Two Wars

Think about it. The browser is one of the primary applications on your computer. You use it every day. Companies that build browsers know that very well and are bidding for you to use their browser. At the beginning of mainstream Internet, everyone was using Netscape, and Microsoft wanted a share of the market, so in 1995, they built Internet Explorer 1.0, released as part of Windows 95 Plus! pack.

© Peter Himschoot 2022
P. Himschoot, *Microsoft Blazor*, https://doi.org/10.1007/978-1-4842-7845-1_1

The First Browser War

Newer versions were released rapidly, and browsers started to add new features such as `<blink>` and `<marquee>` elements. This was the beginning of the first browser war, giving people (especially designers) headaches because some developers were building pages with blinking marquee controls ☺. But developers were also getting sore heads because of incompatibilities between browsers. The first browser war was about having more HTML capabilities than the competition.

But all of this is now behind us with the introduction of HTML5 and modern browsers like Google Chrome, Microsoft Edge, Firefox, Safari, and Opera. HTML5 not only defines a series of standard HTML elements but also rules on how these should render, making it a lot easier to build a website that looks the same in all modern browsers. Then, in 1995, Brendan Eich wrote a little programming language known as *ECMAScript* (initially called LiveScript) in ten days (What!?). It was quickly dubbed JavaScript because its syntax was very similar to Java. I will be using the name JavaScript here because that is what most people call it.

JavaScript and Java are not related. Java and JavaScript have as much in common as ham and hamster (I don't know who formulated this first, but I love this phrasing).

Little did Mr. Eich know how this language would impact the modern Web and even desktop application development. In 1995, Jesse James Garrett wrote a white paper called Ajax (Asynchronous JavaScript and XML), describing a set of technologies where JavaScript is used to load data from the server and that data is used to update the browser's HTML. This avoids full page reloads and allows for client-side web applications, which are applications written in JavaScript that run completely in the browser. One of the first companies to apply Ajax was Microsoft when they built Outlook Web Access (OWA). OWA is a web application almost identical to the Outlook desktop application proving the power of Ajax. Soon other Ajax applications started to appear, with Google Maps stuck in my memory as one of the other keystone applications. Google Maps would download maps asynchronously and with some simple mouse interactions allowed you to zoom and pan the map. Before Google Maps, the server would do the map rendering and a browser displayed the map like any other image by downloading a bitmap from a server.

Building an Ajax website was a major undertaking that only big companies like Microsoft and Google could afford. This soon changed with the introduction of JavaScript libraries like jQuery and knockout.js (knockout was also written by Steve Sanderson, the author of Blazor!). Today, we build rich web apps with Angular, React, and Vue.js. All of them are using JavaScript or higher-level languages like TypeScript which gets transpiled into JavaScript.

Transpiling will take one language and convert it into another language. This is very popular with TypeScript which gives you a modern high-level typed language. You need JavaScript to run it in a browser, so TypeScript gets "transpiled" into JavaScript.

The Second Browser War

This brings us back to JavaScript and the second browser war. JavaScript performance is paramount in modern browsers. Chrome, Edge, Firefox, Safari, and Opera are all competing with one another, trying to convince users that their browser is the fastest with cool-sounding names for their JavaScript engine like V8 and Chakra. These engines use the latest optimization tricks like Just-In-Time (JIT) compilation where JavaScript gets converted into native code as illustrated in Figure 1-1.

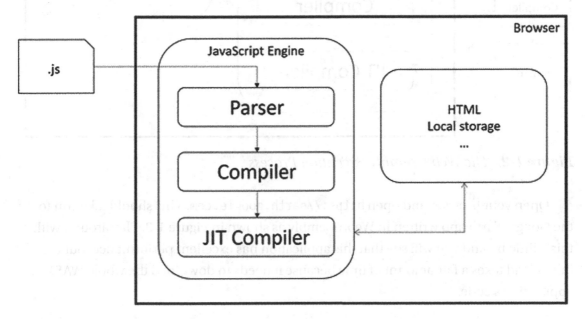

Figure 1-1. *The JavaScript Execution Process*

This process takes a lot of effort because JavaScript needs to be downloaded into the browser, where it gets parsed, then compiled into bytecode, and then Just-In-Time converted into native code. So how can we make this process even faster?

The second browser war is all about JavaScript performance.

Introducing WebAssembly

WebAssembly allows you to take the parsing and compiling to the server, before your users even open up their browser. With WebAssembly, you compile your code in a format called *WASM* (an abbreviation of WebASseMbly), which gets downloaded by the browser where it gets Just-In-Time compiled into native code as in Figure 1-2.

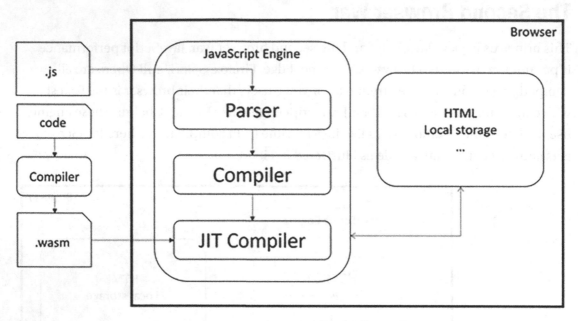

Figure 1-2. *The WebAssembly Execution Process*

Open your browser and open `https://earth.google.com`. This should take you to the Google Earth app written in WebAssembly as shown in Figure 1-3. Play around with this a little bit and you will see that this application has excellent performance, but the initial load takes a fair amount of time because it needs to download the whole WASM application's code.

Figure 1-3. *Google Earth in WebAssembly*

What is WebAssembly? From the official site webassembly.org:

WebAssembly (abbreviated Wasm) is a binary instruction format for a stack-based virtual machine. Wasm is designed as a portable target for compilation of high-level languages like C/C++/Rust, enabling deployment on the web for client and server applications.

So WebAssembly as a new binary format optimized for browser execution, it is NOT JavaScript. It uses a stack-based virtual machine, just like .NET does. There are compilers for languages like C++ and Rust which compile to WASM. Some people have compiled C++ applications to WASM, allowing to run them in the browser. There is even a Windows 2000 operating system (`https://bellard.org/jslinux/vm.html?url=https://bellard.org/jslinux/win2k.cfg&mem=192&graphic=1&w=1024&h=768`) compiled to WASM so you can play minesweeper as shown in Figure 1-4!

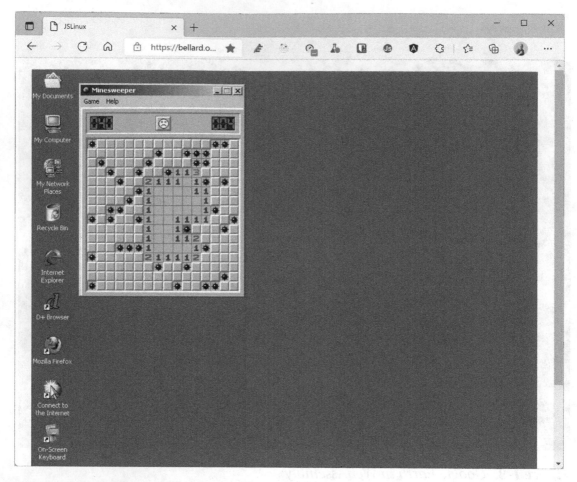

Figure 1-4. *Windows 2000 Running in the Browser*

Which Browsers Support WebAssembly?

WebAssembly is supported by all major browsers: Chrome, Edge, Safari, Opera, and Firefox, including their mobile versions. You can verify support yourself by visiting `https://caniuse.com/?search=WASM` as shown in Figure 1-5.

Edge	Firefox	Chrome	Safari	Opera
		90	13.1	
91	89	91	14	
92	90	92	14.1	77
	91	93	15	
	92	94	TP	
		95		

Figure 1-5. *WebAssembly Support*

As WebAssembly will become more and more important, we will see other browsers follow suit, but don't expect Internet Explorer to support WASM.

WebAssembly and Mono

Mono is an open source implementation of the .NET CLI specification, meaning that Mono is a platform for running .NET assemblies. Mono is used in Xamarin (now called Multi-platform App UI, or MAUI for short) for building mobile applications that run on the Windows, Android, and iOS mobile operating systems. You can also use it to build applications for macOS, Linux, Tizen, and others. Mono also allows you to run .NET on Linux (its original purpose) and is written in C++. This last part is important because we saw that you can compile C++ to WebAssembly. So, what happened is that the Mono team decided to try to compile Mono to WebAssembly, which they did successfully. There are two approaches. One is where you take your .NET code and you compile it together with the Mono runtime into one big WASM application. However, this approach takes a lot of time because you need to take several steps to compile everything into WASM, not so practical for day-to-day development. The other approach takes the Mono runtime and compiles it into WASM, and this runs in the browser where it will execute .NET Intermediate Language just like normal .NET does. The big advantage is that you can simply run .NET assemblies without having to compile them first into WASM.

This is the approach currently taken by Blazor. In the beginning, Blazor used the Mono runtime, but they have now built their own .NET Core runtime for WebAssembly. But Blazor is not the only one taking this approach. For example, there is the Ooui project which allows you to run Xamarin.Forms applications in the browser. The disadvantage of this is that it needs to download a lot of .NET assemblies. This can be solved by using tree shaking algorithms which remove all unused code from assemblies. We will look at this in Chapter 15.

Interacting with the Browser with Blazor

WebAssembly with the .NET runtime allows you to run .NET code in the browser. Steve Sanderson used this to build Blazor. Blazor uses the popular ASP.NET MVC approach for building applications that run in the browser. MVC uses the razor syntax to generate HTML on the server. With Blazor, you build razor files (Blazor = Browser + Razor) which execute inside to browser to dynamically build a web page. With Blazor, you don't need JavaScript to build a web app, which is good news for thousands of .NET developers who want to continue using C# (or F#). To use some browser features, you will still need JavaScript, and we will discuss this in Chapter 10.

How Does It Work?

Let's start with a simple razor file in Listing 1-1 which you can find when you create a new Blazor project (which we will do further on in this chapter, no need to type anything yet).

Note   Each code sample has been formatted for readability, sometimes splitting lines where this is not necessary and using less indentation. I leave it to you how you decide to format your code.

Listing 1-1. The Counter Razor File

```
@page "/counter"

<h1>Counter</h1>

<p role="status">Current count: @currentCount</p>

<button class="btn btn-primary"
        @onclick="IncrementCount">
  Click me
</button>

@code {
  private int currentCount = 0;

  private void IncrementCount()
  {
    currentCount++;
  }
}
```

This file gets compiled into a .NET class (you'll find out how later in this book) which is then executed by the Blazor engine. The result of this execution is a tree-like structure called the *render tree*. The render tree is then sent to JavaScript which updates the DOM to reflect the render tree (creating, updating, and removing HTML elements and attributes). Listing 1-1 will result in h1, p (with the contents set to the value of currentCount), and button HTML elements. When you interact with the page, for example, when you click the button, this will trigger the button's click event which will invoke the IncrementCount method from Listing 1-1. The render tree is then regenerated, and any changes are sent again to JavaScript which will update the DOM. This process is illustrated in Figure 1-6.

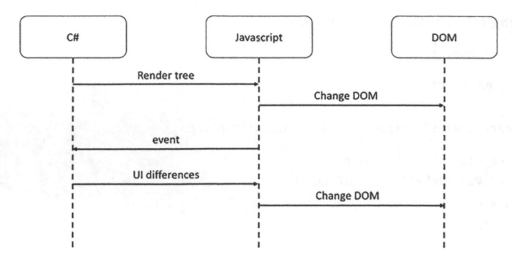

Figure 1-6. *The Blazor WebAssembly DOM Generation Process*

This model is very flexible. It allows you to build Progressive Web Apps, and your app can be embedded in Electron desktop applications of which Visual Studio Code is a prime example.

Blazor Server

At the August 7, 2018, ASP.NET community standup (`www.youtube.com/watch?v=7Eh_ 17jEcCo`), Daniel Roth introduced a new execution model for Blazor now called Blazor Server. In this model, your Blazor site is running on the server resulting in a way smaller download for the browser.

We just saw that Blazor WebAssembly builds a render tree using the .NET runtime running in the browser which then gets sent to JavaScript to update the DOM. With Blazor Server, the render tree is built on the server using regular .NET and then gets serialized to the browser using SignalR (we will look at SignalR in a later chapter). JavaScript in the browser then deserializes the render tree to update the DOM. Pretty similar to the Blazor WebAssembly model. When you interact with the site, events get serialized back to the server which then executes the .NET code, updating the render tree, and the changes get serialized back to the browser. I've illustrated this process in Figure 1-7. The big difference is that there is no need to send the .NET runtime and your Blazor assemblies to the browser. And the programming model stays the same! You can switch Blazor Server-side and Blazor WebAssembly with just a couple of small changes to your code.

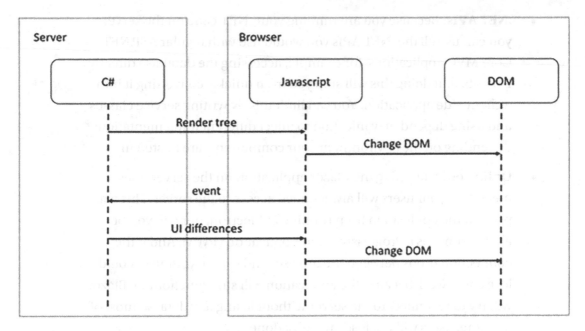

Figure 1-7. *Blazor Server Runtime Model*

Pros and Cons of the Blazor Server

The Blazor Server model has a couple of benefits but also some drawbacks. Let's discuss these here so you can decide which model fits your application's needs.

- **Smaller downloads**: With Blazor Server, your application does not
  need to download dotnet.wasm (the .NET runtime) nor all your .NET
  assemblies. The browser downloads a small JavaScript library which
  sets up the SignalR connection to the server. This means that the
  application will start a lot faster, especially on slower connections,
  but at the price that we continuously need a connection to the server
  to exchange small messages.

- **Development process**: Blazor WebAssembly does not support all
  modern debugging capabilities, resulting in added logging. Because
  your .NET code is running on the server, you can use the regular
  .NET debugger with all of its advanced features. You could start
  building your Blazor application using the server-side model, and
  when it is finished, switch to the client-side model by switching the
  hosting model.

- **.NET APIs**: Because you are running your .NET code on the server, you can use all the .NET APIs you would use with regular ASP.NET Core MVC applications, for example, accessing the database directly. Do note that doing this will stop you from quickly converting it into a client-side application. You can limit this by writing service classes and using dependency injection to inject different implementations depending on the environment your components are hosted in.

- **Online only**: Running the Blazor application on the server does mean that your users will always need access to the server. This will prevent the application from running in Electron, nor will you be able to run it as a Progressive Web Application (PWA). And if the connection drops between the browser and server, your user could lose some work because the application will stop functioning. Blazor will try to reconnect to the server without losing any data, so most of the time, users will not lose any work done.

- **Server scalability**: All your .NET code runs on the server, so if you have thousands of clients, your server(s) will have to handle all the work. Not only that, Blazor uses a stateful model which will require you to keep track of every user's state on the server. So your server will need more resources than with Blazor WebAssembly which can use a stateless model.

Your First Blazor Project

Getting hands-on is the best way to learn. You will first install the prerequisites to developing with Blazor. Then you will create your first Blazor project, run the project to see it work, and finally inspect the different aspects of the project to get a "lay of the land" view for how Blazor applications are developed.

Note   I learned an important lesson from the first edition of this book: never underestimate the speed at which Microsoft innovates! All code samples in the first edition of *Blazor Revealed* became invalid quite rapidly. I do not expect this to happen again with this edition since it is based on the Release To Manufacture (RTM) version of Blazor. If something does not work, simply consult the sources that come with this book. I will keep these up to date. Promise!

The source code for this book is available on GitHub via the book's product page, located at `www.apress.com/ISBN`.

Installing Blazor Prerequisites

Working with Blazor requires you to install some prerequisites, so in this section, you will install what is needed to get going.

Blazor runs on top of *.NET*, optionally providing the web server for your project which will serve the client files that run in the browser and run any server-side APIs that your Blazor project needs. .NET (previously known as .NET Core) is Microsoft's cross-platform solution for working with .NET on Windows, Linux, and OSX.

You can find the installation files at `www.microsoft.com/net/download`. Look for the latest version of the .NET SDK (you'll need at least version 6.0). Follow the installation instructions and install it on your machine, using Windows, OSX, or Linux.

Verify the installation when the installer is done by opening a new command prompt and typing the following command:

```
dotnet --version
```

Output should indicate that you installed the correct version. The version number should be at least 6.0.

Should the command's output show an older version, you will need to download and install a more recent version of .NET SDK. These can run side by side so you will not break other .NET projects doing this.

Using Visual Studio

For people using Windows, *Visual Studio* (from now on, I will refer to Visual Studio as *VS*) is one of the integrated development environments (IDE) we will use throughout this book. If you are using OSX or Linux, you can use Visual Studio Code, and OSX users might prefer Visual Studio for Mac. With any one, you can edit your code, compile it, and run it all from the same application. And the code samples are also the same.

If you want to use Visual Studio, download the latest version of Visual Studio from `www.visualstudio.com/downloads/`. The Community Edition is free and should allow you to do everything done in this book.

Run the installer and make sure that you install the ASP.NET and web development role as shown in Figure 1-8.

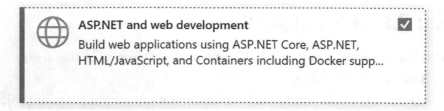

Figure 1-8. *The Visual Studio Installer Workloads Selection*

After installation, run Visual Studio from the Start menu. Then open the Help menu and select About Microsoft Visual Studio. The About Microsoft Visual Studio dialog window should specify at least version 17.0.0 as illustrated in Figure 1-9.

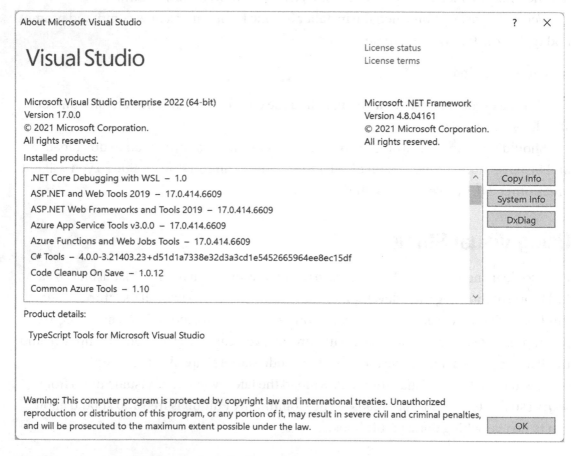

Figure 1-9. *About Microsoft Visual Studio*

Using Visual Studio Code

Visual Studio Code (*VSC*) is a free, modern, cross-platform development environment with an integrated editor, git source control, and debugger. The environment has a huge range of extensions available allowing you to use all kinds of languages and tools directly from VSC. So, if you don't have access to (because you're running a non-Windows operating system or you don't want to use) Visual Studio, use VSC.

Install VSC from www.visualstudio.com/. Install using the defaults.

After installation, you should install a couple of extensions for Code, especially the C# extension. Start Code, and at the left side, select the extensions tab as shown in Figure 1-10.

Figure 1-10. *Visual Studio Code Extensions Tab*

You can search for extensions, so start with C# which is the first extension from Figure 1-11. This extension will give you IntelliSense and debugging for the C# programming language and .NET assemblies. You will probably get a newer version listed, so take the latest.

Click Install.

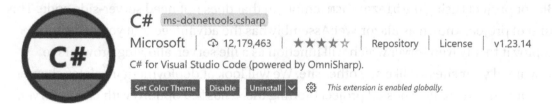

Figure 1-11. *C# for Visual Studio Code*

Understanding the Blazor Templates for VS/Code

Throughout this book, we will create several different Blazor projects. With .NET Core, we can use the *command-line interface* (*CLI*) to create all kinds of projects, including Blazor WebAssembly and Blazor Server.

Let us begin by looking at the installed templates; you can list all installed templates using the following CLI command. You can execute this from a command prompt or from the VSC Terminal.

```
dotnet new --list
```

You will see four columns. The first shows the template's description, the second column displays the name, the third lists the languages for which the template is available, and the last shows the tags, a kind of group name for the template. Among those listed are the following of interest:

```
Template Name                                        Short Name
-------------------------------------------------    -------------------
Blazor Server App                                    blazorserver
Blazor WebAssembly App                               blazorwasm
Class Library                                        classlib
Razor Class Library                                  razorclasslib
Razor Component                                      razorcomponent
xUnit Test Project                                   xunit
```

With Blazor projects, you have a couple of choices. You can create a standalone Blazor project (using the `blazorwasm` template) that does not need server-side code. This kind of project known as Blazor WebAssembly has the advantage that you can simply deploy it to any web server which will function as a file server, allowing browsers to download your site just like any other site. We will look at deployment in a later chapter.

Or you can create a hosted project (adding the `--hosted` option) with client, server, and shared code. This kind of Blazor WebAssembly project will require you to host it where there is .NET Core support because you will execute code on the server as well, for example, to retrieve data from a database.

The third option is to run all Blazor code on the server (using the `blazorserver` template). In this case, the browser will use a SignalR connection to receive UI updates from the server and to send user interaction back to the server for processing.

In this book, we will use the second option (Blazor WebAssembly hosted on ASP.NET MVC Core) most of the time, but the concepts you will learn in this book are the same for all three options. You can even develop for Blazor WebAssembly and Blazor Server at the same time! Why? Because debugging support for Blazor WebAssembly is limited, so you develop with Blazor Server using all debugger features you know and love. But you can test everything with Blazor WebAssembly ensuring you can run everything in the browser later. This is the way I like to work. However, to pull this off, you need some experience with Blazor first, so keep reading.

Generating the Project with Dotnet CLI

To generate the project with dotnet CLI, which works on any machine, start by opening a command line, and change the current directory to wherever you want to create the project. Now execute the following command to create a new Blazor WebAssembly project. The dotnet is the command line, taking the new instruction, with the template being blazorwasm. The --hosted option will generate the server project as well. Finally, we tell it to generate everything in the MyFirstBlazor directory.

```
dotnet new blazorwasm --hosted -o MyFirstBlazor
```

This command will take a little while because it will download a bunch of NuGet packages from the Internet. When the command is ready, you can build your project using

```
cd MyFirstBlazor
dotnet build
```

This should build without any errors.
Now we can run the project from the command line using

```
cd MyFirstBlazor/Server
dotnet run
```

This will show you some output, including the URL of the Blazor application:

```
Building...
info: Microsoft.Hosting.Lifetime[14]
      Now listening on: https://localhost:5001
info: Microsoft.Hosting.Lifetime[14]
```

```
        Now listening on: http://localhost:5000
info: Microsoft.Hosting.Lifetime[0]
        Application started. Press Ctrl+C to shut down.
info: Microsoft.Hosting.Lifetime[0]
        Hosting environment: Development
info: Microsoft.Hosting.Lifetime[0]
        Content root path: C:\Code\GitHub\Microsoft.Blazor.3rd\Ch01\MyFirstBlazor
```

Open your browser on this address (here `https://localhost:5001`), and you are ready to play!

Generating Your Project with Visual Studio

Start Visual Studio and select Create a new project.

Type Blazor in the search box, and select the Blazor WebAssembly App project template as illustrated in Figure 1-12.

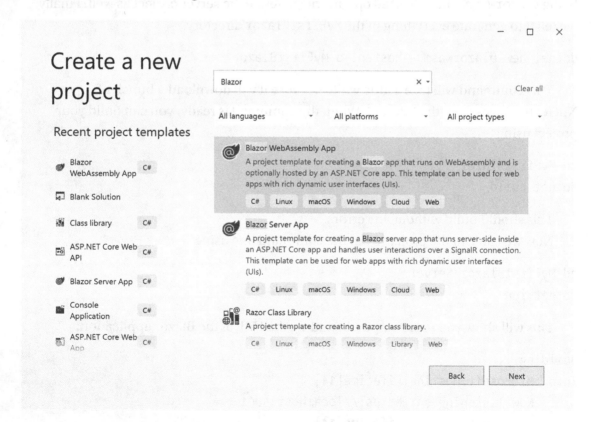

Figure 1-12. *Visual Studio New Project Dialog*

Click Next.

Name your project MyFirstBlazor, choose the location where the project should be generated, and click Next.

On the next screen, you can select the framework to use. Choose the latest version (at the time of writing, that is .NET 6.0), leave Authentication type set to None, check the ASP.NET Core hosted checkbox, and click Create. An example is shown in Figure 1-13.

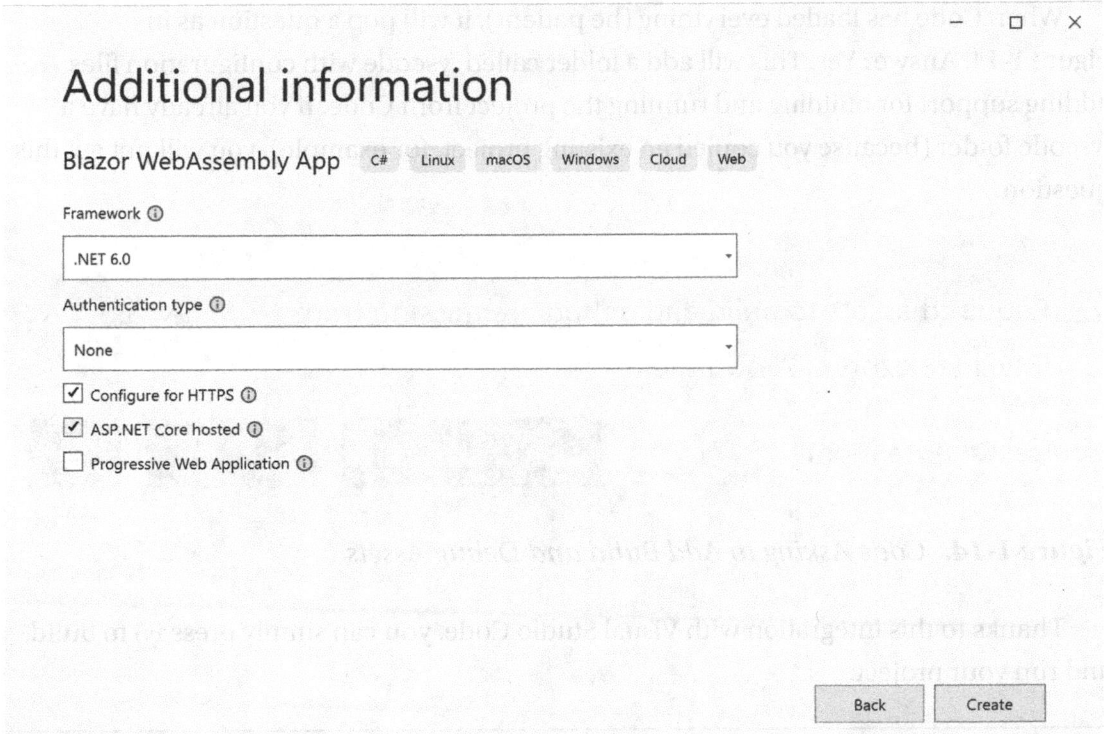

Figure 1-13. *New ASP.NET Core Web Application*

Wait for Visual Studio to complete. Then build and run your solution by pressing F5. After a little while, the browser will open and display the Blazor application.

Running Blazor with Visual Studio Code

After creating the project as we did with the CLI, open your solution's folder (where the MyFirstBlazor.sln file sits) with VSC. You can do this from the command prompt

code .

Or you can open VSC and then select File ➤ Open Folder....

When Code has loaded everything (be patient), it will pop a question as in Figure 1-14. Answer Yes. This will add a folder called .vscode with configuration files adding support for building and running the project from Code. If you already have a .vscode folder (because you copied an existing project, for example), you will not get this question.

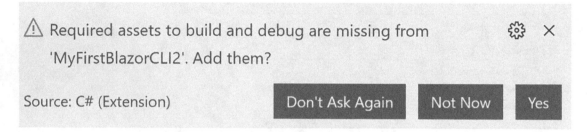

Figure 1-14. *Code Asking to Add Build and Debug Assets*

Thanks to this integration with Visual Studio Code, you can simply press F5 to build and run your project.

Note   VSC now uses Workspace Trust which might pop up a dialog asking if you trust the authors of a project. When opening the provided code download, you will probably encounter this.

Running the Generated Project

Press F5 or Ctrl-F5 (no debugger) to run (this should work for both VS and VSC). Your (default) browser should open and display the home page as shown in Figure 1-15.

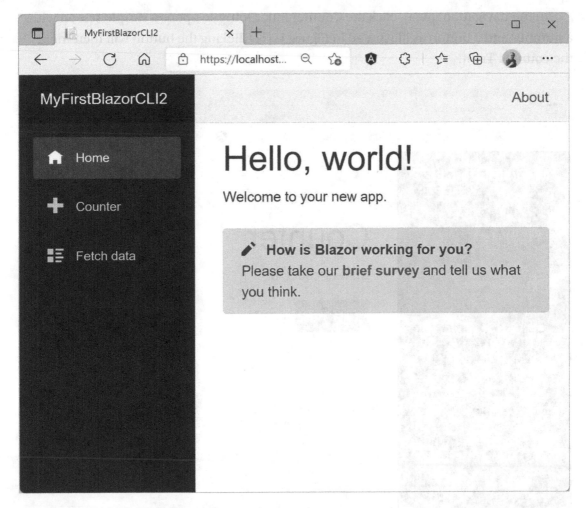

Figure 1-15. *Your First Application – Home Screen*

This generated Single-Page Application (SPA) has on the left side a navigation menu allowing you to jump between different pages. On the right side, you will see the selected component; in Figure 1-15, it is showing the Index component. And in the top right corner, there is an About link to `https://blazor.net/` which is the official Blazor documentation website.

The Index component shows the mandatory "Hello, world!" demo, and it also contains a survey component you can click to fill out a survey (this is a real survey, so please let Microsoft know you like Blazor!). The SurveyPrompt is the first example of a custom Blazor component. We will discuss building components like SurveyPrompt in Chapters 3 and 4.

In the navigation menu, click the Counter link. Doing so opens a simple screen with a number and a button as illustrated in Figure 1-16. Clicking the button will increment the counter. Try it!

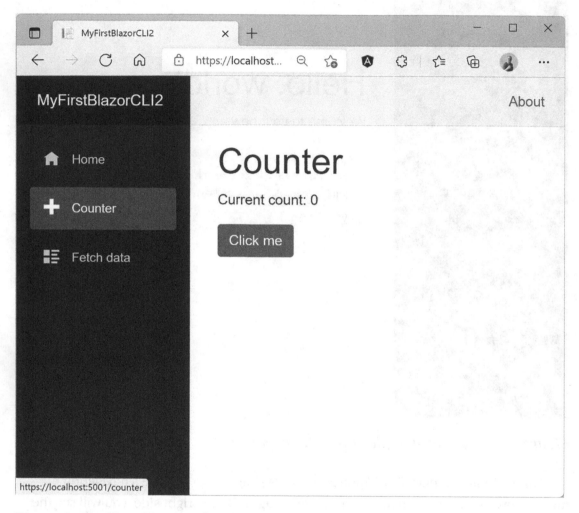

Figure 1-16. *Your First Application – Counter Screen*

In the navigation menu, click the Fetch data link. Here, you can watch a (random and fake) weather forecast as shown in Figure 1-17. This forecast is generated on the server when asked by the client. This is very important because the client (which is running in the browser) cannot access data from a database directly, so many times, you need a server that can access databases and other data storage. Of course, if this was a Blazor Server application, you can access the database directly because you are running on the server.

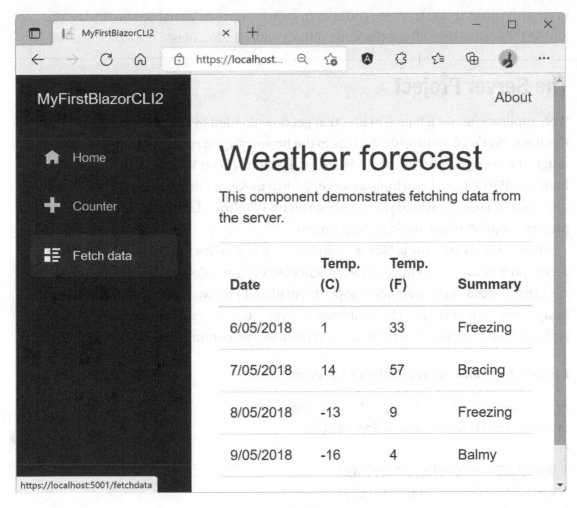

Figure 1-17. *Your First Application – Fetch data Screen*

Examining the Project's Parts

Now being able to play with these pages is all nice, but let us have a look at how all this works. We will look starting with the server project which hosts our Blazor website. Then we will look at the shared project which contains classes used by both server and client. Finally, we will examine the client project which is the actual Blazor implementation.

Visual Studio, Visual Studio Code, and Visual Studio for Mac use solution files to group projects that will form an application. So, a typical Blazor WebAssembly project consists of a server, a client, and a shared project grouped into a single solution. This simplifies building everything since the solution allows tools to figure out in which order to compile everything. Hey, you could even switch between Visual Studio, VS for Mac, and VSC because they all use the same project and solution files!

The Server Project

Web applications are a bunch of files that get downloaded by the browser from a server. It is the server's job to provide the files to the browser upon request. There is a whole range of existing servers to choose from, for example, *IIS* on Windows or *Apache* on Linux. ASP.NET Core has a built-in server known as *Kestrel* that you generated with the `--hosted` option, which you can then run on Windows, Linux, or OSX. This is the preferred option to use during development.

The topic of this book is Blazor, so we're not going to discuss all the details of the server project that got generated (Microsoft has very good documentation on .NET Core at `https://docs.microsoft.com/aspnet/core`), but I do want to show you an important thing. In the server project (MyFirstBlazor.Server), look for Program.cs. Open this file and scroll down to the `Configure` section (look for the comment) shown in Listing 1-2.

Listing 1-2. The Server Project's Program Class

```
// Configure the HTTP request pipeline.
if (app.Environment.IsDevelopment())
{
  app.UseDeveloperExceptionPage();
  app.UseWebAssemblyDebugging();
}
else
{
  app.UseExceptionHandler("/Error");
  app.UseHsts();
}

app.UseHttpsRedirection();

app.UseBlazorFrameworkFiles();
app.UseStaticFiles();

app.UseRouting();
```

```
app.MapRazorPages();
app.MapControllers();
app.MapFallbackToFile("index.html");
```

The `Configure` section is responsible for installing middleware. *Middleware* objects are little .NET components that each have a clear responsibility. When you type in a URL, the browser sends an HTTP request to the server, which then passes it on to the middleware components in the listed order. Some of these will take the request and return a response, and some of them take the response and do something with it. Look at the first lines in Listing 1-3.

Listing 1-3. The UseDeveloperExceptionPage Middleware

```
if (app.Environment.IsDevelopment())
{
  app.UseDeveloperExceptionPage();
  app.UseWebAssemblyDebugging();
}
else
{
  app.UseExceptionHandler("/Error");
  app.UseHsts();
}
```

Would you like to see a detailed error page when the server has an uncaught exception? The `UseDeveloperExceptionPage` method which installs some error handling middleware takes care of that. Of course, you don't need that in production (you should handle all exceptions correctly <grin>), so this middleware is only used when running in a development environment. How does the server know if you are running in development or release? The if statement you see here checks an environment variable called `ASPNETCORE_ENVIRONMENT`, and if the environment variable is set to `Development`, it knows you are running in development mode.

Open the launchSettings.json file in the server project's Properties folder, as shown in Listing 1-4. Look at the MyFirstBlazor.Server profile. One of the settings in the profile sets this environment variable to `Development` which is the proper choice to use while writing your Blazor application.

Listing 1-4. The launchSettings.json File

```json
{
  "iisSettings": {
    "windowsAuthentication": false,
    "anonymousAuthentication": true,
    "iisExpress": {
      "applicationUrl": "http://localhost:39361",
      "sslPort": 44358
    }
  },
  "profiles": {
    "MyFirstBlazor.Server": {
      "commandName": "Project",
      "dotnetRunMessages": true,
      "launchBrowser": true,
      "inspectUri": "{wsProtocol}://{url.hostname}:{url.port}/_framework/
      debug/ws-proxy?browser={browserInspectUri}",
      "applicationUrl": "https://localhost:5001;http://localhost:5000",
      "environmentVariables": {
        "ASPNETCORE_ENVIRONMENT": "Development"
      }
    },
    "IIS Express": {
      "commandName": "IISExpress",
      "launchBrowser": true,
      "inspectUri": "{wsProtocol}://{url.hostname}:{url.port}/_framework/
      debug/ws-proxy?browser={browserInspectUri}",
      "environmentVariables": {
        "ASPNETCORE_ENVIRONMENT": "Development"
      }
    }
  }
}
```

The Blazor bootstrap process requires a bunch of special files, especially dotnet. wasm (dotnet.wasm is the .NET runtime compiled as WebAssembly). This is served by the Blazor middleware, which is installed by the UseBlazorFrameworkFiles instruction. Later in this chapter, you will see why.

Look at the end of Listing 1-2. Here is another important middleware installed. The MapFallbackToFile("index.html") will return the index.html file which takes care of loading everything your Blazor application needs.

Using a Shared Project

The FetchData component downloads weather information from the server. These kinds of requests will be handled by the MVC middleware (MapControllers). We will discuss this in more detail in Chapter 6.

The shape of the forecast data needs to be described in detail (computers are picky things), and in classic projects, you would describe this model's shape twice, once for the client and again for the server because these would use different languages – C# on the server and JavaScript on the client. Not with Blazor! In Blazor, both client and server use C#, so we can describe the model once and share it between client and server as shown in Listing 1-5. As you can see, this is a simple C# class you could easily find in other kinds of projects.

Listing 1-5. The Shared WeatherForecast Class

```
namespace MyFirstBlazor.Shared;
public class WeatherForecast
{
  public DateTime Date { get; set; }

  public int TemperatureC { get; set; }

  public string? Summary { get; set; }

  public int TemperatureF => 32 + (int)(TemperatureC / 0.5556);
}
```

Understanding the Client Blazor Project

Open the client project's wwwroot folder and look for index.html. The contents of that file should appear as shown in Listing 1-6. To be honest, this looks mostly like a normal HTML page. But on closer inspection, you'll see that there is a div tag there with id app. This is where your Blazor application will go.

```
<div id="app">Loading...</div>
```

After this, there is another div; this is used to display errors in case your Blazor application has an uncaught exception.

```
<div id="blazor-error-ui">
  An unhandled error has occurred.
  <a href="" class="reload">Reload</a>
  <a class="dismiss">✖</a>
</div>
```

You will also find an <script> element near the end.

```
<script src="_framework/blazor.webassembly.js"></script>
```

This script will install Blazor by downloading dotnet.wasm. A little further we will look at this in more detail.

Listing 1-6. The index.html File

```
<!DOCTYPE html>
<html>
<head>
  <meta charset="utf-8" />
  <meta name="viewport"
    content="width=device-width, initial-scale=1.0, maximum-scale=1.0,
    user-scalable=no" />
  <title>MyFirstBlazor</title>
  <base href="/" />
  <link href="css/bootstrap/bootstrap.min.css" rel="stylesheet" />
  <link href="css/app.css" rel="stylesheet" />
  <link href="MyFirstBlazor.Client.styles.css" rel="stylesheet" />
</head>
```

```
<body>
  <div id="app">Loading...</div>

  <div id="blazor-error-ui">
    An unhandled error has occurred.
    <a href="" class="reload">Reload</a>
    <a class="dismiss">✗</a>
  </div>
  <script src="_framework/blazor.webassembly.js"></script>
</body>
</html>
```

Open Program.cs from the MyFirstBlazor.Client project as in Listing 1-7. Here, you see that the App component is associated with the app div from index.html. The #app string is a CSS selector which will find that div, and the Blazor runtime will replace it with the App component's render tree.

```
builder.RootComponents.Add<App>("#app");
```

Listing 1-7. The Main Method

```
using Microsoft.AspNetCore.Components.WebAssembly.Hosting;
using MyFirstBlazor.Client;

var builder = WebAssemblyHostBuilder.CreateDefault(args);
builder.RootComponents.Add<App>("#app");

builder.Services.AddScoped(sp => new HttpClient { BaseAddress = new
Uri(builder.HostEnvironment.BaseAddress) });

await builder.Build().RunAsync();
```

The main thing the App component does is to install the Router component as in Listing 1-8. You can find this code in the App.razor file in the client project. The router is responsible for loading a Blazor component depending on the URL in the browser. When the route is not found, it will display the <NotFound> content, which currently shows a simple not found message. For example, if you browse to the "/" URL, the router will look for a component with a matching @page directive.

Listing 1-8. The App Component

```
<Router AppAssembly="@typeof(App).Assembly">
  <Found Context="routeData">
    <RouteView RouteData="@routeData"
               DefaultLayout="@typeof(MainLayout)" />
    <FocusOnNavigate RouteData="@routeData" Selector="h1" />
  </Found>
  <NotFound>
    <LayoutView Layout="@typeof(MainLayout)">
      <p role="alert">Sorry, there's nothing at this address.</p>
    </LayoutView>
  </NotFound>
</Router>
```

In our current MyFirstBlazor project, this will match the Index component which you can find in the Index.razor file from the Pages folder. This component has the matching @page "/" directive so the router will display it for the / URL. This component displays a Hello World message and the survey link as in Listing 1-9.

Listing 1-9. The Index Component

```
@page "/"

<h1>Hello, world!</h1>

Welcome to your new app.

<SurveyPrompt Title="How is Blazor working for you?" />
```

Layout Components

Look at Figures 1-15, 1-16, and 1-17. All have the same menu. This menu is shared among all our Blazor components and is known as a layout component. We will discuss layout components in Chapter 9. But how does Blazor know which component is the layout component? Look again at Listing 1-8. When the route is found, it uses a default layout component called MainLayout. In our project, the layout component can be found in MainLayout.razor from the Shared folder, which I've listed in Listing 1-10.

Listing 1-10. The MainLayout Component

```
@inherits LayoutComponentBase

<div class="page">
  <div class="sidebar">
    <NavMenu />
  </div>
  <main>
    <div class="top-row px-4">
      <a href="http://blazor.net" target="_blank" class="ml-md-auto">
      About</a>
    </div>
    <article class="content px-4">
        @Body
    </article>
  </main>
</div>
```

This component contains a div HTML element with two nested divs. The first nested div with class sidebar contains a single Blazor component: NavMenu. This is where your navigation menu gets defined. The sidebar will display a menu, allowing you to navigate between Home, Counter, and Fetch data. We will look in more detail at navigation and routing in Chapter 9.

The next nested div with class main has two parts. The first is the About link you see on every page. The second part contains the @Body; this is where the selected page will be shown. For example, when you click the Counter link in the navigation menu, the @Body will be replaced with the Counter component.

This is all for now, but the rest of the book will explain each part as we go along.

Debugging Client-Side Blazor

Of course, while building your Blazor app, you will encounter unexpected behavior from time to time. Debugging Blazor Server can be done just like any .NET project using Visual Studio or Code. But with Blazor WebAssembly, your code will be running in the browser. You will be happy to learn that the VS/VSC debugger works with Blazor, although limited. You can put breakpoints in your code, step through your code, and observe variables holding simple types like bool, int, and string. At the time of writing, debugging Blazor WebAssembly only works for Chrome or Edge, both Chromium-based browsers.

Debugging with Visual Studio

To enable debugging with Visual Studio, open the launchSettings.json file from the project you will use as your startup project. With hosted Blazor WebAssembly, this is normally the server project. You will need to set the inspectUri property in here, like in Listing 1-11 (the template normally will configure this for you). This property enables the IDE to detect that this is a Blazor WebAssembly app and instructs the script debugging infrastructure to connect to the browser through the Blazor's debugging proxy.

Listing 1-11. The launchSettings.json File for Debugging (Excerpt)

```
"MyFirstBlazor.Server": {
  "commandName": "Project",
  "dotnetRunMessages": true,
  "launchBrowser": true,
  "inspectUri": "{wsProtocol}://{url.hostname}:{url.port}/_framework/debug/
  ws-proxy?browser={browserInspectUri}",
  "applicationUrl": "https://localhost:5001;http://localhost:5000",
  "environmentVariables": {
    "ASPNETCORE_ENVIRONMENT": "Development"
  }
},
```

Now run your application in VS with the debugger by pressing F5. Be patient while your Blazor site starts to run (in Edge or Chrome!). Now you can put a breakpoint in your code, for example, on the IncrementCount method of the Counter component as in Figure 1-18, line 17. Simply click in the gray area left to your code (also known as the gutter) and a red dot will appear, indicating that the debugger will stop at this code.

```
1    @page "/counter"
2
3    <h1>Counter</h1>
4
5    <p role="status">Current count: @currentCount</p>
6
7    <button class="btn btn-primary"
8            @onclick="IncrementCount">
9      Click me
10   </button>
11
12   @code {
13     private int currentCount = 0;
14
15     private void IncrementCount()
16     {
17       currentCount++;
18     }
19   }
```

Figure 1-18. *Setting a Breakpoint in the IncrementCount Method*

Go back to your Blazor application and click the Counter's Click Me button. The debugger should stop on the IncrementCount method. You can now examine the content of simple variables in the Locals window, like in Figure 1-19.

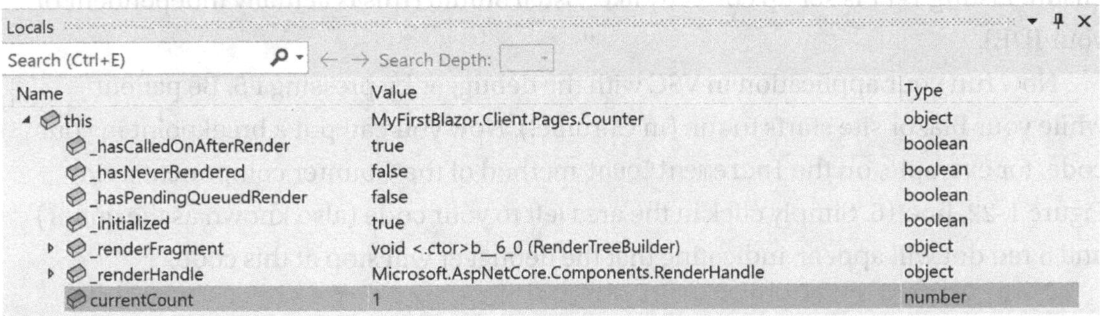

Name	Value	Type
◢ ⬡ this	MyFirstBlazor.Client.Pages.Counter	object
⬡ _hasCalledOnAfterRender	true	boolean
⬡ _hasNeverRendered	false	boolean
⬡ _hasPendingQueuedRender	false	boolean
⬡ _initialized	true	boolean
▷ ⬡ _renderFragment	void <.ctor>b__6_0 (RenderTreeBuilder)	object
▷ ⬡ _renderHandle	Microsoft.AspNetCore.Components.RenderHandle	object
⬡ currentCount	1	number

Locals — Search (Ctrl+E) — Search Depth:

Figure 1-19. *Using the Locals Debugger Window to Inspect Simple Variables*

Debugging with Visual Studio Code

Start VSC. Ensure you have the Microsoft.AspNetCore.Razor.VSCode. BlazorWasmDebuggingExtension debugging extensions installed as in Figure 1-20.

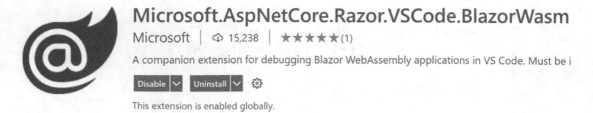

Figure 1-20. *The Blazor WASM Debugging Extension*

You will also have to ensure that the JavaScript Preview Debugger has been enabled (by the time you are reading this, it might no longer be a preview feature). You can find this setting in VSC Settings like in Figure 1-21.

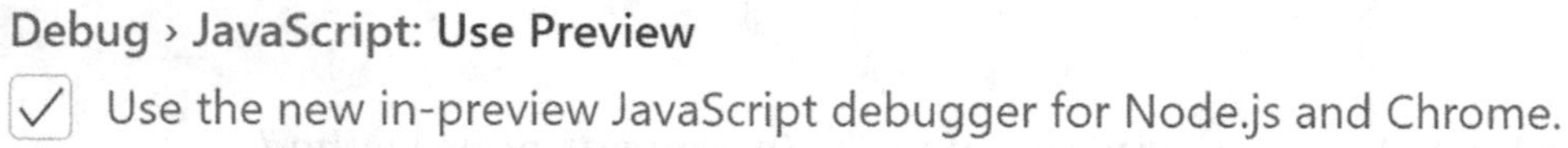

Debug › JavaScript: **Use Preview**

☑ Use the new in-preview JavaScript debugger for Node.js and Chrome.

Figure 1-21. *Enable the JavaScript Preview Debugger*

Open the folder containing the solution file. If it is the first time you open this folder with VSC, be patient, after a while, Figure 1-14 will pop up. Answer Yes. Also ensure Listing 1-11 is set up correctly like Visual Studio (this is actually independent of your IDE).

Now run your application in VSC with the debugger by pressing F5. Be patient while your Blazor site starts to run (in Chrome!). Now you can put a breakpoint in your code, for example, on the `IncrementCount` method of the Counter component as in Figure 1-22, line 16. Simply click in the area left to your code (also known as the gutter) and a red dot will appear, indicating that the debugger will stop at this code.

MyFirstBlazor > Client > Pages > @ Counter.razor

```
1    @page "/counter"
2
3    <h1>Counter</h1>
4
5    <p role="status">Current count: @currentCount</p>
6
7    <button class="btn btn-primary"
8             @onclick="IncrementCount">
9      Click me
10   </button>
11
12   @code {
         2 references
13     private int currentCount = 0;
         1 reference
14     private void IncrementCount()
15     {
16       currentCount++;
17     }
18   }
```

Figure 1-22. *Adding a Breakpoint in VSC*

Go back to your Blazor application and click the Counter's Click Me button. The debugger should stop on the IncrementCount method. You can now examine the content of simple variables in the Locals window, like in Figure 1-23.

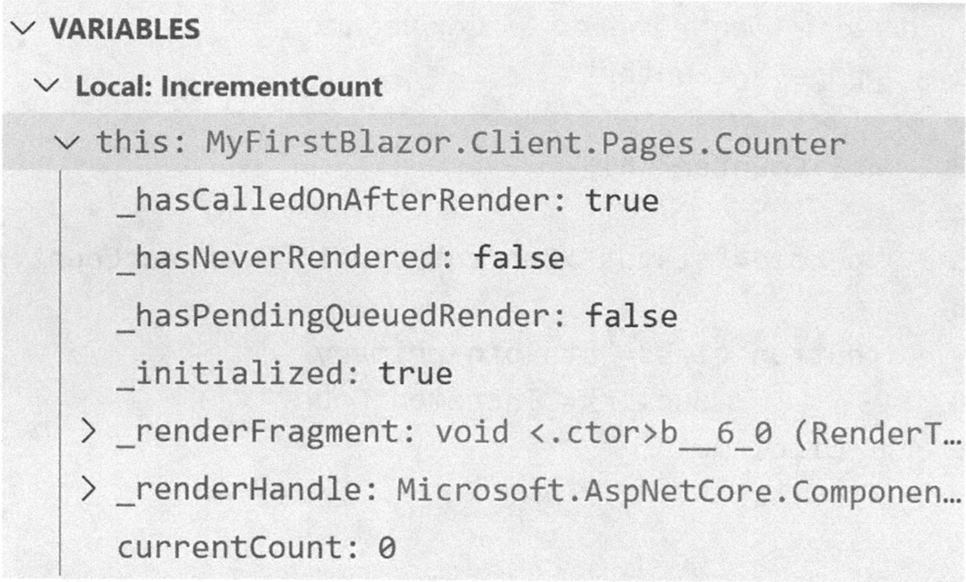

> ∨ **VARIABLES**
>   ∨ **Local: IncrementCount**
>   ∨ `this: MyFirstBlazor.Client.Pages.Counter`
>   `_hasCalledOnAfterRender: true`
>   `_hasNeverRendered: false`
>   `_hasPendingQueuedRender: false`
>   `_initialized: true`
>   > `_renderFragment: void <.ctor>b__6_0 (RenderT…`
>   > `_renderHandle: Microsoft.AspNetCore.Componen…`
>   `currentCount: 0`

Figure 1-23. Inspecting Variables in VSC

Developing with Hot Reload

With .NET Core 6.0, Microsoft introduces a really nice feature called *hot reload*. This allows you to make changes to your code and markup while your application is running. As soon as you make the change, your application will update (hot reloads), even keeping the existing state of the application.

Hot Reload with .NET CLI

Let us start using hot reload using the command-line interface. Open a command prompt and change the directory to the MyFirstBlazor Server project and run

```
dotnet watch
```

This should start the server project (which is hosting the Blazor WebAssembly project), and the browser should also open with your application.

```
watch : Hot reload enabled. For a list of supported edits, see https://aka.
ms/dotnet/hot-reload. Press "Ctrl + Shift + R" to restart.
```

Open the Counter component and increment the counter a couple of times. Now make a change to the Counter component, for example, Listing 1-12.

Listing 1-12. A Simple Change

```
<h1>My First Counter</h1>
```

As soon as you make the change, the browser will update itself, keeping the current count!

You can also change the code, for example, Listing 1-13.

Listing 1-13. Another Simple Change

```
private void IncrementCount()
{
  currentCount+=3;
}
```

Save. Clicking the Increment button will not add 3 to the counter.

If you want to restart again, go back to the command line and press Ctrl-Shift-R.

Hot Reload with Visual Studio

At the time of writing this chapter, hot reload does not work yet for Blazor WebAssembly application with Visual Studio. But, by the time you are reading this, it should work.

The Blazor WASM Bootstrap Process

At the bottom of Listing 1-14, you will find the `<script>` element responsible for bootstrapping Blazor in the browser. Let's look at this process in detail.

Listing 1-14. The index.html File

```
<!DOCTYPE html>
<html>

<head>
    <meta charset="utf-8" />
    <meta name="viewport" content="width=device-width, initial-scale=1.0,
    maximum-scale=1.0, user-scalable=no" />
```

```
    <title>MyFirstBlazor2</title>
    <base href="/" />
    <link href="css/bootstrap/bootstrap.min.css" rel="stylesheet" />
    <link href="css/app.css" rel="stylesheet" />
    <link href="MyFirstBlazor2.Client.styles.css" rel="stylesheet" />
</head>

<body>
    <div id="app">Loading...</div>

    <div id="blazor-error-ui">
        An unhandled error has occurred.
        <a href="" class="reload">Reload</a>
        <a class="dismiss">✕</a>
    </div>
    <script src="_framework/blazor.webassembly.js"></script>
</body>

</html>
```

Run the Blazor application. Open the browser's developer tools (most browsers will open the developer tools when you press F12). We will have a look at what happens at the network layer.

Note   In all screenshots, I will be using the Edge browser which is very similar to Chrome. If you prefer to use another browser, go right ahead since all modern desktop browsers have debugging support.

First, open the browser debugger's Application tab, and press the Clear site data button as in Figure 1-24. This will clear the browser's cache and will give you a better view what happens when someone visits a Blazor WebAssembly application for the first time.

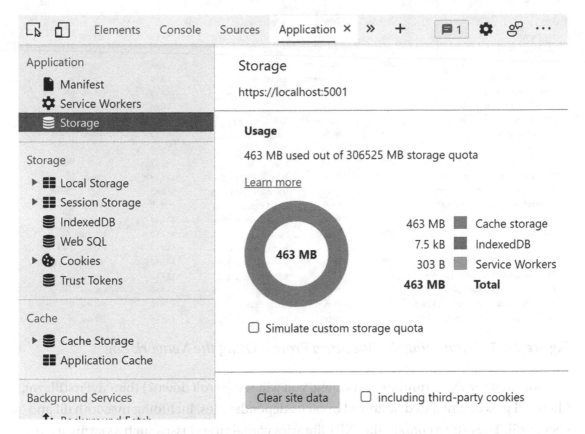

Figure 1-24. *Clearing the Browser's Storage*

Now open the browser debugger's Network tab. Refresh your browser (empty cache and hard refresh) to see what gets downloaded from the server as in Figure 1-25. First, you will see index.html (shown as localhost) being downloaded, which in turn downloads bootstrap.min.css and app.css, and then blazor.webassembly.js. A little lower, you will see that blazor.boot.js gets downloaded, which in turn will download dotnet. wasm. This is the .NET Core runtime compiled to run on WebAssembly!

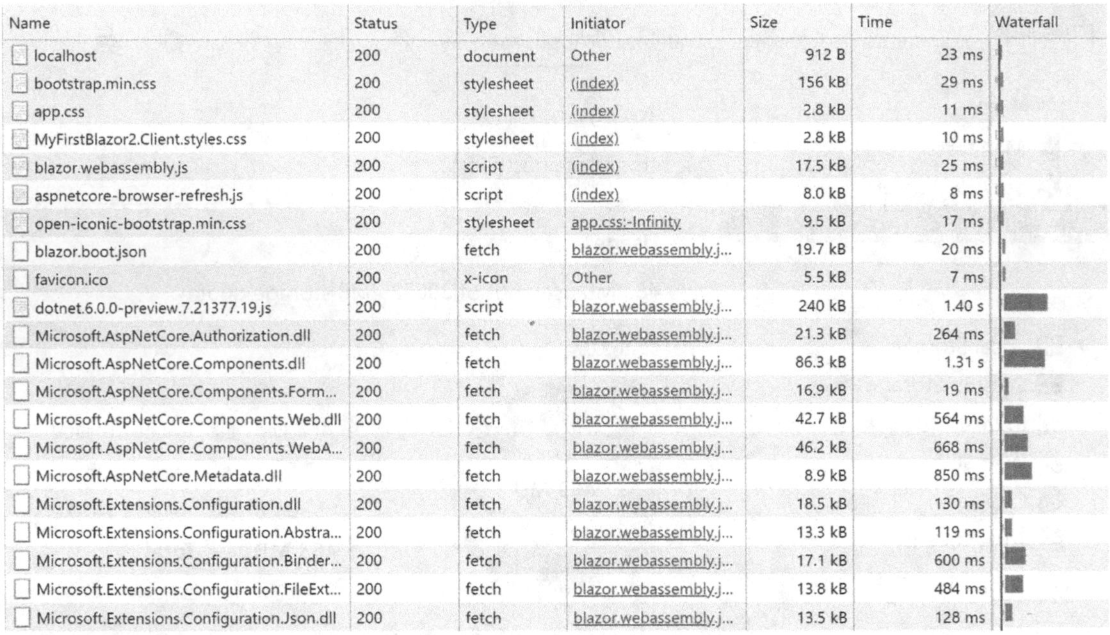

Name	Status	Type	Initiator	Size	Time	Waterfall
localhost	200	document	Other	912 B	23 ms	
bootstrap.min.css	200	stylesheet	(index)	156 kB	29 ms	
app.css	200	stylesheet	(index)	2.8 kB	11 ms	
MyFirstBlazor2.Client.styles.css	200	stylesheet	(index)	2.8 kB	10 ms	
blazor.webassembly.js	200	script	(index)	17.5 kB	25 ms	
aspnetcore-browser-refresh.js	200	script	(index)	8.0 kB	8 ms	
open-iconic-bootstrap.min.css	200	stylesheet	app.css:-Infinity	9.5 kB	17 ms	
blazor.boot.json	200	fetch	blazor.webassembly.j...	19.7 kB	20 ms	
favicon.ico	200	x-icon	Other	5.5 kB	7 ms	
dotnet.6.0.0-preview.7.21377.19.js	200	script	blazor.webassembly.j...	240 kB	1.40 s	
Microsoft.AspNetCore.Authorization.dll	200	fetch	blazor.webassembly.j...	21.3 kB	264 ms	
Microsoft.AspNetCore.Components.dll	200	fetch	blazor.webassembly.j...	86.3 kB	1.31 s	
Microsoft.AspNetCore.Components.Form...	200	fetch	blazor.webassembly.j...	16.9 kB	19 ms	
Microsoft.AspNetCore.Components.Web.dll	200	fetch	blazor.webassembly.j...	42.7 kB	564 ms	
Microsoft.AspNetCore.Components.WebA...	200	fetch	blazor.webassembly.j...	46.2 kB	668 ms	
Microsoft.AspNetCore.Metadata.dll	200	fetch	blazor.webassembly.j...	8.9 kB	850 ms	
Microsoft.Extensions.Configuration.dll	200	fetch	blazor.webassembly.j...	18.5 kB	130 ms	
Microsoft.Extensions.Configuration.Abstra...	200	fetch	blazor.webassembly.j...	13.3 kB	119 ms	
Microsoft.Extensions.Configuration.Binder...	200	fetch	blazor.webassembly.j...	17.1 kB	600 ms	
Microsoft.Extensions.Configuration.FileExt...	200	fetch	blazor.webassembly.j...	13.8 kB	484 ms	
Microsoft.Extensions.Configuration.Json.dll	200	fetch	blazor.webassembly.j...	13.5 kB	128 ms	

Figure 1-25. *Examining the Bootstrap Process Using the Network Log*

Now that the .NET runtime is running, you will see (scroll down?) that MyFirstBlazor.
Client.dll gets downloaded, followed by all its dependencies, including mscorlib.dll and
system.dll. These files contain the .NET libraries containing classes such as string used
to execute all kinds of things, and they are the same libraries you use on the server. This
is very powerful because you can reuse existing .NET libraries in Blazor you or others
built before!

At the bottom of the Network tab, you will see the total download size as in
Figure 1-26. Almost 10 MB! This is because we are using an empty cache; the next
download will show a lot less as shown in Figure 1-27 because now Blazor can retrieve
most of the files from the cache. We will look at reducing the full download size for
production applications in Chapter 15.

226 requests   9.9 MB transferred   23.5 MB resources   Finish: 38.11 s

Figure 1-26. *Total Download Size with Empty Cache*

15 requests 14.5 kB transferred 533 kB resources Finish: 1.63 s

Figure 1-27. *Total Download Size with Filled Cache*

Let us now compare this with Blazor Server.

The Blazor Server Bootstrap Process

Let's look at the bootstrapping process of a Blazor Server project.

Open a command line and run the following command which will create a new Blazor Server project and solution:

```
dotnet new blazorserver -o BlazorServerBootstrap
```

Now we can build and run this application:

```
cd .\BlazorServerBootstrap\
dotnet run
```

Should you get an error like the following line, it means another project is still running. Stop that project first and retry.

```
Failed to bind to address https://127.0.0.1:5001: address already in use
```

Open the browser, and go to `https://localhost:5001`. The Blazor application should be shown. Now open the browser's debugger on the Network tab, disable the cache (on the Network tab, you have a checkbox to disable the cache), and make your page refresh. Now compare what gets downloaded as in Figure 1-28. As you can see, the total download size is a lot smaller, resulting in your page getting loaded faster. You can also see that a WebSocket is opened between server and browser, allowing the Blazor runtime to exchange UI changes and events.

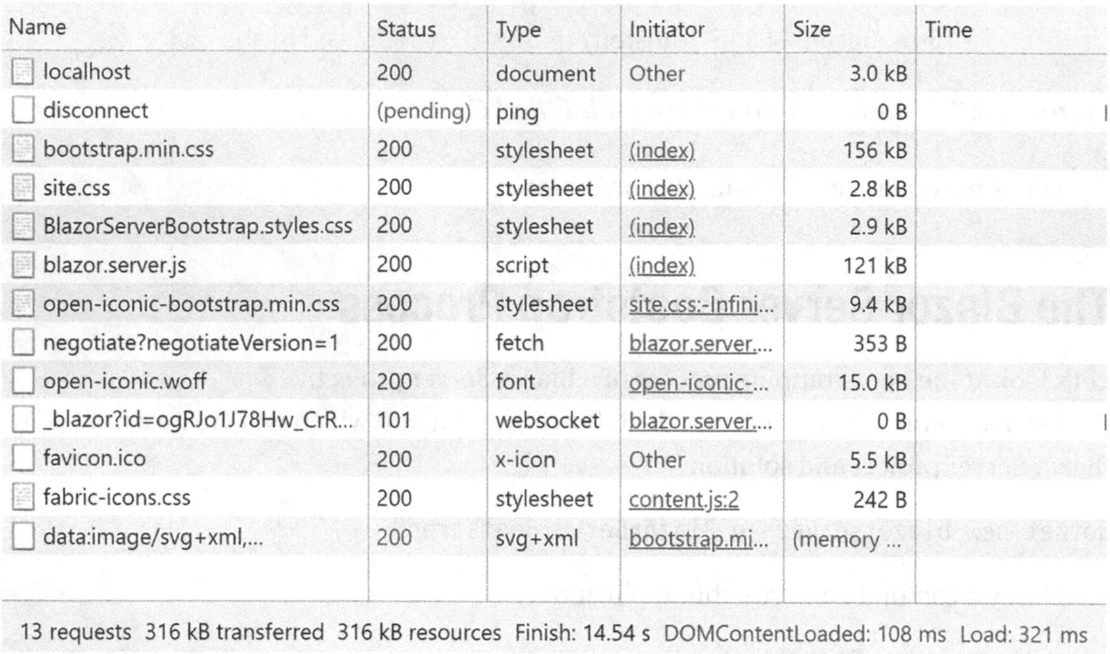

Name	Status	Type	Initiator	Size	Time
localhost	200	document	Other	3.0 kB	
disconnect	(pending)	ping		0 B	
bootstrap.min.css	200	stylesheet	(index)	156 kB	
site.css	200	stylesheet	(index)	2.8 kB	
BlazorServerBootstrap.styles.css	200	stylesheet	(index)	2.9 kB	
blazor.server.js	200	script	(index)	121 kB	
open-iconic-bootstrap.min.css	200	stylesheet	site.css:-Infini...	9.4 kB	
negotiate?negotiateVersion=1	200	fetch	blazor.server....	353 B	
open-iconic.woff	200	font	open-iconic-...	15.0 kB	
_blazor?id=ogRJo1J78Hw_CrR...	101	websocket	blazor.server....	0 B	
favicon.ico	200	x-icon	Other	5.5 kB	
fabric-icons.css	200	stylesheet	content.js:2	242 B	
data:image/svg+xml,...	200	svg+xml	bootstrap.mi...	(memory ...	

13 requests 316 kB transferred 316 kB resources Finish: 14.54 s DOMContentLoaded: 108 ms Load: 321 ms

Figure 1-28. *Looking at Server-Side Blazor Network Activity*

Now click the Counter link in the navigation menu and select the websocket link in the network debugger tab. Each time you click, you will see a couple of SignalR messages appear as in Figure 1-29. These binary messages are all tiny because only changes are transmitted this way. For example, when you click the Increment button in the Counter component, the browser only needs to update the number in the browser.

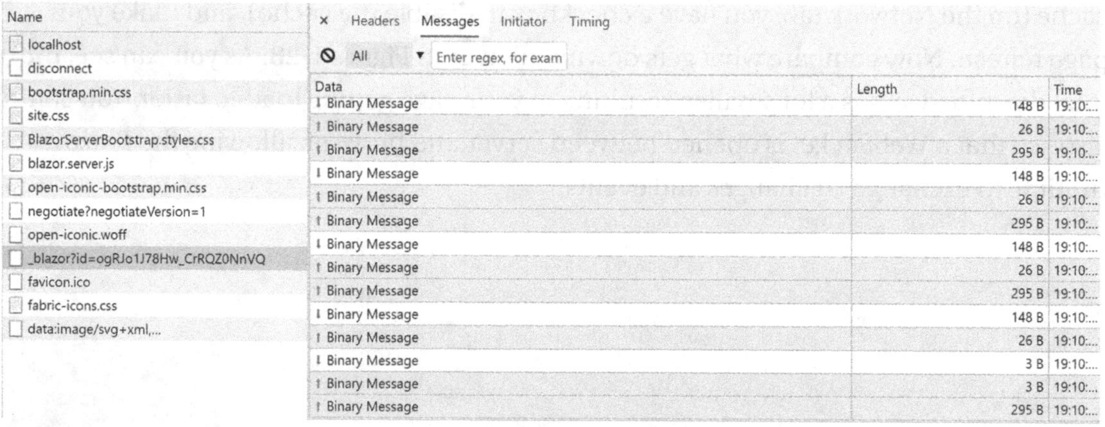

Figure 1-29. *The SignalR Messages*

Nullable Reference Types

Throughout this book, I will be using modern C# with some of the latest features. But there is one C# feature I want to discuss right now. Every developer, from time to time, will encounter a `NullReferenceException`, which is a real bug because you can always avoid it. What if the compiler can help you with this and warn you about a possible `NullReferenceException`? This is what the section "Nullable Reference Types" is all about.

An Apology

Who invented the null pointer? Tony Hoare did, and he apologized in 2009 and denoted this as his billion-dollar mistake (`www.infoq.com/presentations/Null-References-The-Billion-Dollar-Mistake-Tony-Hoare/`):

> *I call it my billion-dollar mistake. It was the invention of the null reference in 1965. At that time, I was designing the first comprehensive type system for references in an object oriented language (ALGOL W). My goal was to ensure that all use of references should be absolutely safe, with checking performed automatically by the compiler. But I couldn't resist the temptation to put in a null reference, simply because it was so easy to implement. This has led to innumerable errors, vulnerabilities, and system crashes, which have probably caused a billion dollars of pain and damage in the last forty years.*

Many object-oriented programming languages still use the `null` pointer, and C# is no exception. Some languages even treated `null` differently. For example, in Objective-C, when a pointer is `null`, the compiler would not invoke a method on it. And it would do this silently! Of course, you would not get a `NullReferenceException`, but it did skip an important piece of functionality.

Using Null in C#

Let us start with the basics. In .NET, there are two different kinds of types: reference types and value types. A reference type uses a reference to point to an object, and a value type holds the value of an object. Because of this, value types cannot be null. But in databases, you can have a column holding a number (a value type) which can be nil. So how do you represent this in C#? For this, we can denote a nullable value type by adding a question mark after the type, for example, in Listing 1-15.

Listing 1-15. A Nullable Value Type

```
int? i = null;
```

Now in C#, we can tell the compiler to treat reference types in the same way, meaning that we will get a warning if we assign a `null` value to a reference type, except when we add a question mark after the type. Listing 1-16 shows both examples.

Listing 1-16. Nullable Reference Types

```
// No warning
string? canBeNull = null;

// Warning:
// Converting null literal or possible null value to non-nullable type
string cannotBeNull = null;
```

Of course, this would break every existing C# application out there, so we need to enable this in our project properties. You can do this in Visual Studio using your project properties as shown in Figure 1-30.

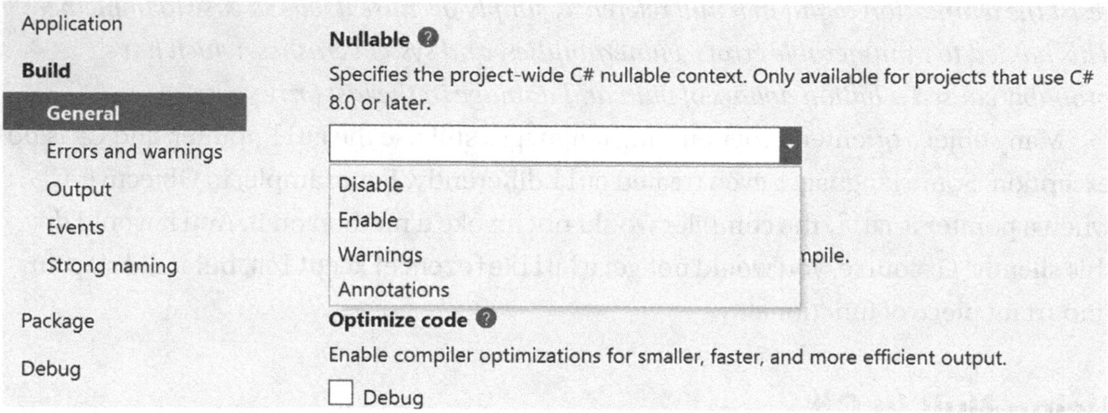

Figure 1-30. *Setting the Nullable Compiler Option*

You can also do this directly in your project as shown in Listing 1-17.

Listing 1-17. Enabling Nullable Reference Types in the Project File

```
<Project Sdk="Microsoft.NET.Sdk">
  <PropertyGroup>
    <OutputType>Exe</OutputType>
    <TargetFramework>net5.0</TargetFramework>
    <Nullable>enable</Nullable>
  </PropertyGroup>
</Project>
```

This causes the compiler to set a nullable flag for every field, property, and method that is of (or returns) a reference type. You can inspect this flag in VS by hovering over it as shown in Figure 1-31.

```
Console.WriteLine( value: canBeNull );
```

[local variable] string? canBeNull
'canBeNull' may be null here.

Figure 1-31. *Inspecting the Nullable Flag*

The compiler then uses that flag to issue warnings if you would attempt to use a nullable reference type, for example, by getting the length of the string. Figure 1-32 will display a warning because the canBeNull reference can be null.

```
Console.WriteLine( value: canBeNull.Length );
```

[local variable] string? canBeNull
'canBeNull' may be null here.
CS8602: Dereference of a possibly null reference.
Show potential fixes (Alt+Enter or Ctrl+.)

Figure 1-32. *Possible Null Reference*

However, if we nest this in a condition as in Figure 1-33 where we check against null, the compiler will no longer issue a warning.

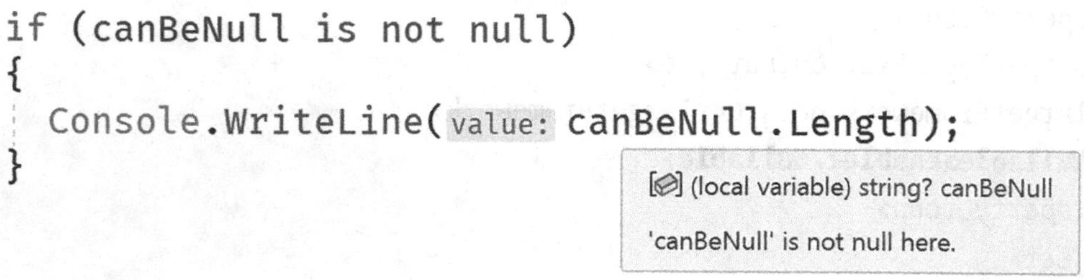

```
if (canBeNull is not null)
{
    Console.WriteLine( value: canBeNull.Length);
}
```

(local variable) string? canBeNull

'canBeNull' is not null here.

Figure 1-33. *No Possible Null Reference*

So the whole idea of nullable reference types is to make the compiler do the analysis and to issue a warning when we can have a possible null being used which would result in a NullReferenceException.

Using References

In C#, we can declare a class with an example in Listing 1-18. But when you do this with nullable reference types enabled, you will get compiler warnings. Why? Because you can create a new instance of a Person with a null FirstName and/or a null LastName. So again, the compiler will warn about this.

Listing 1-18. A Person Class

```
public class Person
{
    public string FirstName { get; set; }

    public string LastName { get; set; }
}
```

There are a couple of ways we can make the compiler stop issuing warnings. We can use a constructor as in Listing 1-19. Now we cannot create a Person instance with a null property. Should someone call this constructor with a null argument, the compiler will again issue a warning.

Listing 1-19. Using a Constructor

```
public class Person
{
  public Person(string firstName, string lastName)
  {
    FirstName = firstName;
    LastName = lastName;
  }

  public string FirstName { get; set; }

  public string LastName { get; set; }
}
```

Sometimes you simply cannot use a constructor to silence the compiler. For example, you might want to use this `Person` class with Entity Framework Core. In this case, you could make `FirstName` and `LastName` nullable as in Listing 1-20.

Listing 1-20. Person with Nullable Name

```
public class Person
{
  public string? FirstName { get; set; }
  public string? LastName { get; set; }
}
```

However, this does not mimic real life. There is another technique we can use.

The Null-Forgiving Operator

Sometimes you just know that a nullable reference is not `null`, and you want to tell the compiler about this. For this, we can use the *null-forgiving operator* by appending the nullable reference with an exclamation mark as in Figure 1-34. This sets the nullable flag to `false`, and the compiler is happy.

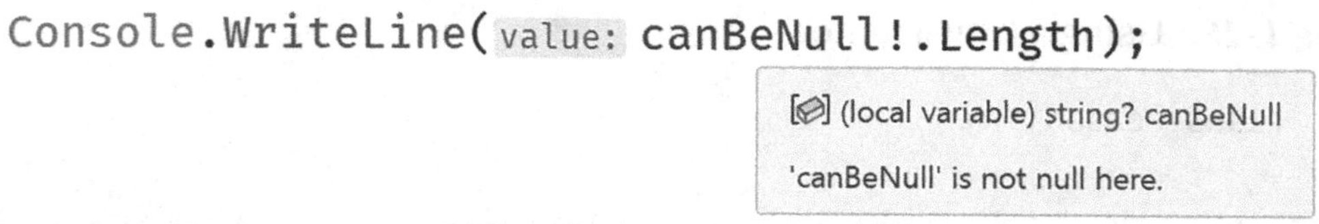

```
Console.WriteLine( value: canBeNull!.Length);
```

> [icon] (local variable) string? canBeNull
>
> 'canBeNull' is not null here.

Figure 1-34. *The Null-Forgiving Operator*

We can even use this to have a `null` value with the nullable flag set to false! What?! Let us look at the `Person` class again. When we want to use this class with a library such as Entity Framework Core and we trust this library to always provide us with non-null values, we can silence the compiler as in Listing 1-21. This looks weird. Here, we assign the `null!` value, whose nullable flag is set to `false` so the compiler does not give us warnings.

Listing 1-21. Using the Null-Forgiving Operator with Types

```
public class Person
{
  public string? FirstName { get; set; } = null!;

  public string? LastName { get; set; } = null!;
}
```

This is exactly the technique we will use to create Blazor components that have reference properties that we cannot initialize using a constructor.

Of course, with string properties, we can also assign them an empty string instead of null as in Listing 1-22. But for other reference types, this is not always possible.

Listing 1-22. The Person Class with Empty Name.

```
public class Person
{
  public string? FirstName { get; set; } = string.Empty;

  public string? LastName { get; set; } = string.Empty;
}
```

Nullable Reference Types and .NET Libraries

Microsoft has gone through a lot of effort to make all their libraries support nullable reference types. I want you to realize that this is all compiler meta-data, so you can use the new libraries supporting nullable reference types with older projects; the compiler will simply ignore this meta-data. You can also use libraries that do not support this meta-data, but you will need to use the null-forgiving operator with a lot of methods. But do yourself a favor – get to use nullable reference types and your code will be shipped with a lot less bugs! You can learn more at `https://docs.microsoft.com/en-us/dotnet/csharp/nullable-references`.

Summary

In this chapter, we looked at the history of the browser wars and how this resulted in the creation of WebAssembly. The .NET runtime allows you to run .NET assemblies, and because it can now also run on WebAssembly, we can now run .NET assemblies in the browser! All of this resulted in the creation of Blazor, where you build razor files containing .NET code which update the browser's DOM, giving us the ability to build Single-Page Applications in .NET, instead of JavaScript.

First, we installed the prerequisites needed for developing and running Blazor applications. We then created our first Blazor project. This project will be used throughout this book to explain all the Blazor concepts you need to know about. We examined this solution, looking at the server-side project, the shared project, and the Blazor project, and compared the bootstrap process for both Blazor WebAssembly and Blazor Server.

Finally, we looked at using nullable reference types and how this can help writing better code with less bugs.

CHAPTER 2

Data Binding

Imagine an application that needs to display data to the user, and capture changes made by that user to save the modified data. One way you could build an application like this is to, once you got the data, iterate over each item of data. For example, for every member of a list, you would generate the same repeating element, and then inside that element, you would generate text boxes, drop-downs, and other UI elements that present data. Later, after the user has made some changes, you would iterate over your generated elements, and for every element, you would inspect the child elements to see if their data was changed. If so, you copy the data back into your objects that will be used for saving that data.

This is an error-prone process and a lot of work if you want to do this with something like jQuery (jQuery is a very popular JavaScript framework which allows you to manipulate the browser's *Document Object Model* (*DOM*)).

Modern frameworks like Angular and React have become popular because they simplify this process greatly through *data binding*. With data binding, most of this work for generating UI and copying data back into objects is done by the framework.

A Quick Look at Razor

Blazor is the combination of *Browser* + *Razor* (with a lot of artistic freedom). So, to understand Blazor, we need to understand browsers and the Razor language. I will assume you understand what a browser is since the Internet has been very popular for over more than a few decades. But Razor (as a computer language) might not be that clear (yet). Razor is a markup syntax that allows you to embed code in a template. Razor can be used to dynamically generate HTML, but you can also use it to generate code and other formats. For example, at the company I work, we generate emails using Razor.

Razor made its appearance in ASP.NET MVC. In ASP.NET Core MVC, razor is executed at the server side to generate HTML which is sent to the browser. But in

51

© Peter Himschoot 2022
P. Himschoot, *Microsoft Blazor*, https://doi.org/10.1007/978-1-4842-7845-1_2

Blazor, this code is executed inside your browser (with *Blazor WebAssembly*) and will dynamically update the web page without having to go back to the server.

Remember the MyFirstBlazor solution we generated from the template in the previous chapter? Open it again with Visual Studio or Code and have a look at SurveyPrompt.razor as shown in Listing 2-1.

Listing 2-1. Examining SurveyPrompt.razor

```
<div class="alert alert-secondary mt-4" role="alert">
  <span class="oi oi-pencil mr-2" aria-hidden="true"></span>
  <strong>@Title</strong>

  <span class="text-nowrap">
    Please take our
    <a target="_blank" class="font-weight-bold" href="https://go.microsoft.
    com/fwlink/?linkid=2148851">brief survey</a>
  </span>
  and tell us what you think.
</div>

@code {
  // Demonstrates how a parent component can supply parameters
  [Parameter]
  public string Title { get; set; }
}
```

As you can see, razor mainly consists of HTML markup. But if you want to have some C# properties or methods, you can embed them in the @code section of a razor file. This works because the razor file is used to generate a .NET class and everything in @code is embedded in that class.

For example, the SurveyPrompt component allows you to set the Title property, which is set in Index.razor as in Listing 2-2.

Listing 2-2. Setting the SurveyPrompt's Title (Excerpt from Index.razor)

```
<SurveyPrompt Title="How is Blazor working for you?" />
```

Because the public `Title` property can be set in another component, the property becomes a parameter, and because of that, you need to apply the `[Parameter]` attribute, as in Listing 2-1. `SurveyPrompt` can then embed the contents of the `Title` property in its HTML markup using the @ syntax (third line in Listing 2-1). This syntax tells razor to switch to C#, and this will get the property as an expression and embed its value in the markup.

One-Way Data Binding

One-way data binding is where data flows from the component to the DOM or vice versa, but only in one direction. Data binding from the component to the DOM is where some data, like the customer's name, needs to be displayed. Data binding from the DOM to the component is where a DOM event took place, like the user clicking a button, and we want some code to run.

One-Way Data Binding Syntax

Let's look at an example of one-way data binding in razor. Open the solution we built in Chapter 1 (MyFirstBlazor.sln), and open Counter.razor, repeated here in Listing 2-3.

Listing 2-3. Examining One-Way Data Binding with Counter.razor

```
@page "/counter"

<h1>Counter</h1>

<p>Current count: @currentCount</p>

<button class="btn btn-primary" @onclick="IncrementCount">
  Click me
</button>

@code {
  private int currentCount = 0;
```

```
private void IncrementCount()
{
  currentCount++;
}
}
```

On this page, you get a simple counter, which you can increment by clicking the button as illustrated in Figure 2-1.

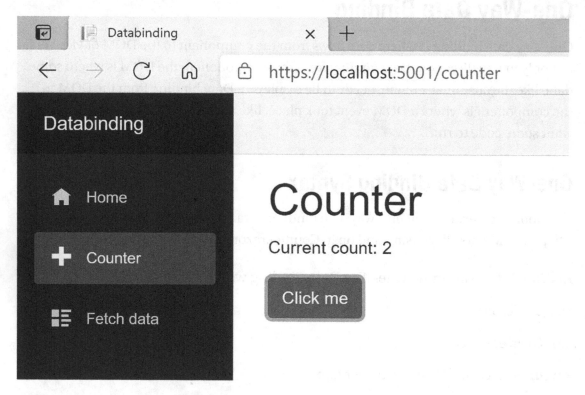

Figure 2-1. *The Counter Page*

Let's look at the workings of this page. The currentCount field is defined in the @code section in Counter.razor. This is not a field that can be set from outside, so there is no need for the [Parameter] attribute, and we can keep it private.

To display the value of the counter in razor, we use the @currentCount razor syntax as shown in Listing 2-4.

Listing 2-4. Data Binding from the Component to the DOM

```
<p>Current count: @currentCount</p>
```

Any time you click the button, the Blazor runtime sees that `currentCount` may have been updated, and it will automatically update the DOM with the latest value of `currentCount`.

Attribute Binding

You can also use this same syntax to bind the value of an HTML attribute.

Open app.css which you can find in the wwwroot/css folder and add these two CSS classes from Listing 2-5.

Listing 2-5. Some Simple Styles

```
.red-background {
  background: red;
  color: white;
}

.yellow-background {
  background: yellow;
  color: black;
}
```

Wrap the `currentCount` in an `<span>` as in Listing 2-6. Every time you change the value of `currentCount` by clicking the button, it changes the `currentCount`'s background color.

Listing 2-6. Binding an HTML Attribute

```
@page "/counter"

<h1>Counter</h1>

<p>Current count: <span class="@BackgroundColor">@currentCount</span></p>

<button class="btn btn-primary" @onclick="IncrementCount">Click me</button>
```

```
@code {
  private int currentCount = 0;

  private void IncrementCount()
  {
    currentCount++;
  }

  private string BackgroundColor
  => (currentCount % 2 == 0) ? "red-background" : "yellow-background";
}
```

Conditional Attributes

Sometimes you can control the browser by adding some attributes to DOM elements. For example, in Listing 2-7, to disable a button, you can simply use the disabled attribute.

Listing 2-7. Disabling a Button Using the `disabled` Attribute

```
<button disabled>Disabled Button</button>
```

With Blazor, you can data bind an attribute to a Boolean expression (e.g., a field, property, or method of type bool), and Blazor will hide the attribute if the expression evaluates to false (or null) and will show the attribute if it evaluates to true. Go back to the Counter.razor and add the code from Listing 2-8.

Listing 2-8. Disabling the Click Me Button

```
<button class="btn btn-primary"
        disabled="@(currentCount > 10)"
        @onclick="IncrementCount">
  Click me
</button>
```

Try it. Clicking the button until the currentCount becomes 10 will disable the button by adding the disabled attribute to the button. As soon as currentCount falls below 10, the button will become enabled again (except there is no way you can do this for the moment).

Event Handling and Data Binding

We update `currentCount` using the `IncrementCount()` method from Listing 2-3. This method gets called by clicking the "Click Me" button. This again is a one-way data binding, but in the other direction, from the button to your component. Blazor allows you to react to DOM events (like the DOM's `click` event) this way, instead of using JavaScript. You can also build your own components that have events, where you can use the same syntax to react to them. This will be discussed in Chapter 3.

Event Binding Syntax

Look at Listing 2-9. Now we are using the `@on<event>` syntax; in this case, we want to bind to the button's `click` DOM event, so we use the `@onclick` attribute on the button element, and we pass it the name of the method we want to call.

Listing 2-9. Data Binding from the DOM to the Component

```
<button class="btn btn-primary" @onclick="IncrementCount">
  Click me
</button>
```

Clicking the button will trigger the DOM's `click` event, which then will call the `IncrementCount` method, which will cause the UI to be updated with the new value of the `currentCount` field. Whenever the user interacts with the site, for example, by clicking a button, Blazor assumes that the event will have some side effect because a method gets called, so it will update the UI with the latest values. Simply calling a method will not cause Blazor to update the UI. We will discuss this later in this chapter.

Event Arguments

In regular .NET, event handlers of type `EventHandler` can find out more information about the event using the `sender` and `EventArgs` arguments. In Blazor, event handlers don't follow the strict event pattern from .NET, but you can declare the event handler method to take an argument of some type derived from `EventArgs`, for example, `MouseEventArgs`, as shown in Listing 2-10. Here, we are using the `MouseEventArgs` instance to see if the Ctrl key is being pressed and, if so, to decrement the `currentCount` field.

Each event uses a specific kind of `EventArgs`, so please refer to online documentation at `https://docs.microsoft.com/aspnet/core/blazor/components/event-handling` for more information about a specific event.

Listing 2-10. A Blazor Event Handler Taking Arguments

```
private void IncrementCount(MouseEventArgs e)
{
  if (e.CtrlKey)
  {
    currentCount--;
  }
  else
  {
    currentCount++;
  }
}
```

Using C# Lambda Functions

Data binding to an event does not always require you to write a method. You can also use C# lambda function syntax with an example shown in Listing 2-11.

Listing 2-11. Event Data Binding with Lambda Syntax

```
<button class="btn btn-primary"
        disabled="@(currentCount > 10)"
        @onclick="@(() => currentCount++)">
  Click me
</button>
```

If you want to use a lambda function to handle an event, you need to wrap it in round braces.

Two-Way Data Binding

Sometimes you want to display some data to the user, and you want to allow the user to make changes to this data. This is common in data entry forms. Here, we will explore Blazor's two-way data binding syntax.

Two-Way Data Binding Syntax

With two-way data binding, we will have the DOM update whenever the component changes, but the component will also update because of modifications in the DOM. The simplest example is with an `<input>` HTML element.

Let's try something. Modify Counter.razor by adding an `increment` field and an `<input>` element using the `@bind` attribute as shown in Listing 2-12. Also modify the `IncrementCount` method to use the `increment` when you click the button.

Listing 2-12. Adding an Increment and an Input

```
@page "/counter"

<h1>Counter</h1>

<p>Current count: <span class="@BackgroundColor">@currentCount</span></p>

<p>
  <input type="number" @bind="@increment" />
</p>

<button class="btn btn-primary"
        disabled="@(currentCount > 10)"
        @onclick="IncrementCount">
  Click me
</button>

@code {
  private int currentCount = 0;
  private int increment = 1;

  private void IncrementCount(MouseEventArgs e)
  {
```

```
  if (e.CtrlKey)
  {
    currentCount -= increment;
  }
  else
  {
    currentCount += increment;
  }
}

private string BackgroundColor
=> (currentCount % 2 == 0) ? "red-background" : "yellow-background";
}
```

Build and run.

Change the value of the input, for example, 3. You should now be able to increment the currentCount with other values as in Figure 2-2.

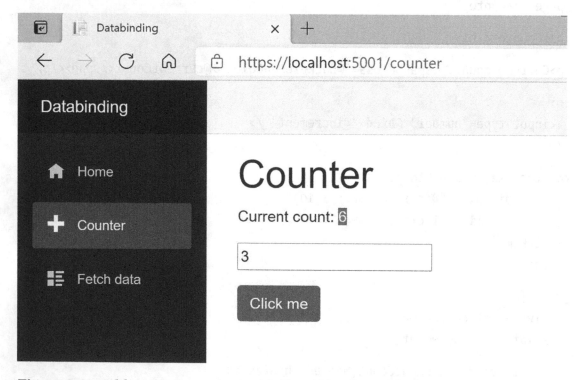

Figure 2-2. *Adding an Increment with Two-Way Data Binding*

Look at the `<input>` element you just added, repeated here in Listing 2-13.

Listing 2-13. Two-Way Data Binding with the @bind Syntax

```
<input type="number" @bind="@increment" />
```

Here, we are using the @bind syntax which is the equivalent of two different one-way bindings as shown in Listing 2-14.

Here, we use one-way data binding (`value="@increment"`) to set the input's value property to the increment variable. When the user modifies the contents of the input element, the change event (@onchange) will trigger and will set the increment variable to the input's value (`increment = int.Parse($"{e.Value}")`). So when one side changes, the other will be updated.

Listing 2-14. Data Binding in Both Directions

```
<input type="number"
      value="@increment"
      @onchange="@((ChangeEventArgs e)
                  => increment = int.Parse($"{e.Value}"))" />
```

This alternative syntax is very verbose and not that handy to use. Using @bind is way more practical. However, don't forget about this technique; using the more verbose syntax can sometimes be a more elegant solution!

Binding to Other Events: @bind:{event}

Blazor will update the value in two-way data binding when the DOM's onchange event occurs. This means that the increment field of the Counter component will be updated when the user changes the focus to another element, for example, the button. But maybe this is too late for you. Let's look at how you can change the event that triggers data binding.

Add a second input by copying the line from Listing 2-14. Run this example and change the value of one input by typing a number into it (don't use the increment/decrement buttons that browsers add for number inputs). The other input's value will not update immediately. Clicking the other input will update it. This is because we're using the onchange event, which triggers when the input loses focus! If you want data binding to occur immediately, you can bind to the oninput event by using the explicit

@bind:event syntax. The oninput event triggers after each change in the input. Update the second input element to match Listing 2-15. Typing in the second input will update the first input after each keystroke.

Listing 2-15. Explicit Binding to Events

```
<input type="number" @bind="@increment" @bind:event="oninput" />
```

Preventing Default Actions

In Blazor, you can react to events, and the browser will also react to these. For example, when you press a key with the focus on an <input> element, the browser will react by adding the keystroke to the <input>.

But what if you don't want the browser to behave as normal? Let's say you want to allow the user to increment and decrement an input's value simply by pressing "+" or "-". Change the <input> from Listing 2-12 to react to the keypress event as in Listings 2-16 and 2-17.

Listing 2-16. Handling keypress Events

```
<p>
  <input type="number"
         @bind="@increment"
         @onkeypress="KeyHandler" />
</p>
```

Listing 2-17. The KeyHandler Method

```
private void KeyHandler(KeyboardEventArgs e)
{
  if (e.Key == "+")
  {
    increment += 1;
  }
  else if (e.Key == "-")
  {
    increment -= 1;
  }
}
```

Build and run. Pressing "+" and "-" will increment and decrement the value in the input, but you will also see any key you just pressed added to the `<input>` HTML element because this is the default behavior for an input. To stop this default behavior, we can add `@{event}:preventDefault` like in Listing 2-18. Here, we use a bool field `shouldPreventDefault` (set to `true`) to stop the default behavior of the input, but you can use any Boolean expression.

Listing 2-18. Stopping the Default Behavior of the Input

```
<p>
  <input type="number"
         @bind="@increment"
         @onkeypress="KeyHandler"
         @onkeypress:preventDefault="@shouldPreventDefault" />
</p>

// add this next to the KeyHandler method
private bool shouldPreventDefault = true;
```

Build and run again. Now pressing "+" will increment the input's value as expected.

You can also leave out the value for `preventDefault`, and then it will always prevent the default action as in Listing 2-19.

Listing 2-19. Shorter Notation

```
<p>
  <input type="number"
         @bind="@increment"
         @onkeypress="KeyHandler"
         @onkeypress:preventDefault />
</p>
```

Stopping Event Propagation

In a browser, events propagate to the parent element, then to that parent element's parent, etc. Again, generally this is desirable, but not always.

Let's look at an example. Start by adding two nested `div` elements to the `Counter` component which each handles the `@onmousemove` event as in Listing 2-20.

Listing 2-20. Event Propagation Example

```
@page "/counter"

<h1>Counter</h1>

<p>Current count:
  <span class="@BackgroundColor">
    @currentCount
  </span>
</p>

<p>
  <input type="number"
         @bind="@increment"
         @onkeypress="KeyHandler"
         @onkeypress:preventDefault="@shouldPreventDefault" />
</p>

<div style="width: 400px; height: 400px; background: yellow"
     @onmousemove="OuterMouseMove">
  @outerPos
  <div style="width: 300px; height: 300px;
              background: green; margin:50px"
       @onmousemove="InnerMouseMove">
    @innerPos
  </div>
</div>

<br/>

<button class="btn btn-primary"
        disabled="@(currentCount > 10)"
        @onclick="IncrementCount">
  Click me
</button>
```

Also add code from Listing 2-21. These event handlers simply show the mouse position in the element.

Listing 2-21. The Event Handlers

```
private void KeyHandler(KeyboardEventArgs e)
{
  if (e.Key == "+")
  {
    increment += 1;
  }
  else if (e.Key == "-")
  {
    increment -= 1;
  }
}

private string outerPos = "Nothing yet";

private void OuterMouseMove(MouseEventArgs e)
  => outerPos = $"Mouse at {e.ClientX}x{e.ClientY}";

private string innerPos = "Nothing yet";

private void InnerMouseMove(MouseEventArgs e)
  => innerPos = $"Mouse at {e.ClientX}x{e.ClientY}";
```

Build and run.

Move the mouse pointer around in the yellow square. Now do the same for the green rectangle. However, moving the mouse in the green square also updates the yellow one! This is because the mousemove event (and others) gets sent to the element where the event occurs and also to its parent element all the way up to the root element! If you want to avoid this, you can stop this propagation by adding the {event}:stopPropagation attribute. Add it to the inner square as in Listing 2-22. From now on, moving the mouse in the inner square does not update the outer square.

Listing 2-22. Stopping the Event from Propagating to the Parent

```
<div style="width: 400px; height: 400px; background: yellow"
    @onmousemove="OuterMouseMove">
  @outerPos
  <div style="width: 300px; height: 300px;
```

```
            background: green; margin:50px"
        @onmousemove="InnerMouseMove"
        @onmousemove:stopPropagation>
      @innerPos
   </div>
</div>
```

If you want to be able to turn this on and off from code, assign a bool expression to this attribute, just like `preventDefault`.

Formatting Dates

Data binding to a `DateTime` value can be formatted with the `@bind:format` attribute as shown in Listing 2-23. If you need to format the date depending on the user's language and culture, keep on reading. This is discussed in Chapter 14.

Listing 2-23. Formatting a Date

```
<p>
  <input @bind="@Today" @bind:format="yyyy-MM-dd" />
</p>

@code {
  private DateTime Today { get; set; } = DateTime.Now;
}
```

Currently, `DateTime` values are the only ones supporting the `@bind:format` attribute.

Change Detection

The Blazor runtime will update the DOM whenever it thinks changes have been made to your data. One example is when an event executes some of your code, it assumes you've modified some values as a side effect and renders the UI. However, Blazor is not always capable of detecting all changes, and in this case, you will have to tell Blazor to apply the changes to the DOM. A typical example is with background threads, so let us look at an example of this.

Open Counter.razor and add another button that will automatically increment the counter when pressed as in Listing 2-24. The AutoIncrement method uses a .NET Timer instance to increment the currentCount every second. A timer instance will run on a background thread, executing the callback delegate at intervals (just like setInterval with JavaScript).

Listing 2-24. Adding Another Button

```
@page "/counter"

<h1>Counter</h1>

<p>Current count: <span class="@BackgroundColor">@currentCount</span></p>

<button class="btn btn-primary"
        disabled="@(currentCount > 10)"
        @onclick="IncrementCount">
  Click me
</button>

<button class="btn btn-secondary"
        @onclick="AutoIncrement">
  Auto Increment
</button>

@code {
  private int currentCount = 0;

  private void IncrementCount()
  {
    currentCount += 1;
    Console.WriteLine("++");
  }

  private string BackgroundColor
  => (currentCount % 2 == 0) ? "red-background"
                            : "yellow-background";
```

```
private void AutoIncrement()
{
    var timer = new System.Threading.Timer(
        callback: (_) => IncrementCount(),
        state: null,
        dueTime: TimeSpan.FromSeconds(1),
        period: TimeSpan.FromSeconds(1));
    }
}
```

You might find the lambda function argument in the `Timer`'s constructor a little strange. I use an underscore when I need to name an argument that is not used in the body of the lambda function. Call it anything you want, for example, `ignore` – it does not matter. I simply like to use underscore because then I don't have to think of a good name for the argument. C# 7 made this official; it is called *discards*, and you can find more at `https://docs.microsoft.com/dotnet/csharp/discards`.

Run this page. Clicking the "Auto Increment" button will start the timer, but the `currentCount` will not update on the screen. Why? Try clicking the "Increment" button. The `currentCount` has been updated, so it is a UI problem. If you open the browser's debugger, you will see in the console tab a ++ appear every second, so the timer works! That's because I've added a `Console.Writeline`, which sends the output to the debugger's console. Sometimes an easy way to see if things are working.

Blazor will re-render the page whenever an event occurs. It will also re-render the page in case of asynchronous operations. However, some changes cannot be detected automatically. In this case, because we are making some changes on a background thread, you need to tell Blazor to update the page by calling the `StateHasChanged` method which every Blazor component inherits from its base class.

Go back to the `AutoIncrement` method and add a call to `StateHasChanged` as in Listing 2-25. `StateHasChanged` tells Blazor that some state has changed (who would have thought!) and that it needs to re-render the page.

Listing 2-25. Adding StateHasChanged

```
private void AutoIncrement()
{
    var timer = new System.Threading.Timer(
        callback: (_) => { IncrementCount(); StateHasChanged(); },
```

```
        state: null,
        dueTime: TimeSpan.FromSeconds(1),
        period: TimeSpan.FromSeconds(1));
}
```

Run again. Now pressing "Auto Increment" will work.

As you can see, sometimes we will need to tell Blazor manually to update the DOM. In general, the Blazor runtime will detect when to update the UI. When the user interacts with your application, events get triggered which will make change detection happen. When an async method completes, change detection will occur. It is only when we go outside the Blazor runtime, for example, using a .NET Timer, that we need to trigger change detection ourselves. More on this when we look at building components in the next two chapters.

The PizzaPlace Single-Page Application

Let us apply this newfound knowledge and build a nice Pizza ordering website. Throughout the rest of this book, we will enhance this site with all kinds of features.

Creating the PizzaPlace Project

Create a new Blazor hosted project, either using Visual Studio or dotnet CLI. Refer to the explanation on creating a project in the first chapter if you don't recall how. Call the project PizzaPlace. You get a similar project to the MyFirstBlazor project. Now let's apply some changes!

First, enable the nullable reference type feature for each project (you might find that the Blazor template has already enabled nullable reference types):

```
<PropertyGroup>
    <TargetFramework>net6.0</TargetFramework>
    <Nullable>enable</Nullable>
</PropertyGroup>
```

With Visual Studio, you can also open your project's properties like in Figure 2-3.

```
Build

General


Conditional compilation symbols ?
Specifies symbols on which to perform conditional compilation. Separate symbols with a semi-colon (';').

 $(DefineConstants)TRACE

 Debug      TRACE;DEBUG;NET;NET6_0;NETCOREAPP
 Release    TRACE;RELEASE;NET;NET6_0;NETCOREAPP


Platform target ?
Specifies the processor to be targeted by the output file. Choose 'x86' for any 32-bit Intel-compatible processor, choose 'x64' for
any 64-bit Intel-compatible processor, or choose 'Any CPU' to specify that any processor is acceptable. 'Any CPU' is the default
value for projects, because it allows the application to run on the broadest range of hardware.

 Any CPU                                          ▾


Nullable ?
Specifies the project-wide C# nullable context. Only available for projects that use C# 8.0 or later.

 Enable                                           ▾
```

Figure 2-3. *Enable Nullable Reference Types*

Out of the box, Blazor uses the popular Bootstrap 4 layout framework
(https://getbootstrap.com/), including open-iconic fonts. Expect to see bootstrap and
open-iconic (oi) CSS classes in the code samples. However, you can use any other layout
framework, because Blazor uses standard HTML and CSS. This book is about Blazor, not
fancy layouts, so we're not going to spend a lot of time choosing nice colors and making
the site look great. Focus!

In the server project, throw away WeatherForecastController.cs. We don't need
weather forecasts to order pizzas. In the shared project, delete WeatherForecast.cs. Same
thing. In the client project, throw away the Counter.razor and FetchData.razor files from
the Pages folder and SurveyPrompt.razor from the Shared folder.

Adding Shared Classes to Represent the Data

In Blazor, it is best to add classes holding data to the Shared project (unless you are
building a Blazor application without a back-end server). These classes are used to send
the data from the server to the client and later to send the data back. You might know
these kinds of classes as models, or Data Transfer Objects (DTO).

What do we need? Since we will build a site around pizzas, creating a class to
represent this makes sense.

Start with classes representing a `Pizza` and how spicy it is as in Listings 2-26 and 2-27.

Listing 2-26. The Spiciness Class

```
namespace PizzaPlace.Shared
{
  public enum Spiciness
  {
    None,
    Spicy,
    Hot
  }
}
```

Listing 2-27. The Pizza Class

```
namespace PizzaPlace.Shared
{
  public class Pizza
  {
    public Pizza(int id, string name, decimal price,
                 Spiciness spiciness)
    {
      this.Id = id;
      this.Name = name;
      this.Price = price;
      this.Spiciness = spiciness;
    }
    public int Id { get; }
    public string Name { get; }
    public decimal Price { get; }
    public Spiciness Spiciness { get; }
  }
}
```

Our application is NOT about editing pizzas yet, so I've made this class immutable, that is, nothing can be changed once a pizza object has been created. In C#, this is easily done by creating properties with only a getter. You can still set these properties, but only in the constructor.

Next, we will need a class representing the menu we offer. Add a new class to the Shared project called Menu with the implementation from Listing 2-28.

Listing 2-28. The Menu Class

```
using System.Collections.Generic;
using System.Linq;

namespace PizzaPlace.Shared
{
  public class Menu
  {
    public List<Pizza> Pizzas { get; set; }
    = new List<Pizza>();

    public void Add(Pizza pizza)
      => Pizzas.Add(pizza);

    public Pizza? GetPizza(int id)
    => Pizzas.SingleOrDefault(pizza => pizza.Id == id);
  }
}
```

As in real life, a restaurant's menu is a list of meals, in this case, a pizza meal.

We will also need a Customer class in the Shared project with implementation from Listing 2-29. In this case, the Customer class is a normal, mutable class unlike the Pizza class. The user will enter some information which we will store in an instance of Customer. And because we are using nullable reference types, we need to remove the compiler's warning when we don't initialize our properties. This is easily done by assigning default! to them. Chapter 1 talks more about this.

Listing 2-29. The Customer Class

```
namespace PizzaPlace.Shared
{
  public class Customer
  {
    public int Id { get; set; }

    public string Name { get; set; } = default!;

    public string Street { get; set; } = default!;

    public string City { get; set; } = default!;

  }
}
```

Each customer has a shopping basket, so add the Basket class to the Shared project as in Listing 2-30.

Listing 2-30. The Basket Class, Representing the Customer's Order

```
using System.Collections.Generic;

namespace PizzaPlace.Shared
{
  public class ShoppingBasket
  {
    public Customer Customer { get; set; } = new Customer();

    public List<int> Orders { get; set; } = new List<int>();

    public bool HasPaid { get; set; }

  }
}
```

Please note that we just keep the pizza id in the Orders collection. You will learn why later.

One more class before we group them all together. We'll use a UI class to keep track of some UI options, so add this class to the Shared project as in Listing 2-31.

Listing 2-31. The UI Options Class

```
namespace PizzaPlace.Shared
{
  public class UI
  {
    public bool ShowBasket { get; set; } = true;
  }
}
```

Finally, we group all these classes into a single State class, again in the Shared project with implementation from Listing 2-32.

Listing 2-32. The State Class

```
namespace PizzaPlace.Shared
{
  public class State
  {
    public Menu Menu { get; } = new Menu();

    public ShoppingBasket Basket { get; } = new ShoppingBasket();

    public UI UI { get; set; } = new UI();
  }
}
```

There is another good reason to put all these classes into the Shared project. There is limited debugging for Blazor. By putting these classes into the Shared project, we can apply unit testing best practices on the shared classes because it is a regular .NET project and even use the Visual Studio debugger to examine weird behavior. The Shared project can also be used by other projects since it is a .NET Standard project, for example, a Windows or MAUI client!

Building the UI to Show the Menu

With these classes in place to represent the data, the next step is to build the user interface that shows the menu. We will start by displaying the menu to the user, and then we will enhance the UI to allow the user to order one or more pizzas.

The problem of displaying the menu is twofold: first, you need to display a list of data. The menu can be thought of as a list, like any other list. Secondly, in our application, we'll need to convert the spiciness choices from their numeric values into URLs leading to the icons used to indicate different levels of hotness.

Open Index.razor. Remove the <SurveyPrompt> element. Add the @code section to hold our restaurant's (limited) menu with code from Listing 2-33 by initializing the State instance. We also override the OnInitialized method to add our menu items to our State Menu. This method allows you to make some changes to the component before it is rendered for the first time.

Listing 2-33. Building Our Application's Menu

```
@page "/"

<h1>Hello, world!</h1>

Welcome to your new app.

@code {
  private State State { get; } = new State();

  protected override void OnInitialized()
  {
    State.Menu.Add(
      new Pizza(1, "Pepperoni", 8.99M, Spiciness.Spicy ));
    State.Menu.Add(
      new Pizza(2, "Margarita", 7.99M, Spiciness.None));
    State.Menu.Add(
      new Pizza(3, "Diabolo", 9.99M, Spiciness.Hot));
  }
}
```

If you compile now, you will get a bunch of compiler errors. These will tell you that the compiler cannot find the class State. What would you do if this was a C# file? You would add a using statement at the top. We can do the same in a razor file, with an example shown in Listing 2-34.

Listing 2-34. Adding a using Statement to a Razor Component

```
@page "/"
@using PizzaPlace.Shared

<h1>Hello, world!</h1>
```

However, with razor, we can do even better. We can add this using statement to all the components at once!

Open the _Imports.razor file and add a @using like in Listing 2-35. All razor files in the directory (and child directories) of _Imports.razor will now automatically recognize the PizzaPlace.Shared namespace.

Listing 2-35. Add using Statements to _Imports.razor

```
@using System.Net.Http
@using System.Net.Http.Json
@using Microsoft.AspNetCore.Components.Forms
@using Microsoft.AspNetCore.Components.Routing
@using Microsoft.AspNetCore.Components.Web
@using Microsoft.AspNetCore.Components.Web.Virtualization
@using Microsoft.AspNetCore.Components.WebAssembly.Http
@using Microsoft.JSInterop
@using PizzaPlace.Client
@using PizzaPlace.Client.Shared

@using PizzaPlace.Shared
```

The PizzaPlace menu is a list like any other list. You can display it by adding some razor markup in Index.razor to generate the menu as HTML as shown in Listing 2-36. I like to use comments to show the start and end of each section on my page. This makes it easier to find a certain part of my page when I come back to it later. In the next chapter, we will convert each section in its own Blazor component, making future maintenance a lot easier to do.

What we are doing here is iterating over each pizza in the menu and generate a row with four columns, one for the name, one for the price, one for the spiciness, and finally one for the order button. There are still some compiler errors which we will fix next.

Listing 2-36. Generating the HTML with Razor

```
@page "/"

<!-- Menu -->

<h1>Our selection of pizzas</h1>

@foreach (var pizza in State.Menu.Pizzas)
{
  <div class="row">
    <div class="col">
      @pizza.Name
    </div>
    <div class="col text-right">
      @($"{pizza.Price:0.00}")
    </div>
    <div class="col"></div>
    <div class="col">
      <img src="@SpicinessImage(pizza.Spiciness)"
          alt="@pizza.Spiciness" />
    </div>
    <div class="col">
      <button class="btn btn-success pl-4 pr-4"
          @onclick="@(() => AddToBasket(pizza))">
        Add
      </button>
    </div>
  </div>
}
```

```
<!-- End menu -->
@code {
  private State State { get; } = new State();

  protected override void OnInitialized()
  {
    State.Menu.Add(
      new Pizza(1, "Pepperoni", 8.99M, Spiciness.Spicy ));
    State.Menu.Add(
      new Pizza(2, "Margarita", 7.99M, Spiciness.None));
    State.Menu.Add(
      new Pizza(3, "Diabolo", 9.99M, Spiciness.Hot));
  }
}
```

Converting Values

We still have a little problem. We need to convert the spiciness value to an URL, which is done by the SpicinessImage method as shown in Listing 2-37. Add this method to the @code area of the Index.razor file.

Listing 2-37. Converting a Value with a Converter Function

```
private string SpicinessImage(Spiciness spiciness)
  => $"images/{spiciness.ToString().ToLower()}.png";
```

This converter function simply converts the name of the enumeration's value from Listing 2-26 into the URL of an image file which can be found in the Blazor project's images folder as shown in Figure 2-4. Add this folder (which can be found in this book's download) to the wwwroot folder.

hot.png   none.png

spicy.png

Figure 2-4. *The Content of the Images Folder*

Adding Pizzas to the Shopping Basket

Having the menu functioning leads naturally to the adding of pizzas to the shopping basket. When you click the Add button, the AddToBasket method will be executed with the chosen pizza. You can find the implementation of the AddToBasket method in Listing 2-38 which is part of Index.razor.

Listing 2-38. Ordering a Pizza

```
@code {
  private State State { get; } = new State();

  protected override void OnInitialized()
  {
    State.Menu.Add(
      new Pizza(1, "Pepperoni", 8.99M, Spiciness.Spicy ));
    State.Menu.Add(
      new Pizza(2, "Margarita", 7.99M, Spiciness.None));
    State.Menu.Add(
      new Pizza(3, "Diabolo", 9.99M, Spiciness.Hot));
  }

  private string SpicinessImage(Spiciness spiciness)
    => $"images/{spiciness.ToString().ToLower()}.png";

  private void AddToBasket(Pizza pizza)
    => State.Basket.Add(pizza.Id);
}
```

Our ShoppingBasket class now needs an Add method as in Listing 2-39.

Listing 2-39. The Basket's Add Method

```
using System.Collections.Generic;

namespace PizzaPlace.Shared
{
  public class ShoppingBasket
  {
    public Customer Customer { get; set; } = new Customer();

    public List<int> Orders { get; set; } = new List<int>();

    public bool HasPaid { get; set; }

    public void Add(int pizzaId)
    => Orders.Add(pizzaId);
  }
}
```

Look at the @onclick event handler (@onclick="@(() => AddToBasket(pizza))") for the button from Listing 2-36. Why is this event handler using a lambda? When you order a pizza, you want of course to have your chosen pizza added to the basket. So how can we pass the pizza to AddToBasket from Listing 2-38? By using a lambda function, we can simply pass the pizza variable used in the @foreach loop to it. Using a normal method wouldn't work because there is no easy way to send the selected pizza. This is also known as a closure (very similar to JavaScript closures) and can be very practical!

Run the application. You should see Figure 2-5.

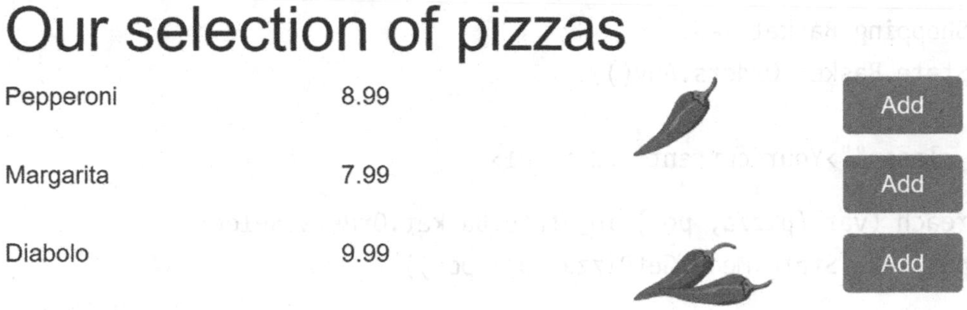

Our selection of pizzas

Pepperoni	8.99		Add
Margarita	7.99		Add
Diabolo	9.99		Add

Figure 2-5. *Our PizzaPlace's Menu*

When you click the Add button, you're adding a pizza to the shopping basket. But how can we be sure (since we're not displaying the shopping basket yet)?

We can use the debugger, just like any other .NET project! Add a breakpoint to the AddToBasket method as in Figure 2-6, and run your project with the debugger. Wait for the browser to display the PizzaPlace page and click one of the Add buttons. The debugger should stop the breakpoint. Now you can inspect the argument of the AddToBasket method, which should be the selected pizza. Most of the usual debugging stuff works with Blazor!

```
135     private string SpicinessImage(Spiciness spiciness)
136     ⇒ $"images/{spiciness.ToString().ToLower()}.png";
137
138     private void AddToBasket(Pizza pizza)
139     ⇒ State.Basket.Add(pizza.Id);
140
141     private void RemoveFromBasket(int pos)
142     ⇒ State.Basket.RemoveAt(pos);
```

Figure 2-6. *Adding a Breakpoint to Your Component*

Displaying the Shopping Basket

The next thing on the menu (some pun intended) is displaying the shopping basket. We are going to use a feature from C# called *tuples*. I will explain tuples in a moment.

Add Listing 2-40 after the menu from Listing 2-36 (the comments should make this quite easy to find).

Listing 2-40. Displaying the Shopping Basket

```
<!-- End menu -->
<!-- Shopping Basket -->
@if (State.Basket.Orders.Any())
{
  <h1 class="">Your current order</h1>

  @foreach (var (pizza, pos) in State.Basket.Orders.Select(
(id, pos) => (State.Menu.GetPizza(id), pos)))
  {
    <div class="row mb-2">
      <div class="col">
        @pizza.Name
      </div>
      <div class="col text-right">
        @($"{pizza.Price:0.00}")
      </div>
      <div class="col"></div>

      <div class="col"></div>
      <div class="col">
        <button class="btn btn-danger"
            @onclick="@(() => RemoveFromBasket(pos))">
          Remove
        </button>
      </div>
    </div>
  }

  <div class="row">
    <div class="col"></div>
    <div class="col"><hr /></div>
    <div class="col"> </div>
    <div class="col"> </div>
  </div>
```

```
<div class="row">
  <div class="col"> Total:</div>
  <div class="col text-right font-weight-bold"> @($"{State.
  TotalPrice:0.00}") </div>
  <div class="col"> </div>
  <div class="col"> </div>
  <div class="col"> </div>
</div>
}

<!-- End shopping basket -->
```

Most of this stuff is very similar, but now we are iterating over a list of tuples (keep reading, a very handy new feature in C# https://docs.microsoft.com/dotnet/csharp/tuples).

Tuples are very similar to anonymous types from C#, in that they let you store and return intermediate multi-part results without you having to build a helper class.

Let's look at this code in a little more detail:

```
@foreach (var (pizza, pos) in State.Basket.Orders.Select(
 (id, pos) => (State.Menu.GetPizza(id), pos)))
```

We are using LINQ's Select to iterate over the list of orders (which contain pizza ids). To display the pizza in the shopping basket, we need a pizza, so we convert the id to a pizza with the GetPizza method from the Menu.

Let's look at the lambda function used in the Select:

```
(id, pos) => (State.Menu.GetPizza(id), pos))
```

The LINQ Select method has two overloads, and we're using the overload taking an element from the collection (id) and the position in the collection (pos). We use these to create tuples. Each tuple represents a pizza from the basket and its position in the basket! We could have done the same, creating a little helper class with the pizza and position, but this is now done for us! And it is efficacious, using less memory than a class because it is a value type!

The pizza is used to display its name and price, while the position is used in the Delete button. This button invokes the RemoveFromBasket method from Listing 2-41.

Listing 2-41. Removing Items from the Shopping Basket

```
@code {
  private State State { get; } = new State();

  protected override void OnInitialized()
  {
    State.Menu.Add(
      new Pizza(1, "Pepperoni", 8.99M, Spiciness.Spicy ));
    State.Menu.Add(
      new Pizza(2, "Margarita", 7.99M, Spiciness.None));
    State.Menu.Add(
      new Pizza(3, "Diabolo", 9.99M, Spiciness.Hot));
  }

  private string SpicinessImage(Spiciness spiciness)
    => $"images/{spiciness.ToString().ToLower()}.png";

    private void AddToBasket(Pizza pizza)
    => State.Basket.Add(pizza.Id);

    private void RemoveFromBasket(int pos)
    => State.Basket.RemoveAt(pos);
}
```

And of course, we need to add the RemoveAt method to the ShoppingBasket class as in Listing 2-42.

Listing 2-42. The Basket Class's RemoveAt Method

```
using System.Collections.Generic;

namespace PizzaPlace.Shared
{
  public class ShoppingBasket
  {
    public Customer Customer { get; set; } = new Customer();

    public List<int> Orders { get; set; } = new List<int>();
```

```
    public bool HasPaid { get; set; }

    public void Add(int pizzaId)
    => Orders.Add(pizzaId);

    public void RemoveAt(int pos)
      => Orders.RemoveAt(pos);
  }
}
```

At the bottom of the shopping basket, the total order amount is shown. This is calculated by the State class. Add the TotalPrice method from Listing 2-43 to the State class. Please note the use of the null-forgiving operator (!) because I am assuming that the ShoppingBasket will always contain valid pizza ids.

Listing 2-43. Calculating the Total Price in the State Class

```
using System.Linq;

namespace PizzaPlace.Shared
{
  public class State
  {
    public Menu Menu { get; } = new Menu();

    public ShoppingBasket Basket { get; } = new ShoppingBasket();

    public UI UI { get; set; } = new UI();

    public decimal TotalPrice
      => Basket.Orders.Sum(id => Menu.GetPizza(id)!.Price);
  }
}
```

Run the application and order some pizzas. You should see your current order similar to Figure 2-7.

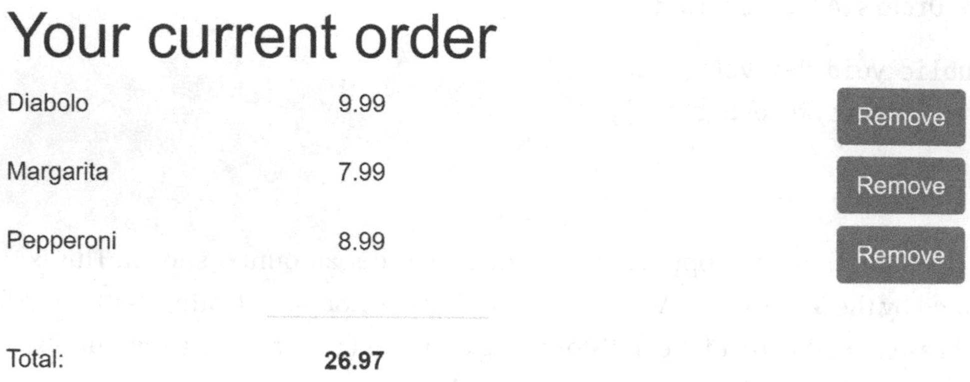

Your current order

Diabolo	9.99	Remove
Margarita	7.99	Remove
Pepperoni	8.99	Remove
Total:	**26.97**	

Figure 2-7. *Your Shopping Basket with a Couple of Pizzas*

Entering the Customer Information

Of course, to complete the order, we need to know a couple of things about the customer, especially we need to know the customer's name and address because we need to deliver the order.

Start by adding the following razor to your Index.razor page as in Listing 2-44.

Listing 2-44. Adding Form Elements for Data Entry

```
<!-- End shopping basket -->
<!-- Customer entry -->

<h1>Please enter your details below</h1>

<fieldset>
  <div class="row mb-2">
    <label class="col-2" for="name">Name:</label>
    <input class="col-6" id="name"
      @bind="State.Basket.Customer.Name" />
  </div>
  <div class="row mb-2">
    <label class="col-2" for="street">Street:</label>
```

```
    <input class="col-6" id="street"
      @bind="State.Basket.Customer.Street" />
  </div>
  <div class="row mb-2">
    <label class="col-2" for="city">City:</label>
    <input class="col-6" id="city"
      @bind="State.Basket.Customer.City" />
  </div>

  <button @onclick="PlaceOrder">Checkout</button>

</fieldset>

<!-- End customer entry -->
```

This adds three `<label>`s and their respective `<input>`s for name, street, and city.

You will also need to add the `PlaceOrder` method to your `@code` as shown in Listing 2-45.

Listing 2-45. The PlaceOrder Method

```
@code {
  private State State { get; } = new State();

  protected override void OnInitialized()
  {
    State.Menu.Add(
      new Pizza(1, "Pepperoni", 8.99M, Spiciness.Spicy));
    State.Menu.Add(
      new Pizza(2, "Margarita", 7.99M, Spiciness.None));
    State.Menu.Add(
      new Pizza(3, "Diabolo", 9.99M, Spiciness.Hot));
  }

  private string SpicinessImage(Spiciness spiciness)
    => $"images/{spiciness.ToString().ToLower()}.png";

  private void AddToBasket(Pizza pizza)
  => State.Basket.Add(pizza.Id);
```

```
private void RemoveFromBasket(int pos)
=> State.Basket.RemoveAt(pos);

private void PlaceOrder()
{
  Console.WriteLine("Placing order");
}
}
```

The PlaceOrder method doesn't do anything useful yet; we'll send the order to the server later. This does however show a valid debugging technique in Blazor, where we place Console.WriteLine statements to see what gets executed.

Run the application and enter your details, for example, as in Figure 2-8.

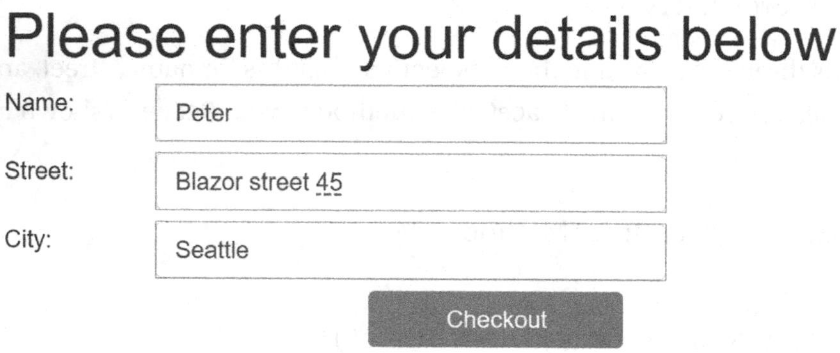

Please enter your details below

Name:	Peter
Street:	Blazor street 45
City:	Seattle

Checkout

Figure 2-8.   *Filling Out the Customer Detail*

Debugging Tip

Even with modern debuggers, you want to see the State object because it contains the customer's details and order as you are interacting with the application. Will we send the correct information to the server when we press the Checkout button? For this, we'll use a simple trick by displaying the State on our page, so you can review it at any time.

Start by adding a new static class DebuggingExtensions to your Blazor client project as in Listing 2-46.

Listing 2-46. The DebuggingExtensions Class

```
using System.Text.Json;

namespace PizzaPlace.Client
{
  public static class DebuggingExtensions
  {
    private static JsonSerializerOptions options = new
JsonSerializerOptions { WriteIndented = true };

    public static string ToJson(this object obj)
      => JsonSerializer.Serialize(obj, options);
  }
}
```

And at the bottom of Index.razor, add a simple paragraph as in Listing 2-47.

Listing 2-47. Showing State

```
<!-- End customer entry -->
@State.ToJson()

@code {
```

Run your project. As you interact with the page, you'll see State change with an example shown in Figure 2-9.

```
{ "Menu": { "Pizzas": [ { "Id": 1, "Name": "Pepperoni", "Price": 8.99, "Spiciness": 1 }, { "Id": 2,
"Name": "Margarita", "Price": 7.99, "Spiciness": 0 }, { "Id": 3, "Name": "Diabolo", "Price": 9.99,
"Spiciness": 2 } ] }, "Basket": { "Customer": { "Id": 0, "Name": "Peter", "Street": "Blazor street
45", "City": "Seattle" }, "Orders": [ 2, 3, 1 ], "HasPaid": false }, "UI": { "ShowBasket": true },
"TotalPrice": 26.97 }
```

Figure 2-9. *Watching State Changes*

It should be obvious that we remove this debugging feature when the page is ready ☺. For example, you could add an #if DEBUG inside the ToJson method to only make it work outside release builds.

Blazor Validation

But wait! Clicking the Checkout button works, even while there is no customer name, address, or city! We need to do some validation! So, let's start with an introduction to Blazor *validation*.

Letting Entities Validate Themselves

Classes like Customer should validate themselves because they have the best knowledge about the validity of their properties. .NET has a couple of built-in validation mechanisms, and here we are going to use the standard System.ComponentModel. DataAnnotations. In Chapter 3, we will look at using other validation mechanisms. With data annotations, you add attributes to your entity's properties, indicating what kind of validation is required.

Start by adding the System.ComponentModel.Annotations package to the PizzaPlace.Shared project.

Now add [Required] attributes to the Customer class as in Listing 2-48. These annotations make the Name, Street, and City properties mandatory. Use the ErrorMessage property to set the validation error message. You can add other attributes like [CreditCard], [EmailAddress], [MaxLength], [MinLength], [Phone], [Range], [RegularExpression], [StringLength], and [Url] for further validation.

Listing 2-48. Adding Annotations for Validation

```
using System.ComponentModel.DataAnnotations;

namespace PizzaPlace.Shared
{
  public class Customer
  {
    public int Id { get; set; }

    [Required(ErrorMessage = "Please provide a name")]
    public string Name { get; set; } = default!;

    [Required(ErrorMessage = "Please provide a street with house number.")]
    public string Street { get; set; } = default!;
```

```
    [Required(ErrorMessage = "Please provide a city")]
    public string City { get; set; } = default!;
  }
}
```

Using FormField and InputText to Enable Validation

Blazor comes with some built-in components that will perform validation for you. Replace the customer entry UI with Listing 2-49. Here, we replace the <input> HTML elements with built-in editing components. The EditForm component wraps around all the InputText components and will render as the HTML <form> element. The EditForm component has a Model property which you set to the instance you need to validate. When the user clicks the Submit button, the EditForm component performs validation, and when there are no validation errors, it will call the OnValidSubmit event.

Use the InputText component for each field, binding one to each property of the model using the @bind-Value attribute. This is the syntax used to tell the component to use two-way data binding between the Value property of the InputText component and the property of the model. Listing 2-49 has three such InputText components, one for Name, Address, and City.

Other input components also exist for other types, such as InputTextArea, InputRadio, InputRadioGroup, InputDate, InputCheckbox, InputSelect, and InputNumber. You can even build your own.

Listing 2-49. Using EditForm and InputText

```
<!-- Customer entry -->

<h1 class="mt-2 mb-2">Please enter your details below</h1>

<EditForm Model="@State.Basket.Customer"
        OnValidSubmit="PlaceOrder">

  <fieldset>
    <div class="row mb-2">
      <label class="col-2" for="name">Name:</label>
      <InputText class="form-control col-6"
        @bind-Value="@State.Basket.Customer.Name" />
    </div>
```

91

```
  <div class="row mb-2">
    <label class="col-2" for="street">Street:</label>
    <InputText class="form-control col-6"
      @bind-Value="@State.Basket.Customer.Street" />
  </div>
  <div class="row mb-2">
    <label class="col-2" for="city">City:</label>
    <InputText class="form-control col-6"
      @bind-Value="@State.Basket.Customer.City" />
  </div>
  <div class="row mb-2">
    <button class="mx-auto w-25 btn btn-success"
      @onclick="PlaceOrder">Checkout</button>
  </div>
</fieldset>
</EditForm>

<!-- End customer entry -->
```

Showing Validation Errors

If you run the application right now, you will see that there is no validation yet. Why? Because Blazor allows you to choose between different validation systems (and even build your own), and we did not pick one! Here, we want to use data annotations for validation, so add the DataAnnotationsValidator component to the EditForm as in Listing 2-50.

Listing 2-50. Adding DataAnnotationsValidator

```
<EditForm Model="@State.Basket.Customer"
        OnValidSubmit="PlaceOrder">

  <DataAnnotationsValidator />

  <fieldset>
```

Run the application again, and click the Checkout button. You will see that the inputs now receive a red border, because of validation errors. As a user, you would now wonder what you did wrong. So we need to show some error as feedback.

To show the validation message for each input, you add a `ValidationMessage` component and you set the `For` property to a delegate that returns the field to show validation messages for as in Listing 2-51.

Listing 2-51. Showing Validation Messages

```
<EditForm Model="@State.Basket.Customer"
          OnValidSubmit="PlaceOrder">

  <DataAnnotationsValidator />

  <fieldset>
    <div class="row mb-2">
      <label class="col-2" for="name">Name:</label>
      <InputText class="form-control col-6"
        @bind-Value="@State.Basket.Customer.Name" />
    </div>
    <div class="row mb-2">
      <div class="col-6 offset-2">
        <ValidationMessage
          For="@(() => State.Basket.Customer.Name)" />
      </div>
    </div>
    <div class="row mb-2">
      <label class="col-2" for="street">Street:</label>
      <InputText class="form-control col-6"
        @bind-Value="@State.Basket.Customer.Street" />
    </div>
    <div class="row mb-2">
      <div class="col-6 offset-2">
        <ValidationMessage
          For="@(() => State.Basket.Customer.Street)" />
      </div>
    </div>
```

```
    <div class="row mb-2">
      <label class="col-2" for="city">City:</label>
      <InputText class="form-control col-6"
        @bind-Value="@State.Basket.Customer.City" />
    </div>
    <div class="row mb-2">
      <div class="col-6 offset-2">
        <ValidationMessage
          For="@(() => State.Basket.Customer.City)" />
      </div>
    </div>
    <div class="row mb-2">
      <button class="mx-auto w-25 btn btn-success"
        @onclick="PlaceOrder">Checkout</button>
    </div>
  </fieldset>
</EditForm>
```

Build and run the PizzaPlace project. Click the Checkout button. You should get validation errors as shown in Figure 2-10. Blazor validation also adds some styles, and by default, this will put a red border around inputs with validation errors.

Please enter your details below

Name:

Please provide a name

Street:

Please provide a street with house number.

City:

Please provide a city

Checkout

Figure 2-10. *Showing Validation Errors*

Note that the Checkout button does not invoke the `PlaceOrder` method if there are validation errors.

Now enter a name, street, and city. You should see the validation errors go away. You will also see green borders appear since the inputs are now valid.

You can also use a `ValidationSummary` component which shows all the validation errors together as an unordered list. For example, you can add the `ValidationSummary` component below the `DataAnnotationsValidator` as in Listing 2-52. This will show all validation errors as in Figure 2-11.

Listing 2-52. Using the `ValidationSummary` Component

```
<EditForm Model="@State.Basket.Customer"
          OnValidSubmit="PlaceOrder">

  <DataAnnotationsValidator />
  <ValidationSummary/>
```

Please enter your details below

- Please provide a name
- Please provide a street with house number.
- Please provide a city

Figure 2-11. *The ValidationSummary's Output*

Customizing the Validation Feedback

When you enter a value in an `InputText` element (or one of the other input components), Blazor validation gives you feedback about the validity of the value by adding certain CSS classes. Let us have a look at how this is implemented. Run the PizzaPlace project, right-click one of the inputs, and then select Inspect from the browser's menu.

Initially, an untouched input will have the `valid` class, as in Listing 2-53 (the other classes come from the class attribute in Listing 2-51).

Listing 2-53. Validation Uses the Valid CSS Class

```
<input class="form-control col-6 valid" ...>
```

When you make a valid change to an input, the `modified` class is added as in Listing 2-54.

Listing 2-54. Validation Adds the Modified Class After a Change

```
<input class="form-control col-6 modified valid" ...>
```

With an invalid input, you get the `invalid` class, as in Listing 2-55.

Listing 2-55. Bad Input Uses the Invalid CSS Class

```
<input class="form-control col-6 modified invalid" ...>
```

Finally, validation messages get the `validation-message` CSS class, as in Listing 2-56.

Listing 2-56. Validation Messages Use the validation-message Class

```
<div class="validation-message">Please provide a name</div>
```

Out of the box, Blazor uses the following CSS styling for validation, as shown in Listing 2-57. You can find these CSS rules in wwwroot/css/app.css. Simply put, these add a green outline to an input if it has valid modifications and a red outline when the input has an invalid value.

Listing 2-57. Blazor's built-in CSS Validation Rules

```
.valid.modified:not([type=checkbox]) {
    outline: 1px solid #26b050;
}

.invalid {
    outline: 1px solid red;
}

.validation-message {
    color: red;
}
```

So, if you want to customize how your feedback looks like, you customize these CSS rules. For example, you can use the following CSS to wwwroot/css/app.css from Listing 2-58 to make validation look like Figure 2-12.

Listing 2-58. Some Custom CSS Rules to Change Validation Feedback

```css
.valid.modified:not([type=checkbox]) {
  border-left: 5px solid #42A948; /* green */
}

.invalid {
  border-right: 5px solid #a94442; /* red */
}

.validation-message {
  color: #a94442;
}
```

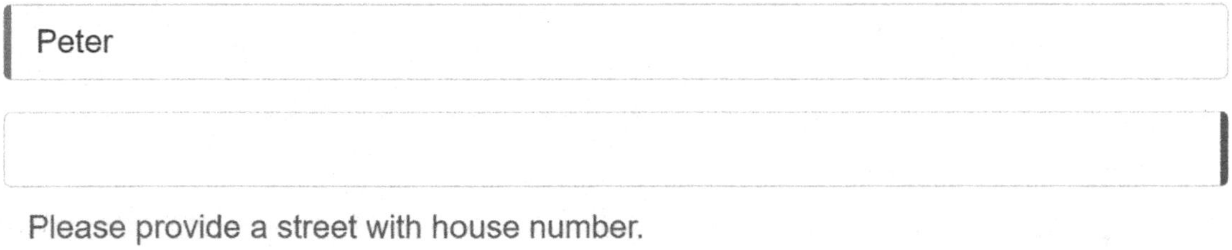

Please provide a street with house number.

Figure 2-12. *Customized Validation Feedback*

Summary

In this chapter, we looked at data binding in Blazor. We started with one-way data binding where we can embed the value of a property or a field in the UI using the @ SomeProperty syntax. We then looked at event binding where you bind an element's event to a method using the on<event>="@SomeMethod" syntax. Blazor also has support for two-way data binding where we can update the UI with the value of a property and vice versa using the @bind="SomeProperty" syntax. Finally, we examined validation where we can use standard .NET validation techniques.

CHAPTER 3

Components and Structure for Blazor Applications

In the previous chapter on data binding, you have built a single monolithic application called PizzaPlace with Blazor. After a while, this will become harder and harder to maintain because everything is in one place, resulting in one big razor file.

In modern web development, we build applications by constructing them from *components*, which typically are again built from smaller components. A Blazor component is a self-contained chunk of user interface. *Blazor components* are classes built from razor and C# with one specific purpose (also known as *single responsibility principle*) and are easier to understand, debug, and maintain. And of course, you can reuse the same component in different pages, which can be a huge advantage.

In this chapter, we will explore how to build Blazor components.

What Is a Blazor Component?

To put it in a simple manner, each razor file in Blazor is a component. It's that simple! A razor file in Blazor contains markup and has code in the @code section. Each page we have been using from the MyFirstBlazor project is a component! And components can be built by adding other components as children.

Any class that derives from the ComponentBase class becomes a Blazor component; a little later, we will build an example of this. When you use a razor file, the generated class will also derive from ComponentBase.

Remember the MyFirstBlazor project from the previous chapter? Create a new one just like it in Visual Studio (or Code), and let's have a look at some of the components in there.

© Peter Himschoot 2022
P. Himschoot, *Microsoft Blazor*, https://doi.org/10.1007/978-1-4842-7845-1_3

Open Index.razor as in Listing 3-1. See SurveyPrompt? That is one of the components that are part of the Blazor template. It takes one parameter Title which we can set where we want to use the component. Let us have a good look at the SurveyPrompt component.

Listing 3-1. The Index Page

```
@page "/"

<h1>Hello, world!</h1>

Welcome to your new app.

<SurveyPrompt Title="How is Blazor working for you?" />
```

Examining the SurveyPrompt Component

Open SurveyPrompt.razor as in Listing 3-2, which can be found in the Shared folder of the client project. The component is called SurveyPrompt because a component gets named after the razor file it is in.

Listing 3-2. The SurveyPrompt Component

```
<div class="alert alert-secondary mt-4" role="alert">
  <span class="oi oi-pencil mr-2" aria-hidden="true"></span>
  <strong>@Title</strong>

  <span class="text-nowrap">
    Please take our
    <a target="_blank" class="font-weight-bold"
       href="https://go.microsoft.com/fwlink/?linkid=2148851">
      brief survey
    </a>
  </span>
  and tell us what you think.
</div>
```

```
@code {
    // Demonstrates how a parent component can supply parameters
    [Parameter]
    public string Title { get; set; }
}
```

Look at the Razor markup. This is a simple Blazor component that displays an icon in front of the Title as shown in Figure 3-1 and then displays a link to the survey (a real survey which you should take 😊 – this will show Microsoft that you're interested in Blazor).

Hello, world!

Welcome to your new app.

> ✏️ **How is Blazor working for you?**
> Please take our **brief survey** and tell us what you think.

Figure 3-1. *The SurveyPrompt Component*

The @code section simply contains a property Title that uses one-way data binding for rendering in the component. Do note the [Parameter] attribute on the Title property. This is required for components that want to expose their *public* properties to the parent component. This way, we can pass data to nested components, for example, how the Index component passes the Title to the SurveyPrompt component.

Building a Simple Alert Component with Razor

Let us build our own Blazor component that will show a simple alert. Alerts are used to draw the attention of the user to some message, for example, a warning.

Creating a New Component with Visual Studio

Open the MyFirstBlazor solution. Right-click the Pages folder and select Add ➤ New Item.... The Add New Item window should open as in Figure 3-2.

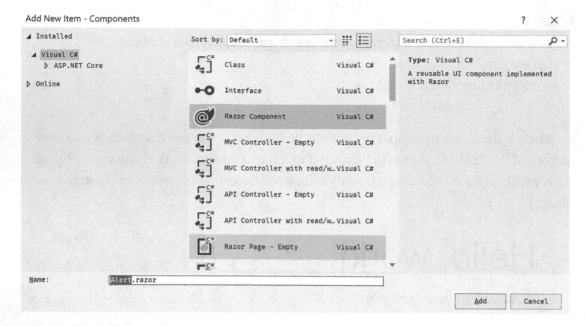

Figure 3-2. *The Add New Item Window*

Select Razor Component and name it Alert.razor. Click Add.

Creating a New Component with Code

Right-click the Pages folder of the client project and select New File. Name it Alert.razor. Unlike Visual Studio, this will not generate any code in this file. There are extensions available for creating Blazor components. I will let you explore which one you like best (e.g., `https://visualstudiomagazine.com/articles/2020/04/08/vs-code-blazor.aspx`).

Implementing the Alert Component

Remove all existing content from Alert.razor and replace it with Listing 3-3. Let us have a look at this component.

The first line in the `Alert` component uses an `@if` to hide or show its inner content. This is a common technique if you want to conditionally display content. So, if the `Show` public property (actually parameter) is `false`, the whole component is not shown. This allows us to "hide" the component until needed.

Our `Alert` component will show some content in a `<div>` element as an alert (using bootstrap styles), so how do we pass this content to the `Alert` component?

Inside the @if, there is a <div> element with @ChildContent as its child. You use @ChildContent if you want to access the nested element in the Alert component, as you'll see when we use the Alert component in Listing 3-4.

Blazor dictates that this property/parameter should be named @ChildContent and it needs to be of type RenderFragment because this is the way the Blazor engine passes it (we will look at this later in this chapter).

Listing 3-3. The Alert Component

```
@if (Show)
{
  <div class="alert alert-secondary mt-4" role="alert">
    @ChildContent
  </div>
}
@code {
  [Parameter]
  public bool Show { get; set; }

  [Parameter]
  public RenderFragment ChildContent { get; set; } = default!;
}
```

Note   The default Blazor templates use Bootstrap 4 for styling. Bootstrap (http://getbootstrap.com) is a very popular CSS framework, originally built for Twitter, giving an easy layout for web pages. However, Blazor does not require you to use bootstrap, so you can use whatever styling you prefer. In that case, you would have to update all the razor files in the solution using the other styles, just like in regular web development. In this book, we will use bootstrap, simply because it is there.

Go back to Index.razor to add the element.

As you start to type, Visual Studio and Code are smart enough to provide you with IntelliSense, as illustrated in Figure 3-3, for the Alert component and its parameters!

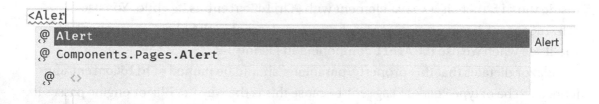

Figure 3-3. *Visual Studio IntelliSense Support for Custom Blazor Components*

Complete the Alert and add a button as in Listing 3-4.

Listing 3-4. Using Our Alert Component in Index.razor

```
@page "/"

<h1>Hello, world!</h1>

<Alert Show="@ShowAlert">
  <span class="oi oi-check mr-2" aria-hidden="true"></span>
  <strong>Blazor is so cool!</strong>
</Alert>

<button @onclick="ToggleAlert" class="btn btn-success">Toggle</button>

@code {
  public bool ShowAlert { get; set; } = true;

  public void ToggleAlert() => ShowAlert = !ShowAlert;
}
```

Inside the <Alert> tag, there is a <span> displaying a checkmark icon using the open-iconic font and a <strong> element displaying a simple message. These will be set as the @ChildContent property of the Alert component.

Build and run your project. When you click the <button>, it calls the ToggleAlert method which will hide and show the Alert as in Figure 3-4.

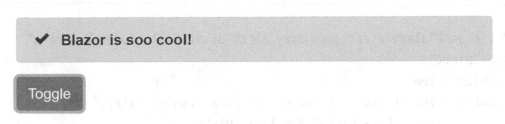

Figure 3-4. *Our Simple Alert Component Before Clicking the Toggle Button*

Separating View and View Model

You might not like this mixing of markup (*view*) and code (*view model*). If you like, you can use two separate files, one for the view using razor and another for the view model using C#. The view will display the data from the view model, and event handlers in the view will invoke methods from the view model.

Some people prefer this way of working because it's more like the *MVVM* pattern.

Each Blazor razor file gets generated into a C# partial class. If you want to separate the code from the razor file, put the code in a partial class with the same name as the component. The C# compiler will merge code from both files into a single class. Let's try this!

Creating a DismissibleAlert Component

If you haven't done so yet, open the MyFirstBlazor solution. With Visual Studio, right-click the Pages folder and select Add ➤ New Item…. The Add New Item dialog should open as shown in Figure 3-2. This time, select Razor Component and name it DismissibleAlert.razor. Also, add a new C# class, and call the file DismissibleAlert. razor.cs.

With Visual Studio Code, right-click the Pages folder, select New File, and name it DismissibleAlert.razor. Do this again to create a new file called Dismissible.razor.cs.

A `Dismissible` is an alert with a little x button, which the user can click to dismiss the alert. It is quite similar to the previous `Alert` component. Replace the markup in the razor file with Listing 3-5.

105

Listing 3-5. The Markup for Dismissible.razor

```
@if (Show)
{
  <div class="alert alert-secondary alert-dismissible fade show mt-4"
  role="alert">
    @ChildContent
    <button type="button" class="close" data-dismiss="alert"
            aria-label="Close" @onclick="Dismiss">
      <span aria-hidden="true">&times;</span>
    </button>
  </div>
}
```

There is no @code section, because you will write this in the .cs file.

Replace the C# code in Dismissible.razor.cs with Listing 3-6.

Listing 3-6. The Code for Dismissible.razor.cs

```
using Microsoft.AspNetCore.Components;

namespace Components.Pages
{
  public partial class Dismissible
  {
    [Parameter]
    public bool Show { get; set; }

    [Parameter]
    public RenderFragment ChildContent { get; set; } = default!;

    public void Dismiss()
      => Show = false;
  }
}
```

Do note that this is a *partial* class with the same name as the Blazor component! So instead of putting your code in the @code section of a razor file, you can put the code in a partial class.

Which model is best? I don't think either one is better than the other; it is more a matter of taste. Choose the one you like. I do like the code separation model a little more (my personal opinion) because I think the C# editor has better features for keeping my code maintainable and clean.

Understanding Parent-Child Communication

Parent and child components typically communicate through data binding. For example, in Listing 3-7, we are using our Dismissible, which communicates with the parent component through the parent's ShowAlert property. Clicking the Toggle button will hide and show the alert. You can try this by replacing the contents of Index.razor (simply replace Alert with Dismissible) with Listing 3-7.

Listing 3-7. Using Dismissible

```
@page "/"

<h1>Hello, world!</h1>

<Dismissible Show="@ShowAlert">
  <span class="oi oi-check mr-2" aria-hidden="true"></span>
  <strong>Blazor is so cool!</strong>
</Dismissible>

<button @onclick="ToggleAlert" class="btn btn-success">Toggle</button>

@code {
  public bool ShowAlert { get; set; } = true;

  public void ToggleAlert() => ShowAlert = !ShowAlert;
}
```

Adding a Timer Component

Start by adding a new class called Timer to the Pages folder as shown in Listing 3-8. The timer will not have any visual part, so we don't even need a .razor file to build the view.

A Blazor component is a class that inherits the ComponentBase class. Since we want to use the Timer class as a Blazor component, we need to inherit from ComponentBase.

This `Timer` class will invoke a delegate (`Tick`) after a certain number of seconds (`TimeInSeconds`) have expired. The `Tick` parameter is of type `Action`, which is one of the built-in delegate types of .NET. An `Action` is simply a method returning a void with no parameters. There are other generic `Action` types, such as `Action<T>` which is a method returning void with one parameter of type T. This allows the parent component to set the `Action`, so the child will execute the `Action` (in this case, after `TimeInSeconds` has expired).

Listing 3-8. The Timer Class

```
using Microsoft.AspNetCore.Components;
using System;
using System.Threading;

namespace Components.Pages
{
  public class Timer : ComponentBase
  {
    [Parameter]
    public double TimeInSeconds { get; set; }

    [Parameter]
    public Action Tick { get; set; } = default!;

    protected override void OnInitialized()
    {
      var timer = new System.Threading.Timer(
        callback: (_) => InvokeAsync(() => Tick?.Invoke()),
        state: null,
        dueTime: TimeSpan.FromSeconds(TimeInSeconds),
        period: Timeout.InfiniteTimeSpan);
    }
  }
}
```

Now add the `Timer` component to the Index page as in Listing 3-9. With this change, the `Timer` component will invoke the `ToggleAlert` method after 5 seconds.

Listing 3-9. Adding the Timer Component to Dismiss the Alert

```
@page "/"

<h1>Hello, world!</h1>

<Dismissible Show="@ShowAlert">
  <span class="oi oi-check mr-2" aria-hidden="true"></span>
  <strong>Blazor is so cool!</strong>
</Dismissible>

<button @onclick="ToggleAlert" class="btn btn-success">Toggle</button>

<Timer TimeInSeconds="5" Tick="ToggleAlert"/>

@code {
  public bool ShowAlert { get; set; } = true;

  public void ToggleAlert()
  {
    Console.WriteLine("*** Toggle ***");
    ShowAlert = !ShowAlert;
  }
}
```

Run the application and wait at least 5 seconds. The alert does not hide! Why?!

Look at the markup, which is in Listing 3-9, for Dismissible. It shows the component based on the Show parameter, and this one gets set through data binding. Does the ToggleAlert method get called? Run the Blazor website again, and immediately open the browser's debugger on the console tab. After a little while, you should see the Console.WriteLine output appear. So the ToggleAlert method does get called.

Think about this. We invoke a method asynchronously using a Timer. When the timer fires, we set the Index component ShowAlert property to false. But we still need to update the UI. You can manually trigger the UI to update by calling the StateHasChanged method.

This is very important! The Blazor runtime updates the UI automatically when an event triggers, like the button click. The Blazor runtime also updates the UI for its own asynchronous methods, but not for other asynchronous methods like Timer.

Time to fix our application. Add a call to StateHasChanged in the ToggleAlert method as in Listing 3-10.

Listing 3-10. Adding StateHasChanged

```
public void ToggleAlert()
{
  ShowAlert = !ShowAlert;
  StateHasChanged();
}
```

Run again and wait, and after 5 seconds, the alert disappears!

To be honest, I don't like the previous solution to our problem. Because a child component calls the ToggleAlert method, we manually need to call StateHasChanged. Is there no better way? And we haven't even solved another problem. When the user dismissed the alert before the timer triggered the Tick method, it should reappear after 5 seconds because it will set ShowAlert back to true!

We will fix both problems, but first, we need to understand two-way data binding between components.

Using Two-Way Data Binding Between Components

When the user clicks the Dismissible component's close button, it sets its own Show property to false, as intended. The problem is that the parent Index component's ShowAlert stays true. Changing the value of the Dismissible local Show property will not update the Index component's ShowAlert property. What we need is two-way data binding between components, and Blazor has that.

With two-way data binding, changing the value of the Show parameter will update the value of the ShowAlert property of the parent and vice versa.

You can use the @bind-<<NameOfProperty>> syntax (which we already used with the InputTitle component in the previous chapter) to data bind any property of a child component. This will use two-way data binding. So update the Index page to use two-way data binding as in Listing 3-11.

Listing 3-11. Using Two-Way Data Binding

```
<Dismissible @bind-Show="ShowAlert">
  <span class="oi oi-check mr-2" aria-hidden="true"></span>
  <strong>Blazor is so cool!</strong>
</Dismissible>
```

Run the website. However, you will not see any valid page. The Blazor runtime encountered a problem. You can discover the problem by opening the browser's debugger. Check the console. You will see a bunch of red messages, one of which is stating:

```
Object of type 'Components.Pages.Dismissible' does not have a property
matching the name 'ShowChanged'.
```

Properties that support two-way data binding need a way to tell the parent that the property has changed. The child component uses for that a delegate, so the parent component through the Blazor runtime can install its own change handler (just like an event) when the property has changed. This change handler will then update the parent component's data bound property. The child component is responsible for invoking the Changed delegate when the property changes.

Open the `Dismissible` class and its implementation to match Listing 3-12. There are two changes. First of all, the Show property now uses the "full" implementation of a property, because we need to implement the setter that it will call the ShowChanged delegate when its value changes.

Second we add an extra parameter which should be called `<<yourproperty>>Changed` of type `Action<<typeofyourproperty>>`. For example, the property is named Show of type bool, so we add ShowChanged of type Action<bool>.

Listing 3-12. The Dismissible Class with Two-Way Binding Support

```
using Microsoft.AspNetCore.Components;
using System;

namespace Components.Pages
{
  public partial class Dismissible
  {
    private bool show;
```

```
[Parameter]
public bool Show
{
  get => show;
  set
  {
    if (value != show)
    {
      show = value;
      ShowChanged?.Invoke(show);
    }
  }
}

[Parameter]
public Action<bool>? ShowChanged { get; set; }

[Parameter]
public RenderFragment ChildContent { get; set; } = default!;

public void Dismiss()
  => Show = false;
}
}
```

Whenever someone or something changes the Show property's value, the property's setter triggers the ShowChanged delegate. This means the parent component can inject some code (which it does for you when you use two-way data binding) into the ShowChanged delegate property which will invoke when the property is changed (internally or externally).

Note   The property setter checks if the value has changed. Only trigger the Changed delegate when there is an actual change. This will avoid a possible endless loop of Changed handling.

Now, when the Dismissible Show property changes, Blazor will update the parent's ShowAlert property because we are using two-way data binding.

We still need to fix the problem when the Timer fires.

One way (but there is a better way) is in Listing 3-13. Here, we call StateHasChanged whenever the ShowAlert property gets a new value. This is better because anywhere we update the ShowAlert property, we update the UI.

Listing 3-13. Update the UI when ShowAlert Changes the Value

```
@page "/"

<h1>Hello, world!</h1>

<DismissibleAlert @bind-Show="ShowAlert">
  <span class="oi oi-check mr-2" aria-hidden="true"></span>
  <strong>Blazor is so cool!</strong>
</DismissibleAlert>

<button @onclick="ToggleAlert" class="btn btn-success">Toggle</button>

<Timer TimeInSeconds="5" Tick="ToggleAlert" />

@code {
  private bool showAlert = true;

  public bool ShowAlert
  {
    get => showAlert; set
    {
      if (value != showAlert)
      {
        showAlert = value;
        StateHasChanged();
      }
    }
  }

  public void ToggleAlert()
  {
    ShowAlert = !ShowAlert;
  }
}
```

Run. Wait 5 seconds.

The Alert should automatically hide as illustrated in Figures 3-5 and 3-6.

Figure 3-5. The Alert Being Shown

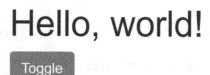

Figure 3-6. The Alert Automatically Hides After 5 Seconds

Should your project still not update, you can debug a client-side Blazor project by adding breakpoints or some `Console.WriteLine` statements. These will appear in the browser's console window. You can see examples of this in the book's code which you can download from the Apress site.

Using EventCallback<T>

Now, with the `DismissibleAlert` component from the previous section, we have been using two-way data binding between components with the `@bind-Show` syntax, and we used the `ShowChanged` callback to notify the parent component that the `Show` property has changed. To make the parent update its UI, we also added a call to `StateHasChanged` when the parent's `ShowAlert` property gets modified. But there is a better way!

Blazor has the `EventCallback` type for this, which was added to Blazor in .NET Core 3.0 Preview 3 (https://github.com/aspnet/AspNetCore/issues/6351). The big difference between `Action<T>` and `EventCallback<T>` is that the latter will invoke `StateHasChanged` for you!

Update the DismissibleAlert component's ShowChanged as in Listing 3-14.

Listing 3-14. Using EventCallback<T>

```
using Microsoft.AspNetCore.Components;
using System;

namespace Components.Pages
{
  public partial class DismissibleAlert
  {
    private bool show;

    [Parameter]
    public bool Show
    {
      get => show;
      set
      {
        if (value != show)
        {
          show = value;
          ShowChanged?.InvokeAsync(show);
        }
      }
    }

    [Parameter]
    public EventCallback<bool>? ShowChanged { get; set; }

    [Parameter]
    public RenderFragment ChildContent { get; set; } = default!;

    public void Dismiss()
      => Show = false;
  }
}
```

So instead of using an `Action<T>` delegate, we use the `EventCallback<T>` type. First of all, this type is a value type, so we don't need to check for `null`. And instead of an `Invoke` method, it has an `InvokeAsync` method which solves some special problems which are not important at this point in time.

If you want to learn more about these problems, open your browser on `https://github.com/dotnet/aspnetcore/issues/6351`.

You should also update the `Timer` component to use an `EventCallback` as in Listing 3-15.

Listing 3-15. The Improved Timer Component

```
using Microsoft.AspNetCore.Components;
using System;
using System.Threading;

namespace Components.Pages
{
  public class Timer : ComponentBase
  {
    [Parameter]
    public double TimeInSeconds { get; set; }

    [Parameter]
    public EventCallback Tick { get; set; } = default!;

    protected override void OnInitialized()
    {
      var timer = new System.Threading.Timer(
        callback: (_) => InvokeAsync(() => Tick.InvokeAsync()),
        state: null,
        dueTime: TimeSpan.FromSeconds(TimeInSeconds),
        period: Timeout.InfiniteTimeSpan);
    }
  }
}
```

Finally, update the Index component's `ShowAlert` property by removing the call to `StateHasChanged` as in Listing 3-16 (we can use an automatic property again).

Listing 3-16. Index with Simple ShowAlert Property

```
@page "/"

<h1>Hello, world!</h1>

<DismissibleAlert @bind-Show="ShowAlert">
  <span class="oi oi-check mr-2" aria-hidden="true"></span>
  <strong>Blazor is so cool!</strong>
</DismissibleAlert>

<button @onclick="ToggleAlert" class="btn btn-success">Toggle</button>

<Timer TimeInSeconds="5" Tick="ToggleAlert" />

@code {

  public bool ShowAlert { get; set; } = true;

  public void ToggleAlert()
  {
    ShowAlert = !ShowAlert;
  }
}
```

Build and run. Wait 5 seconds. The alert should hide!

In general, you should prefer `EventCallback<T>` over normal delegates for parent-child communication, such as events and two-way data binding. There are exceptions to the rule (e.g., the fact that `EventCallback` triggers component, re-rendering might be a problem, and then using a delegate can be the solution).

Referring to a Child Component

Generally, you should prefer data binding to have components communicate with one another. This way, one component does not need to know anything about another component, except the data bindings. It also makes the Blazor runtime take care of updating components with changes.

However, you can also directly interact with a *child component*. Let's look at an example: we want the dismissible alert to disappear by calling its `Dismiss` method. Update your code to match Listing 3-17, where we use the `@ref` syntax to place a reference to a component in a field. Please make sure that field is of the component's type.

Listing 3-17. Referring to a Child Component

```
@page "/"

<h1>Hello, world!</h1>

<DismissibleAlert @bind-Show="ShowAlert" @ref="alert">
  <span class="oi oi-check mr-2" aria-hidden="true"></span>
  <strong>Blazor is so cool!</strong>
</DismissibleAlert>

<button @onclick="ToggleAlert" class="btn btn-success">Toggle</button>

<Timer TimeInSeconds="5" Tick="@(() => alert.Dismiss())" />

@code {

  public bool ShowAlert { get; set; } = true;

  public void ToggleAlert()
  {
    ShowAlert = !ShowAlert;
  }

  private DismissibleAlert alert = default!;
}
```

In this example, the Blazor runtime will put a reference to the `DismissibleAlert` component in the `alert` field. You can instruct Blazor to do this using the `@ref` syntax. When the timer calls its `Tick` parameter after 5 seconds, we use this reference to call the `DismissibleAlert`'s `Dismiss` method.

Communicating with Cascading Parameters

When a higher-level component wants to pass data to an immediate child, life is easy. Simply use data binding. But when a higher-level component needs to share some data with a deeper nested component, passing data using data binding requires each intermediate component to expose that data through a parameter and pass it down to the next level. Not only is this inconvenient when you have several levels of components, but who says that you are in control of these components? Blazor solves this problem with cascading values and parameters. Let us look at an example.

Open MyFirstBlazor and add the `CounterData` class from Listing 3-18.

Listing 3-18. The CounterData Class

```
using System;

namespace Components
{
  public class CounterData
  {
    private int count;
    public int Count
    {
      get => this.count;
      set
      {
        if (value != count)
        {
          this.count = value;
          CountChanged?.Invoke(this.count);
        }
      }
    }
    public Action<int>? CountChanged { get; set; }
  }
}
```

Using the CascadingValue Component

Our top-level component (called GrandMother) wants to pass this data as a cascading value to any descendant component. You can use the Blazor built-in CascadingValue component for this. Look at Listing 3-19 for an example of using the CascadingValue component. Here, we pass GrandMother's data field (of type CounterData) as a cascading value. Any component which is part of the ChildContent will now be able to access the CounterData instance from GrandMother.

Listing 3-19. Use the CascadingValue Component to Pass Data to Descendants

```
<h3>GrandMother</h3>

@data.Count

<CascadingValue Value="@this.data">
  @ChildContent
</CascadingValue>

@code {
    public CounterData data = new CounterData { Count = 10 };

    protected override void OnInitialized()
    {
      this.data.CountChanged += (newCount) =>
        this.StateHasChanged();
    }

    [Parameter]
    public RenderFragment ChildContent { get; set; } = default!;
}
```

Open Index.razor and add the GrandMother component as in Listing 3-20. This component has two child components, one is a direct GrandChild component (which we will build after this) and another is a GrandChild component wrapped in a DismissibleAlert component. This last component knows nothing about CounterData or GrandMother. Still, the GrandMother component will be able to pass its cascading value to the GrandChild component.

Listing 3-20. Using the GrandMother Component

```
@page "/"

<h1>Hello, world!</h1>

<DismissibleAlert @bind-Show="ShowAlert" @ref="alert">
  <span class="oi oi-check mr-2" aria-hidden="true"></span>
  <strong>Blazor is so cool!</strong>
</DismissibleAlert>

<button @onclick="ToggleAlert" class="btn btn-success">Toggle</button>

<Timer TimeInSeconds="5" Tick="@(() => alert.Dismiss())" />

<GrandMother>
  <GrandChild/>
  <DismissibleAlert Show="true">
    <GrandChild/>
  </DismissibleAlert>
</GrandMother>
@code {
  public bool ShowAlert { get; set; } = true;

  public void ToggleAlert()
  {
    ShowAlert = !ShowAlert;
  }

  private DismissibleAlert alert = default!;
}
```

The GrandChild component can be found in Listing 3-21 (please add this as another component in the Pages folder). This component has a property of type CounterData, and it will receive it from GrandMother by adding the CascadingParameter attribute. Both GrandMother and GrandChild(ren) now are sharing the same instance of CounterData. If this looks like magic, the CascadingParameter will search all cascading properties of the CascadingParameter's type. If there are multiple cascading properties, you can add a name to get a more specific match, as we will discuss next.

Listing 3-21. Receiving the Cascading Value

```
<h3>GrandChild</h3>

<button @onclick="Increment">Inc</button>

@code {

    [CascadingParameter()]
    public CounterData gmData { get; set; } = default!;

    private void Increment()
    {
      gmData.Count += 1;
    }
}
```

When you click the Inc button of `GrandChild`, the `CounterData`'s Count property increments. The `GrandMother` component wants to display this value every time it gets incremented, so `CounterData` notifies the `GrandMother` of changes. The `GrandMother` component subscribes to these changes and calls `StateHasChanged` to update itself. How the shared object handles this notification is up to you; for example, `CounterData` uses a delegate. You could also use `INotifyPropertyChanged`. If you're not familiar with this interface, it is used in a lot of .NET applications to notify interested parties that a property has changed. For example, Windows Presentation Foundation (WPF) heavily relies on this interface. If you would like to learn more, any good book on WPF will explain this, or you can find more information at `https://docs.microsoft.com/dotnet/api/system.componentmodel.inotifypropertychanged`.

Resolving Ambiguities

What if there are several components exposing the same type of cascading value? In this case, you can name the cascading value. For example, you can name the `GrandMother`'s cascading value like in Listing 3-22.

Listing 3-22. Use a Named Cascading Value in GrandMother

```
<CascadingValue Value="@this.data" Name="gm">
  @ChildContent
</CascadingValue>
```

The GrandChild component should then receive the cascading value like in Listing 3-23.

Listing 3-23. Receive the Named Cascading Value

```
[CascadingParameter(Name = "gm")]
public CounterData gmData { get; set; } = default!;
```

Component Life Cycle Hooks

A Blazor component has a life cycle just like any other .NET object. A component is born, goes through a couple of changes, and then dies. A Blazor component has a couple of methods you can override to capture the life cycle of the component. In this section, we will look at these life cycle hooks because it's very important to understand them well. Putting code in the wrong life cycle hook will likely break your component.

You should also remember that each life cycle method gets called at least once for every component. Even a component with no parameters will see methods like SetParametersAsync and OnParametersSetAsync called at least once.

Life Cycle Overview

Let us start with the big picture. I have created a LifeCycle component from Listings 3-24 and 3-25 to experiment with and that shows each life cycle hook on the browser's console. So every life cycle method is listed, except the asynchronous versions of two life cycle methods: OnInitializedAsync and OnParametersSetAsync. If you want to follow along, you can use the sample code that comes with the book.

Listing 3-24. The LifeCycle Component's Code

```
using Microsoft.AspNetCore.Components;
using System;
using System.Threading.Tasks;

namespace Components.Pages
{
  public partial class LifeCycle
  {
    public LifeCycle()
    {
      Console.WriteLine("Inside constructor");
    }

    private int counter;

    [Parameter]
    public int Counter
    {
      get => counter;
      set
      {
        counter = value;
        Console.WriteLine($"Counter set to {counter}");
      }
    }

    public override Task SetParametersAsync(ParameterView parameters)
    {
      Console.WriteLine("SetParametersAsync called");
      return base.SetParametersAsync(parameters);
    }

    protected override void OnParametersSet()
      => Console.WriteLine("OnParametersSet called");
```

```
    protected override void OnInitialized()
        => Console.WriteLine("OnInitialized called");

    protected override void OnAfterRender(bool firstRender)
        => Console.WriteLine($"OnAfterRender called with firstRender =
{firstRender}");

    protected override bool ShouldRender()
    {
        Console.WriteLine($"ShouldRender called");
        return true;
    }

    public void Dispose()
        => Console.WriteLine("Disposed");
    }
}
```

Listing 3-25. The LifeCycle Component's Markup

```
@implements IDisposable

<h3>LifeCycle @Counter</h3>
```

Listing 3-25 also shows how you can implement an interface in a component using the @implements syntax. I also added this component to the Index component as in Listing 3-26. Let us run this and examine the output.

Listing 3-26. Using the LifeCycle Component

```
@page "/"

...

  <LifeCycle Counter="@counter" />

<button class="btn btn-primary" @onclick="Increment">Increment</button>

@code {

  private int counter = 1;
```

```
public void Increment()
{
  counter += 1;
}

...
}
```

When the Index component gets created, it will create the nested LifeCycle component, resulting in this output:

```
Inside constructor
SetParametersAsync called
Counter set to 1
OnInitialized called
OnParametersSet called
OnAfterRender called with firstRender = True
```

The LifeCycle component gets constructed (constructor called), and then Blazor calls the SetParametersAsync method. This method normally will result in the parameter setters being called, and that is why we see the Counter property's output.

Then the Blazor runtime calls the OnInitialized method (and the asynchronous OnInitializedAsync which I left out for simplicity). After this, the OnParametersSet method is called (and also the asynchronous OnParametersSetAsync method). Now the component is ready to be rendered, and the Blazor runtime renders it. Finally, rendering the OnAfterRender method is called which gets passed a Boolean which is true on the first render.

This whole process is illustrated in Figure 3-7.

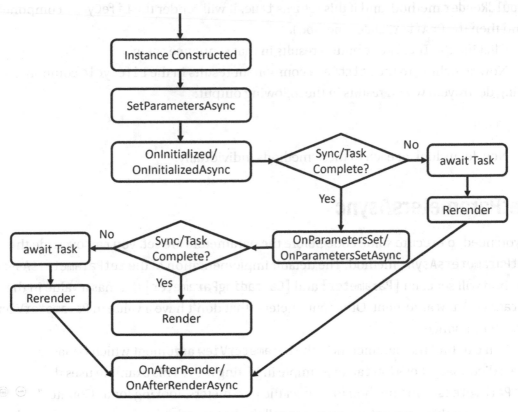

Figure 3-7. *The Component Life Cycle Overview*

My Index component has an Increment button, and when I click this button, this is the output:

```
SetParametersAsync called
Counter set to 2
OnParametersSet called
ShouldRender called
OnAfterRender called with firstRender = False
```

Because I clicked the Increment button of the Index component, it invokes the click handler and then re-renders itself. But first it sets the parameters on the LifeCycle component which results in the SetParametersAsync method being called again (which sets the Counter parameter). After this, it invokes the OnParametersSet method to indicate all parameters have been updated (and also the asynchronous OnParametersSetAsync method).

Now, should the Blazor runtime render the component? For this, it calls the ShouldRender method, and if this returns true, it will render the LifeCycle component (and then the OnAfterRender method).

Clicking the Increment button results in that sequence again.

Now switching to the FetchData component results in the LifeCycle component being destroyed, which results in the following output:

Disposed

Now let us look at each of these methods individually.

SetParametersAsync

If you need to execute some code before the parameters are set, you can override the SetParametersAsync method. The default implementation of the SetParametersAsync method will set each [Parameter] and [CascadingParameter] that has a value in the ParameterView argument. Other parameters (that don't have a value in ParameterView) are left unchanged.

You can find the parameters in the ParameterView argument which behaves like a dictionary. Let's look at an example in Listing 3-27. This example uses the SetParametersAsync method to inspect the parameters, looking for a "Counter" parameter. If this parameter is even, we call the base method; otherwise, we don't do anything, resulting in an even valued Counter.

There is one snag; when you don't call the base method, the UI doesn't update, so you should call StateHasChanged if you want the component to update. Initially, our LifeCycle component could receive an odd value, and that is why we call StateHasChanged for the first time.

One more remark: should the LifeCycle component have other parameters, your implementation is still responsible for setting these parameters since we don't call the base SetParametersAsync method in every case.

Listing 3-27. Overriding SetParametersAsync

```
private bool firstParametersSet = true;

public override Task SetParametersAsync(ParameterView parameters)
{
  Console.WriteLine("SetParametersAsync called");
```

```
if (parameters.TryGetValue(nameof(Counter), out int counter))
{
  // ignore odd values
  if (counter % 2 == 0)
  {
    return base.SetParametersAsync(parameters);
  }
  if(firstParametersSet)
  {
    firstParametersSet = false;
    StateHasChanged(); // Force render
  }
}
return Task.CompletedTask;
}
```

OnInitialized and OnInitializedAsync

When your component has been created and the parameters have been set, the
OnInitialized and OnInitializedAsync methods are called. Implement one of these
methods if you want to do some one-time extra initialization after the component
has been created, for example, fetching some data from a server like the FetchData
component from the project. The OnInitialized methods are *only called once*, right
after the creation of the component.

Use OnInitialized for *synchronous* code as in Listing 3-28. Here, we execute
synchronous code like fetching the current DateTime.

Listing 3-28. The OnInitialized Life Cycle Hook

```
DateTime created;

protected override void OnInitialized()
{
  created = DateTime.Now;
}
```

Use `OnInitializedAsync` (Listing 3-29) to call *asynchronous* methods, for example, making asynchronous REST calls (we will look at making REST calls in further chapters).

Listing 3-29. The OnInitializedAsync Life Cycle Hook

```
protected override async Task OnInitializedAsync()
{
  forecasts = await Http.GetFromJsonAsync<WeatherForecast[]>
                ("sample-data/weather.json");
}
```

OnParametersSet and OnParametersSetAsync

When you need one or more parameters to look up data after a change to the parameters, you use `OnParametersSet` or `OnParametersSetAsync` instead of the `On Initialized/OnInitializedAsync` methods. Every time data binding updates one or more of your parameters, these methods get called again, so they are ideal for calculated properties, filtering, etc. For example, you could have a `DepartmentSelector` component that allows the user to select a department from a company and another `EmployeeList` component that takes the selected department as a parameter. The `EmployeeList` component can then fetch the employees for that department in its `OnParametersSetAsync` method.

Use `OnParametersSet` (Listing 3-30) if you are only calling synchronous methods.

Listing 3-30. The OnParametersSet Method

```
DateTime lastUpdate;

protected override void OnParametersSet()
{
  lastUpdate = DateTime.Now;
  Console.WriteLine("OnParametersSet called");
}
```

Use `OnParametersSetAsync` (Listing 3-31) if you need to call asynchronous methods. For example, retrieving values from a database that depend on a parameter value should be done in an asynchronous way. In general, any use of methods that take longer than 60 milliseconds should be done asynchronously.

Listing 3-31. The OnParametersSetAsync Method

```
[Parameter]
public DateTime Date { get; set; }

protected override async Task OnParametersSetAsync()
{
  forecasts = await weatherService.GetForcasts(Date);
}
```

ShouldRender

The ShouldRender method returns a Boolean value, indicating if the component should be re-rendered. Do realize that the first render ignores this ShouldRender method, so a component will render at least once. The default implementation always returns true. You want to override this method to stop the component from re-rendering.

Let's make a change to the LifeCycle component as in Listing 3-32. We only want it to show odd values. So when counter is even, we tell the Blazor engine not to render this component.

Listing 3-32. Implementing the ShouldRender Method

```
public override Task SetParametersAsync(ParameterView parameters)
{
  shouldRender = true;
  if (parameters.TryGetValue(nameof(Counter), out int counter))
  {
    // ignore odd values
    if (counter % 2 == 0)
    {
      shouldRender = false;
    }
  }
  return base.SetParametersAsync(parameters);
}
```

```
private bool shouldRender;

protected override bool ShouldRender()
{
  return shouldRender;
}
```

OnAfterRender and OnAfterRenderAsync

The OnAfterRender and OnAfterRenderAsync methods are called after Blazor has completely rendered the component. This means that the browser's DOM has been updated with changes made to your Blazor component. Use these methods to invoke JavaScript code that needs access to elements from the DOM (which we will cover in the JavaScript chapter 10). This method takes a Boolean firstRender argument, which allows you to attach JavaScript event handlers only once.

Note   Avoid calling StateHasChanged in this method, as it can cause an infinite loop.

Use OnAfterRender shown in Listing 3-33 to call synchronous methods, for example, in JavaScript.

Listing 3-33. The OnAfterRender Life Cycle Hook

```
protected override void OnAfterRender(bool firstRender)
{
}
```

Use OnAfterRenderAsync as shown in Listing 3-34 to call asynchronous methods, for example, JavaScript methods that return promises or observables.

Listing 3-34. The OnAfterRenderAsync Life Cycle Hook

```
protected override Task OnAfterRenderAsync(bool firstRender)
{
}
```

IDisposable

If you need to run some *cleanup* code when your component is removed from the UI, implement the IDisposable interface. You can implement this interface in razor using the @implements syntax, for example, in Listing 3-25. Normally, you put the @implements at the top of the .razor file, but if you use code separation, you can also declare it on the partial class.

Most of the time, dependency injection will take care of calling Dispose, so generally, you won't need to implement IDisposable if you only need to dispose of your dependencies.

The IDisposable interface requires you to implement a Dispose method as in Listing 3-35.

Listing 3-35. Implementing the Dispose Method

```
public void Dispose()
{
  // Cleanup code here
}
```

A Word on Asynchronous Methods

When the Blazor runtime calls asynchronous methods like OnInitializedAsync and OnParametersSetAsync, it will await this method and will also render the component. The only exception to this is the OnAfterRenderAsync method, which will not trigger a render (otherwise, this will cause an infinite render loop).

This is the reason you should always check variables that get initialized in an asynchronous method for null values. A nice example of this is the FetchData component as in Listing 3-36. The forecasts field gets initialized in the OnInitializedAsync method, so until this method completes, the forecast field is null. This means that we should check this field for null values as in Listing 3-37.

Listing 3-36. Initializing `forecasts`

```
private WeatherForecast[]? forecasts;

protected override async Task OnInitializedAsync()
{
  forecasts = await Http.GetFromJsonAsync<WeatherForecast[]>("sample-data/
  weather.json");
}
```

Listing 3-37. Checking `forecasts` for Null

```
@if (forecasts == null)
{
  <p><em>Loading...</em></p>
}
```

Refactoring PizzaPlace into Components

In the previous chapter on data binding, we built a website for ordering pizzas. This used only one component with three different sections. Let us split up this component into smaller, easier to understand components and try to maximize reuse.

Creating a Component to Display a List of Pizzas

Open the PizzaPlace Blazor project from the previous chapter. You can also start with the code examples from this book; look for Chapter 2 which contains the finished version. Start by reviewing Index.razor. This is our main component, and you can say that it has three main sections: a menu, a shopping basket, and customer information.

The menu iterates over the list of pizzas and displays each one with a button to order. The shopping basket also displays a list of pizzas (but now from the shopping basket) with a button to remove it from the order. Looks like both have something in common; they need to display pizzas with an action you choose by clicking the button. So let's create a component to display a list of pizzas, using a nested component to display a pizza's details.

We have also seen that we can split components into a razor file with the markup and a C# file with the code. Let us do that here!

Add a new component to the Pages folder called PizzaItem.razor. Also create a new class called PizzaItem.razor.cs. Replace this class with the code from Listing 3-38. You should be able to copy most of the code from Index.

Listing 3-38. The Code for the PizzaItem Component

```
using Microsoft.AspNetCore.Components;
using PizzaPlace.Shared;

namespace PizzaPlace.Client.Pages
{
  public partial class PizzaItem
  {
    [Parameter]
    public Pizza Pizza { get; set; } = default!;

    [Parameter]
    public string ButtonTitle { get; set; } = default!;

    [Parameter]
    public string ButtonClass { get; set; } = default!;

    [Parameter]
    public EventCallback<Pizza> Selected { get; set; }

    private string SpicinessImage(Spiciness spiciness)
        => $"images/{spiciness.ToString().ToLower()}.png";
  }
}
```

Now replace the razor file with contents from Listing 3-39. You can copy most of the markup from the Index component (the part within the first @foreach) with some changes.

Listing 3-39. The PizzaItem Component

```
<div class="row">
  <div class="col">
    @Pizza.Name
  </div>
```

```
<div class="col text-right">
  @($"{Pizza.Price:0.00}")
</div>
<div class="col"></div>
<div class="col">
  <img src="@SpicinessImage(Pizza.Spiciness)"
       alt="@Pizza.Spiciness" />
</div>
<div class="col">
  <button class="@ButtonClass"
          @onclick="@(() => Selected.InvokeAsync(Pizza))">
    Add
  </button>
</div>
</div>
```

The PizzaItem component will display a pizza, so it should not come as a surprise that it has a Pizza parameter. This component also displays a button, but how this button looks and behaves will differ where we use it. And that is why it has a ButtonTitle and ButtonClass parameter to change the button's look, and it also has a Selected event callback of type EventCallback<Pizza> which gets invoked when you click the button. Do you remember why we are using EventCallback<T> instead of Action<T>? Do note that this component does one thing well, and only one thing: display the pizza and allow an action on the pizza by clicking the button.

We can now use this component to display the menu (a list of pizzas). Add a new component to the Pages folder called PizzaList.razor (and PizzaList.razor.cs) as in Listings 3-40 and 3-41.

Listing 3-40. The PizzaList Component's Code

```
using Microsoft.AspNetCore.Components;
using PizzaPlace.Shared;
using System.Collections.Generic;

namespace PizzaPlace.Client.Pages
{
  public partial class PizzaList
```

```
  {
    [Parameter]
    public string Title { get; set; } = default!;

    [Parameter]
    public IEnumerable<Pizza> Items { get; set; } = default!;

    [Parameter]
    public string ButtonClass { get; set; } = default!;

    [Parameter]
    public string ButtonTitle { get; set; } = default!;

    [Parameter]
    public EventCallback<Pizza> Selected { get; set; }
  }
}
```

Listing 3-41. The PizzaList Component's Markup

```
@if (Items is null || !Items.Any())
{
  <div>Loading...</div>
}
else
{
  <h1>@Title</h1>

  @foreach (var pizza in Items)
  {
    <PizzaItem Pizza="@pizza"
          ButtonClass="@ButtonClass"
          ButtonTitle="@ButtonTitle"
          Selected="@Selected" />
  }
}
```

First note the use of the @if. Here, we need to decide what to do should the Items property (which is an IEnumerable<Pizza>) be null of empty. In that case, we will display a loading UI, assuming the Items collection will be filled in later.

Otherwise, the PizzaList component displays a Title and all the pizzas from the Items collection, so it takes these as parameters. It also takes a Selected event callback which you invoke by clicking the button next to a pizza. Note that the PizzaList component reuses the PizzaItem component to display each pizza and that the PizzaList Selected event callback is passed directly to the PizzaItem Selected event callback. Same thing for the button parameters. The Index component will set this callback, and it will be executed by the PizzaItem component.

With the PizzaItem and PizzaList components ready, we can use them in Index, which you can find in Listing 3-42.

Listing 3-42. Using the PizzaList Component in Index.razor

```
<!-- Menu -->

<PizzaList Title="Our Selection of Pizzas"
          Items="@State.Menu.Pizzas"
          ButtonTitle="Order"
          ButtonClass="btn btn-success pl-4 pr-4"
          Selected="@AddToBasket" />

<!-- End menu -->
```

Run the application and try to order a pizza. Your selected pizza should be added to the shopping basket. Thanks to the EventCallback<T> type, there is no need to call StateHasChanged. Had we used an Action<T> or Func<T>, the UI would not update, and you would need to call StateHasChanged whenever you receive events from a child component!

Showing the ShoppingBasket Component

Add a new razor component called ShoppingBasket.razor (and code behind file) to the Pages folder and change its contents to Listings 3-43 and 3-44.

Listing 3-43. The ShoppingBasket Component's Code

```
using Microsoft.AspNetCore.Components;
using PizzaPlace.Shared;
using System;
using System.Collections.Generic;
using System.Linq;

namespace PizzaPlace.Client.Pages
{
  public partial class ShoppingBasket
  {
    [Parameter]
    public IEnumerable<int> Orders { get; set; } = default!;

    [Parameter]
    public EventCallback<int> Selected { get; set; } = default!;

    [Parameter]
    public Func<int, Pizza> GetPizzaFromId { get; set; }
      = default!;

    private IEnumerable<(Pizza pizza, int pos)> Pizzas
      { get; set; } = default!;

    private decimal TotalPrice { get; set; } = default!;

    protected override void OnParametersSet()
    {
      Pizzas = Orders.Select((id, pos)
                  => (pizza: GetPizzaFromId(id), pos: pos));
      TotalPrice = Pizzas.Select(tuple
                      => tuple.pizza.Price).Sum();
    }
  }
}
```

Listing 3-44. The ShoppingBasket Component's Markup

```
@if (Orders is not null && Orders.Any())
{
  <h1 class="">Your current order</h1>

  @foreach (var (pizza, pos) in Pizzas)
  {
    <div class="row mb-2">
      <div class="col">
        @pizza.Name
      </div>
      <div class="col text-right">
        @($"{pizza.Price:0.00}")
      </div>
      <div class="col"></div>

      <div class="col"></div>
      <div class="col">
        <button class="btn btn-danger"
            @onclick="@(() => Selected.InvokeAsync(pos))">
          Remove
        </button>
      </div>
    </div>
  }

  <div class="row">
    <div class="col"></div>
    <div class="col"><hr /></div>
    <div class="col"> </div>
    <div class="col"> </div>
  </div>

  <div class="row">
    <div class="col"> Total:</div>
    <div class="col text-right font-weight-bold">@
($"{TotalPrice:0.00}")</div>
```

```
    <div class="col"> </div>
    <div class="col"> </div>
    <div class="col"> </div>
  </div>
}
```

The `ShoppingBasket` component is similar to the `PizzaList` component, but there are some big differences (and that is why we are not reusing the `PizzaList` component. We will do this in the next chapter). The `ShoppingBasket` class (the one from the shared project) keeps track of the order using only ids of pizzas, so we need something to get the pizza object. This is done through the `GetPizzaFromId` delegate (again, we don't want this component to know a lot about the other classes). Another change is the `OnParametersSet` method. The `OnParametersSet` method gets called when the component's parameters have been set. Here, we override it to build a list of (pizza, position) tuples which we need during data binding and to calculate the total price of the order.

Tuples are just another type in C#. But with modern C#, we get this very convenient syntax; for example, `IEnumerable<(Pizza pizza, int pos)>` means we have a type that is a list of pizza and position pairs. Think of tuples as a nice replacement for anonymous types, which allow you to quickly have compiler-generated types.

Using the `ShoppingBasket` component in `Index` is easy, as you can see in Listing 3-45.

Listing 3-45. Using the ShoppingBasket Component

```
<!-- Shopping Basket -->

<ShoppingBasket Orders="@State.Basket.Orders"
                GetPizzaFromId="@State.Menu.GetPizza"
                Selected="@RemoveFromBasket" />

<!-- End shopping basket -->
```

Run your project again. Everything should still work (and look the same).

Adding the CustomerEntry Component

Add a new CustomerEntry component to the Pages folder as in Listings 3-46 and 3-47.

Listing 3-46. The CustomerEntry Component's Code

```
using Microsoft.AspNetCore.Components;
using PizzaPlace.Shared;

namespace PizzaPlace.Client.Pages
{
  public partial class CustomerEntry
  {
    [Parameter]
    public string Title { get; set; } = default!;

    [Parameter]
    public string ButtonTitle { get; set; } = default!;
    [Parameter]
    public string ButtonClass { get; set; } = default!;

    [Parameter]
    public Customer Customer { get; set; } = default!;

    [Parameter]
    public EventCallback ValidSubmit { get; set; } = default!;
  }
}
```

Listing 3-47. The CustomerEntry Component's Markup

```
<h1 class="mt-2 mb-2">@Title</h1>

<EditForm Model="@Customer"
          OnValidSubmit="@ValidSubmit">

  <DataAnnotationsValidator />

  <fieldset>
    <div class="row mb-2">
```

```
      <label class="col-2" for="name">Name:</label>
      <InputText class="form-control col-6"
        @bind-Value="@Customer.Name" />
    </div>
    <div class="row mb-2">
      <div class="col-6 offset-2">
        <ValidationMessage For="@(() => Customer.Name)" />
      </div>
    </div>
    <div class="row mb-2">
      <label class="col-2" for="street">Street:</label>
      <InputText class="form-control col-6"
        @bind-Value="@Customer.Street" />
    </div>
    <div class="row mb-2">
      <div class="col-6 offset-2">
        <ValidationMessage For="@(() => Customer.Street)" />
      </div>
    </div>
    <div class="row mb-2">
      <label class="col-2" for="city">City:</label>
      <InputText class="form-control col-6"
        @bind-Value="@Customer.City" />
    </div>
    <div class="row mb-2">
      <div class="col-6 offset-2">
        <ValidationMessage For="@(() => Customer.City)" />
      </div>
    </div>
    <div class="row mb-2">
      <button class="@ButtonClass">@ButtonTitle</button>
    </div>
  </fieldset>
</EditForm>
```

143

The CustomerEntry component uses a `<label>`, InputText, and ValidationMessage for each customer property.

Now we are ready to complete the Index component. Listing 3-48 shows you the whole Index.razor file.

Listing 3-48. The Index Component

```
@page "/"

<!-- Menu -->
<PizzaList Title="Our Selection of Pizzas"
           Items="@State.Menu.Pizzas"
           ButtonTitle="Order"
           ButtonClass="btn btn-success pl-4 pr-4"
           Selected="@AddToBasket" />
<!-- End menu -->
<!-- Shopping Basket -->
<ShoppingBasket Orders="@State.Basket.Orders"
                GetPizzaFromId="@State.Menu.GetPizza"
                Selected="@RemoveFromBasket" />
<!-- End shopping basket -->
<!-- Customer entry -->
<CustomerEntry Title="Please enter your details below"
               Customer="@State.Basket.Customer"
               ButtonTitle="Checkout"
               ButtonClass="mx-auto w-25 btn btn-success"
               ValidSubmit="PlaceOrder" />
<!-- End customer entry -->
@State.ToJson()

@code {
  private State State { get; } = new State();

  protected override void OnInitialized()
  {
    State.Menu.Add(
      new Pizza(1, "Pepperoni", 8.99M, Spiciness.Spicy));
    State.Menu.Add(
```

```
    new Pizza(2, "Margarita", 7.99M, Spiciness.None));
  State.Menu.Add(
    new Pizza(3, "Diabolo", 9.99M, Spiciness.Hot));
}

private void AddToBasket(Pizza pizza)
=> State.Basket.Add(pizza.Id);

private void RemoveFromBasket(int pos)
=> State.Basket.RemoveAt(pos);

private void PlaceOrder()
{
  Console.WriteLine("Placing order");
}
}
```

Build and run the PizzaPlace application. Things should work like before, except for one thing. Remember the debugging tip from the previous chapter? When you change the name of the customer, this tip does not update correctly. Only after pressing the button will this update. Let's fix this.

Using Cascading Properties

The problem is as follows. Whenever the user edits properties from the customer, we want the CustomerEntry component to trigger a CustomerChanged event callback. This way, other components in the UI will update because of changes to the customer. But how can we detect these changes? If we were using <input> elements, we could use the onchanged event, but unfortunately, the InputText component does not have this event. It does have the ValueChanged event, but I don't want to use that here (otherwise, I could not show you the use of a cascading property for this).

Look at the CustomerEntry component again. You see an EditForm with nested InputText components. The EditForm provides a cascading value of type EditContext, and the InputText components use this EditContext for things like validation.

Note   If you like, all of the source code for the InputText and other components in Blazor is available on GitHub (`https://github.com/dotnet/aspnetcore/tree/master/src/Components`) since Blazor is open source. That is what I did to figure out the solution to the problem.

Whenever one of the Input components changes, it calls the `EditContext.NotifyFieldChanged` method. And here is where things get interesting because `EditContext` has an `OnFieldChanged` event, which triggers every time a model's property changes.

Let us build a component that uses the `EditContext`'s `OnFieldChanged` event to notify us of changes. This way, we don't have to implement the `ValueChanged` event for each Input.

Add a new class to the client project's Pages folder, and name it `InputWatcher` with the implementation shown in Listing 3-49. The `InputWatcher` class has one parameter `FieldChanged`, of type `EventCallback<string>`. The `InputWatcher` receives the same `EditContext` instance (as a cascading parameter) as the one used by the `InputText` component. By subscribing to the `EditContext`'s `FieldChanged` event, all the work will be done by the `EditContext` instance.

Listing 3-49. The InputWatcher Component

```
using Microsoft.AspNetCore.Components;
using Microsoft.AspNetCore.Components.Forms;

namespace PizzaPlace.Client.Pages
{
  public class InputWatcher : ComponentBase
  {
    private EditContext editContext = default!;

    [CascadingParameter]
    public EditContext EditContext
    {
      get => this.editContext;
      set
      {
```

```
      this.editContext = value;
      EditContext.OnFieldChanged += async (sender, e) =>
      {
        await FieldChanged.InvokeAsync(e.FieldIdentifier
                                    .FieldName);
      };
    }
  }

  [Parameter]
  public EventCallback<string> FieldChanged { get; set; }

  public bool Validate()
    => EditContext?.Validate() ?? false;
  }
}
```

When the EditContext property gets set, the InputWatcher simply registers for the FieldChanged event and calls its own FieldChanged event callback.

Let's use the InputWatcher in our CustomerEntry component. Add the InputWatcher component inside the EditForm component, and add a FieldChanged event callback as in Listings 3-50 and 3-51. The InputWatcher component invokes the FieldChanged method, which triggers the CustomerChanged callback.

Listing 3-50. Make the Customer Parameter Two-Way Bindable

```
using Microsoft.AspNetCore.Components;
using PizzaPlace.Shared;

namespace PizzaPlace.Client.Pages
{
  public partial class CustomerEntry
  {
    ...

    [Parameter]
    public EventCallback<Customer> CustomerChanged { get; set; }

    private void FieldChanged(string fieldName)
```

```
  {
    CustomerChanged.InvokeAsync(Customer);
  }
 }
}
```

Listing 3-51. The CustomerEntry Component with CustomerChanged Callback

```
<EditForm Model="@Customer"
          OnValidSubmit="@ValidSubmit">

  <DataAnnotationsValidator />

  <InputWatcher FieldChanged="@FieldChanged" />
```

To complete the story, use two-way data binding in the Index component for the Customer property as in Listing 3-52.

Listing 3-52. Use Two-Way Data Binding for the Customer

```
<CustomerEntry Title="Please enter your details below"
               @bind-Customer="@State.Basket.Customer"
               ButtonTitle="Checkout"
               ButtonClass="mx-auto w-25 btn btn-success"
               ValidSubmit="PlaceOrder" />
```

Build and run. When you make a change to the customer, you should see the customer update in the debugging tip when you tab out of a control. Hey, this was not hard at all!

Disabling the Submit Button

You might want to disable the Submit button as long as there are validation errors. Our freshly introduced InputWatcher allows us to do that. Look for the Validate method in Listing 3-49. This method calls the EditContext.Validate method. We are going to use this to enable/disable the Submit button.

Start by making the changes from Listings 3-53 and 3-54. First, we add a reference to the InputWatcher because we need to call the Validate method every time a field changes. Also, add a Boolean field isInvalid, and use it to disable the button by binding it to the button's disabled attribute. Finally, every time a field changes, we update the isInvalid by calling the Validate method.

Listing 3-53. Disabling the Submit Button

```
using Microsoft.AspNetCore.Components;
using PizzaPlace.Shared;

namespace PizzaPlace.Client.Pages
{
  public partial class CustomerEntry
  {
    ...

    private void FieldChanged(string fieldName)
    {
      CustomerChanged.InvokeAsync(Customer);
      isInvalid = !inputWatcher.Validate();
    }

    private InputWatcher inputWatcher = default!;

    bool isInvalid = true;
  }
}
```

Listing 3-54. Disabling the Submit Button

```
<h1 class="mt-2 mb-2">@Title</h1>

<EditForm Model="@Customer"
          OnValidSubmit="@ValidSubmit">

  <DataAnnotationsValidator />

  <InputWatcher FieldChanged="@FieldChanged" @ref="@inputWatcher" />

  <fieldset>
    <div class="row mb-2">
      <label class="col-2" for="name">Name:</label>
```

```
      <InputText class="form-control col-6"
        @bind-Value="@Customer.Name" />
    </div>
    <div class="row mb-2">
      <div class="col-6 offset-2">
        <ValidationMessage For="@(() => Customer.Name)" />
      </div>
    </div>
    <div class="row mb-2">
      <label class="col-2" for="street">Street:</label>
      <InputText class="form-control col-6"
        @bind-Value="@Customer.Street" />
    </div>
    <div class="row mb-2">
      <div class="col-6 offset-2">
        <ValidationMessage For="@(() => Customer.Street)" />
      </div>
    </div>
    <div class="row mb-2">
      <label class="col-2" for="city">City:</label>
      <InputText class="form-control col-6"
        @bind-Value="@Customer.City" />
    </div>
    <div class="row mb-2">
      <div class="col-6 offset-2">
        <ValidationMessage For="@(() => Customer.City)" />
      </div>
    </div>
    <div class="row mb-2">
      <button class="@ButtonClass" disabled="@isInvalid">
        @ButtonTitle
      </button>
    </div>
  </fieldset>
</EditForm>
```

Run your application, and leave some of the `Customer` properties invalid (that is to say blank). When you press the Submit button (a.k.a. Checkout), you will get validation errors and the button will disable itself. When you fix the validation errors, the Submit button will again be enabled. If you want the button to be enabled right away, change the initial value of `isInvalid` to `false`.

Summary

In this chapter, we covered building Blazor components. We discussed how components can communicate with each other through parameters and data binding. We look at how a component can reference a child component. Cascading values are a very nice way of sharing data between components in a hierarchy. Finally, we saw the life cycle hooks that Blazor components have and allow us to intercept the important events in a component's life.

We applied this by dividing the monolithic `Index` component of the PizzaPlace application into smaller components.

CHAPTER 4

Advanced Components

In Chapter 3, we looked at building components for Blazor. But we are not done yet. There is still a lot more we need to discuss about components. One of the things we really need to look at is templated components and Razor templates. Then we will look at component libraries, virtualization, and dynamic components.

Using Templated Components

Components are Blazor's building block for reuse. In C#, generics are heavily used for reuse; just think about all the collections like List<T> you use with generics. Would it not be cool if Blazor had something like generic components? Yes, Blazor does!

Blazor supports *templated components* where you can specify one or more UI templates as parameters, making templated components even more reusable! For example, your application could be using grids all over the place. You can now build a templated component for a Grid taking the type used in the grid as a parameter (very much like you can build a generic type in .NET) and specify the UI used for each item separately! Let's look at an example.

Creating the Grid Templated Component

Create a new Blazor project; call it Components.Advanced. Now add a new razor component to the project's Pages folder and name it Grid as in Listings 4-1 and 4-2.

This is a templated component because it states the TItem as a *type parameter* using the @typeparam TItem syntax in the razor file. Look at the partial Grid<TItem> class for this from Listing 4-1. This is a *generic type* stated in C#. Compare this with class List<T> where T is a type parameter. You can have as many type parameters as you like; simply list each type parameter using the @typeparam syntax, but for this Grid<TITem> component, we only need one.

© Peter Himschoot 2022

P. Himschoot, *Microsoft Blazor*, https://doi.org/10.1007/978-1-4842-7845-1_4

Listing 4-1. The Templated Grid Component's Code

```
using Microsoft.AspNetCore.Components;
using System.Collections.Generic;

namespace Components.Advanced.Pages
{
  public partial class Grid<TItem>
  {
    [Parameter]
    public RenderFragment Header { get; set; } = default!;

    [Parameter]
    public RenderFragment<TItem> Row { get; set; } = default!;

    [Parameter]
    public RenderFragment Footer { get; set; } = default!;

    [Parameter]
    public IReadOnlyList<TItem> Items { get; set; } = default!;
  }
}
```

Listing 4-2. The Templated Grid Component's Markup

```
@typeparam TItem

<table border="1">
  <thead>
    <tr>@Header</tr>
  </thead>
  <tbody>
    @foreach (var item in Items)
    {
      <tr>@Row(item)</tr>
    }
  </tbody>
```

```
<tfoot>
  <tr>@Footer</tr>
</tfoot>
</table>
```

The Grid component has four parameters. The Header and Footer parameters are of type RenderFragment which represents some markup (HTML, Blazor components) which we can specify when we use the Grid component (we will look at an example right after explaining the Grid component further). Look for the <thead> element in Listing 4-2 in the Grid component. Here, we use the @Header razor syntax telling the Grid component to put the markup for the Header parameter here. Same thing for the Footer.

The Row parameter is of type RenderFragment<TItem> which is a generic version of RenderFragment. In this case, you can specify markup with access to the TItem instance allowing you access to properties and methods of the TItem. The Items parameter here is an IReadOnlyList<TItem> which can be data bound to any class with the IReadOnlyList<TItem> interface, for example, a List<T>. Look for the <tbody> element in Listing 4-2. We iterate over all the items (of type TItem) of the IReadOnlyList<TItem> using a foreach loop, and we use the @Row(item) razor syntax to apply the Row parameter, passing the current item as an argument.

Using the Grid Templated Component

Now let's look at an example of using the Grid templated component. Open the FetchData component in the Components.Advanced project. Replace the <table> with the Grid component as in Listing 4-3.

Note   The FetchData component uses a couple of things such as @page and @ inject we will discuss in later chapters, so bear with the example.

The FetchData component uses the Grid component specifying the Items parameter as the forecasts array of WeatherForecast instances. Look again at the type of Items in the Grid component: IReadOnlyList<TItem>. The compiler is smart enough to infer from this that the Grid's type parameter (TItem) is the WeatherForecast type. I love type inference!

Listing 4-3. Using the Grid Templated Component in the FetchData Component

```
@page "/fetchdata"
@inject HttpClient Http

<h1>Weather forecast</h1>

<p>This component demonstrates fetching data from the server.</p>

@if (forecasts == null)
{
  <p><em>Loading...</em></p>
}
else
{
  <Grid Items="forecasts">
    <Header>
      <th>Date</th>
      <th>Temp. (C)</th>
      <th>Temp. (F)</th>
      <th>Summary</th>
    </Header>
    <Row>
      <!-- by default called context -->
      <td>@context.Date</td>
      <td>@context.TemperatureC</td>
      <td>@context.TemperatureF</td>
      <td>@context.Summary</td>
    </Row>
    <Footer>
      <td colspan="4">Spring is in the air!</td>
    </Footer>
  </Grid>
}

@code {
  private WeatherForecast[] forecasts;
```

```
protected override async Task OnInitializedAsync()
{
  forecasts =
   await Http.GetFromJsonAsync<WeatherForecast[]>
     ("sample-data/weather.json");
}

public class WeatherForecast
{
  public DateTime Date { get; set; }

  public int TemperatureC { get; set; }

  public string Summary { get; set; }

  public int TemperatureF => 32 + (int)(TemperatureC / 0.5556);
 }
}
```

Now look at the Header parameter of the Grid component in Listing 4-3. This syntax will bind whatever is inside the <Header> element to the Grid's Header parameter which is of type RenderFragment. In this example, we specify some HTML table headers (<th>). The grid will put these inside the table row (<tr>) element from Listing 4-2. The Footer parameter is similar.

Examine the Row parameter in Listing 4-3. Inside the <Row> element, we want to use the current item from the iteration in Listing 4-2. But how should we access the current item? By default, Blazor will pass the item as the context argument (of type TItem), so you would access the date of the forecast instance as @context.Date.

You can override the name of the argument as shown in Listing 4-4. This is what we do with the Context parameter (provided by Blazor) using <Row Context="forecast">. Now the item from the iteration can be accessed using the forecast argument. Can you guess what the output of the Grid will be?

Listing 4-4. Overriding the Context Argument

```
<Grid Items="forecasts">
  <Header>
    <th>Date</th>
    <th>Temp. (C)</th>
```

```
    <th>Temp. (F)</th>
    <th>Summary</th>
  </Header>
  <Row Context="forecast">
    <!-- by default called context, but now called forecast -->
    <td>@forecast.Date</td>
    <td>@forecast.TemperatureC</td>
    <td>@forecast.TemperatureF</td>
    <td>@forecast.Summary</td>
  </Row>
  <Footer>
    <td colspan="4">Spring is in the air!</td>
  </Footer>
</Grid>
```

Run your solution and select the Fetch data link from the navigation menu. Admire your new templated component as in Figure 4-1!

Weather forecast

This component demonstrates fetching data from the server.

Date	Temp. (C)	Temp. (F)	Summary
5/6/2018 12:00:00 AM	1	33	Freezing
5/7/2018 12:00:00 AM	14	57	Bracing
5/8/2018 12:00:00 AM	-13	9	Freezing
5/9/2018 12:00:00 AM	-16	4	Balmy
5/10/2018 12:00:00 AM	-2	29	Chilly
Spring is in the air!			

Figure 4-1. *Showing Forecasts with the Grid Templated Component*

Now we have a reusable Grid component that we can use to show any list of items passing the list to the Items parameters and specifying what should be shown in the Header, Row, and Footer parameters! But there is more!

Specifying the Type Parameter's Type Explicitly

Normally, the compiler can infer the type of the TItem type parameter, but if this does not work as you expect, you can specify the type explicitly. Please note that this is the name of the type parameter, same as List<TItem>. You can use any name that makes sense. Simply specify the type of your type parameter by specifying it as TItem (the name of the type parameter used in the templated component) when you use the component as in Listing 4-5.

Listing 4-5. Explicitly Specifying the Type Parameter

```
<Grid Items="forecasts" TItem="WeatherForecast">
  <Header>
```

Using Generic Type Constraints

With C# generics, you can specify constraints on a generic type using the where syntax. Listing 4-6 shows an example using plain C#. A constraint states that whatever type will be used for T should implement the IDisposable interface. You can learn more about it at https://docs.microsoft.com/dotnet/csharp/programming-guide/generics/constraints-on-type-parameters.

Listing 4-6. Generics Using a Constraint

```
public class DisposableList<T> where T : IDisposable
```

We can do the same for templated components. For example, we could state that TItem should implement IDisposable for the Grid templated component as shown in Listing 4-7.

Listing 4-7. Using Constraints with a Templated Component

```
@typeparam TItem where TItem: IDisposable
```

Razor Templates

In templated components, you can have parameters of type RenderFragment, which can then be given a value using markup. You can also give a RenderFragment or RenderFragment<TItem> a value using a Razor template.

A *Razor template* is a way to define a UI snippet, for example, @Hello!, which you can then pass into a RenderFragment. A Razor template generally uses the @<element>...</element> syntax. In the example's case, we specify a RenderFragment without any arguments, for example, to use in the Grid's Header parameter. But if you need to pass an argument to the RenderFragment<TItem>, you create a Razor template using a syntax that looks a lot like a lambda function.

Think of a Razor template as special C# syntax for creating a RenderFragment.

Let's look at an example. Start by adding a new component called ListView as in Listings 4-8 and 4-9. This will show an unordered list of items (of type TItem) using <ul> and <li> HTML elements.

Listing 4-8. The Template ListView Component's Code

```
using Microsoft.AspNetCore.Components;
using System.Collections.Generic;

namespace Components.Advanced.Pages
{
  public partial class ListView<TItem>
  {
    [Parameter]
    public RenderFragment<TItem> ItemTemplate { get; set; }
    = default!;

    [Parameter]
    public IReadOnlyList<TItem> Items { get; set; }
    = default!;
  }
}
```

Listing 4-9. The Templated ListView Component's Markup

```
@typeparam TItem

<ul>
  @foreach (var item in Items)
  {
    <li>
      @ItemTemplate(item)
    </li>
  }
</ul>
```

Now add the `ListView` to the `FetchData` component as in Listing 4-10 (I have left out most of the unchanged parts). The `ItemTemplate` parameter now uses the `forecastTemplate` `RenderFragment` which is specified in the @code section. Look at the `forecastTemplate` in Listing 4-10. This uses a syntax very similar to a C# lambda function taking the `forecast` as an argument and returns a `RenderFragment<TItem>` using the `(forecast) => @<span>@forecast.Summary</span>` razor syntax.

In the `ListView` component's `ItemTemplate`, we simply invoke the template as if it was a lambda function. So you could say that a Razor template is like an invokable function returning a `RenderFragment`!

Listing 4-10. Using the ListView Component with a RenderFragment

```
@page "/fetchdata"
  ...

  <ListView Items="forecasts">
    <ItemTemplate>
      @forecastTemplate(context)
    </ItemTemplate>
  </ListView>
}
```

```
@code {

  private RenderFragment<WeatherForecast> forecastTemplate =
    (forecast) => @<span>@forecast.Summary</span>;

  ...
```

Wig-Pig Syntax

Let's go wild: can we have a RenderFragment<RenderFragment>? Currently, our
ListView<TItem> is using an <ul> to wrap the items, but what if the user of the
ListView<TItem> wants to use an <ol> or something different?

Looking at Listing 4-9, this means that we want to be able to replace the outer
(<ul>) markup with a template, loop over the items, and use another template to render
each item.

Create a new component called ListView2 as in Listings 4-11 and 4-12 (kind of
enhanced version of ListView). Note that in Listing 4-11 the ListTemplate parameter is
of type RenderFragment<RenderFragment>. Why would we want this? Because we want
to use the ListTemplate as a wrapper around another RenderFragment, so RenderFragm
ent<RenderFragment> makes sense!

Listing 4-11. Using a RenderFragment<RenderFragment>

```
using Microsoft.AspNetCore.Components;
using System.Collections.Generic;

namespace Components.Advanced.Pages
{
  public partial class ListView2<TItem>
  {
    [Parameter]
    public RenderFragment<RenderFragment>? ListTemplate
    { get; set; }

    [Parameter]
    public RenderFragment<TItem> ItemTemplate
    { get; set; } = default!;
```

```
  [Parameter]
  public IReadOnlyList<TItem> Items
  { get; set; } = default!;
  }
}
```

Listing 4-12. The ListView2 Component

```
@typeparam TItem

@if(ListTemplate is null )
{

<ul>
  @foreach (var item in Items)
  {
    <li>
      @ItemTemplate(item)
    </li>
  }
</ul>
} else
{

}
```

The markup for ListView2 currently will use a default <ul> list in case the
ListTemplate is not used (and that is why it is set as nullable). But now we need to talk
about using the ListTemplate. What do we want? We want the ListTemplate to wrap the
foreach loop which then calls the ItemTemplate. So we need to pass a RenderFragment
to it that will contain the foreach loop. But how can we do this in our component?

Let me introduce you to the *pig-wig syntax*: @:@{. It is called like that because it looks
like a grumpy pig with a wig (not my invention!).

Inside our ListView2 component, we will invoke the ListTemplate as in Listing 4-13,
which uses the pig-wig syntax passing a RenderFragment that loops over each item and
calls the ItemTemplate. The pig-wig syntax consists of two parts. The @: part tells razor to
switch to C# mode, and the @{ tells the C# compiler to create a Razor template.

Listing 4-13. Using the Pig-Wig Syntax

```
@typeparam TItem

@if(ListTemplate is null )
{
  ...
} else
{
  @ListTemplate(
    @:@{
      foreach(var item in Items)
      {
        @ItemTemplate(item)
      }
    }
  )
}
```

Time to use the `ListView2` component as in Listing 4-14. Please add this to the `FetchData` component below the first `ListView`. Since the `ListTemplate` takes a `RenderFragment` as an argument, we call the context (called `innerTemplate`) here, wrapped in the markup for the list. This will call the `foreach` loop which will call the `ItemTemplate`. So as the consumer of a `ListView2` component, you provide the `ListTemplate`, but also call the `innerTemplate` to allow the `ListView2` component to render its pig-wig template. Phew...

Listing 4-14. Using a Templated Component with ListTemplate

```
<ListView2 Items="forecasts">
  <ListTemplate Context="innerTemplate">
    <ol>
      @innerTemplate
    </ol>
  </ListTemplate>
```

```
<ItemTemplate Context="forecast">
  <li>@forecast.Summary</li>
</ItemTemplate>
</ListView2>
```

Using Blazor Error Boundaries

With reusable components like templated components, you allow the user of your component to inject their own logic. But what is that logic is flawed and starts throwing exceptions?

Blazor error boundaries allow you to handle exceptions within your component and to provide some nice UI indicating the problem, without the exception taking the rest of the page down with it.

Let us use an example: start by updating the class to throw an exception when it is too cold as in Listing 4-15.

Listing 4-15. Emulating Some Flawed Logic

```
public class WeatherForecast
{
  public DateTime Date { get; set; }

  public int TemperatureC { get; set; }

  public string? Summary { get; set; }

  public int TemperatureF
  => TemperatureC > 0 ? 32 + (int)(TemperatureC / 0.5556)
                      : throw new DivideByZeroException();
}
```

Running the application and choosing the FetchData component will crash the whole page. Not a nice user experience.

Update the Grid templated component to use the ErrorBoundary component as in Listing 4-16. To protect any place where you want to display an error UI if the inner element throws an exception, wrap it with an ErrorBoundary.

Listing 4-16. Using an ErrorBoundary

```
@typeparam TItem

<table border="1">
  <thead>
    <tr>@Header</tr>
  </thead>
  <tbody>
    @foreach (var item in Items)
    {
      <ErrorBoundary>
        <tr>@Row(item)</tr>
      </ErrorBoundary>
    }
  </tbody>
  <tfoot>
    <tr>@Footer</tr>
  </tfoot>
</table>
```

Running the application and choosing the FetchData component will now result in errors being shown as in Figure 4-2.

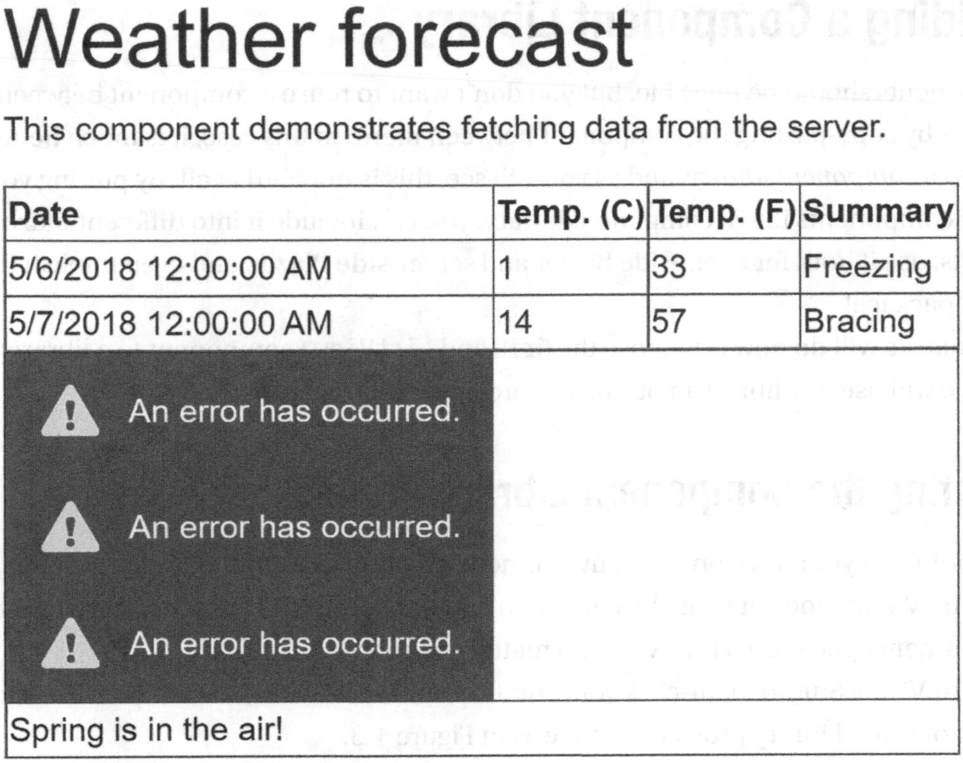

Weather forecast

This component demonstrates fetching data from the server.

Date	Temp. (C)	Temp. (F)	Summary
5/6/2018 12:00:00 AM	1	33	Freezing
5/7/2018 12:00:00 AM	14	57	Bracing
⚠ An error has occurred.			
⚠ An error has occurred.			
⚠ An error has occurred.			
Spring is in the air!			

Figure 4-2. *Using the ErrorBoundary*

By default, the ErrorBoundary's error UI uses an empty div with the blazor-error-boundary CSS class. You can customize this CSS class to change the error UI for the whole application.

You can also customize the error UI of a specific ErrorBoundary component using its ErrorContent parameter, with an example shown in Listing 4-17.

Listing 4-17. Customizing an ErrorBoundary

```
<ErrorBoundary>
    <ChildContent>
  <tr>@Row(item)</tr>
  </ChildContent>
    <ErrorContent>
        <div>Too cold!</div>
    </ErrorContent>
</ErrorBoundary>
```

167

Building a Component Library

Components should be reusable. But you don't want to reuse a component between projects by copy-pasting the component between them. In this case, it is much better to build a *component library*, and as you will see, this is not hard at all! By putting your Blazor components into a component library, you can include it into different Blazor projects, use it both for client-side Blazor and server-side Blazor, and even publish it as a *NuGet* package!

What we will do now is to move the Grid and ListView2 component to a library, and then we will use this library in our Blazor project.

Creating the Component Library Project

Depending on your development environment, creating a component library is different. We will look at using Visual Studio and the dotnet CLI (which is development environment agnostic, so this works no matter your choice of IDE).

With Visual Studio, right-click your solution, and select Add New Project. Look for the Razor Class Library project template as in Figure 4-3.

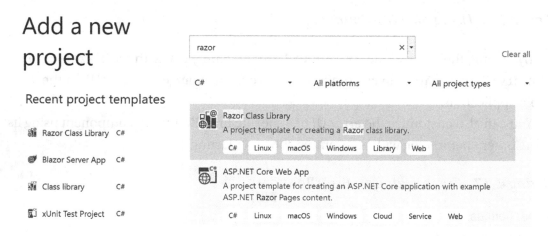

Figure 4-3. *Add a New Component Library Project*

Click Next. Name this project Components.Library, select the folder next to your other project, and click Next. In the next screen, click Create.

With dotnet CLI, open a command prompt or use the integrated terminal from Visual Studio Code (you can use Ctrl-` as a shortcut to toggle the terminal in Code).

Change the current directory to the folder where your other projects are. Type in the following command:

```
dotnet new razorclasslib -n Components.Library
```

The `dotnet new` command will create a new project based on the `razorclasslib` template. If you want the project to be created in a subdirectory, you can specify it using the `-o <<subdirectory>>` parameter.

Executing this command should show you output like

```
The template "Razor Class Library" was created successfully.
```

Change to the solution's directory. Add it to your solution by typing in the next command (with `<<path-to>>` a place holder for you to replace):

```
dotnet sln add <<path-to>>Components.Library
```

Adding Components to the Library

First, open the Components.Library project file and add support for nullable reference types:

```
<Project Sdk="Microsoft.NET.Sdk.Razor">

  <PropertyGroup>
    <TargetFramework>net6.0</TargetFramework>
    <Nullable>enable</Nullable>
  </PropertyGroup>
```

Also remove all existing files (except the _Imports.razor file and wwwroot folder) in the library project.

Previously, we built a couple of templated components. Some of these are very reusable, so we will move them to our library project. Start with `Grid`.

Move (you can use Shift-Drag-and-Drop) the Grid.razor and Grid.razor.cs files from your Components.Advanced project to the Components.Library project.

Do the same for `ListView2` component. Both components are still using the client's namespace, so update their namespace to `Components. Library`.

Building the library project should succeed. Building the solution will still get compiler errors from the client project because we need to add a reference from the client project to the component library, which we will fix in the next part.

Referring to the Library from Your Project

Now that our library is ready, we are going to use it in our project. The way the library works means we can also use it in other projects (just like any other library project in .NET). Hey, you could even make it into a NuGet package (if you want more information, look at https://docs.microsoft.com/dotnet/core/deploying/creating-nuget-packages) and let the rest of the world enjoy your work!

To use our component library in a project, we have two options.

Using Visual Studio, start by right-clicking the client project and select Add ➤ Project Reference. Make sure you check Components.Library and click OK. Blazor component libraries are just another kind of library/assembly.

Using the project file (e.g., with Visual Studio Code), open the Components.Advanced.csproj file and add the `<ProjectReference>` element to it as in Listing 4-18.

Listing 4-18. Add a Reference to Another Project

```
<Project Sdk="Microsoft.NET.Sdk.BlazorWebAssembly">

  ...

  <ItemGroup>
    <ProjectReference Include="..\Components.Library\Components.Library.
    csproj" />
  </ItemGroup>

</Project>
```

Using the Library Components

Now that you have added the reference to the component library, you can use these components like any other component, except that these components live in another namespace. Just like in C#, you can use the fully qualified name to refer to a component like in Listing 4-19.

Listing 4-19. Using the Fully Qualified Component Name

```
<Components.Library.Grid>
  ...
</Components.Library.Grid>
```

And like in C#, you can add a @using statement so you can use the component's name as in Listing 4-20. Add @using statements to the top of the razor file.

Listing 4-20. Add a @using Statement in Razor

```
@page "/fetchdata"
@inject HttpClient Http
@using Components.Library

...

  <Grid Items="forecasts">
...
```

With razor, you can add the @using statement to the _Imports.razor file as in Listing 4-21 which will enable you to use the namespace in all the .razor files which are in the same directory or subdirectory. The easiest way to think about this is that Blazor will copy the contents of the _Imports.razor file to the top of every .razor file in that directory and subdirectory.

Listing 4-21. Add a @using to _Imports.razor

```
@using System.Net.Http
@using System.Net.Http.Json
@using Microsoft.AspNetCore.Components.Forms
@using Microsoft.AspNetCore.Components.Routing
@using Microsoft.AspNetCore.Components.Web
@using Microsoft.AspNetCore.Components.Web.Virtualization
@using Microsoft.AspNetCore.Components.WebAssembly.Http
@using Microsoft.JSInterop
@using Components.Advanced
@using Components.Advanced.Shared

@using Components.Library @* Added using *@
```

Your solution should compile now and run just like before.

Why did we move our components into a component library? To make the components in the component library reusable for other projects. Simply add a reference to the library and its components can be used!

Static Resources in a Component Library

Maybe you want to use an image (or some other static file like CSS or JavaScript) in your component library. The Blazor runtime requires you to put static resources in the project's **wwwroot** folder. If you want static resources in your application instead of the library, you should put these resources in the wwwroot folder of the application's project. For both cases, you need to put these in the wwwroot folder; the only difference is that for library projects, you need to use a different URL.

I downloaded an image of a cloud from `https://openclipart.org/` and copied it into the wwwroot folder (any image will do). You can then refer to this static resource using a URL that uses the content path to the resource. If your resource is in the Blazor application's project, the path starts at the wwwroot folder, but for library projects, the URL should start with `_content/{LibraryProjectName}` and refers to the wwwroot folder from your library project. For example, to refer to the `cloud.png` file in the Components.Library project, open Index.razor and add the image from Listing 4-22.

Listing 4-22. Referring to a Static Resource in a Component Library

```
@page "/"

<h1>Hello, world!</h1>

Welcome to your new app.

<SurveyPrompt Title="How is Blazor working for you?" />

<img src="_content/Components.Library/cloud.png" alt="Cloud"/>
```

Run your project. You should see your image.

You can also refer to this static content inside the component library from your main project using the same URL.

Virtualization

Sometimes you need to display a lot of data, maybe thousands of rows. If you are going to use a simple foreach loop to create the UI for each row, you will get a noticeable delay between loading the data and the rendering of the data, because the Blazor runtime will have to create the UI for each row. Here, we will look at the built-in virtualization which will only render visible rows.

Displaying a Large Number of Rows

Let us start by building the class for the data and a class that will generate large number of instances of this data.

Add a new Data folder to the Components.Advanced project and add the Measurement class from Listing 4-23. You can also copy this class from the book's sources to save some typing.

Listing 4-23. The Measurement Class

```
using System;

namespace Components.Advanced.Data
{
  public class Measurement
  {
    public Guid Guid { get; set; }
    public double Min { get; set; }
    public double Avg { get; set; }
    public double Max { get; set; }
  }
}
```

Now add the MeasurementsService class from Listing 4-24 to the Data folder. The MeasurementsService class has a single GetMeasurements method that returns many rows. You can change the nrOfRows constant to play with the number of rows. So why does the GetMeasurements method return a ValueTask<T>? Because this allows me later to change my mind and call some asynchronous method, for example, to retrieve the data using a REST call. Think of ValueTask<T> as the union of T and Task<T>, giving

173

the choice whether to implement a method synchronously or asynchronously. You can learn more about ValueTask<T> at https://devblogs.microsoft.com/dotnet/understanding-the-whys-whats-and-whens-of-valuetask/.

Listing 4-24. The MeasurementsService Class

```
using System;
using System.Collections.Generic;
using System.Threading.Tasks;

namespace Components.Advanced.Data
{
  public class MeasurementsService
  {
    public ValueTask<List<Measurement>> GetMeasurements()
    {
      const int nrOfRows = 5000;

      var result = new List<Measurement>();
      var rnd = new Random();
      for (int i = 0; i < nrOfRows; i += 1)
      {
        result.Add(new Measurement()
        {
          Guid = Guid.NewGuid(),
          Min = rnd.Next(0, 100),
          Avg = rnd.Next(100, 300),
          Max = rnd.Next(300, 400),
        });
      }
      return new ValueTask<List<Measurement>>(result);
    }
  }
}
```

Add a razor component called NonVirtualMeasurements from Listing 4-25 to the Pages folder. Again, you can copy this from the provided sources. This component looks a lot like the FetchData component where we fetch the data, and then iterate over it with a foreach loop. The NonVirtualMeasurements component also has some logic to display the amount of time it took to render the component using the .NET Stopwatch class. This class has a Start and Stop method and will measure the amount of time between them.

Listing 4-25. Component Displaying Many Rows

```
@using Components.Advanced.Data
@using System.Diagnostics

@if (measurements is null)
{
<p><em>Loading...</em></p>
}
else
{
<table class="table">
    <thead>
        <tr>
            <th>Guid</th>
            <th>Min</th>
            <th>Avg</th>
            <th>Max</th>
        </tr>
    </thead>
    <tbody>
        @foreach (var measurement in measurements)
        {
        <tr>
            <td>@measurement.Guid.ToString()</td>
            <td>@measurement.Min</td>
            <td>@measurement.Avg</td>
            <td>@measurement.Max</td>
        </tr>
        }
    </tbody>
</table>
}
```

```
@code {
  private List<Measurement>? measurements;
  private Stopwatch timer = new Stopwatch();

  protected override async Task OnInitializedAsync()
  {
    MeasurementsService measurementService =
      new MeasurementsService();
    measurements = await measurementService.GetMeasurements();
    timer.Start();
  }

  protected override void OnAfterRender(bool firstRender)
  {
    timer.Stop();
    Console.WriteLine($"Full rendering took {timer.
ElapsedMilliseconds} ms.");
  }
}
```

To complete this part of the demo, add the NonVirtualMeasurements component to your Index.razor file as in Listing 4-26.

Listing 4-26. Using the NonVirtualMeasurements Component

```
@page "/"

<h1>Hello, world!</h1>

Welcome to your new app.

<NonVirtualMeasurements/>
```

Build and run the application. Depending on the speed of your computer, you will see a noticeable delay while Blazor is building the UI (you might even run out of memory or crash the browser!). We can also look at the browser's debugging console to see how it took to render. On my machine, I got the following output:

```
Full rendering took 746 ms.
```

This is not so bad thinking about the number of rows being created.

Using the Virtualize Component

So how can we lighten the load? Blazor has a `Virtualize` component just for this! The `Virtualize` component will only create the UI for visible rows, and depending on the height of your screen, the rendered rows in this demo should be about 20 rows. Way better than 5000 rows! When you scroll, the `Virtualize` component will then dynamically render the new rows which become visible. There are some limits to this. First, all rows should have the same height; otherwise, the `Virtualize` component cannot calculate which row to render without rendering all other preceding rows. You should only use this component when there are many rows which are not visible. Time to see this in action. Copy-paste the NonVirtualMeasurements.razor file and name it VirtualMeasurements.razor. Replace the foreach loop as in Listing 4-27. The `Virtualize` component is a templated component that receives its items through the `Items` parameter and uses the `Virtualize.ItemContent` parameter to render each item. Think of `<ItemContent>` as the body of a for loop.

Listing 4-27. Replace the foreach with the Virtualize Component

```
<Virtualize Items="@measurements" Context="measurement">
  <ItemContent>
    <tr>
      <td>@measurement.Guid.ToString()</td>
      <td>@measurement.Min</td>
      <td>@measurement.Avg</td>
      <td>@measurement.Max</td>
    </tr>
  </ItemContent>
</Virtualize>
```

Replace the `NonVirtualMeasurements` component in Index.razor with the `VirtualMeasurements` component.

Build and run. Now the UI renders almost instantly, and when I look in my browser's debugger console, I see

```
Full rendering took 28 ms.
```

This is way faster! Try scrolling. It scrolls smoothly! With the `Virtualize` component, you get a lot of features with almost no work. But that is not all of it!

Adding Paging

There is more we can do. Our component is loading all the data from the service, while we are only displaying a tiny fraction of rows. With the Virtualize component, we can change the service, so it only returns rows that are being displayed. We do this by setting the ItemsProvider parameter on the Virtualize component, which is an asynchronous delegate taking an ItemsProviderRequest and returns an ItemsProviderResult<T>.

Let us change our measurements to do this. First, implement the GetMeasurementsPage method in the MeasurementsService class as in Listing 4-28. This method returns a tuple containing the segment of rows and the total number of rows (all of them, not just the segment size).

Listing 4-28. Adding Paging to the MeasurementsService

```
public ValueTask<(List<Measurement>, int)> GetMeasurementsPage
  (int from, int count, CancellationToken cancellationToken)
{
  const int maxMeasurements = 5000;
  var result = new List<Measurement>();
  var rnd = new Random();
  count = Math.Max(0, Math.Min(count, maxMeasurements - from));
  for (int i = 0; i < count; i += 1)
  {
    result.Add(new Measurement()
    {
      Guid = Guid.NewGuid(),
      Min = rnd.Next(0, 100),
      Avg = rnd.Next(100, 300),
      Max = rnd.Next(300, 400),
    });
  }
  return new ValueTask<(List<Measurement>, int)>((result, maxMeasurements));
}
```

Copy-paste the VirtualMeasurements.razor file and name it PagedVirtualMeasurements.razor. Update the `Virtualize` component with the `ItemsProvider` parameter as in Listing 4-29. Now the `Virtualize` component will ask the `ItemsProvider` to fetch several rows. Of course, it has to do an estimate on how many rows fit on the screen, and that is why I also provide the `ItemSize` parameter.

The `ItemsProvider` is an async method taking an `ItemsProviderRequest` which has three properties, a `StartIndex`, a `Count`, and a `CancellationToken`. We use these properties to call the `GetMeasurementPage` method which returns a collection of rows and the total number of rows. This is then returned as an `ItemsProviderResult`.

Listing 4-29. Using the ItemsProvider

```
@using Components.Advanced.Data
@using System.Diagnostics

<table class="table">
    <thead>
        <tr>
            <th>Guid</th>
            <th>Min</th>
            <th>Avg</th>
            <th>Max</th>
        </tr>
    </thead>
    <tbody>
      <Virtualize ItemsProvider="@LoadMeasurements"
                  ItemSize="25"
                  Context="measurement">
        <ItemContent>
          <tr>
            <td>@measurement.Guid.ToString()</td>
            <td>@measurement.Min</td>
            <td>@measurement.Avg</td>
            <td>@measurement.Max</td>
          </tr>
        </ItemContent>
```

```
        <Placeholder>
            <tr><td colspan="4">Loading...</td></tr>
        </Placeholder>
    </Virtualize>
  </tbody>
</table>
@code {
  private async ValueTask<ItemsProviderResult<Measurement>>
    LoadMeasurements(ItemsProviderRequest request)
  {
    MeasurementsService measurementService =
      new MeasurementsService();
    var (measurements, totalItemCount) =
      await measurementService.GetMeasurementsPage
      (request.StartIndex, request.Count,
       request.CancellationToken);
    return new ItemsProviderResult<Measurement>(
      measurements, totalItemCount);
  }

  private Stopwatch timer = new Stopwatch();

  protected override void OnInitialized()
  {
    timer.Start();
  }

  protected override void OnAfterRender(bool firstRender)
  {
    timer.Stop();
    Console.WriteLine($"Full rendering took {timer.
ElapsedMilliseconds} ms.");
  }
}
```

Replace the VirtualMeasurements component with the PagedVirtualMeasurements component in Index.razor. Now we are ready to run. Again the experience is pretty smooth. The UI renders instantaneously and scrolling is very fast. Of course, there is a little cheat going on. We don't have a delay to fetch the rows we would have if we were to retrieve the rows over a network connection. Let's emulate this. Slow down the GetMeasurementsPage method by adding the delay from Listing 4-30. Here, we add a call to Task.Delay to emulate a delay. You can play with the delay constant to make things even more slow.

Listing 4-30. Emulating a Slow Fetch with Task.Delay

```
public async ValueTask<(List<Measurement>, int)> GetMeasurementsPage
  (int from, int count, CancellationToken cancellationToken)
{
  const int maxMeasurements = 5000;
  // Start Add delay
  const int delay = 50;
  await Task.Delay(delay, cancellationToken);
  // End Add delay
  var result = new List<Measurement>();
  var rnd = new Random();
  count = Math.Max(0, Math.Min(count, maxMeasurements - from));
  for (int i = 0; i < count; i += 1)
  {
    result.Add(new Measurement()
    {
      Guid = Guid.NewGuid(),
      Min = rnd.Next(0, 100),
      Avg = rnd.Next(100, 300),
      Max = rnd.Next(300, 400),
    });
  }
  return (result, maxMeasurements);
}
```

Run this and start scrolling. Because of the delay, the `Virtualize` component might not have the row to render, so there is a `Placeholder` parameter which is displayed in its place. Of course, the moment the row is loaded, it gets replaced with the `ItemContent`.

Dynamic Components

Sometimes you might not know the component which you need to render a UI. Maybe you need to wait for the user to make a choice, and then you display the component, depending on the user's choice. How would you do that? You could use an elaborate `if` statement for each choice, but this will become a maintenance nightmare soon! However, Blazor now has the `DynamicComponent` component that makes it easy to select a component at runtime. Imagine you want to open a pet hotel, so people need to be able to register their pet(s). Initially, you will board cats and dogs, but in the long run, you might want to board other animals. So you start with the following enum from Listing 4-31.

Listing 4-31. An AnimalKind Enumeration

```
namespace Components.Advanced.Data
{
  public enum AnimalKind
  {
    Unknown,
    Dog,
    Cat
  }
}
```

Next, you add classes from Listing 4-32 for each kind of `Animal`, using inheritance to make it easier to reuse some of the properties.

Listing 4-32. Different Kinds of Animals

```
namespace Components.Advanced.Data
{
  public class Animal
  {
    public string Name { get; set; } = string.Empty;
  }

  public class Dog : Animal
  {
    public bool IsAGoodDog { get; set; }
  }

  public class Cat : Animal
  {
    public bool Scratches { get; set; }
  }
}
```

You also need some components, one for each kind of animal. Let us start with the base component for Animal which is in Listing 4-33. Yes, you can also use inheritance with Blazor components if they somehow inherit from ComponentBase!

Listing 4-33. The Base AnimalComponent

```
using Components.Advanced.Data;
using Microsoft.AspNetCore.Components;

namespace Components.Advanced.Pages
{
  public partial class AnimalComponent : ComponentBase
  {
    [Parameter]
    public EventCallback ValidSubmit { get; set; }

  }
}
```

Now we derive from this the CatComponent as in Listings 4-34 and 4-35. All of this should be familiar by now, except that in the markup you will see the syntax to inherit from another component: the @inherits AnimalComponent tells the compiler to derive from AnimalComponent instead of ComponentBase.

Listing 4-34. The CatComponent Code

```
using Components.Advanced.Data;
using Microsoft.AspNetCore.Components;

namespace Components.Advanced.Pages
{
  public partial class CatComponent
  {
    [Parameter]
    public Cat Instance { get; set; } = default!;
  }
}
```

Listing 4-35. The CatComponent Markup

```
@inherits AnimalComponent

<EditForm Model="@Instance"
          OnValidSubmit="@ValidSubmit">

  <DataAnnotationsValidator />

  <fieldset>
    <div class="row mb-2">
      <label class="col-2" for="name">Name:</label>
      <InputText class="form-control col-6"
        @bind-Value="@Instance.Name" />
    </div>
```

```
      <div class="row mb-2">
        <div class="col-6 offset-2">
          <ValidationMessage For="@(() => Instance.Name)" />
        </div>
      </div>
      <div class="row mb-2">
        <label class="col-2" for="scratches">Scratches</label>
        <div class="col-1 pl-0 w-auto">
          <InputCheckbox class="form-control col-6"
          @bind-Value="@Instance.Scratches" />
        </div>
      </div>
      <div class="row mb-2">
        <div class="col-2">
          <button class="btn btn-success">Save</button>
        </div>
      </div>
    </fieldset>
  </EditForm>
```

In a very similar fashion (meaning you can copy-paste most of this), we have the DogComponent in Listings 4-36 and 4-37.

Listing 4-36. The DogComponent's Code

```
using Components.Advanced.Data;
using Microsoft.AspNetCore.Components;

namespace Components.Advanced.Pages
{
  public partial class DogComponent
  {
    [Parameter]
    public Dog Instance { get; set; } = default!;
  }
}
```

Listing 4-37. The DogComponent's Markup

```
@inherits AnimalComponent

<EditForm Model="@Instance"
          OnValidSubmit="@ValidSubmit">

  <DataAnnotationsValidator />

  <fieldset>
    <div class="row mb-2">
      <label class="col-2" for="name">Name:</label>
      <InputText class="form-control col-6"
        @bind-Value="@Instance.Name" />
    </div>
    <div class="row mb-2">
      <div class="col-6 offset-2">
        <ValidationMessage For="@(() => Instance.Name)" />
      </div>
    </div>
    <div class="row mb-2">
      <label class="col-2" for="isagooddog">Is a good dog</label>
      <div class="col-1 pl-0 w-auto">
        <InputCheckbox class="form-control col-6"
          @bind-Value="@Instance.IsAGoodDog" />
      </div>
    </div>
    <div class="row mb-2">
      <div class="col-2">
        <button class="btn btn-success">Save</button>
      </div>
    </div>
  </fieldset>
</EditForm>
```

Now add a new component called AnimalSelector as in Listing 4-38. This is the component where we will use the DynamicComponent. Why? Because we will ask the user to select a kind of animal, and then we will display the component that matches that animal.

Listing 4-38. The AnimalSelector Markup

```
<div class="row">
  <div class="col-2">
    Please select:
  </div>
  <div class="col-6 pl-0 pr-0">
    <select class="form-control"
      @onchange="@((ChangeEventArgs e)
        => AnimalSelected(e.Value))">
      @foreach (AnimalKind kind in
        Enum.GetValues(typeof(AnimalKind)))
      {
        <option value="@kind">@kind.ToString()</option>
      }
    </select>
  </div>
</div>
```

Now when the user selects a kind of animal, we call the `AnimalSelected` method which is in Listing 4-39. This method gets passed a string instance containing an `AnimalKind` value, so we parse this string into an `AnimalKind` and we use this value to select an instance of the `ComponentMetaData` class.

Listing 4-39. The AnimalSelector's Code

```
using Components.Advanced.Data;
using System;

namespace Components.Advanced.Pages
{
  public partial class AnimalSelector
  {
```

```
    ComponentMetaData? MetaData;

    private void AnimalSelected(object? value)
    {
      string? val = value?.ToString();
      if (Enum.TryParse<AnimalKind>(val, out AnimalKind kind))
      {
        MetaData = kind.ToMetaData();
      }
    }
  }
}
```

What does ComponentMetaData from Listing 4-40 contain? It contains a Type property (yes, of type Type) and a Parameters property called Dictionary<string,object>. These are used by DynamicComponent to select a Component to display (e.g., when Type is CatComponent, the DynamicComponent will replace itself with the CatComponent). Now CatComponent has a [Parameter] property (called Instance), so DynamicComponent needs to provide this parameter. The ComponentMetaData's Parameters dictionary will contain a key called Instance, with the value set for the Instance parameter.

Listing 4-40. The ComponentMetaData Class

```
using System;
using System.Collections.Generic;

namespace Components.Advanced.Data
{
  public class ComponentMetaData
  {
    public ComponentMetaData(Type type,
      Dictionary<string, object> parameters)
    {
      Type = type;
      Parameters = parameters;
    }
```

```
    public Type Type { get; set; }

    public Dictionary<string, object> Parameters { get; }
  }
}
```

One more thing to complete this example: look at the `AnimalSelected` method from Listing 4-39. How do we convert the `AnimalKind` to a `ComponentMetaData` instance? For this, I have a `ToMetaData` extension method in class `AnimalMetaData` from Listing 4-41. This method uses the new C# pattern matching `switch` statement which is ideal for this kind of thing. Here, we switch on the AnimalKind value. If it is a Dog, we return the ComponentMetaData for a dog, similar for a Cat, and for all the rest (using the _ discard syntax), we return a null value.

Listing 4-41. The AnimalMetaData Class

```csharp
using Components.Advanced.Pages;
using System.Collections.Generic;

namespace Components.Advanced.Data
{
  public static class AnimalMetaData
  {
    private static Dictionary<string, object> ToParameters
      (this object instance)
      => new Dictionary<string, object>
      {
        { "Instance", instance }
      };

    public static ComponentMetaData? ToMetaData
      (this AnimalKind animal)
      => animal switch
      {
        AnimalKind.Dog =>
          new ComponentMetaData(typeof(DogComponent),
            new Dog().ToParameters()),
        AnimalKind.Cat =>
```

```
        new ComponentMetaData(typeof(CatComponent),
          new Cat().ToParameters()),
      _ => null
    };
  }
}
```

To complete the AnimalSelector component, we will look at the value of the MetaData property (in Listing 3-39) and use a DynamicComponent to select the appropriate component for the selected animal and set its parameters as in Listing 4-42.

Listing 4-42. Completing the AnimalSelector Component

```
<div class="row">
  <div class="col-2">
    Please select:
  </div>
  <div class="col-6 pl-0 pr-0">
    <select class="form-control" @onchange="@((ChangeEventArgs e)
                                 => AnimalSelected(e.Value))">
      @foreach (AnimalKind kind in Enum.GetValues(typeof(AnimalKind)))
      {
        <option value="@kind">@kind.ToString()</option>
      }
    </select>
  </div>
</div>

@if (MetaData is not null)
{
  <div class="mt-2">
    <DynamicComponent
      Type="@MetaData.Type" Parameters="@MetaData.Parameters" />
  </div>
}
```

Add the AnimalSelector to your Index component (as in Listing 4-43).

Listing 4-43. The Index Component with AnimalSelector

```
@page "/"
<div>
  <AnimalSelector />
</div>
```

Run the application. Now when you select a kind of animal, the appropriate editor is shown as in Figure 4-4.

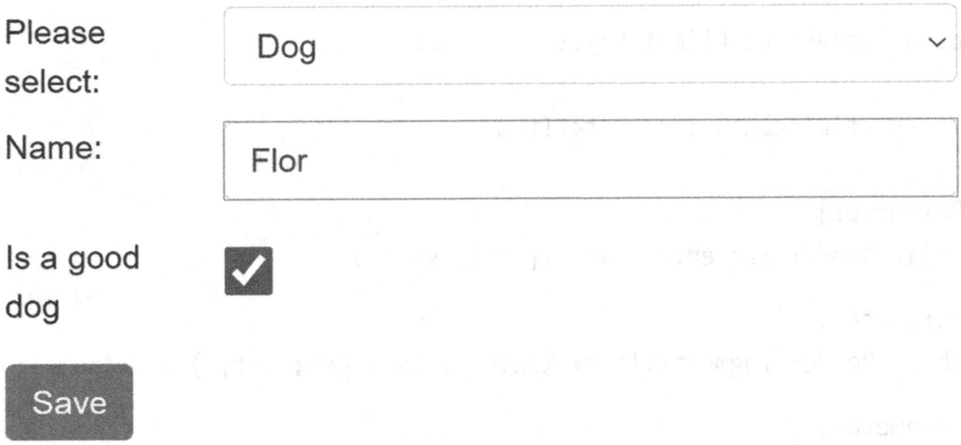

Please select:	Dog ⌄
Name:	Flor
Is a good dog	✅

Save

Figure 4-4. *The AnimalSelector After Selecting a Dog*

Component Reuse and PizzaPlace

In Chapter 3, we built a couple of components for the PizzaPlace application. There was an opportunity to have more reuse, and we are going to take that here. We will build a templated component for showing lists of pizza and then reuse it to show the menu and the shopping basket. Open the PizzaPlace solution from the previous chapter (or the sources that come with this book).

Let's first refresh out memory. We have a PizzaItem component to show the details of a Pizza. We also have the PizzaList component that shows the pizzas from the menu, and we have the ShoppingBasket component to list the pizzas from the order. Both PizzaList and ShoppingBasket iterate over a list, so there is an opportunity here for reuse. Create a new component called ItemList from Listings 4-44 and 4-45. Here, we have a Header and Footer of type RenderFragment? and a RowTemplate parameter of

191

type RenderFragment<TItem>. The Header and Footer parameters are optional, and that is why we use an @if. There is also the Items parameter of type IEnumerable<TItem>, and this parameter allows the compiler to infer the type of TItem when we assign it a collection. We iterate over this parameter using a @foreach, and we call the RowTemplate RenderFragment.

Listing 4-44. The ItemList Component's Code

```
using Microsoft.AspNetCore.Components;
using System.Collections.Generic;

namespace PizzaPlace.Client.Pages
{
  public partial class ItemList<TItem>
  {
    [Parameter]
    public RenderFragment? Header { get; set; }

    [Parameter]
    public RenderFragment<TItem> RowTemplate { get; set; } = default!;

    [Parameter]
    public RenderFragment? Footer { get; set; }

    [Parameter]
    public IEnumerable<TItem> Items { get; set; } = default!;
  }
}
```

Listing 4-45. The ItemList Component's Markup

```
@typeparam TItem

@if (Header is not null)
{
  @Header
}
@foreach (TItem item in Items)
{
```

```
  @RowTemplate(item)
}
@if (Footer is not null)
{
  @Footer
}
```

Now that we have this templated component, we can use it for both the `PizzaList` and `ShoppingBasket` components.

Update the markup for the `PizzaList` component as in Listing 4-46.

Listing 4-46. The PizzaList Component Using the ItemList

```
<ItemList Items="@Items">
  <Header>
    <h1>@Title</h1>
  </Header>
  <RowTemplate Context="pizza">
    <PizzaItem Pizza="@pizza"
               ButtonClass="@ButtonClass"
               ButtonTitle="@ButtonTitle"
               Selected="@Selected" />
  </RowTemplate>
</ItemList>
```

And replace the `ShoppingBasket` markup with Listing 4-47.

Listing 4-47. The ShoppingBasket Component Using the ItemList

```
@if (Pizzas.Any())
{
  <ItemList Items="@Pizzas">
    <Header>
      <h1 class="">Your current order</h1>
    </Header>
    <RowTemplate Context="tuple">
      <PizzaItem Pizza="@tuple.pizza"
                 ButtonClass="btn btn-danger"
```

```
                ButtonTitle="Remove"
                Selected="@(() =>
                    Selected.InvokeAsync(tuple.pos))" />
    </RowTemplate>
    <Footer>
      <div class="row">
        <div class="col"></div>
        <div class="col"><hr /></div>
        <div class="col"> </div>
        <div class="col"> </div>
      </div>
      <div class="row">
        <div class="col"> Total:</div>
        <div class="col text-right font-weight-bold">
          @($"{TotalPrice:0.00}")
        </div>
        <div class="col"> </div>
        <div class="col"> </div>
        <div class="col"> </div>
      </div>
    </Footer>
  </ItemList>
}
```

Now we have enhanced our PizzaPlace application by adding a templated component which we reuse for both the PizzaList and ShoppingBasket components. Compile and run. The PizzaPlace application should work as before.

Summary

In this chapter, we saw that in Blazor you can build templated components, which resemble generic classes. These templated components can be parameterized to render different UIs, which makes them quite reusable! We discussed Razor templates, which allows us to write markup in C# and had a look at the weird pig-wig syntax. We can build component libraries to maximize reuse of our components. Finally, we looked at virtualization which is a great way to work with large lists and how dynamic components give flexibility at runtime.

We applied this knowledge by building a simple templated component for showing lists of pizzas which we need in several places.

CHAPTER 5

Services and Dependency Injection

Dependency inversion is one of the basic principles of good *object-oriented design*. The big enabler is *dependency injection.* In this chapter, we will discuss dependency inversion and injection and why it is a fundamental part of Blazor. We will illustrate this by building a *Service* that encapsulates where the data gets retrieved and stored.

What Is Dependency Inversion?

Currently, our Blazor PizzaPlace app retrieves its data from hard-coded sample data. But in a real-life situation, this data will probably be stored in a *database* on the server. Retrieving and storing this data could be done in the component itself, but this is a bad idea. Why? Because technology changes quite often, and different customers for your application might want to use their specific technology, requiring you to update your app for every customer.

Instead, we will put this logic into a *Service object*. A Service object's role is to encapsulate specific business rules or how data is communicated between the client and the server. A Service object is also a lot easier to test since we can write *unit tests* that run on their own, without requiring a user to interact with the application for testing.

But first, let's talk about the dependency inversion principle and how dependency injection allows us to apply this principle.

© Peter Himschoot 2022
P. Himschoot, *Microsoft Blazor*, https://doi.org/10.1007/978-1-4842-7845-1_5

Understanding Dependency Inversion

Imagine a ProductList component that uses a service class, and the component creates the service using the new operator, as in Listing 5-1.

Listing 5-1. A Component Using a ProductsService

```
@using Dependency.Inversion.Shared

@foreach (var product in productsService.GetProducts())
{
  <div>@product.Name</div>
  <div>@product.Description</div>
  <div>@product.Price</div>
}

@code {
  private ProductsService productsService =
    new ProductsService();
}
```

This component is now completely dependent on the ProductsService! This is known as *tight coupling*; see Figure 5-1.

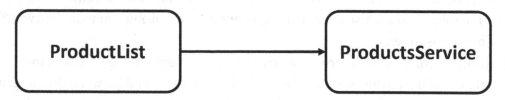

Figure 5-1. *Tight Coupling*

Now you want to test the ProductList component, and ProductsService requires a server on the network to talk to. In this case, you will need to set up a server just to run the test. And if the server is not ready yet (the developer in charge of the server hasn't come around to it), you cannot test your component! Or you are using the ProductsService in several places in your location, and you need to replace it with another class. Now you will need to find every use of the ProductsService and replace the class. What a maintenance nightmare!

Using the Dependency Inversion Principle

The *dependency inversion* principle states:

A. High-level modules should not depend on low-level modules. Both should depend on abstractions.

B. Abstractions should not depend on details. Details should depend on abstractions.

What this means is that the ProductsList component (the higher-level module) should not directly depend on the ProductsService (the lower-level module). Instead, it should rely on an *abstraction*. Using C# terminology: it should rely on an *interface* describing what a ProductsService should be able to do, not a class describing how it should work.

The IProductsService interface would look like Listing 5-2.

Listing 5-2. The Abstraction As Described in an Interface

```
public interface IProductsService
{
  IEnumerable<Product> GetProducts();
}
```

And we change the ProductsList component to rely on this abstraction, as in Listing 5-3. Please note that we still need to assign an instance to the productService variable.

Listing 5-3. The ProductList Component Using the IProductsService Interface

```
@using Dependency.Inversion.Shared

@foreach (var product in productsService.GetProducts())
{
  <div>@product.Name</div>
  <div>@product.Description</div>
  <div>@product.Price</div>
}

@code
{
  private IProductsService productsService;
}
```

199

Now the `ProductList` component (the high-level module from earlier) only relies on the `IProductsService` interface, an abstraction. And the abstraction does not reveal how we will implement the `GetProducts` method.

Of course, now we make the `ProductsService` (which is the low-level module) implement the `IProductsService` interface as in Listing 5-4.

Listing 5-4. The ProductsService Implementing the IProductsService Interface

```
public class ProductsService : IProductsService
{
  public IEnumerable<Product> GetProducts()
    => ...
}
```

If you want to test the `ProductList` component implemented using dependency inversion, you build a hard-coded version of the `IProductsService` and run the test without needing a server, for example, in Listing 5-5. We will discuss some of these techniques for testing in a later chapter.

Listing 5-5. A Hard-Coded IProductsService Used for Testing

```
public class HardCodedProductsService : IProductsService
{
  public IEnumerable<Product> GetProducts()
  {
    yield return new Product
    {
      Name = "Isabelle's Homemade Marmelade",
      Description = "...",
      Price = 1.99M
    };
    yield return new Product
```

```
  {
    Name = "Liesbeth's Applecake",
    Description = "...",
    Price = 3.99M
  };
}
}
```

If you are using the IProductsService interface in different places in your application (instead of the ProductsService class), all you need to do to replace its implementation is to build another class that implements the IProductsService interface and tell your application to use the other class!

By applying the *dependency inversion principle* (see Figure 5-2), we gained a lot more flexibility.

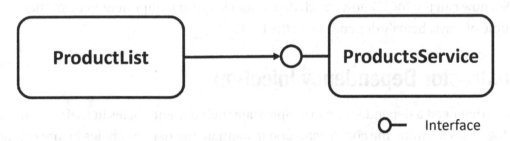

Figure 5-2. *Loosely Coupled Objects Through Dependency Inversion*

Adding Dependency Injection

If you were to run this application, you would get a NullReferenceException. Why? Because the ProductsList component from Listing 5-3 still needs an instance of a class implementing IProductsService! We could pass the ProductsService in the constructor of the ProductList component, for example, in Listing 5-6.

Listing 5-6. Passing the ProductsService in the Constructor

```
new ProductList(new ProductsService())
```

But if the ProductsService also depends on another class, it quickly becomes like Listing 5-7. This is of course not a practical way of working! Because of that, we will use an Inversion-of-Control Container (I didn't invent this name!).

Listing 5-7. Creating a Deep Chain of Dependencies Manually

```
new ProductList( new ProductsService(new Dependency()))
```

Using an Inversion-of-Control Container

An *Inversion-of-Control Container* (IoCC) is just another object, which specializes in creating objects for you. You simply ask it to create for you an instance of a type, and it will take care of creating any dependencies it requires.

It is a little bit like in a movie where a surgeon, in the middle of an operation, needs a scalpel. The surgeon in the movie holds out his (or her) hand and asks for "Scalpel number 5!". The nurse (the Inversion-of-Control Container) who is assisting simply hands the surgeon the scalpel. The surgeon doesn't care where the scalpel comes from or how it was built.

So, how can the IoCC know which dependencies your component needs? There are a couple of ways, heavily depending on the IoCC.

Constructor Dependency Injection

Classes that need a dependency can simply state their dependencies in their constructor. The IoCC will examine the constructor and instantiate the dependencies before calling the constructor. And if these dependencies have their own dependencies, then the IoCC will also build them! For example, if the `ProductsService` has a constructor that takes an argument of type `Dependency`, as in Listing 5-8, then the IoCC will create an instance of type `Dependency` and will then call the `ProductsService`'s constructor with that instance. The `ProductsService` constructor then stores a reference to the dependency in some field, as in Listing 5-8. Should the `ProductsService`'s constructor take multiple arguments, then the IoCC will pass an instance for each argument. Constructor injection is normally used for required dependencies.

Listing 5-8. The ProductsService's Constructor with Arguments

```
public class ProductsService
{
  private readonly Dependency dep;

  public ProductsService(Dependency dep)
  {
    this.dep = dep;
  }
}
```

Property Dependency Injection

If the class that the IoCC needs to build has properties that indicate a dependency, then these properties are filled in by the IoCC. The way a property does that depends on the IoCC (in .NET, there are a couple of different IoCC frameworks; some of these use an attribute on the property), but in Blazor, you can have the IoCC inject an instance with the @inject directive in your razor file, for example, the second line of code in Listing 5-9.

Listing 5-9. Injecting a Dependency with the @inject Directive

```
@using Dependency.Inversion.Shared
@inject IProductsService productsService

 @foreach (var product in productsService.GetProducts())
{
  <div>@product.Name</div>
  <div>@product.Description</div>
  <div>@product.Price</div>
}

@code
{
}
```

If you're using code separation, you can add a property to your class and apply the [Inject] attribute as in Listing 5-10. Since this listing is using nullable reference types, we need to assign a default! to remove the compiler warning.

Listing 5-10. Using the Inject Attribute for Property Injection

```
public partial class ProductList
{
  [Inject]
  public IProductsService ProductsService { get; set; }
    = default!;
}
```

You can then use this property directly in your razor file, as in Listing 5-11.

Listing 5-11. Using the ProductsService Property that Was Dependency Injected

```
@foreach (var product in productsService.GetProducts())
{
  <div>@product.Name</div>
  <div>@product.Description</div>
  <div>@product.Price</div>
}
```

Configuring Dependency Injection

There is one more thing we need to discuss. When your dependency is a class, then the IoCC can easily know that it needs to create an instance of the class with the class's constructor. But if your dependency is an interface, which it generally needs to be if you are applying the principle of dependency inversion, then which class does it use to create the instance? Without your help, it cannot know.

An IoCC has a mapping between interfaces and classes, and it is your job to configure this mapping. You configure the mapping in your Blazor WebAssembly project's Program class (and in the Startup class for Blazor Server). So open Program.cs, as in Listing 5-12.

Listing 5-12. The Program Class

```
using Microsoft.AspNetCore.Components.WebAssembly.Hosting;
using Microsoft.Extensions.DependencyInjection;
using System;
using System.Net.Http;
using System.Threading.Tasks;

namespace Dependency.Inversion.Client
{
  public class Program
  {
    public static async Task Main(string[] args)
    {
      var builder = WebAssemblyHostBuilder.CreateDefault(args);
      builder.RootComponents.Add<App>("#app");

      builder.Services.AddScoped(sp => new HttpClient
      {
        BaseAddress =
          new Uri(builder.HostEnvironment.BaseAddress)
      });

      await builder.Build().RunAsync();
    }
  }
}
```

The Program class creates a builder instance, which has a property Services of type IServiceCollection. It is this IServiceCollection we need to configure. If you are familiar with ASP.NET Core, it is the same type used in the ConfigureServices method from the Startup class.

To configure the mapping for the IoCC, you use extension methods on the IServiceCollection instance. Which extension method you call depends on the lifetime you want to give the dependency. There are three options for the lifetime of an instance which we will discuss next.

Note   The lifetime of instances is different for Blazor WebAssembly and Blazor Server. It is even different from the lifetime you know from ASP.NET Core!

Singleton Dependencies

Singleton classes are classes that only have one instance (in the application's scope). These are typically used to manage some global state. For example, you could have a class that keeps track of how many times people have clicked a certain product. Having multiple instances of this class would complicate things because they will have to start communicating with each other to keep track of the clicks. Singleton classes can also be classes that don't have any state and that only have behavior (utility classes such as one that does conversions between imperial and metric units). In this case, you could have multiple instances, but this is just wasteful and will make the garbage collector work harder.

You configure dependency injection to reuse the same instance all the time with the `AddSingleton` extension method, for example, Listing 5-13. Every time the IoCC needs an instance of the `IProductsService` interface, it will use an instance of the `ProductService` class.

Listing 5-13. Adding a Singleton to Dependency Injection

```
builder.Services
        .AddSingleton<IProductsService, ProductsService>();
```

There is an overload available (Listing 5-14) that allows you to create the singleton instance yourself and then tell IoCC to use that instance.

Listing 5-14. Create the Singleton Yourself

```
ProductsService productsService = new ProductsService();
builder.Services
        .AddSingleton<IProductsService>(productsService);
```

In case your class does not have an interface, you can also use Listing 5-15.

Listing 5-15. Adding a Singleton to Dependency Injection

```
builder.Services
    .AddSingleton<ProductsService>();
```

Why not use static methods instead of singletons you say? Static methods and properties are very hard to replace with fake implementations during testing (have you ever tried to test a method that uses a date with DateTime.Now, and you want to test it with February 29 of some quantum leap year?). During testing, you can easily replace the real class with a fake class because it implements an interface!

Now about the difference between Blazor WebAssembly and Blazor Server. In Blazor WebAssembly, your application is running in a browser's tab. You can even have multiple copies of the same Blazor application running in different tabs of your browser (even different browsers). Each tab will have its own singleton instance, in the memory of that browser tab. So you cannot use singletons to share state between tabs with Blazor WASM. And when you refresh the tab, the application will re-initialize with a new instance for the singleton.

With Blazor Server, the application is running on the server. So here the singleton is actually shared among every user running the Blazor application on the same server! But even here your application can be hosted with several servers, and each server will have its own singleton!

Transient Dependencies

Transient means short lived. In .NET, there are a lot of objects which are short lived, which might not even survive beyond a single method call. For example, when you are concatenating a couple of strings, the intermediate strings are thrown away almost instantly after being created. Using transient objects makes a lot of sense when you don't want to be affected by the previous state of an object. Instead, you start with a fresh slate by creating a new instance.

When you configure dependency injection to use a transient lifetime for a class, each time an instance is needed by the IoCC, it will create a fresh instance.

You configure dependency injection to use transient instances with the AddTransient extension method, as in Listing 5-16.

Listing 5-16. Adding a Transient Class to Dependency Injection

```
builder.Services
        .AddTransient<IProductsService, ProductsService>();
```

However, in Blazor we are working client side, and in that case, the UI stays put for the entire interaction. This means that you will have components that only have one created instance and only one instance of the dependency. You might think in that case transient and singleton will do the same thing. But there can be another component that needs the same type of dependency. If you are using a singleton, then both components will share the same instance of the dependency, while transient each gets a unique instance! You should be aware of this.

Scoped Dependencies

When you configure dependency injection to use a *scoped* dependency, the IoCC will reuse the same instance per scope but uses new instances between different scopes. But what does a scope mean?

Again there is a difference between Blazor WASM and Blazor Server. In Blazor WASM, the scope is the application (running in the browser) itself. With Blazor WASM, a scoped instance will have the same lifetime as a singleton.

Blazor Server uses a *circuit* which is the SignalR connection to keep track of a single user's application (somewhat like a session). This circuit spans across HTTP requests but not across the SignalR connection used with Blazor Server.

You configure the dependency to use scoped lifetime with the `AddScoped` extension method as in Listing 5-17.

Listing 5-17. Registering a Class to Use Scoped Lifetime

```
builder.Services
        .AddScoped<IProductsService, ProductsService>();
builder.Services
        .AddScoped<ProductsService>();
```

Understanding Blazor Dependency Lifetime

Let's look at the lifetime of the injected dependencies in Blazor. For this, I have written a demo app which you can find in the included sources for this book.

The source code for this book is available on GitHub via the book's product page, located at www.apress.com/ISBN.

I started by building three services, each one with a different lifetime (determined through the configuration of dependency injection). For example, see Listing 5-18. Every time an instance gets created, it gets assigned a GUID. By displaying the instance's GUID, it becomes easy to see which instance gets replaced with a new instance. These classes also implement IDisposable so we can see when they get disposed by looking in the browser's debugger console.

Listing 5-18. One of the Dependencies Used for the Experiment

```
using System;

namespace Blazor.LifeTime.Shared
{
  public class SingletonService : IDisposable
  {
    public Guid Guid { get; set; } = Guid.NewGuid();

    public void Dispose()
      => Console.WriteLine("ScopedService Disposed");
  }
}
```

Then I added these three services to the service collection, as in Listing 5-19 (Blazor WASM) and Listing 5-20 (Blazor Server).

Listing 5-19. Adding the Dependencies for Blazor WASM

```
using Blazor.LifeTime.Shared;
using Microsoft.AspNetCore.Components.WebAssembly.Hosting;
using Microsoft.Extensions.DependencyInjection;
using System;
using System.Net.Http;
using System.Threading.Tasks;
```

```
namespace Blazor.Wasm.LifeTime
{
  public class Program
  {
    public static async Task Main(string[] args)
    {
      var builder = WebAssemblyHostBuilder.CreateDefault(args);
      builder.RootComponents.Add<App>("#app");

      builder.Services.AddScoped(sp => new HttpClient
      {
        BaseAddress = new Uri(builder.HostEnvironment.BaseAddress)
      });

      builder.Services.AddSingleton<SingletonService>();
      builder.Services.AddTransient<TransientService>();
      builder.Services.AddScoped<ScopedService>();

      await builder.Build().RunAsync();
    }
  }
}
```

Listing 5-20. Adding the Dependencies for Blazor Server (Excerpt)

```
public void ConfigureServices(IServiceCollection services)
{
  services.AddRazorPages();
  services.AddServerSideBlazor();
  services.AddSingleton<WeatherForecastService>();

  services.AddSingleton<SingletonService>();
  services.AddTransient<TransientService>();
  services.AddScoped<ScopedService>();
}
```

And finally, I consume these services in the Index component from Listing 5-21. This will display GUIDs for each dependency (don't forget to add the proper @using to _Imports.razor).

Listing 5-21. The Component Consuming the Dependencies

```
@page "/"

@inject SingletonService  singletonService
@inject TransientService transientService
@inject ScopedService scopedService

<div>
  <h1>Singleton</h1>
  Guid: @singletonService.Guid
  <h1>Transient</h1>
  Guid: @transientService.Guid
  <h1>Scoped</h1>
  Guid: @scopedService.Guid
</div>
```

Blazor WebAssembly Experiment

Run the Blazor.Wasm.Lifetime project, which will start Blazor WebAssembly. We get Figure 5-3 on the first page (your GUIDs will be different). Switching to the Counter page and back shows Figure 5-4.

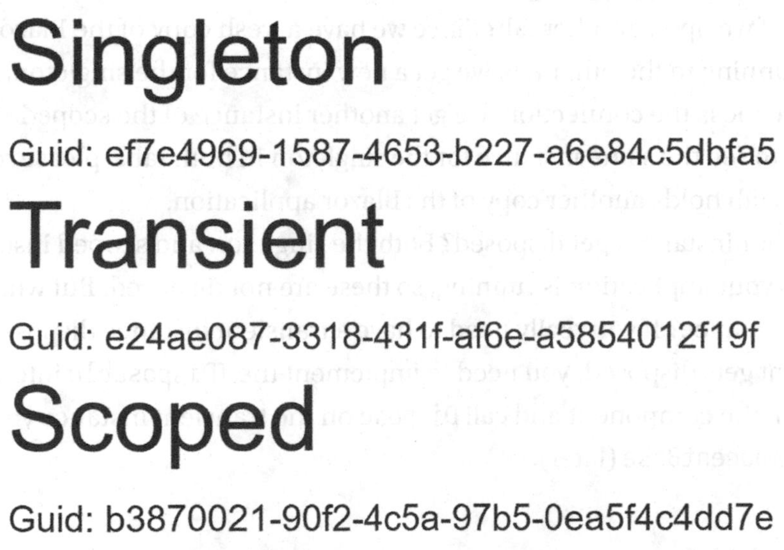

Singleton

Guid: ef7e4969-1587-4653-b227-a6e84c5dbfa5

Transient

Guid: e24ae087-3318-431f-af6e-a5854012f19f

Scoped

Guid: b3870021-90f2-4c5a-97b5-0ea5f4c4dd7e

Figure 5-3. *Displaying Client-Side Blazor Dependencies*

Singleton

Guid: ef7e4969-1587-4653-b227-a6e84c5dbfa5

Transient

Guid: 09c774af-d651-4192-bc90-f2c72bb7f645

Scoped

Guid: b3870021-90f2-4c5a-97b5-0ea5f4c4dd7e

Figure 5-4. *The Dependencies from the Other Page*

Each time the Index component gets created, it will ask dependency injection for instances of the SingletonService, TransientService, and ScopedService. The SingletonService instance gets reused all the time because we see the same GUID. The TransientService instance gets replaced each time (because each time we get a different GUID). We also see the same instance for the ScopedService. In Blazor WebAssembly, scoped instances are scoped by default to the browser's tab (the application); they behave like singletons, so there is no difference.

And what if we open another tab? Since we have a fresh copy of the Blazor application running in the other tab, we get a new instance for the singleton, and because the scope is the connection, we get another instance of the scoped instance. If you expected to see the same instance for the singleton in both tabs, please remember that here each tab holds another copy of the Blazor application.

When do our instances get disposed? Both the singleton and scoped instance will live as long as your application is running, so these are not disposed. But what about the transient instance? If you really need to have a transient instance disposed when the component gets disposed, you need to implement the IDisposable interface as in Listing 5-22 on the component and call Dispose on the transient instance yourself! Or use OwningComponentBase (later).

Listing 5-22. Implementing IDisposable on a Component

```
@page "/"

@inject SingletonService  singletonService
@inject TransientService transientService
@inject ScopedService scopedService

@implements IDisposable

<div>
  <h1>Singleton</h1>
  Guid: @singletonService.Guid
  <h1>Transient</h1>
  Guid: @transientService.Guid
  <h1>Scoped</h1>
  Guid: @scopedService.Guid
</div>

@code {
  public void Dispose()
    => transientService.Dispose();
}
```

Blazor Server Experiment

Now run the Blazor.Server.LifeTime project; make sure you are running the server using Kestrel and not IIS. Your browser should open on the Index page as in Figure 5-5. Select the Counter page and back to the Index page to see Figure 5-6 (again, you will have different GUIDs).

Singleton

Guid: 02aa5f6c-561d-4b4e-8426-624b7d1e4f34

Transient

Guid: f2414328-c83b-499e-a2b4-0be0232c0601

Scoped

Guid: c22e470f-4752-43d8-8a92-ea9703c8850f

Figure 5-5. *Displaying Server-Side Dependencies*

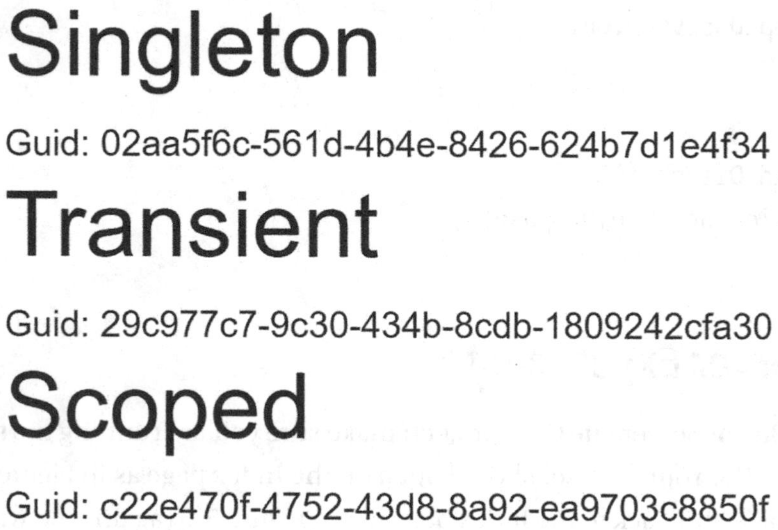

Singleton

Guid: 02aa5f6c-561d-4b4e-8426-624b7d1e4f34

Transient

Guid: 29c977c7-9c30-434b-8cdb-1809242cfa30

Scoped

Guid: c22e470f-4752-43d8-8a92-ea9703c8850f

Figure 5-6. *After Clicking the Other Link*

Here, we see similar behavior like the one we saw for Blazor WASM. But don't get fooled. This is not the same, and we can see that by opening another tab. You should see the same GUID for the singleton instance as in Figure 5-7. Now we are running on the server, and the server will have one instance of the singleton for all users. Open the page in another browser; again, you will see the same GUID.

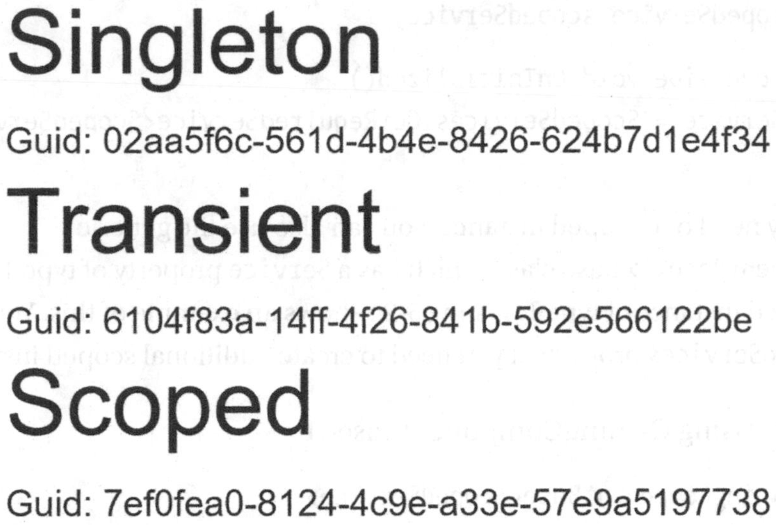

Singleton

Guid: 02aa5f6c-561d-4b4e-8426-624b7d1e4f34

Transient

Guid: 6104f83a-14ff-4f26-841b-592e566122be

Scoped

Guid: 7ef0fea0-8124-4c9e-a33e-57e9a5197738

Figure 5-7. *Opening Another Tab with Server-Side on the Home Page*

Using OwningComponentBase

What if you want a service instance that belongs to your component and you want this instance to be disposed automatically when the component gets disposed? You can make your component create its own scope by deriving from the OwningComponentBase class. Look at Listing 5-23 which is the OwningComponent which you can find in the provided project. Here, we inherit from OwningComponentBase. Instead of using regular dependency injection, the OwningComponentBase class has the ScopedServices property which is an IServiceProvider. Any scoped instances should be created through the ScopedServices' GetService or GetRequiredService method. These instances now belong to the component's scope and will automatically be disposed when the component is disposed.

Listing 5-23. A Component Deriving from OwningComponentBase

```
@using Microsoft.Extensions.DependencyInjection
@inherits OwningComponentBase

<h1>OwningComponent</h1>
Guid: @scopedService.Guid

@code {
```

215

```
private ScopedService scopedService;

protected override void OnInitialized()
=> scopedService = ScopedServices.GetRequiredService<ScopedService>();
}
```

If you only need one scoped instance, you can also use the generic
OwningComponentBase<T> base class, which has a Service property of type T which will
hold the scoped instance of type T. Listing 5-24 shows an example of this. You can still
use the ScopedServices property if you need to create additional scoped instances.

Listing 5-24. Using OwningComponentBase<T>

```
@inherits OwningComponentBase<ScopedService>

<h1>OwningComponent2</h1>
Guid: @Service.Guid
```

Now add both these components to the Index component as in Listing 5-25. You can
choose between Blazor Server and Blazor WebAssembly.

Listing 5-25. Using OwningComponentBase Derived Components

```
@page "/"

@inject SingletonService  singletonService
@inject TransientService transientService
@inject ScopedService scopedService

<div>
  <h1>Singleton</h1>
  Guid: @singletonService.Guid
  <h1>Transient</h1>
  Guid: @transientService.Guid
  <h1>Scoped</h1>
  Guid: @scopedService.Guid
  <OwningComponent/>
  <OwningComponent2/>
</div>
```

Run your project and make sure you have the console open. Now click the Counter component. The console should show the ScopedService instances being disposed. Also note that each time the OwningComponent and OwningComponent2 get instantiated, they receive a new instance of the ScopedService.

Note   Don't implement IDisposable on components deriving from OwningComponentBase because this will cease the automatic disposal of the scoped instances!

The Result of the Experiment

Now the experiment is complete, let us draw some conclusions about the lifetime of the injected dependencies. Every time an instance gets created, it gets a new GUID. This makes it easy to see if a new instance gets created or the same instance gets reused.

Transient lifetime is easy. Transient lifetime means you get a new instance every time. This is the same for both Blazor WASM and Blazor Server.

Singleton lifetime means that in Blazor WASM you get one instance for the entire duration of the application. If you really need to share an instance between all the uses and tabs, you need to put this on the server and access it through calls to the server. But with Blazor Server, everyone uses the same instance. Please make sure you don't put any user's information in a singleton because this will bleed to other users (bad!).

Scoped lifetime with Blazor WASM means the same as singleton lifetime. But with Blazor Server, we need to be careful. Blazor Server uses a SignalR connection (called a circuit) between the browser and the server, and scoped instances are linked to the circuit. You can derive from the OwningComponentBase class if you need scoped behavior for a specific component.

For both Blazor WebAssembly and Blazor Server, if you need to have the same instance, no matter which tab the user is using, you cannot rely on dependency injection to do this for you. You will need to do some state handling yourself! More about this in Chapter 11.

Building Pizza Services

Let's go back to our PizzaPlace project and introduce it to some services. I can think of at least two services, one to retrieve the menu and one to place the order when the user clicks the Order button. For the moment, these services will be very simple, but later we will use these to set up communication with a server.

Start by reviewing the Index component, which is Listing 5-26 with the markup left out for conciseness.

Listing 5-26. The Index Component

```
@code {
  private State State { get; } = new State();

  protected override void OnInitialized()
  {
    State.Menu.Add(
      new Pizza(1, "Pepperoni", 8.99M, Spiciness.Spicy));
    State.Menu.Add(
      new Pizza(2, "Margarita", 7.99M, Spiciness.None));
    State.Menu.Add(
      new Pizza(3, "Diabolo", 9.99M, Spiciness.Hot));
  }

  private void AddToBasket(Pizza pizza)
  => State.Basket.Add(pizza.Id);

  private void RemoveFromBasket(int pos)
  => State.Basket.RemoveAt(pos);

  private void PlaceOrder()
  {
    Console.WriteLine("Placing order");
  }
}
```

Pay special attention to the State property. We will initialize the State.Menu property from the MenuService service (which we will build next), and we will use dependency injection to pass the service.

Adding the MenuService and IMenuService Abstraction

If you are using Visual Studio, right-click the PizzaPlace.Shared project and select Add ➤ New Item. If you are using Code, right-click the PizzaPlace.Shared project and select Add File. Add a new interface class IMenuService and complete it as in Listing 5-27.

Listing 5-27. The IMenuService Interface

```
using System.Threading.Tasks;

namespace PizzaPlace.Shared
{
  public interface IMenuService
  {
    ValueTask<Menu> GetMenu();
  }
}
```

This interface allows us to retrieve a menu. Note that the GetMenu method returns a ValueTask<Menu>; that is because we expect the service to retrieve our menu from a server (we will build this in the following chapters) and we want the method to support an asynchronous call.

Let's elaborate on this. First, update the Index component's OnInitializedAsync method (don't forget the @inject at the top) as in Listing 5-28. This is an asynchronous method using the async keyword in its declaration.

Never call asynchronous services in your Blazor component's constructor; always use OnInitializedAsync or OnParametersSetAsync.

Inside the OnInitializedAsync method, we call the GetMenu method using the await keyword which requires GetMenu to return a Task<Menu> or ValueTask<T>. But why a ValueTask<T> and not Task<T>? Because I don't know how someone will implement the GetMenu method. They may do this synchronously, for example, by retrieving it from a cache, and then using a Task<T> is more expensive than a ValueTask<T>. Also, the ValueTask<T> is a value type, meaning that this one does not end up on the heap in the synchronous case. If you want to learn more about this, Apress has an excellent book about all of this called *Pro .NET Memory Management: For Better Code, Performance, and Scalability.*

Listing 5-28. Using the IMenuService

```
@page "/"
@inject IMenuService MenuService

<!-- Menu -->

<PizzaList Title="Our Selection of Pizzas"
           Items="@State.Menu.Pizzas"
           ButtonTitle="Order"
           ButtonClass="btn btn-success pl-4 pr-4"
           Selected="@AddToBasket" />

<!-- End menu -->
<!-- Shopping Basket -->

<ShoppingBasket Orders="@State.Basket.Orders"
                GetPizzaFromId="@State.Menu.GetPizza"
                Selected="@RemoveFromBasket" />

<!-- End shopping basket -->
<!-- Customer entry -->

<CustomerEntry Title="Please enter your details below"
               @bind-Customer="@State.Basket.Customer"
               ButtonTitle="Checkout"
               ButtonClass="mx-auto w-25 btn btn-success"
               ValidSubmit="PlaceOrder" />

<!-- End customer entry -->
@State.ToJson()

@code {
  private State State { get; } = new State();

  protected override async Task OnInitializedAsync()
  {
    Menu menu = await MenuService.GetMenu();
```

```
  foreach(Pizza pizza in menu.Pizzas)
  {
    State.Menu.Add(pizza);
  }
}

private void AddToBasket(Pizza pizza)
=> State.Basket.Add(pizza.Id);

private void RemoveFromBasket(int pos)
=> State.Basket.RemoveAt(pos);

private void PlaceOrder()
{
  Console.WriteLine("Placing order");
}
}
```

We are not ready to run this application yet because we still not to configure dependency injection. But run it anyway! When you get the error, look at the browser's debugger console. You should see the following error:

```
Unhandled exception rendering component: Cannot provide a value for
property 'MenuService' on type 'PizzaPlace.Client.Pages.Index'. There is no
registered service of type 'PizzaPlace.Shared.IMenuService'.
```

Dependency injection could not provide an instance for IMenuService. Of course, it can't! We did implement this interface.

Add a new HardCodedMenuService class to the PizzaPlace.Shared project, as in Listing 5-29. The GetMenu method returns a new ValueTask<Menu> containing three different kinds of pizza.

Listing 5-29. The HardCodedMenuService Class

```
using System.Collections.Generic;
using System.Threading.Tasks;

namespace PizzaPlace.Shared
{
  public class HardCodedMenuService : IMenuService
```

```
    {
      public ValueTask<Menu> GetMenu()
        => new ValueTask<Menu>(
          new Menu
          {
            Pizzas = new List<Pizza> {
              new Pizza(1, "Pepperoni", 8.99M, Spiciness.Spicy),
              new Pizza(2, "Margarita", 7.99M, Spiciness.None),
              new Pizza(3, "Diabolo", 9.99M, Spiciness.Hot)
            }
          });
    }
}
```

Now we are ready to use the IMenuService in our Index component.

Open Program.cs from the client project. We'll use a transient object as stated in Listing 5-30.

Listing 5-30. Configuring Dependency Injection for the MenuService

```
using Microsoft.AspNetCore.Components.WebAssembly.Hosting;
using Microsoft.Extensions.DependencyInjection;
using PizzaPlace.Shared;
using System;
using System.Net.Http;
using System.Threading.Tasks;

namespace PizzaPlace.Client
{
  public class Program
  {
    public static async Task Main(string[] args)
    {
      var builder = WebAssemblyHostBuilder.CreateDefault(args);
      builder.RootComponents.Add<App>("#app");

      builder.Services.AddScoped(sp => new HttpClient
      {
```

```
    BaseAddress = new Uri(
      builder.HostEnvironment.BaseAddress)
  });

  builder.Services
      .AddTransient<IMenuService, HardCodedMenuService>();

  await builder.Build().RunAsync();
    }
  }
}
```

Run your Blazor project. Everything should still work! In the next chapters, we will replace this with a service to retrieve everything from a database on the server.

Ordering Pizzas with a Service

When the user makes a selection of pizzas and fulfills the customer information, we want to send the order to the server, so they can warm up the oven and send some nice pizzas to the customer's address. Start by adding an IOrderService interface to the PizzaPlace. Shared project as in Listing 5-31.

Listing 5-31. The IOrderService Abstraction As a C# Interface

```
using System.Threading.Tasks;

namespace PizzaPlace.Shared
{
  public interface IOrderService
  {
    ValueTask PlaceOrder(ShoppingBasket basket);
  }
}
```

To place an order, we just send the basket to the server. In the next chapter, we will build the actual server-side code to place an order; for now, we will use a fake implementation that simply writes the order to the browser's console. Add a class called ConsoleOrderService to the PizzaPlace.Shared project as in Listing 5-32.

Listing 5-32. The ConsoleOrderService

```
using System;
using System.Threading.Tasks;

namespace PizzaPlace.Shared
{
  public class ConsoleOrderService : IOrderService
  {
    public ValueTask PlaceOrder(ShoppingBasket basket)
    {
      Console.WriteLine($"Placing order for {basket.Customer.Name}");
      return new ValueTask();
    }
  }
}
```

The PlaceOrder method simply writes the basket to the console. However, this method implements the asynchronous pattern from .NET, so we need to return a new ValueTask instance.

Inject the IOrderService into the Index component as in Listing 5-33.

Listing 5-33. Injecting the IOrderService

```
@page "/"
@inject IMenuService MenuService
@inject IOrderService orderService
```

And use the order service when the user clicks the Order button by replacing the implementation of the PlaceOrder method in the Index component. Since the orderService returns a ValueTask (same with Task), we need to invoke it using the await syntax, as in Listing 5-34.

Listing 5-34. The Asynchronous PlaceOrder Method

```
private async Task PlaceOrder()
{
  await orderService.PlaceOrder(State.Basket);
}
```

As the final step, configure dependency injection. Again, we will make the IOrderService transient as in Listing 5-35.

Listing 5-35. Configuring Dependency Injection for the OrderService

```
builder.Services
        .AddTransient<IMenuService, HardCodedMenuService>();
builder.Services
        .AddTransient<IOrderService, ConsoleOrderService>();
```

Think about this. How hard will it be to replace the implementation of one of the services? There is only one place that says which class we will be using, and that is in Program (or Startup with Blazor Server). In a later chapter, we will build the server-side code needed to store the menu and the orders, and in the chapter after that, we will replace these services with the real deal!

Build and run your project again, open your browser's debugger, and open the console tab. Order some pizzas and click the Order button. You should see some feedback being written to the console.

Summary

In this chapter, we discussed dependency inversion, which is a best practice for building easily maintainable and testable object-oriented applications. We also saw that dependency injection makes it very easy to create objects with dependencies, especially objects that use dependency inversion. Then we looked at the dependency injection that comes with Blazor. When you configure dependency injection, you need to be careful with the lifetime of your instances, so let's repeat that.

Transient objects are always different; a new instance is provided to every component and every service.

Scoped objects are the same for a user's connection, but different across different users and connections. You can derive from the OwningComponentBase class if you need scoped behavior for a specific component.

Singleton objects are the same for every object and every request, but still have different lifetime between Blazor WebAssembly and Blazor Server.

CHAPTER 6

Data Storage and Microservices

In general, client-side browser applications need to store some of their data. In some cases, such as games, the application can store its data in the browser itself, using browser local storage. But in most cases, storage will happen on the server, which has access to database engines such as SQL Server. In this chapter, you will learn the basics of storing data using Entity Framework Core and exposing that data using REST and microservices built on top of ASP.NET Core.

What Is REST?

Storing data on the Web is ubiquitous. But how can applications communicate with one another? Representational State Transfer (REST) is a protocol built on top of the HTTP protocol for invoking functionality on servers, such as retrieving and storing data from/in a database.

Understanding HTTP

Before talking about REST, you should have a good understanding of the Hypertext Transfer Protocol, better known as HTTP. HTTP was created by Tim Berners-Lee at CERN in 1989. CERN is a center for elementary physics research, and what do researchers do when they have completed their research? They publish papers with their research findings. Before the Internet, publishing a paper was done literally on paper (hence the name), and it took a lot of time between writing the paper and getting it published in a research magazine. Instead, Tim Berners-Lee devised a way to put papers on a server and allow users to read these papers using a program, now known as a browser.

227

© Peter Himschoot 2022
P. Himschoot, *Microsoft Blazor*, https://doi.org/10.1007/978-1-4842-7845-1_6

Also, scientific papers contain a lot of references, and when you want to read a paper like this, it helps to be able to access the referenced papers. The Internet facilitates reading papers through the use of *HyperText Markup Language* (HTML). Hypertext is an electronic document format that can contain links to other documents. You simply click the link to read the other paper, and you can go back to the first paper simply by clicking the back button in your browser.

Universal Resource Identifiers and Methods

Browsers are applications that know how to talk HTTP, and the first thing you do after opening a browser is you type in a *Universal Resource Identifier* (URI). A URI allows a browser to talk to a server, but more is needed. As the name suggests, a URI identifies a resource universally, but you also need to use an *HTTP method* to instruct the server to do something with the URI. The most common method is GET. As Figure 6-1 shows, when you type in a URI in the browser, it will do a GET on the server.

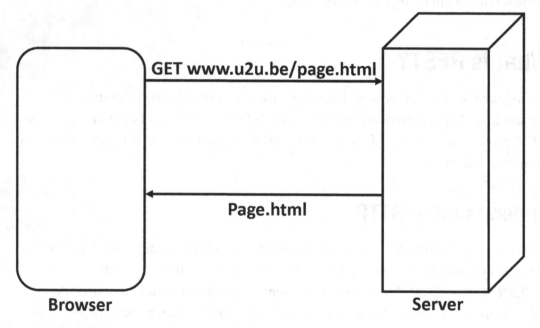

Browser   **Server**

Figure 6-1. *The Browser Uses the GET Method to Retrieve a Document*

Each time you click a hyperlink in the HTML document, the browser repeats this process with another URI.

But there are other methods. If you want to publish a new paper, you can use the POST method to send the paper to the server, supplying it with a URI. In this case, the server will store the paper at the requested URI. If you want to make a change to your paper, for example, to correct a spelling mistake, you can use the PUT method. Now the server will overwrite the contents identified by the URI. And finally, you can delete the paper using the DELETE method and its URI.

Note   Using the GET, POST, PUT, and DELETE methods like this is a convention. Nothing states that you have to do things like this, and there are REST services out there that use different methods and status codes.

HTTP Status Codes

What happens when you ask a server about something it doesn't have? What should the server return? Servers not only return HTML, but they also return a status code about the result. When the server can process the request successfully, it will in general return status code 200 (other successful status codes exist – you can find the full list at https://en.wikipedia.org/wiki/List_of_HTTP_status_codes). When the server can't find the resource, it will return a status code 404. Status code 404 simply means "Not Found". The client will receive this status code and can react appropriately. When the browser receives a status code 200 ("OK"), it displays the HTML; when it receives a 404, it displays a not found screen; etc.

Invoking Server Functionality Using REST

Think about these methods we just talked about. With POST, you can CREATE something on a server; with GET, you can READ it back; with PUT, you can UPDATE something on the server; and with DELETE, you can DELETE things on the server. They are also known as CRUD operations (CREATE-READ-UPDATE-DELETE). Roy Fielding, the inventor of REST, realized that using the HTTP protocol you can also use HTTP to work with data stored in a database. For example, if you use the GET method with a URI http://someserver/categories, the server can execute some code to retrieve data from the categories relational table and return it. Of course, the server would use a format more appropriate for transferring data, such as XML or JSON. Because there are many different formats for data, the server also needs a way to convey which format it is sending. (At the beginning of the Web, only HTML was used as the format.) This is done through HTTP headers.

HTTP Headers

HTTP headers are instructions exchanged between the client and the server. Headers are key/value pairs, where the client and server agree on the key. Many standard HTTP headers exist which you can find at `https://en.wikipedia.org/wiki/List_of_HTTP_header_fields`. For example, a server can use the `Content-Type` header to tell the client to expect a specific format. Another header is the `Accept` header, which is sent by the client to the server to politely ask the server to send the content in that format; this is also known as *content negotiation*. Currently, the most popular format is *JavaScript Object Notation* (JSON). And this is the exchange format you will use with Blazor.

JavaScript Object Notation

JSON is a compact format for transferring data. Look at the example in Listing 6-1.

Listing 6-1. An Example of JSON

```
{ "book" : {
  "title" : "Microsoft Blazor",
  "chapters" : [ "Your first Blazor project", "Data Binding"]
  }
}
```

This JSON format describes a book, which can easily be transformed into an object in memory. The simplest JSON object is a string, for example, "Hello world!", but we can also create complex objects and arrays of JSON objects.

Objects are denoted using curly braces, and inside the curly braces, you will see a comma-separated list of properties. Each property uses a `key : value` notation. Listing 6-1 contains a single `book` object with as value another nested JSON object. This nested JSON object contains two properties: `title` and `chapters`. The `title` is a string "Microsoft Blazor". Note that the property name is also transferred as a string. And finally, the chapters property is an array of strings, where you use square brackets to indicate an array.

The JSON format is used for transferring data between two machines but today is also heavily used for configuring tools, such as ASP.NET Core (just look at appsettings. json in an ASP.NET server project). JSON today is way more popular on the Web than XML, probably because of its simplicity.

Some Examples of REST Calls

You need a list of pizzas from a server, and the server exposes the pizzas at URI http:// someserver/pizza. To get a list of pizzas, you use the GET method, and you use the Accept header with value application/json to request the JSON format. Look at Figure 6-2 for this example.

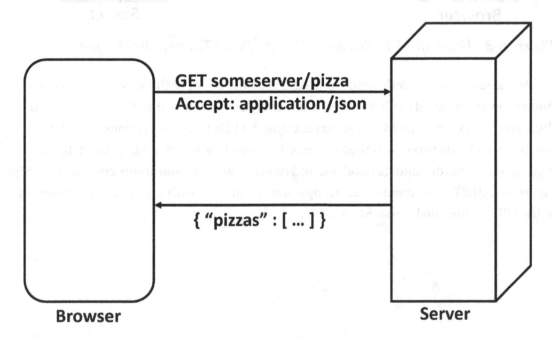

GET someserver/pizza
Accept: application/json

{ "pizzas" : [...] }

Browser   **Server**

Figure 6-2. *Using REST to Retrieve a List of Pizzas*

Maybe your client wants to display the details of a pizza with id number 5. In this case, it can append the id to the URI and perform a GET. Should the server not have any pizza with that id, it can return a status code 404, as illustrated in Figure 6-3.

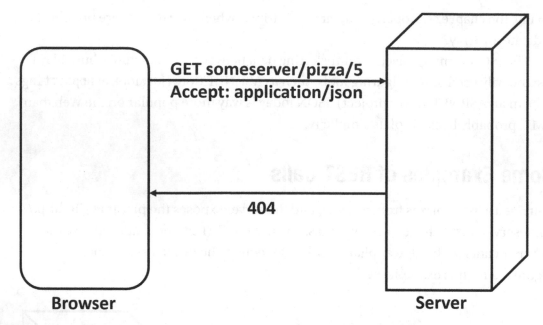

Figure 6-3. *Using REST to Retrieve a Specific Pizza Through Its Unique Id*

As the last example, let's send some data from the client to the server. Imagine that the customer has filled in all the details for the order and clicks the Order button. You then send the order as JSON to the server using the POST method (remember POST means insert). The server can then process the order in any way it likes; for instance, it can insert the order into its database and return a 201: Created status code, as in Figure 6-4. REST recommends returning a status code 201 with the Location header set to the URI for the newly created resource.

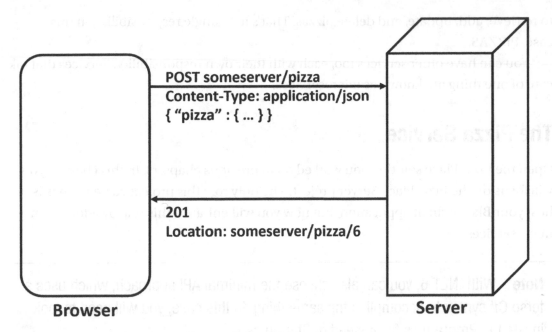

Figure 6-4. *POSTing an Order to the Server*

Building a Simple Microservice Using ASP.NET Core

So, how do you build a REST service? Your (hosted) Blazor project uses ASP.NET Core for hosting the Blazor client, and adding a REST service to your server project is easy. But first, let's do a little intro to microservices.

Services and Single Responsibility

A service is something (here, it will be a piece of software) that listens for requests; when it receives a request, the service handles the request and returns with a response. In Chapter 5, we built a menu service which can return a list of pizzas. In real life, you also encounter services, and they are very similar. Consider a bank. You step into a bank, and you give the teller your account number, some ID, and request $100. The teller will check your account; if you have enough money in your account, the teller will deduct the money and give you the cash. Should your account be too low, the teller will refuse. In both cases, you got a response.

Services should also adhere to the principle of single responsibility. They should do one thing very well, and that's it. For example, the pizza service will allow clients to retrieve, add, update, and delete pizzas. That's it. A single responsibility, in this case, PIZZAS.

You can have other services too, each with their own responsibility. Services that take care of one thing are known as microservices.

The Pizza Service

Open the PizzaPlace solution you worked on in previous chapters. In this chapter, you will focus on the PizzaPlace.Server project. The only role this project currently has is to host your Blazor client application, but now you will enhance this role by adding some microservices.

Note   With .NET 6, you can also choose the minimal API approach, which uses a terse C# syntax to accomplish the same thing. In this case, you will need to look inside the Program.cs file instead of Startup.cs.

Open Startup.cs and look at the Configure method, as in Listing 6-2.

Listing 6-2. The Startup Class's Configure Method

```
public void Configure(IApplicationBuilder app,
                      IWebHostEnvironment env)
{
  if (env.IsDevelopment())
  {
    app.UseDeveloperExceptionPage();
    app.UseWebAssemblyDebugging();
  }
  else
  {
    app.UseExceptionHandler("/Error");
    // The default HSTS value is 30 days. ...
    app.UseHsts();
  }
```

```
app.UseHttpsRedirection();
app.UseBlazorFrameworkFiles();
app.UseStaticFiles();

app.UseRouting();

app.UseEndpoints(endpoints =>
{
  endpoints.MapRazorPages();
  endpoints.MapControllers();
  endpoints.MapFallbackToFile("index.html");
});
}
```

The last line with the endpoints.MapFallbackToFile("index.html") method takes care of your Blazor client project. But right before it, you see the endpoints. MapControllers() method that is used for hosting your services.

How the MapControllers method works is not the topic of this book, but I will cover what you need to know. If you want to learn more about ASP.NET Core, there are many good books about this topic, such as *Pro ASP.NET Core MVC* by Adam Freeman (www.apress.com/gp/book/9781430265290).

In a nutshell, ASP.NET MVC will give the HTTP request to a controller class which should inherit the ControllerBase class, and then the controller will execute one of its methods. How does it decide? The MapControllers method will take the request's URL, for example, /pizzas, and use the first segment of the URL to search for a controller with a matching name, for example, PizzasController. Because we are using REST, the chosen controller will pick the method that matches the verb, for example, GET. If your method is called Get(), it will be invoked, but you can also use the HttpGet attribute on a method. In that case, the method's name is not important. With the HttpGet attribute, you can specify what the URL should look like, which allows you to pass arguments in the URL to the method. We will look at an example shortly.

Next in line is the Controllers folder of the server project. Initially, this folder is empty, and the idea is that you put your service classes here. In ASP.NET, service classes are known as controllers, hence the name of the folder.

If you are using Visual Studio, right-click this folder and select Add ➤ Controller. Select API Controller - Empty from Figure 6-5 and click Add.

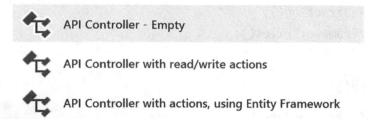

Figure 6-5. *Adding a New Controller*

Type `PizzasController` and click Add again.

If you are using Code, simply right-click the Controllers folder and select Add File. Name it PizzasController.cs. Now complete the class as in Listing 6-3.

This will add a new class called `PizzasController`, inheriting from `ControllerBase`, which you can see in Listing 6-3. This class also has two attributes on it. The `[ApiController]` attribute tells the ASP.NET runtime that this is a controller for a REST service. The `[Route]` attribute tells the ASP.NET runtime that the URI where it will expose itself is "api/pizzas". The "[controller]" part of the route is a placeholder for the name of the controller (Pizzas), but without the "Controller" part.

Listing 6-3. The Empty PizzasController

```
using Microsoft.AspNetCore.Mvc;

namespace PizzaPlace.Server.Controllers
{
  [Route("api/[controller]")]
  [ApiController]
  public class PizzasController : ControllerBase
  {
  }
}
```

Let's add a GET method to retrieve a list of pizzas. For the moment, you will hard-code the list, but in the next section, you will retrieve it from a database. Modify the `PizzasController` as shown in Listing 6-4.

Listing 6-4. Adding a Method to the PizzaController to Retrieve a List of Pizzas

```
using Microsoft.AspNetCore.Mvc;
using PizzaPlace.Shared;
using System.Collections.Generic;
using System.Linq;

namespace PizzaPlace.Server.Controllers
{
  [Route("api/[controller]")]
  [ApiController]
  public class PizzasController : ControllerBase
  {
    private static readonly List<Pizza> pizzas = new List<Pizza>
    {
      new Pizza(1, "Pepperoni", 8.99M, Spiciness.Spicy ),
      new Pizza(2, "Margarita", 7.99M, Spiciness.None ),
      new Pizza(3, "Diabolo", 9.99M, Spiciness.Hot )
    };

    [HttpGet("/pizzas")]
    public IQueryable<Pizza> GetPizzas()
      => pizzas.AsQueryable();
  }
}
```

Let's walk through this implementation. First, you declare a hard-coded static list of pizzas. Next is the GetPizzas method, which has attribute HttpGet("/pizzas"). This attribute says that when you perform a GET HTTP method on the server with the /pizzas URI, the server should call the GetPizzas method. This attribute overrides the Route attribute on the class, so the default api/pizzas will not invoke the GetPizzas method.

The GetPizzas method returns an IQueryable<Pizza>, and ASP.NET Core will send this result back to the client as a list of pizzas. The IQueryable<Pizza> interface is used in .NET to represent data that can be queried, such as database data, and is returned by LINQ queries. Why IQueryable<Pizza>? Because later in this chapter, we will return data from a database which is exposed as this type.

Note that the `GetPizzas` method contains nothing about HOW the data will be transferred to the client. This is all taken care of for you by ASP.NET Core! By default, your implementation in ASP.NET Core will use JSON, which is what you want. ASP.NET Core allows you to pick other formats, including your custom format. The client can request a certain format, such as XML or JSON using the Accept header in the request. Here, we will be using the default JSON format.

Time to see if it works. First, ensure that the PizzaPlace.Server project is the startup project (with Visual Studio, right-click the PizzaPlace.Server project and select Set as Startup Project from the drop-down menu. The PizzaPlace.Server project should be shown as bold).

Now run your project and wait for the browser to open because you will perform a GET; you can use the browser for the GET method, but for other methods, you will use a nice tool called Postman.

Change the URI in the browser to http://localhost:xxxx/pizzas where xxxx is the original port number in your browser (the port number gets selected by the host and might be different than mine). You should see the result shown in Figure 6-6.

```
[{"id":1,"name":"Pepperoni","price":8.99,"spiciness":1},
 {"id":2,"name":"Margarita","price":7.99,"spiciness":0},
 {"id":3,"name":"Diabolo","price":9.99,"spiciness":2}]
```

Figure 6-6. *The Results of Getting a List of Pizzas from the Pizza Service*

A JSON-encoded list of pizzas! It works! So here we see an array of objects, and each object has the properties of our `Pizza` class (except the properties use lowercase which is the convention with JSON).

Now you are ready to retrieve the data from a real database using Entity Framework Core.

What Is Entity Framework Core?

Entity Framework Core is the framework Microsoft recommends for working with databases. Entity Framework Core (EF) is an *Object-Relational Mapper* which allows you to write classes as normal C# classes and then store and retrieve .NET objects from a database without having to be an SQL expert. It will take care of querying, inserting, updating, and deleting objects in the database for you. This is also known as *persistence ignorance*, where your code does not need to know how and where data gets stored! Entity Framework Core has support for SQL Server, SQLite, and more.

Using the Code-First Approach

But of course, you need to explain to Entity Framework Core what kind of data you want to store. Entity Framework Core uses a technique called *Code First*, where you write code to describe the data and how it should be stored in the database. Then, you can use this to generate the database, the tables, and the constraints. If you want to make changes to the database, you can update the database schema with *code-first migrations*.

If you already have a database, you can also generate the code from the database, also known as EF *Database First*, but this is not the target of this book.

With code-first approach, you describe the classes (also known as *entities*) that will map to database tables. You already have the `Pizza` class (which you can find in the PizzaPlace.Shared project) to describe the Pizza table in the database. But you need to do more.

In this part, you will be using *SQL Server*, or *SQLite* if you don't have access to SQL Server. If you installed Visual Studio on your Windows machine, SQL Server was installed too.

You can check if SQL Server was installed as follows: start Visual Studio and select View ➤ SQL Server Object Explorer from the menu. Now click Add SQL Server. Expand the local node. If you have SQL Server, locally it should be listed.

If you don't have SQL Server on your machine, you can install a free version of SQL Server or use a SQL Server instance in the cloud, for example, SQL Server on Azure (`https://azure.microsoft.com/get-started`). You can even install SQL Server on Linux and OSX! There are some nice articles on the Web (e.g., `https://database.guide/how-to-install-sql-server-on-a-mac/`) that explain how. And if you don't want to bother installing SQL Server, you can also use *SQLite*, which is available out of box with .NET Core, so you don't need to install anything for SQLite.

Let us start by adding Entity Framework Core to the PizzaPlace.Server project. If you are using Visual Studio, right-click the server project and select Manage NuGet Packages. The NuGet window will open in Visual Studio. NuGet is a very practical way for installing dependencies such as Entity Framework Core to your project. It will not only install the *Microsoft.EntityFrameworkCore.SqlServer* library but also all its dependencies.

Select the Browse tab and type *Microsoft.EntityFrameworkCore.SqlServer* in the search box (or *Microsoft.EntityFrameworkCore.Sqlite* if you are using that). You should see this library as the top search result (if not, look at the top right corner of the NuGet window where you will see *Package Source*; select nuget.org as the source). Select it, then select the Latest stable version from the Version drop-down, and click the Install button.

With Code, you open the command prompt with the current folder set to where the PizzaPlace.Server project is, and type in the following command:

```
dotnet add package Microsoft.EntityFrameworkCore.SqlServer
```

If you opted to use SQLite, use this command:

```
dotnet add package Microsoft.EntityFrameworkCore.Sqlite
```

Add a new class called `PizzaPlaceDbContext` to the PizzaPlace.Server project, as shown in Listing 6-5. This class represents the database, and you do need to give a couple of hints about how you want your data to be stored in SQL Server (or some other database engine; this uses the same code).

Note   The whole idea of using Entity Framework is to abstract away the underlying database. In general, to switch to a different database engine, you install a different NuGet package which will take care of communicating with the database. The code stays the same and EF is really efficient!

Listing 6-5. The PizzaPlaceDbContext Class

```
using Microsoft.EntityFrameworkCore;
using PizzaPlace.Shared;

namespace PizzaPlace.Server
{
  public class PizzaPlaceDbContext : DbContext
  {
    public PizzaPlaceDbContext(DbContextOptions<PizzaPlaceDbContext> options)
      : base(options) { }

    public DbSet<Pizza> Pizzas { get; set; } = default!;
```

```
protected override void OnModelCreating(
  ModelBuilder modelBuilder)
{
  base.OnModelCreating(modelBuilder);

  var pizzaEntity = modelBuilder.Entity<Pizza>();

  pizzaEntity.HasKey(pizza => pizza.Id);
  pizzaEntity.Property(pizza => pizza.Name)
    .HasMaxLength(80);
  pizzaEntity.Property(pizza => pizza.Price)
    .HasColumnType("money");
  pizzaEntity.Property(pizza => pizza.Spiciness)
    .HasConversion<string>();
  }
 }
}
```

First, you need to create a constructor for the PizzaPlaceDbContext class taking a Db
ContextOptions<PizzaPlaceDbContext> argument. This is used to pass some options
and the connection to the database server, which you will do later in this section.

Next, you add a table to the database to represent your pizzas using a public property
of type DbSet<Pizza>. DbSet<T> is the collection class used by Entity Framework Core
to represent a table in the database, but you can think of it as a List<T> (one of the cool
things with Entity Framework Core is that you work with collections instead of using SQL
to talk to the database). Entity Framework Core will use the DbSet<T> to interact with a
database table, in this case, the Pizzas table.

Finally, you override the OnModelCreating method, which takes a modelBuilder
argument. In the OnModelCreating method, you describe how each DbSet<T> should
be mapped to the database; for example, you can tell it which table to use, how each
column should be called, which type to use in the database, etc. In this case, you tell
the modelBuilder that the Pizza table should have a primary key, the Id property of
the Pizza class. We tell it to make the Name maximum 80 characters and how the Price
property should be mapped to a SQL type. You will use the MONEY type for that. Finally,
we tell EF that the Spiciness enumeration should be mapped to a string using the
HasConversion<string>() method. This way, we end up with nice readable entries
for spiciness, instead of a number. For the moment, this is enough for your current

241

implementation. You don't have to explain everything about every property because there are a lot of defaults available. For example, the string type from .NET will be mapped to a type used for strings in the database.

Preparing Your Project for Code-First Migrations

Now you are ready to tell the PizzaPlaze.Server project to use SQL Server (or SQLite) as the database. You do this with dependency injection. In ASP.NET Core, you configure dependency injection in the Startup class's ConfigureServices method. Let's have a look at this method which is shown in Listing 6-6.

Listing 6-6. The Startup.ConfigureServices Method

```
public void ConfigureServices(IServiceCollection services)
{
  services.AddControllersWithViews();
  services.AddRazorPages();
}
```

Remember IServiceCollection from Chapter 5? Here, dependencies for ASP. NET Core are added, such as dependencies for Controllers and razor pages, which are required for your service.

The Startup class also comes with a constructor as in Listing 6-7.

Listing 6-7. The Startup Class's Constructor

```
public class Startup
{
  public Startup(IConfiguration configuration)
  {
    Configuration = configuration;
  }

  public IConfiguration Configuration { get; }
```

You need this constructor to have access to the project's configuration file. The configuration will contain the connection string for the database to talk to.

Now we will provide the `PizzaPlaceDbContext` class as a dependency in the `ConfigureServices` method. If you are using SQL Server, add the following code from Listing 6-8 at the end of the `ConfigureServices` method.

Listing 6-8. Adding Entity Framework Dependencies

```
public void ConfigureServices(IServiceCollection services)
{
  services.AddControllersWithViews();
  services.AddRazorPages();
  services.AddDbContext<PizzaPlaceDbContext>(options =>
    options.UseSqlServer(
      Configuration.GetConnectionString("PizzaPlaceDb")));
}
```

This single statement tells ASP.NET Core that you will be using the `PizzaPlaceDbContext` and that you will be storing it in SQL Server. This code also looks up the connection string for the database in configuration, which you still need to add.

Should you opt for SQLite, you need to add the code from Listing 6-9.

Listing 6-9. Using SQLite As the Database

```
public void ConfigureServices(IServiceCollection services)
{
  services.AddControllersWithViews();
  services.AddRazorPages();
  services.AddDbContext<PizzaPlaceDbContext>(options =>
   options.UseSqlite(
     Configuration.GetConnectionString("PizzaPlaceDbLite"))
   );
}
```

ASP.NET Core allows you to place your configuration settings in many different places, such as a JSON configuration file, environment variables, etc. Our server project already has a configuration file called appsettings.json, so open it.

You need to add a connection string that will allow access to the database. A database connection string tells your code where to find the database server, which database to use, and which credentials should be used to log in. Update the appsettings.json configuration file as in Listing 6-10. This actually contains two connection strings, one for SQL Server and one for SQLite. The SQL Server connection string uses the (localdb)\\MSSQLLocalDB server, which is the server installed with Visual Studio. Of course, if you are using another database server, you will also have to change the server name. There are a lot of examples on www.connectionstrings.com/, or read on to find out how to get the connection string with Visual Studio. The SQLite connection string is a lot simpler, containing the name of the file where we will store the data using SQLite.

Listing 6-10. The appsettings.json Configuration File

```
{
  "Logging": {
    "LogLevel": {
      "Default": "Information",
      "Microsoft": "Warning",
      "Microsoft.Hosting.Lifetime": "Information"
    }
  },
  "AllowedHosts": "*",
  "ConnectionStrings": {
    "PizzaPlaceDb": "Server=(localdb)\\MSSQLLocalDB;Database=PizzaPlaceDb;
    Trusted_Connection=True;MultipleActiveResultSets=true",
    "PizzaPlaceDbLite": "Data Source=PizzaPlace.db"
  }
}
```

Finding Your Database Server's Connection String

If you are not sure which connection string to use, you can find the connection string for SQL Server in Visual Studio by selecting View ➤ SQL Server Object Explorer.

You can connect to a database by clicking the server icon with the little green + sign, shown in Figure 6-7.

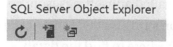

Figure 6-7. *SQL Server Object Explorer*

You can look for available database servers by expanding the Local, Network, or Azure expanders as in Figure 6-8. I recommend that you try to find the MSSQLLocalDB database server. If you use another database server, you might need to change how to log in to your database. When you're ready, click Connect.

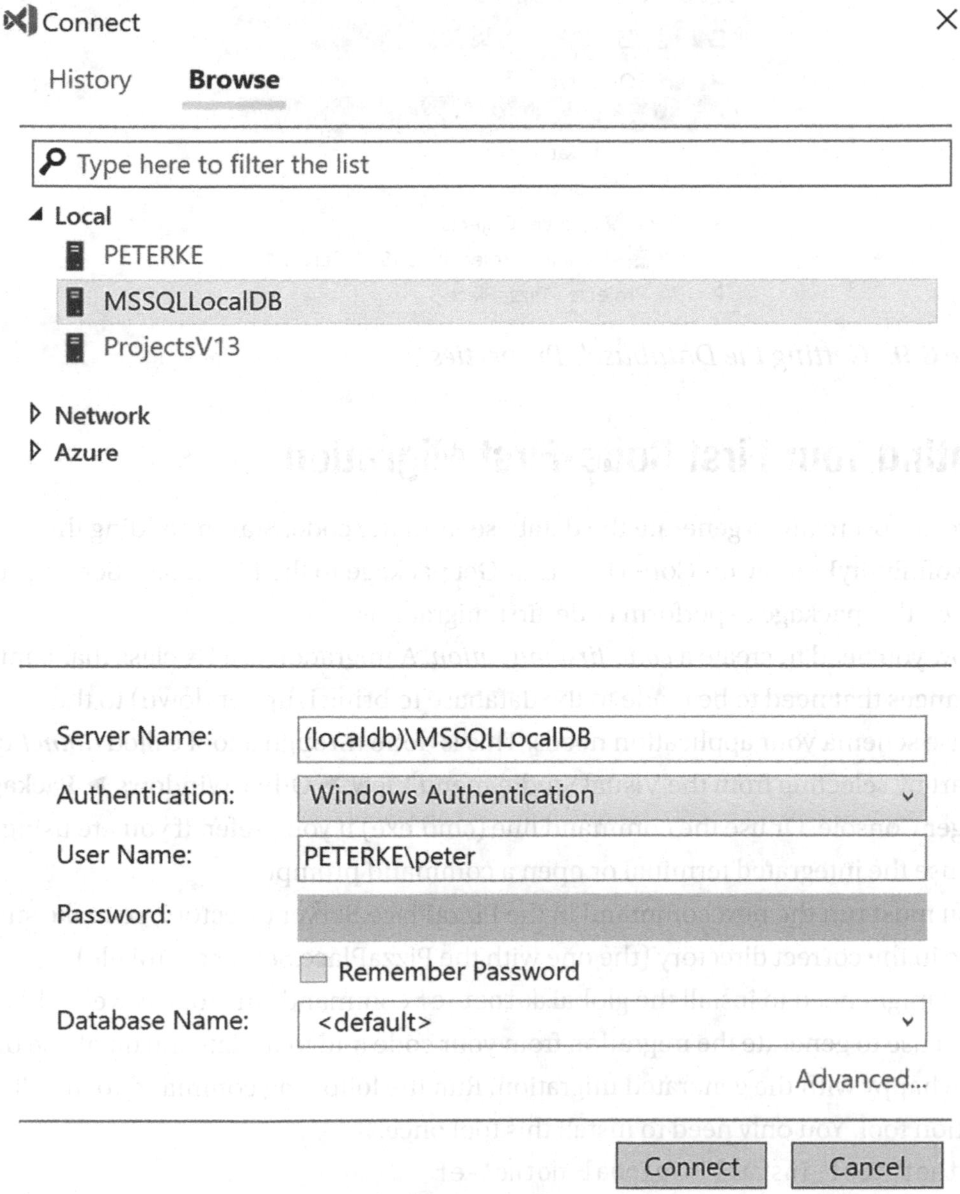

Figure 6-8. *Finding the Connection String for a Database*

Next, expand SQL Server in SQL Server Object Explorer from Figure 6-9 and select your server. Right-click it and select Properties. Now copy the connection string from the properties window, paste it in appsettings.json, and change the database name to PizzaPlaceDb.

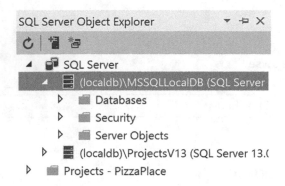

Figure 6-9. *Getting the Database's Properties*

Creating Your First Code-First Migration

You are almost ready to generate the database from the code. Start by adding the Microsoft.EntityFrameworkCore.Design NuGet package to the PizzaPlace.Server project. You need this package to perform code-first migrations.

Now you need to create a *code-first migration*. A migration is a C# class that contains the changes that need to be made to the database to bring it up (or down) to the database schema your application needs. This is done through a tool called *dotnet-ef*.

Start by selecting from the Visual Studio menu View ➤ Other Windows ➤ Package Manager Console. Or use the command line (cmd.exe) if you prefer. If you are using Code, use the integrated terminal or open a command prompt.

You must run the next command in the PizzaPlace.Server directory, so make sure you are in the correct directory (the one with the PizzaPlace.Server.csproj file).

You might need to install the global `dotnet-ef` command-line tool as well. This is the tool you use to generate the migration from your code and to update the database once you are happy with the generated migration. Run the following command to install the migration tool. You only need to install this tool once.

```
dotnet tool install --global dotnet-ef
```

Now execute the following command to create the migration:

```
dotnet-ef migrations add CreatingPizzaPlaceDb
```

Here, you use the `dotnet-ef` tool to add a new migration called CreatingPizzaPlaceDb. You can pick any name you want for the migration; do pick one that makes sense. You should see the following output:

```
Build started...
Build succeeded.
Done. To undo this action, use 'ef migrations remove'
```

Should you get an error or warnings, please review the code for the `Pizza` and the `PizzaPlaceDbContext` classes (and maybe compare with the provided sources for the book), ensure that all the Entity Framework packages are using the same version, and try again.

This tool created a new Migrations folder in the PizzaPlace.Server project with two files similar to Figure 6-10 but with a different timestamp.

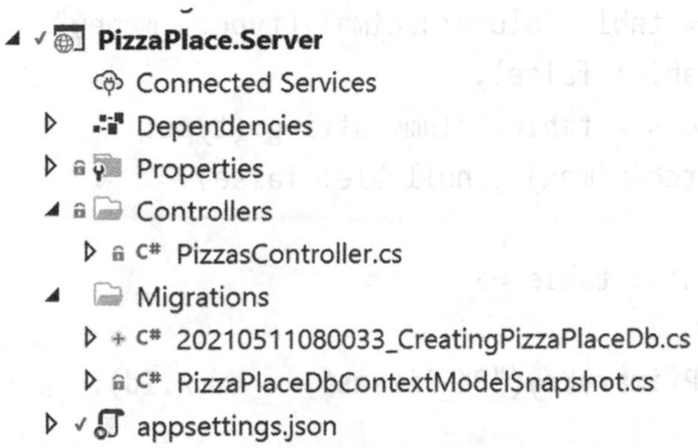

Figure 6-10. The Result of Adding the First Migration

Open the CreatingPizzaDb.cs file from Listing 6-11 and look at what the tool did. If you have been using SQLite, consult Listing 6-12.

Listing 6-11. The CreatingPizzaDb.cs File for SQL Server

```csharp
using Microsoft.EntityFrameworkCore.Migrations;

namespace PizzaPlace.Server.Migrations
{
  public partial class CreatingPizzaPlaceDb : Migration
  {
    protected override void Up(MigrationBuilder migrationBuilder)
    {
      migrationBuilder.CreateTable(
          name: "Pizzas",
          columns: table => new
          {
            Id = table.Column<int>(type: "int", nullable: false)
                .Annotation("SqlServer:Identity", "1, 1"),
            Name = table.Column<string>(type: "nvarchar(80)",
              maxLength: 80, nullable: false),
            Price = table.Column<decimal>(type: "money",
              nullable: false),
            Spiciness = table.Column<string>(type:
              "nvarchar(max)", nullable: false)
          },
          constraints: table =>
          {
            table.PrimaryKey("PK_Pizzas", x => x.Id);
          });
    }

    protected override void Down(MigrationBuilder migrationBuilder)
    {
      migrationBuilder.DropTable(
          name: "Pizzas");
    }
  }
}
```

A migration class has two methods: Up and Down. The Up method will upgrade the database schema. In this case, it will create a new table called Pizzas with Id, Name, Price, and Spiciness columns.

The Down method downgrades the database schema, in this case, by dropping the column. As you are developing, you will make small changes to the database schema; each change becomes a migration. We can then use these migrations to update the database or go back to a previous schema of the database. You can also apply a whole series of changes when you want to update your production database to match the development database's schema.

Listing 6-12. The Migration Class for SQLite

```
using Microsoft.EntityFrameworkCore.Migrations;

namespace PizzaPlace.Server.Migrations
{
  public partial class Created : Migration
  {
    protected override void Up(MigrationBuilder migrationBuilder)
    {
      migrationBuilder.CreateTable(
        name: "Pizzas",
        columns: table => new
        {
          Id = table.Column<int>(type: "INTEGER",
                            nullable: false)
                  .Annotation("Sqlite:Autoincrement", true),
          Name = table.Column<string>(type: "TEXT",
                                    maxLength: 80,
                                    nullable: false),
          Price = table.Column<decimal>(type: "money",
                                      nullable: false),
          Spiciness = table.Column<string>(type: "TEXT",
                                      nullable: false)
        },
```

```
      constraints: table =>
      {
        table.PrimaryKey("PK_Pizzas", x => x.Id);
      });
  }

  protected override void Down(
    MigrationBuilder migrationBuilder)
  {
    migrationBuilder.DropTable(
        name: "Pizzas");
  }
 }
}
```

Generating the Database

Now you are ready to generate the database from your migration. With Visual Studio, go back to the Command Line or Package Manager Console window (View ➤ Other Windows ➤ Package Manager Console), or with Code, open the integrated terminal (View ➤ Terminal). Ensure you are in the folder that contains the PizzaPlace.Server project and type the following command:

```
dotnet-ef database update
```

This just created the database for you! Let's have a look at the database. First, let's look at SQL Server.

From Visual Studio, open View ➤ SQL Server Object Explorer and expand the tree for the PizzaPlaceDb database as in Figure 6-11 (you might need to refresh the database: right-click Databases and select Refresh).

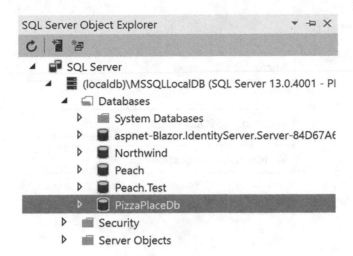

Figure 6-11. *SQL Server Object Explorer Showing the PizzaPlaceDb Database*

If you don't have Visual Studio, you can download *Azure Data Studio* from https://docs.microsoft.com/sql/azure-data-studio/download-azure-data-studio. After installation ends, start Azure Data Studio and create a new connection. Enter your server name and select PizzaPlaceDb from the drop-down list, as shown in Figure 6-12.

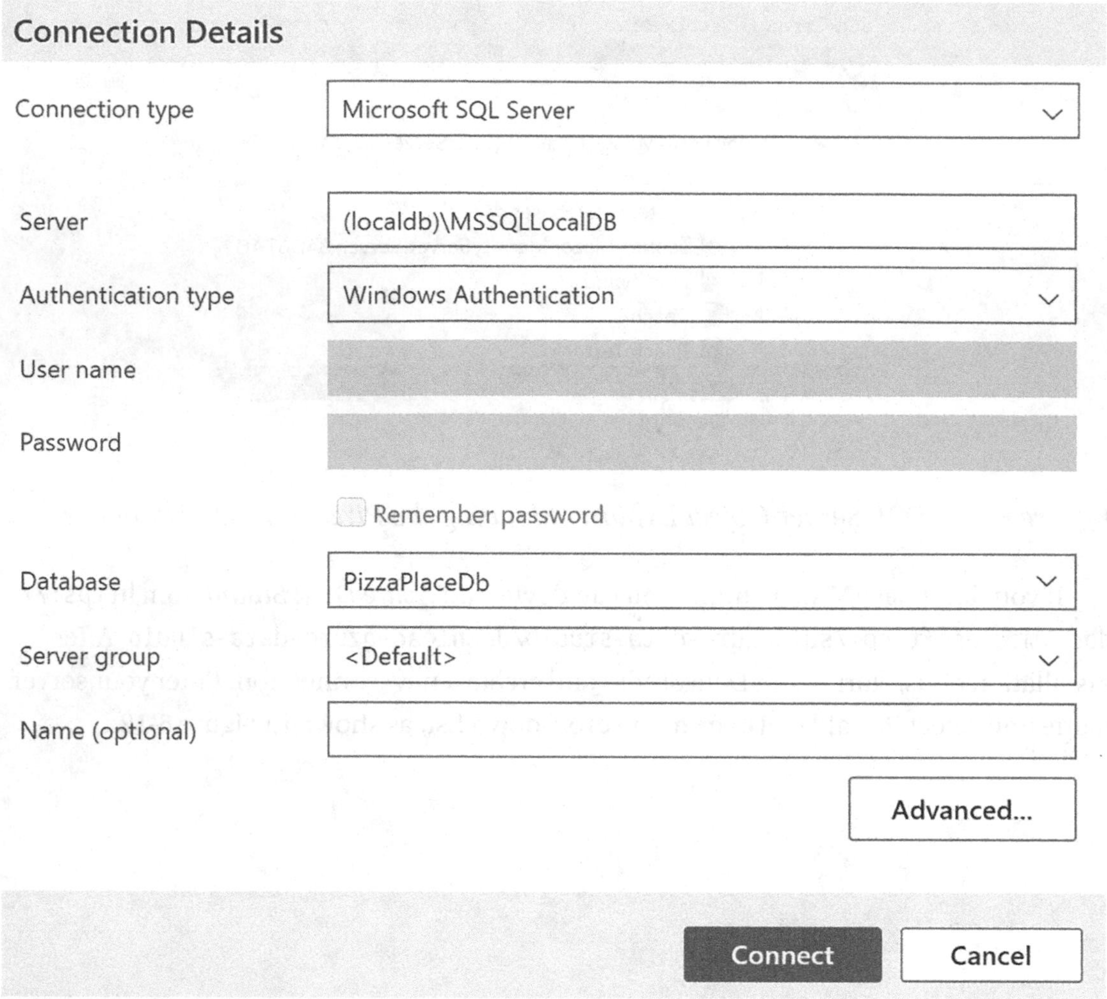

Connection Details

Connection type	Microsoft SQL Server ⌄
Server	(localdb)\MSSQLLocalDB
Authentication type	Windows Authentication ⌄
User name	
Password	
	▢ Remember password
Database	PizzaPlaceDb ⌄
Server group	<Default> ⌄
Name (optional)	

Advanced...

Connect   Cancel

Figure 6-12. *Connection with SQL Operations Studio*

To look at the SQLite database, you will need to download and install the SQLite database browser from https://sqlitebrowser.org/.

Now run DB Browser, and open the PizzaPlace.db. You can now use this tool to explore the database as in Figure 6-13.

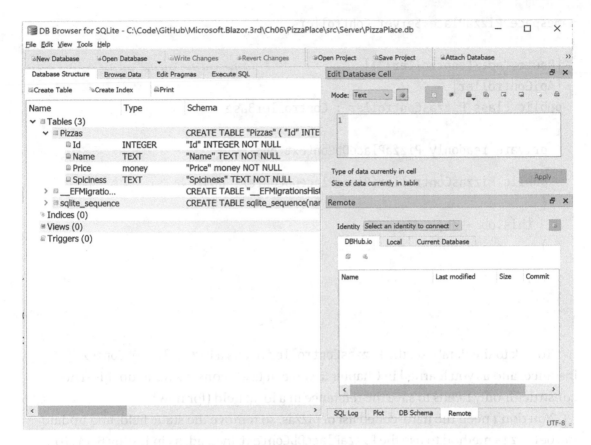

Figure 6-13. *Using DB Browser for SQLite*

Enhancing the Pizza Microservice

Let's add some functionality to the Pizza microservice so it uses the database instead of
hard-coded data and add a method to insert a pizza in your database.

Open the PizzaController class, which sits in the Controllers folder of
the PizzaPlace.Server project. Start by adding a constructor that takes the
PizzaPlaceDbContext as an argument, as in Listing 6-13.

Listing 6-13. Injecting a PizzaPlaceDbContext Instance into the Controller

```
using Microsoft.AspNetCore.Mvc;
using PizzaPlace.Shared;
using System.Collections.Generic;
using System.Linq;
```

```
namespace PizzaPlace.Server.Controllers
{
  [Route("api/[controller]")]
  [ApiController]
  public class PizzasController : ControllerBase
  {
    private readonly PizzaPlaceDbContext db;

    public PizzasController(PizzaPlaceDbContext db)
    {
      this.db = db;
    }

    ...

  }
}
```

To talk to the database, the PizzasController needs a PizzaPlaceDbContext instance, and as you learned in Chapter 5, you can use a constructor to do this. The constructor only needs to save the reference in a local field (for now).

You don't need the hard-coded list of pizzas, so remove the static field, and update the GetPizza method to use the PizzaPlaceDbContext instead, as in Listing 6-14. To get all the pizzas, you can simply use the Pizzas property of the PizzaPlaceDbContext. The Entity Framework will access the database when it accesses the Pizzas property and return all the rows in the Pizza table. Also remove the Route attribute, since the GetPizzas method specifies its URL.

Listing 6-14. Retrieving the Pizzas from the Database

```
using Microsoft.AspNetCore.Mvc;
using PizzaPlace.Shared;
using System.Collections.Generic;
using System.Linq;

namespace PizzaPlace.Server.Controllers
{
  [ApiController]
  public class PizzasController : ControllerBase
```

```
{
  private readonly PizzaPlaceDbContext db;

  public PizzasController(PizzaPlaceDbContext db)
  {
    this.db = db;
  }

  [HttpGet("/pizzas")]
  public IQueryable<Pizza> GetPizzas()
    => db.Pizzas;
  }
}
```

Now let's add a method to insert a new pizza in the database. Add the InsertPizza method from Listing 6-15 to the PizzasController class. This method will receive a pizza instance from the client as part of the POST request body, so you add the HttpPost attribute with the URI that you should post to. The pizza object will be posted in the request body, and this is why the InsertPizza method's pizza argument has the FromBody attribute to tell ASP.NET MVC Core to convert the body of the request to a pizza instance. The method adds the pizza to the PizzaPlaceDbContext Pizzas table and then saves it to the database using the SaveChanges method. The InsertPizza method then returns a 201 Created status code with the URI of the pizza as the response, as is the convention with REST. There are many possible HTTP status codes that you could return from a controller's method. But the most common of them have special helper methods that make it easy to return a certain status code, for instance, Ok(), NotFound(). In this case, you return a 201 – Created status code. You will examine this response with Postman in the next part of this chapter.

Listing 6-15. The InsertPizza Method

```
using Microsoft.AspNetCore.Mvc;
using PizzaPlace.Shared;
using System.Collections.Generic;
using System.Linq;

namespace PizzaPlace.Server.Controllers
{
```

```
[Route("api/[controller]")]
[ApiController]
public class PizzasController : ControllerBase
{
  private readonly PizzaPlaceDbContext db;

  public PizzasController(PizzaPlaceDbContext db)
  {
    this.db = db;
  }

  [HttpGet("/pizzas")]
  public IQueryable<Pizza> GetPizzas()
    => db.Pizzas;

  [HttpPost("/pizzas")]
  public IActionResult InsertPizza([FromBody] Pizza pizza)
  {
    db.Pizzas.Add(pizza);
    db.SaveChanges();
    return Created($"pizzas/{pizza.Id}", pizza);
  }
}
}
```

This is an introduction to REST services. Building real services with all the different approaches and best practices can take up a whole book. The idea of this chapter is to get you up and running.

Testing Your Microservice Using Postman

So now you have your first microservice. But how do you test it? Previously, you used the browser to test the GetPizzas method, which uses the GET method. For other methods, such as POST, PUT, and DELETE, you need a better tool. Here, you will use Postman, which is a tool specifically for testing REST services.

Open your favorite browser and go to www.getpostman.com. Download the application and install it. By the time you read this book, the installation procedure may have changed a bit, so please follow the instructions from the installer.

After it has installed, run Postman.

Postman will open, and it will ask you what you want to do. Select Create New, as shown in Figure 6-14.

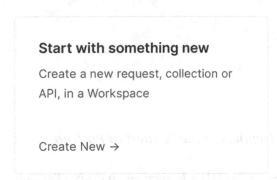

Get started with Postman

Start with something new

Create a new request, collection or API, in a Workspace

Create New →

Figure 6-14. *Select Create New to Get Started with Postman*

Now select Create a request as in Figure 6-15.

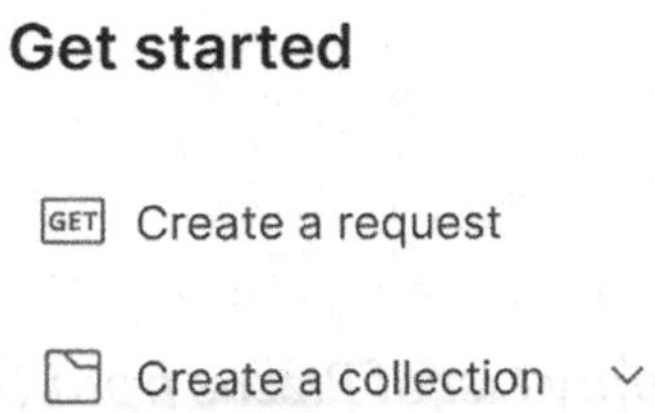

Get started

GET   Create a request

☐   Create a collection   ⌄

Figure 6-15. *Create a Request with Postman*

Now run the PizzaPlace solution and copy the URI from the browser. Paste it in Postman's URL field and append /pizzas as in Figure 6-16. Don't forget that you most likely will have a different port number!

https://localhost:5001/pizzas   💾 Save ⌄ | ✏️ 💬

GET   ⌄   https://localhost:5001/pizzas   Send ⌄

Figure 6-16. *Making a GET Request with Postman*

Before you click Send, let's add the Accept header. Click the Headers tab and enter Accept as the key and application/json as the value. Please refer to Figure 6-17 for reference.

Figure 6-17. *Adding Headers to the Request in Postman*

Now you can click Send. You should receive an empty list as in Figure 6-18. Also note the 200 OK status code, meaning the method was executed successfully! We simply don't have any pizzas in our database yet.

Body ∨						200 OK 59 ms 169 B Save Response ∨
Pretty	Raw	Preview	Visualize	JSON ∨		

```
1   []
```

Figure 6-18. *Receiving an Empty List of Pizzas from the Server*

Let's add a couple of pizzas to the database. At the top of Postman, you will find a tab with a plus sign. Click it to add another tab. Select POST as the method and copy the URI from the previous tab, as shown in Figure 6-19.

Figure 6-19. *Starting with the POST Request*

Now select the Headers section and add a new header with key Content-Type and value application/json like in Figure 6-20.

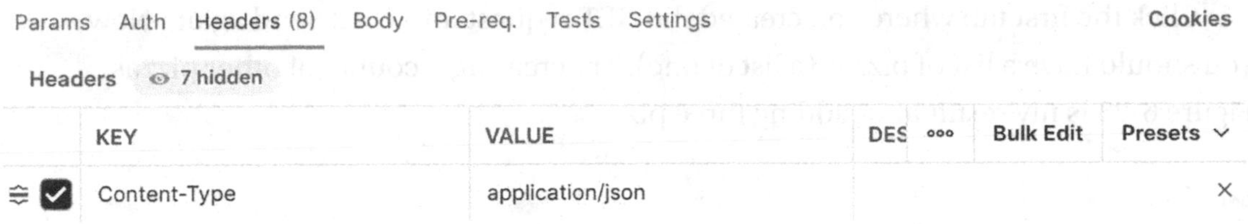

Figure 6-20. Adding the Content-Type Header for the POST Request

Now select the Body section, select the raw format using the drop-down, and enter a pizza object using JSON. Please refer to Figure 6-21. Note that this raw string contains the pizza's properties serialized as JSON and that you don't need to send the Id property because the server will generate the id when it gets inserted into the database.

Figure 6-21. Entering a Pizza Using JSON

Ensure your PizzaPlace application is still running, and then click the Send button. If all is well, you should receive a positive 201 Created response as in Figure 6-22. In the response area of Postman, select the Headers tab. Look for the Location header. It will show the new URI given to this pizza. This Location header is returned by the Created method you called as the last line of Listing 6-15.

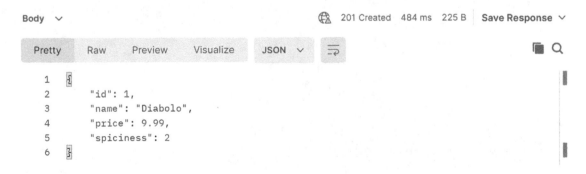

Figure 6-22. The POST Response in Postman

Click the first tab where you created the GET request and click Send again. Now you should have a list of pizzas (a list of one). Try creating a couple of other pizzas. Figure 6-23 is my result after adding three pizzas.

Body   Cookies   Headers (4)   Test Results   Status: 200 OK   Time: 17 ms   Size: 318 B   Save Response ⌄

Pretty   Raw   Preview   Visualize   JSON ⌄   ⇥

```
 1  [
 2      {
 3          "id": 1,
 4          "name": "Diabolo",
 5          "price": 9.9900,
 6          "spiciness": 2
 7      },
 8      {
 9          "id": 2,
10          "name": "Margarita",
11          "price": 7.9900,
12          "spiciness": 0
13      },
14      {
15          "id": 3,
16          "name": "Pepperoni",
17          "price": 8.9900,
18          "spiciness": 1
19      }
20  ]
```

Figure 6-23. *A List of Pizzas Stored in the Database*

Summary

In this chapter, you had a look at how to store data on the server using Entity Framework Core and how to expose that data using Web API, REST, and microservices. You added a pizza service to the PizzaPlace application and then went on testing it with Postman.

In the next chapter, you will learn how to talk to your service(s) from Blazor.

CHAPTER 7

Communication with Microservices

In the previous chapter, you built a microservice using ASP.NET Core and Entity Framework Core to retrieve the menu of pizzas from the server. In this chapter, you will add support to the Blazor client to talk to that microservice. You will also complete the project by adding support for completing the order.

Using the HttpClient Class

Start by creating a fresh Blazor WASM project (with hosting enabled) just like you created in the first chapter (call it *Blazor.Communication*). You will use this project to examine the template that was created for you. You will start by looking at the server side of the solution, then the shared project's code, and then the client side.

Examining the Server Project

Look at the Blazor.Communication.Server project and look for the WeatherForecastController class, which is in Listing 7-1.

Listing 7-1. The WeatherForecastController Class

```
using Blazor.Communication.Shared;
using Microsoft.AspNetCore.Mvc;

namespace Blazor.Communication.Server.Controllers;
[ApiController]
[Route("[controller]")]
public class WeatherForecastController : ControllerBase
```

261

© Peter Himschoot 2022
P. Himschoot, *Microsoft Blazor*, https://doi.org/10.1007/978-1-4842-7845-1_7

```
{
  private static readonly string[] Summaries = new[]
  {
    "Freezing", "Bracing", "Chilly", "Cool", "Mild", "Warm",
    "Balmy", "Hot", "Sweltering", "Scorching"
  };

  private readonly ILogger<WeatherForecastController> _logger;

  public WeatherForecastController(
    ILogger<WeatherForecastController> logger)
  {
    _logger = logger;
  }

  [HttpGet]
  public IEnumerable<WeatherForecast> Get()
  {
    return Enumerable.Range(1, 5)
                .Select(index => new WeatherForecast
    {
      Date = DateTime.Now.AddDays(index),
      TemperatureC = Random.Shared.Next(-20, 55),
      Summary = Summaries[Random.Shared.Next(Summaries.Length)]
    })
    .ToArray();
  }
}
```

Does this look somewhat familiar? Of course, it does; this is an API controller like we saw in the previous chapter. What URL you should use to access the list of WeatherForecasts?

The WeatherForecastController class exposes one REST endpoint at URI /WeatherForecast to retrieve a list of WeatherForecast objects. This time, the WeatherForecastController uses the [Route("[controller]")] attribute to set up the endpoint to generically listen to an URI that contains the name of the controller (without the suffix "Controller") and then uses the [HttpGet] attribute to expect the GET method.

To invoke this method, you should use a GET on the `/weatherforecast` URI, which you can try with your browser (or if you prefer, Postman). Run the solution and type the URI in your browser (don't forget you might have a different port number) which will result in Figure 7-1 (expect different weather; it is random).

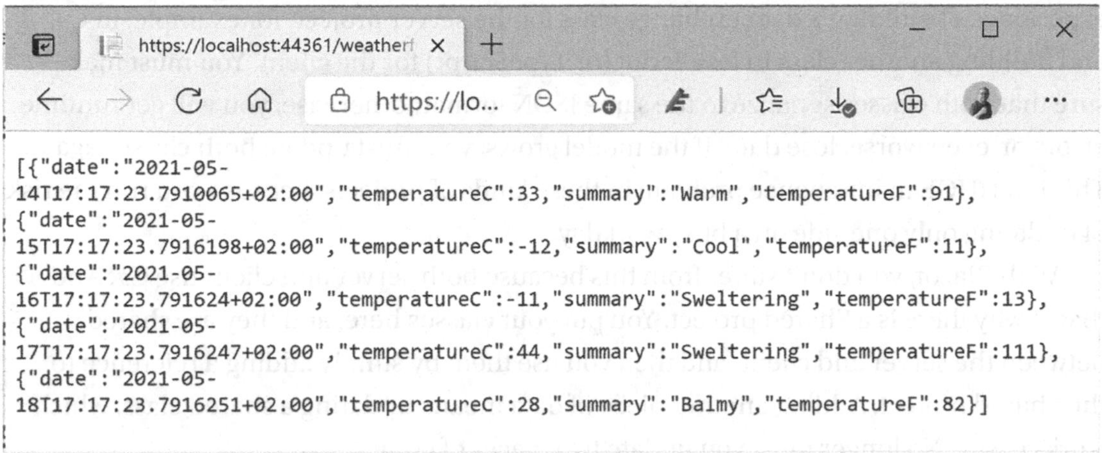
https://localhost:44361/weatherf
https://lo...
[{"date":"2021-05-14T17:17:23.7910065+02:00","temperatureC":33,"summary":"Warm","temperatureF":91},
{"date":"2021-05-15T17:17:23.7916198+02:00","temperatureC":-12,"summary":"Cool","temperatureF":11},
{"date":"2021-05-16T17:17:23.791624+02:00","temperatureC":-11,"summary":"Sweltering","temperatureF":13},
{"date":"2021-05-17T17:17:23.7916247+02:00","temperatureC":44,"summary":"Sweltering","temperatureF":111},
{"date":"2021-05-18T17:17:23.7916251+02:00","temperatureC":28,"summary":"Balmy","temperatureF":82}]

Figure 7-1. *Invoking the Service Using the Browser*

The `Get` method from Listing 7-1 uses a random choice of temperatures and summaries to generate these forecasts, which is great for a demo.

Using a Shared Project. Why?

Now open the `WeatherForecast` class from the Blazor.Communication.Shared project, which is in Listing 7-2.

Listing 7-2. The Shared WeatherForecast Class

```
namespace Blazor.Communication.Shared;
public class WeatherForecast
{
  public DateTime Date { get; set; }

  public int TemperatureC { get; set; }

  public string? Summary { get; set; }

  public int TemperatureF => 32 + (int)(TemperatureC / 0.5556);
}
```

This WeatherForecast class is straightforward, containing the Date of the forecast, the temperature in Celsius and Fahrenheit, and a Summary, but I want to draw your attention to the fact that this class lives in the Shared project. This shared project is used both by the server and the client project.

If you ever created a web app with JavaScript, you should be familiar with the experience of building a data exchange class for the server project, for example, in C#, and building another class in JavaScript (or TypeScript) for the client. You must make sure that both classes serialize to the same JSON format; otherwise, you will get runtime errors or, even worse, lose data! If the model grows, you must update both classes again. This is a HUGE maintenance problem in these kinds of projects, because you run the risk of updating only one side on a busy workday.

With Blazor, you don't suffer from this because both server and client use C#. And that is why there is a Shared project. You put your classes here, and they are shared between the server and client, and then you use them by simply adding a reference to the Shared project. Adding another piece of data means updating a shared class, which works easily! No longer must you update two pieces of code.

Looking at the Client Project

Now look at the Blazor.Communication.Client project. Inside the Pages folder, you will find the FetchData component from Listing 7-3.

Listing 7-3. The FetchData Component

```
@page "/fetchdata"
@using Blazor.Communication.Shared
@inject HttpClient Http

<h1>Weather forecast</h1>

<p>This component demonstrates fetching data from the server.</p>

@if (forecasts == null)
{
  <p><em>Loading...</em></p>
}
```

```
else
{
  <table class="table">
    <thead>
      <tr>
        <th>Date</th>
        <th>Temp. (C)</th>
        <th>Temp. (F)</th>
        <th>Summary</th>
      </tr>
    </thead>
    <tbody>
      @foreach (var forecast in forecasts)
      {
        <tr>
          <td>@forecast.Date.ToShortDateString()</td>
          <td>@forecast.TemperatureC</td>
          <td>@forecast.TemperatureF</td>
          <td>@forecast.Summary</td>
        </tr>
      }
    </tbody>
  </table>
}
@code {
  private WeatherForecast[]? forecasts;

  protected override async Task OnInitializedAsync()
  {
    forecasts = await Http
      .GetFromJsonAsync<WeatherForecast[]>("WeatherForecast");
  }

}
```

Let's look at this line by line. The first line adds the path for routing. You will look at routing in a later chapter. For the moment, you should know that when the URI is / fetchdata, the FetchData component will be shown in the browser.

The second line in Listing 7-3 adds a Razor @using statement for the Shared project's namespace to the component. You need this because you use the WeatherForecast class from the Shared project. Just like in C#, you use using statements in Razor to refer to classes from another namespace.

On the third line, you inject the HttpClient instance using the @inject syntax from Razor. The HttpClient class is the one you will use to talk to the server. You will learn about the HttpClient class in more detail later in this chapter.

I do want to point out that you should never instantiate an instance of the HttpClient class yourself. Blazor sets up the HttpClient class in a special way, and if you create an instance yourself, it simply will not work as expected! Another reason not to create an instance yourself is that this is a dependency of the FetchData component, and we learned in Chapter 5 that classes and components should never create dependencies themselves!

A little lower down in Listing 7-3, you will find an @if statement. Because you fetch the data from the server using an asynchronous way, the forecasts field will initially hold a null reference. So, if the forecasts field has not been set, you tell the user to wait. If you have a slow network, you can see this happening. When you test your Blazor application on your own machine, the network is fast, but you can emulate a slow network using the browser (in this case, using Google Chrome).

Emulating a Slow Network in Chrome

Start your Blazor project so the browser opens the Index page. Now open the debugger tools from the browser (on Windows with Chrome, you do this by pressing F12) and select the Network tab as in Figure 7-2. On the right side, you should see a drop-down list that allows you to select which kind of network to emulate. Select *Slow 3G*.

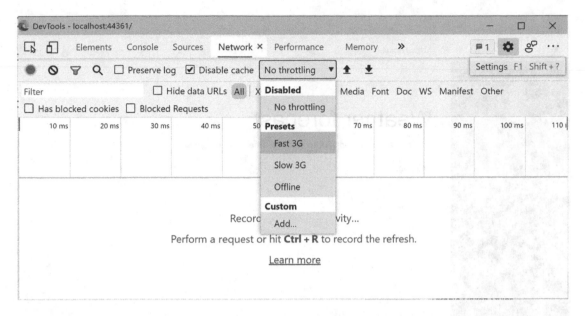

Figure 7-2. *Using the Chrome Browser Debugger to Emulate a Slow Network*

Next, select the Fetch data tab on your Blazor site (should you already be on this tab, select another tab and then the Fetch data tab). Because you now are using a slow network, the Loading... feedback will appear, as shown in Figure 7-3.

After testing your Blazor website with a slow network, don't forget to select *No throttling* from the drop-down from Figure 7-2 to restore your network to its normal speed.

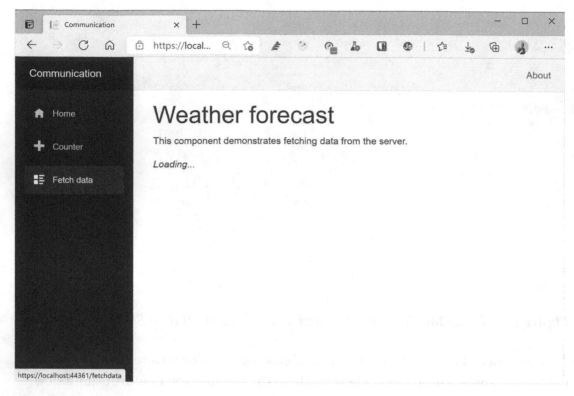

Figure 7-3. *The Loading... Feedback with a Slow Network*

When the OnInitializedAsync method finished, the forecasts field holds data, and your razor file will show a table with the forecasts by iterating over them, as you can see in the else part of Listing 7-3.

Onto the @code section of the FetchData razor file. First, you declare a field called forecasts to hold an array of WeatherForecast instances. You then override the OnInitializedAsync life cycle method. Because you fetch the data from the server using an asynchronous API, you need to put your code in OnInitializedAsync. The OnInitializedAsync method is prefixed with C#'s async keyword, which makes it a breeze to call async APIs with the await keyword.

Asynchronous communication means that the client might need to wait a fair amount (for a computer) for the result to be returned. Asynchronous calls might take a long time, and we don't want to block the application so we use an asynchronous call. Instead of using a call that will stop Blazor from completing other request (freezing the user interface), you use the OnInitializedAsync method, which will wait in the background for the result.

You use the `Http.GetFromJsonAsync<WeatherForecast[]>("WeatherForecast")` to invoke the server's GET endpoint at the URI, and you tell the `GetFromJsonAsync` method (using generics) to expect an array of `WeatherForecast` objects. When the result comes back from the server, you put the result into the forecasts field, and Blazor will take care of re-rendering the UI with your new data, as shown in Figure 7-4.

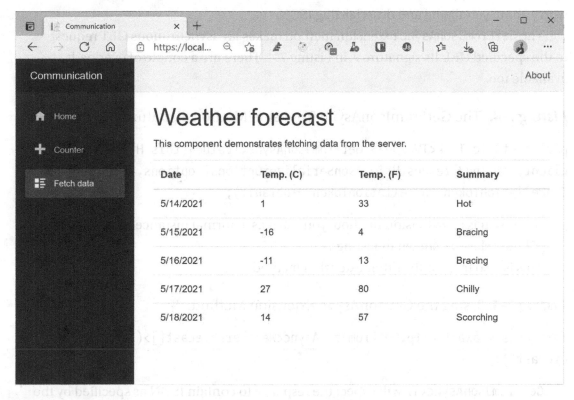

Figure 7-4. *Displaying the WeatherForecast Objects*

Understanding the HttpClient Class

All communication between the client and server passes through the `HttpClient` class. This is the same class other applications in .NET use, and its role is to make the HTTP request to the server and to expose the result from the server. It also allows you to exchange binary or other formatted data, but in Blazor, we normally use JSON. With Blazor WASM, the `HttpClient` class uses the browser's network stack to talk on the network.

The HttpClientJsonExtensions Methods

To make it a lot easier to talk to JSON microservices, .NET provides you with a bunch of handy *extension methods* that take care of converting between .NET objects and JSON, which you can find in the HttpClientJsonExtensions class. This class lives in the System.Net.Http.Json namespace. I advise you use these methods, so you don't have to worry about serializing and deserializing JSON.

The GetFromJsonAsync extension method makes an asynchronous GET request to the specified URI. Its signature is in Listing 7-4. There are a couple of overloads available too.

Listing 7-4. The GetFromJsonAsync Extension Method Signature

```
public static Task<TValue?> GetFromJsonAsync<TValue>(this HttpClient
client, string? requestUri, JsonSerializerOptions? options,
CancellationToken cancellationToken = default);
```

Because it is an extension method, you call it as a normal instance method on the HttpClient class, as shown in Listing 7-5.

This is also true for the other extension methods.

Listing 7-5. Using the GetJsonAsync Extension Method

```
forecasts = await Http.GetFromJsonAsync<WeatherForecast[]>("WeatherF
orecast");
```

GetFromJsonAsync<T> will expect the response to contain JSON as specified by the generic argument. For example, in Listing 7-5, it expects an array of WeatherForecast instances. You normally invoke the GetFromJsonAsync method by prefixing it with the await keyword. Don't forget that you can only use the await keyword in methods and lambda functions that are async.

As you can see in Listing 7-4, there are additional arguments which we discuss later in this section.

You can always inspect the request and response using your browser's debugger. Run your Blazor project and open the browser's debugger on the Network tab. Now select the Fetch data tab in your Blazor website to make it load the data and look at the browser's Network tab as in Figure 7-5.

You can always clear the Network tab from previous requests before making the request using the clear button, which in Chrome looks like a circle with a slash through it (the forbidden sign).

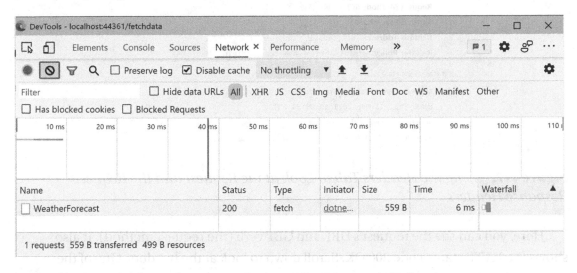

***Figure 7-5.** Inspecting the Network Using the Browser's Debugger*

See the WeatherForecasts entry in Figure 7-5? Now you can click that entry to look at the request and response. Let's start with the request preview shown in Figure 7-6. Using the Preview tab, you can see the server's response.

Name	× Headers **Preview** Response Initiator Timing
☐ WeatherForecast	▼ [,…]
	▶ 0: {date: "2021-05-14T17:57:29.1027301+02:00", temperatureC: 32, summary: "Freezing", t
	▶ 1: {date: "2021-05-15T17:57:29.1027403+02:00", temperatureC: 25, summary: "Mild", tempe
	▶ 2: {date: "2021-05-16T17:57:29.1027418+02:00", temperatureC: 54, summary: "Cool", tempe
	▶ 3: {date: "2021-05-17T17:57:29.1027434+02:00", temperatureC: 33, summary: "Freezing", t
	▶ 4: {date: "2021-05-18T17:57:29.102745+02:00", temperatureC: -1, summary: "Mild", temper

***Figure 7-6.** Using the Preview Tab to Look at the Response*

If you want to look at the request and response headers, you can click the Headers tab, as shown in Figure 7-7.

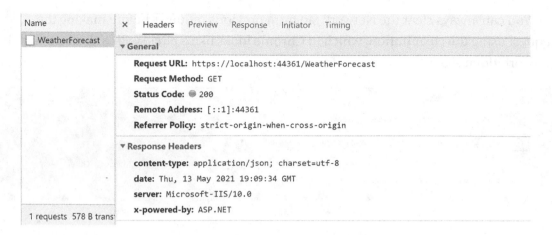

Figure 7-7. *Using the Headers Tab to Look at the Request and the Request/Response Headers*

Here, you can see the request's URL and GET verb (the request method). It also shows the HTTP status code 200 OK. Scroll down to look at the headers. One of the response headers is Content-Type with a value of application/json, which was set by the server telling the client to expect JSON.

The `PostAsJsonAsync` extension method makes a POST request with the content argument serialized in the request body as JSON to the specified URI. Its signature is in Listing 7-6.

Listing 7-6. The PostAsJsonAsync Method's Signature

```
public static Task<HttpResponseMessage> PostAsJsonAsync<TValue>(this
HttpClient client, string? requestUri, TValue value, JsonSerializerOptions?
options = null, CancellationToken cancellationToken = default);
```

The `PutAsJsonAsync` extension method makes a PUT request with the content argument serialized as JSON in the request body to the specified URI. Its signature is in Listing 7-7. Its usage is very similar to PostJsonAsync; the only difference is that it uses the PUT verb.

Listing 7-7. The PutAsJsonAsync Method's Signature

```
public static Task<HttpResponseMessage> PutAsJsonAsync<TValue>(this
HttpClient client, string? requestUri, TValue value, JsonSerializerOptions?
options = null, CancellationToken cancellationToken = default);
```

Customizing Serialization with JsonSerializerOptions

Each of these methods takes an optional `JsonSerializerOptions` which allows you to control how JSON serialization works. For example, the default options will serialize the property names with the casing of the property name. However, there are services that require camel casing for properties. Let us see how we can control this with Listing 7-8. To change the casing, you can set the `PropertyNamingPolicy` property. Here, we set it to `JsonNamingPolicy.CamelCase`. This example also shows how you can control the serialization of enumerations. Normally, enumerations get serialized with their int value. For example, `Spiciness.Spicy` will get serialized as 1. But if you like, you can also use the name of the enumeration value, so `Spiciness.Spicy` will get serialized as "Spicy". Do this by using the `JsonStringEnumConverter` as in Listing 7-8. Don't forget you will have to pass the `JsonSerializerOptions` as an extra argument using the `GetFromJsonAsync` and similar methods.

Listing 7-8. Controlling Casing with JsonSerializerOptions

```
protected readonly JsonSerializerOptions options =
  new JsonSerializerOptions
  {
    PropertyNamingPolicy = JsonNamingPolicy.CamelCase,
    Converters =
    {
        new JsonStringEnumConverter()
    }
  };
```

Retrieving Data from the Server

So now you are ready to implement the client-side `IMenuService` you introduced earlier. Open the PizzaPlace solution and look in the PizzaPlace.Client project for Program.cs, which is shown in Listing 7-9.

Listing 7-9. Your Blazor Project's Program Class

```
using Microsoft.AspNetCore.Components.WebAssembly.Hosting;
using Microsoft.Extensions.DependencyInjection;
using PizzaPlace.Shared;
using System;
using System.Net.Http;
using System.Threading.Tasks;

namespace PizzaPlace.Client
{
  public class Program
  {
    public static async Task Main(string[] args)
    {
      var builder = WebAssemblyHostBuilder.CreateDefault(args);
      builder.RootComponents.Add<App>("#app");

      builder.Services.AddScoped(sp => new HttpClient
      {
        BaseAddress =
          new Uri(builder.HostEnvironment.BaseAddress)
      });

      builder.Services
            .AddTransient<IMenuService, HardCodedMenuService>();
      builder.Services
            .AddTransient<IOrderService, ConsoleOrderService>();

      await builder.Build().RunAsync();
    }
  }
}
```

I would like to point out the third line of the Main method. Previously, I told you that you should never create the HttpClient instance yourself. But here we do! This method makes it very easy to configure your HttpClient instance so the service does not have to set the BaseAddress property. This works for other HttpClient properties too.

In the Main method, you added two services, HardCodedMenuService and ConsoleOrderService. Let's replace these fake implementations with real services that talk to the server.

Implementing the MenuService

With Visual Studio, right-click the PizzaPlace.Client project and select Add ➤ New Folder from the drop-down menu. With Code, right-click the PizzaPlace.Client project and select New Folder. Name this folder *Services*. Now add a new class to this folder called MenuService, which can be found in Listing 7-10.

Again, you are applying the principle of single responsibility where you encapsulate how you talk to the server in a service. This way, you can easily replace this implementation with another one should the need occur.

Listing 7-10. The MenuService Class

```
using PizzaPlace.Shared;
using System.Linq;
using System.Net.Http;
using System.Net.Http.Json;
using System.Threading.Tasks;

namespace PizzaPlace.Client.Services
{
  public class MenuService : IMenuService
  {
    private readonly HttpClient httpClient;

    public MenuService(HttpClient httpClient)
    {
      this.httpClient = httpClient;
    }

    public async ValueTask<Menu> GetMenu()
    {
      var pizzas = await httpClient
```

```
                        .GetFromJsonAsync<Pizza[]>("/pizzas");
      return new Menu { Pizzas = pizzas!.ToList() };
    }
  }
}
```

You start by adding a constructor to this class taking the MenuService's dependency on HttpClient, and you store it in a field named httpClient. Then you implement the IMenuService interface's GetMenu method where you talk to the server calling the GetFromJsonAsync on the server's /pizza endpoint. Note that the /pizza endpoint is relative to the site's base (<base href="/" />), which can be found in the index.html file. You can change this base address in Program.cs (see Listing 7-11). Because the MenuService service returns a menu and not a list of pizzas, you wrap the list of pizzas you got from the server into a Menu object. That's it!

Note   Using the principle of single responsibility results in many small classes, which are easier to understand, maintain, and test.

You have the service; now you need to tell dependency injection to use the MenuService. In the Program class's Main method, replace it as shown in Listing 7-11.

Listing 7-11. Replacing the HardCodedMenuService with the MenuService

```
using Microsoft.AspNetCore.Components.WebAssembly.Hosting;
using Microsoft.Extensions.DependencyInjection;
using PizzaPlace.Client.Services;
using PizzaPlace.Shared;
using System;
using System.Net.Http;
using System.Threading.Tasks;

namespace PizzaPlace.Client
{
  public class Program
  {
    public static async Task Main(string[] args)
    {
```

```
var builder = WebAssemblyHostBuilder.CreateDefault(args);
builder.RootComponents.Add<App>("#app");

builder.Services.AddScoped(sp => new HttpClient
{
    BaseAddress = new Uri(builder.HostEnvironment
                                .BaseAddress)
});

builder.Services
        .AddTransient<IMenuService, MenuService>();
builder.Services
        .AddTransient<IOrderService, ConsoleOrderService>();

await builder.Build().RunAsync();
    }
  }
}
```

Run your project. You should see the list of pizzas (retrieved from your database) as in Figure 7-8! To switch between two implementations (a fake and a real one), all we have to do is to reconfigure dependency injection! Unlimited power!!!

Our Selection of Pizzas

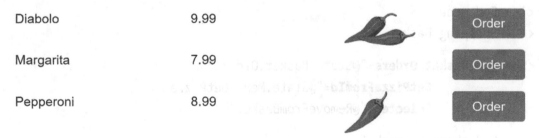

Diabolo	9.99		Order
Margarita	7.99		Order
Pepperoni	8.99		Order

Figure 7-8. *The PizzaPlace App Showing the Pizzas from the Database*

Showing a Loading UI

You will probably first see an empty menu, especially on a slow network. This might confuse some customers, so let's add some UI to tell the customer to wait a bit. Update Index.razor to look like Listing 7-12. Here, we use an @if to check if the menu has been loaded, and as long as there are no pizzas on the menu, we use a bootstrap spinner in the else part. You can replace this with any kind of "loading" UI if you like. For example, you could use https://tobiasahlin.com/spinkit/.

Listing 7-12. Adding a Loading UI to the Index Component

```
@page "/"
@inject IMenuService MenuService
@inject IOrderService orderService

@if (State.Menu.Pizzas.Any())
{
  <!-- Menu -->

  <PizzaList Title="Our Selection of Pizzas"
          Items="@State.Menu.Pizzas"
          ButtonTitle="Order"
          ButtonClass="btn btn-success pl-4 pr-4"
          Selected="@AddToBasket" />

  <!-- End menu -->
  <!-- Shopping Basket -->

  <ShoppingBasket Orders="@State.Basket.Orders"
             GetPizzaFromId="@State.Menu.GetPizza"
             Selected="@RemoveFromBasket" />

  <!-- End shopping basket -->
  <!-- Customer entry -->

  <CustomerEntry Title="Please enter your details below"
             @bind-Customer="@State.Basket.Customer"
             ButtonTitle="Checkout"
             ButtonClass="mx-auto w-25 btn btn-success"
```

```
            ValidSubmit="PlaceOrder" />

  <!-- End customer entry -->

  @State.ToJson()
}
else
{
  <div class="mx-auto text-center mb-3 mt-3">
    <div class="spinner-border text-danger" role="status">
      <span class="visually-hidden">Loading...</span>
    </div>
  </div>
}

@code {
  private State State { get; } = new State();

  protected override async Task OnInitializedAsync()
  {
    Menu menu = await MenuService.GetMenu();
    foreach (Pizza pizza in menu.Pizzas)
    {
      State.Menu.Add(pizza);
    }
  }

  private void AddToBasket(Pizza pizza)
  => State.Basket.Add(pizza.Id);

  private void RemoveFromBasket(int pos)
  => State.Basket.RemoveAt(pos);

  private async Task PlaceOrder()
  {
    await orderService.PlaceOrder(State.Basket);
  }
}
```

If the menu has not been loaded yet, it will display a spinner like in Figure 7-9.

Figure 7-9. *Showing a Loading Progress Bar While Loading the Menu*

Storing Changes

Now onto storing the order from the customer. Because you don't have a microservice yet for storing the order, you will build this first, and then you will implement the client service to send the order to the server.

Updating the Database with Orders

What is an order? Every order has a customer, and an order has one or more pizzas. A pizza can belong to more than one order, which can result in a specific problem: you need a many-to-many relation between pizzas and orders, as illustrated in Figure 7-10. But with Entity Framework Core, this is easy; again, this is taken care of for you.

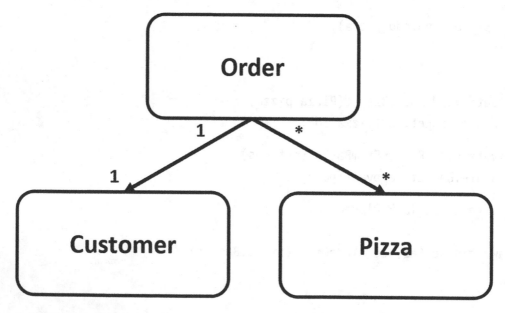

Figure 7-10. *Modeling the Relationships*

Add a new class to the PizzaPlace.Shared project called Order, as shown in Listing 7-13. As expected, we have a property to store the Customer and a collection of Pizza instances. There is also an Id property because a database always needs an identifying field, known as the primary key.

Listing 7-13. The PizzaOrder Class

```
using System.Collections.Generic;

namespace PizzaPlace.Shared
{
  public class Order
  {
    public int Id { get; set; }

    public Customer Customer { get; set; } = default!;

    public ICollection<Pizza> Pizzas { get; set; } = default!;
  }
}
```

Next, update the Pizza class, as shown in Listing 7-14. Here, we are adding a collection to hold the orders. However, we don't need to retrieve the orders from the server, and that is why we add the [JsonIgnore] attribute. This tells the JSON serialization to ignore it when converting to JSON.

Listing 7-14. The Pizza Class

```
using System.Collections.Generic;
using System.Text.Json.Serialization;

namespace PizzaPlace.Shared
{
  public class Pizza
  {
    public Pizza(int id, string name, decimal price,
              Spiciness spiciness)
    {
      this.Id = id;
```

```
      this.Name = name;
      this.Price = price;
      this.Spiciness = spiciness;
    }

    public int Id { get; }
    public string Name { get; }
    public decimal Price { get; }
    public Spiciness Spiciness { get; }

    [JsonIgnore]
    public ICollection<Order>? Orders { get; set; }
  }
}
```

Now you can add these tables to the PizzaPlaceDbContext class, which can be found in Listing 7-15.

Listing 7-15. The Updated PizzaPlaceDbContext Class

```
using Microsoft.EntityFrameworkCore;
using PizzaPlace.Shared;

namespace PizzaPlace.Server
{
  public class PizzaPlaceDbContext : DbContext
  {
    public PizzaPlaceDbContext(
      DbContextOptions<PizzaPlaceDbContext> options)
      : base(options) { }

    public DbSet<Pizza> Pizzas { get; set; } = default!;
    public DbSet<Order> Orders { get; set; } = default!;
    public DbSet<Customer> Customers { get; set; } = default!;

    protected override void OnModelCreating(
      ModelBuilder modelBuilder)
    {
      base.OnModelCreating(modelBuilder);
```

```
    var pizzaEntity = modelBuilder.Entity<Pizza>();

    pizzaEntity.HasKey(pizza => pizza.Id);
    pizzaEntity.Property(pizza => pizza.Name)
        .HasMaxLength(80);
    pizzaEntity.Property(pizza => pizza.Price)
        .HasColumnType("money");
    pizzaEntity.Property(pizza => pizza.Spiciness)
        .HasConversion<string>();

    var ordersEntity = modelBuilder.Entity<Order>();

    ordersEntity.HasKey(order => order.Id);
    ordersEntity.HasOne(order => order.Customer);
    ordersEntity.HasMany(order => order.Pizzas)
                .WithMany(pizza => pizza.Orders);

    var customerEntity = modelBuilder.Entity<Customer>();
    customerEntity.HasKey(customer => customer.Id);
    customerEntity.Property(customer => customer.Name)
        .HasMaxLength(100);
    customerEntity.Property(customer => customer.Street)
        .HasMaxLength(50);
    customerEntity.Property(customer => customer.City)
        .HasMaxLength(50);
    }
  }
}
```

Here you have added the Customers and Orders tables, and in the OnModelCreating method, you explain to Entity Framework Core how things should be mapped.

A Customer has a primary key Id and its string properties which we limit in length. An Order has a primary key Id and a single Customer, and it has a many-to-one relationship with Pizza (one Order can have many Pizzas, and each Pizza can belong to many Orders).

Build your project and fix any compiler error(s) you might have.

Now it is time to create another migration. This migration will update your database with your new tables. In Visual Studio, open the Package Manager Console (which you can find via View ➤ Other Windows ➤ Package Manager Console). With Code, open the integrated terminal. Or use the command line if you prefer (I really like the new terminal in Windows 10). Change the directory to the PizzaPlace.Server project.

Now type the following command:

```
dotnet-ef migrations add Orders
```

This will create a migration for your new database schema.

Apply the migration to your database by typing the following command:

```
dotnet-ef database update
```

This concludes the database part.

Building the Order Microservice

Time to build the microservice for taking orders. With Visual Studio, right-click the Controllers folder of the PizzaPlace.Server project and select New ➤ Controller. Select an Empty API Controller and name it OrdersController. With Code, right-click the Controllers folder of the PizzaPlace.Shared project and select New File, naming it OrdersController. This class can be found in Listing 7-16.

Listing 7-16. The OrdersController Class

```
using Microsoft.AspNetCore.Http;
using Microsoft.AspNetCore.Mvc;
using PizzaPlace.Shared;
using System;
using System.Collections.Generic;
using System.Linq;
using System.Threading.Tasks;

namespace PizzaPlace.Server.Controllers
{
  [Route("api/[controller]")]
  [ApiController]
  public class OrdersController : ControllerBase
  {
```

284

```
  private readonly PizzaPlaceDbContext db;

  public OrdersController(PizzaPlaceDbContext db)
  {
    this.db = db;
  }

  [HttpPost("/orders")]
  public IActionResult InsertOrder([FromBody] ShoppingBasket basket)
  {
    Order order = new Order();
    order.Customer = basket.Customer;
    order.Pizzas = new List<Pizza>();
    foreach (int pizzaId in basket.Orders)
    {
      var pizza = db.Pizzas.Single(p => p.Id == pizzaId);
      order.Pizzas.Add(pizza);
    }
    db.Orders.Add(order);
    db.SaveChanges();
    return Created("/orders", order.Id);
  }
 }
}
```

The `OrdersController` needs a `PizzaPlaceDbContext`, so you add a constructor taking the instance and you let dependency injection take care of the rest. To create a new order, you use the POST verb for the `InsertOrder` method taking a `ShoppingBasket` instance in the request body.

Upon receipt of a basket instance, you create the order, and then set the order's customer. Next, you fill up the order's `Pizzas` collection with pizzas. We receive the Ids for the Pizzas, so we look them up with it. Then we add the new order instance to the `PizzaPlaceDbContext Orders` collection. Now when we call **SaveChanges**, Entity Framework will INSERT it in the `Orders` table. That's it. Entity Framework Core does all the work of storing the data!

Talking to the Order Microservice

Add a new class called OrderService to the Services folder of the PizzaPlace.Client project. This *OrderService* uses a POST request to the server, as shown in Listing 7-17.

Listing 7-17. The OrderService Class

```
using PizzaPlace.Shared;
using System.Net.Http;
using System.Net.Http.Json;
using System.Threading.Tasks;

namespace PizzaPlace.Client.Services
{
  public class OrderService : IOrderService
  {
    private readonly HttpClient httpClient;

    public OrderService(HttpClient httpClient)
    {
      this.httpClient = httpClient;
    }

    public async ValueTask PlaceOrder(ShoppingBasket basket)
    {
      await httpClient.PostAsJsonAsync("/orders", basket);
    }
  }
}
```

First, you add a constructor to the OrderService class, taking the HttpClient dependency, which you store in the httpClient field of the OrderService class. Next, you implement the IOrderService interface by adding the PlaceOrder method, taking a ShoppingBasket as a parameter. Finally, you invoke the asynchronous PostAsJsonAsync method using the await keyword.

Now open the Program class from the PizzaPlace.Client project and replace the ConsoleOrderService class with your new OrderService class, as shown in Listing 7-18.

Listing 7-18. Configuring Dependency Injection to Use the OrderService Class

```
using Microsoft.AspNetCore.Components.WebAssembly.Hosting;
using Microsoft.Extensions.DependencyInjection;
using PizzaPlace.Client.Services;
using PizzaPlace.Shared;
using System;
using System.Net.Http;
using System.Threading.Tasks;

namespace PizzaPlace.Client
{
  public class Program
  {
    public static async Task Main(string[] args)
    {
      var builder = WebAssemblyHostBuilder.CreateDefault(args);
      builder.RootComponents.Add<App>("#app");

      builder.Services.AddScoped(sp => new HttpClient
      {
        BaseAddress = new Uri(builder.HostEnvironment
                                    .BaseAddress)
      });

      builder.Services.AddTransient<IMenuService,
                                    MenuService>();
      builder.Services.AddTransient<IOrderService,
                                    OrderService>();

      await builder.Build().RunAsync();
    }
  }
}
```

Run your PizzaPlace application and place an order for a couple of pizzas. Now open SQL Server Object Explorer in Visual Studio (or SQL Operations Studio) and examine the Customers and Orders tables. They should contain your new order. You will also see another table in the database, the *OrderPizza* table. This table was generated by Entity Framework to store the many-to-many relationship between Orders and Pizzas.

Summary

In this chapter, you learned that in Blazor you talk to the server using the `HttpClient` class, calling the `GetFromJsonAsync` and `PostAsJsonAsync` extension methods. You also learned that you should encapsulate calling the server using a client-side service class so you can easily change the implementation by switching the service type using dependency injection.

CHAPTER 8

Unit Testing

In previous chapters, we have been building a PizzaPlace application, which contains a number of components. We have tested these components by running the application and interacting with it. Here, we will look at writing unit tests for Blazor components using bUnit and MOQ.

Where Can We Find Bugs?

When building software, what are the causes of bugs? As it turns out, in every step of building software, bugs can be introduced. So let us walk over the lifetime of a software project as shown in Figure 8-1. Figure 8-1 also illustrates another obvious fact: the sooner you can find a bug, the cheaper it is to fix it.

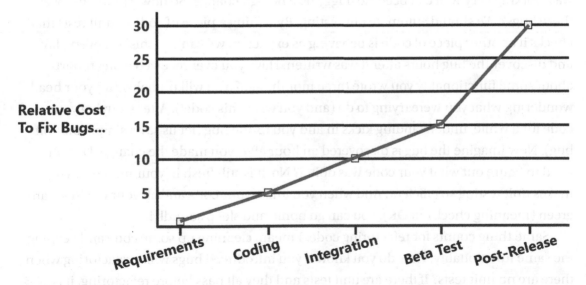

Figure 8-1. *The Cost of Fixing Bugs*

P. Himschoot, *Microsoft Blazor*, https://doi.org/10.1007/978-1-4842-7845-1_8

Requirements

Sometimes bugs are introduced even before a single line of code is written. Writing good requirements is hard, because these need to explain business concepts to developers who are typically not well versed in this domain. The same thing counts for advanced engineering concepts, like rocket building. Let's look at an example. NASA lost its $125,000,000 Mars Climate Orbiter because of a simple missing piece of information in the requirements: which units to use. One team was using metric units (meters, kilogram), while another team was using imperial units (inch, pounds), and there was no conversion in place because each team thought the other team was using the same units! You can read more about it here: `www.latimes.com/archives/la-xpm-1999-oct-01-mn-17288-story.html`.

This bug could easily be averted! Since the specifications never mentioned the units, if someone had asked which units to use and add this to the specifications, this Mars Climate Orbiter would probably be spinning around Mars right now! So as a developer, if you think something is confusing or ambiguous, ask! Never assume anything!

Coding

It is easy to introduce bugs during coding. That is part of developing software. Code that was working very well can become buggy by a benign change. So how can we discover these bugs? We should automate our testing. By writing a piece of code (a unit test) that checks if another piece of code is behaving as expected, we can run this test every day and discover the bug hours after it was written. Have you ever received a bug report about some functionality you wrote three months ago? You will probably rub your head wondering what you were trying to do (and you write this code!). After studying your code for a while, understanding kicks in and you fix the bug (let us say a simple one-off bug). Now imagine the bug is discovered an hour after you made the change. Do you need to figure out what your code was doing? No, it is still fresh in your memory. That makes unit testing so efficient. And when you finish your code and all your unit tests are green (meaning check out OK), you can go home and sleep soundly!

Same thing counts for refactoring code. I mean, cleaning up some code and keeping the same functionality. How do you know if you introduced bugs while refactoring when there are no unit tests? If there are unit tests and they all pass before refactoring, it is easy to see after refactoring if you broke something. Just run the unit tests, and if they all pass, you did not break anything that was known to be working! Again, you can go home and sleep knowing you made your code more maintainable and did not introduce any new bugs!

Integration

Your code works on your machine. And your colleague's code also works on their machine. But will your code work together with your colleague's code? That is what integration is all about. A long time ago, teams would integrate code from different teams at the end of the project. Guess what!? This never went well, resulting in project overruns, sometimes by months. So development teams started to integrate at the end of each month and then at the end of the week. Integrations started to become automated using build systems. Now we can do continuous integration where we integrate changes to the code after each commit in source code. And when we have unit tests, we can run these after the compilation ends and use that to catch breaking changes. Again, this should illustrate the role of good unit tests. You use them to see if your code is working and also to see if everyone's code keeps on working.

Beta Testing

At a certain point in time, you should expose end users to your application. Why? Because developers are not normal people. End users want things to be as simple as possible. For example, look at google.com. This site only has one text box where you type your question and a button to do the search. This simplicity made Google the most used search engine (sorry Microsoft). Developers are control freaks; they want power, not simplicity! Just open the options screen in Visual Studio. You can tweak just about anything! And most end users are not as proficient using computers as developers, sometimes resulting in surprises. Let me tell you about a personal experience I once had. We had built software that runs in a factory, and on a Sunday (they work in that factory continuously), I get a call from an end user. He told me "The button does not work!". After half an hour on the phone, I decided to drive over there and see for myself. I get there and I click the button, and it works! So what was the problem? The button was small because we needed to cram a lot on the screen, and the end user has a bit of a tremor and moved the mouse when clicking, resulting in a click outside of the button. So we fixed the bug by making the button bigger. This is a nice example of a usability problem, where we as developers are not always aware of. So expose your software to your users often, and gain their feedback. We are building it for our end users, right?

Post-release

Perfect software does not exist. Have you ever writing an application that is bug-free? No? I have! It is called "Hello World!". Anything beyond that is impossible. But having an end user discover a bug is bad news. It will lower the trust in the development team and in the quality of the software. So how do we stop bugs from making it into production? You can't! The only thing you can do is to test as much as possible and warn the users that they may encounter bugs, especially early after release.

Why Should We Use Unit Tests?

So how do you test your Blazor application? Hit run and interact with the UI? No problem there, except every time you make a change to your application, you should test everything again. Who has time for that? Can't someone else do it? Yes, that machine in front of you can! With *unit testing*, we automate this unit testing process.

What Makes a Good Unit Test?

When you practice unit testing, your development life cycle looks like this: make some change to the code, build, fix compiler errors, build again, and then run all your tests. Then fix the bugs discovered by your tests. And then you start again. How long does building your application take? A couple of seconds? Now imagine that your unit tests take 5 minutes. Would you want to wait for that? Would you be tempted to disable running the unit tests? *A good unit test should be fast* so we don't have to wait very long. What makes unit tests slow? Typically, this is caused by accessing slow resources, like databases, disks, and the network. So with a unit test, we will avoid using slow resources. What if your unit tests need some setup? Every time you need to run the tests, you would have to prepare some things manually. Again, we don't have time for that. *A good unit test should also be automatic and repeatable*, meaning that the test should report on success or failure and that again we avoid things that need some manual setup. What could that be? Again databases, files on disk, and the network! Another aspect of a good unit test is *consistency*. If your unit test fails, this should be because of a bug in your code, not because someone tripped over a network cable making the database or network inaccessible! So again, we should avoid things like databases, file shares, and networks.

Tests which do not have all the aspects from earlier do exist. You will have to write a test to interact with the database (but don't start testing the framework used to access the database; that is the framework's author's job!). Their tests are known as *integration tests*, because we will run them during the build, not during the development life cycle.

Unit Testing Blazor Components

Let us create a couple of tests for a Blazor application. In the code download for this chapter, you can find the *testing* solution. Open it with your favorite editor. Everything in the project should look familiar. There is the Counter component and the FetchData component which uses an IWeatherService to retrieve the weather forecasts from a server.

Adding a Unit Test Project

Let us look at an example using *xUnit*, which is a popular testing library for .NET which we will also use for testing our Blazor components.

When you are using Visual Studio, right-click the test folder and select Add new project. In the Add New Project dialog, search for the *xUnit Test Project* template. Now click Next. Set the Location to the test folder and name it Testing.ComponentTests.

If you are using Code, open the command prompt to the test folder and execute the following command:

```
dotnet new xunit -n Testing.ComponentTests
```

Now change the directory to the parent directory and execute

```
dotnet sln add .\test\Testing.ComponentTests
```

No matter which tool you are using, add project references to the client and the Shared project. The test project file should look like Listing 8-1, where I also enabled nullable reference types. Since I will test components that have nullable reference types enabled, I think the unit test project should too.

Listing 8-1. The Testing.ComponentTests Project

```
<Project Sdk="Microsoft.NET.Sdk">

  <PropertyGroup>
    <TargetFramework>net6.0</TargetFramework>
    <Nullable>enable</Nullable>
    <IsPackable>false</IsPackable>
  </PropertyGroup>
  <ItemGroup>
    <PackageReference Include="Microsoft.NET.Test.Sdk" Version="16.8.3" />
    <PackageReference Include="xunit" Version="2.4.1" />
    <PackageReference Include="xunit.runner.visualstudio" Version="2.4.3">
      <IncludeAssets>runtime; build; native; contentfiles; analyzers;
      buildtransitive</IncludeAssets>
      <PrivateAssets>all</PrivateAssets>
    </PackageReference>
    <PackageReference Include="coverlet.collector" Version="1.3.0">
      <IncludeAssets>runtime; build; native; contentfiles; analyzers;
      buildtransitive</IncludeAssets>
      <PrivateAssets>all</PrivateAssets>
    </PackageReference>
  </ItemGroup>
  <ItemGroup>
    <ProjectReference Include="..\..\src\Client\Testing.Client.csproj" />
    <ProjectReference Include="..\..\src\Shared\Testing.Shared.csproj" />
  </ItemGroup>
</Project>
```

Adding bUnit to the Test Project

With the current unit test project, we can test our services and other non-Blazor classes. In order to test Blazor components, we need to add *bUnit*. So use your favorite method to add the *bUnit* package (choose latest stable version).

You also need to change the SDK for your project as in Listing 8-2. We need to do this because we will use razor syntax to build unit tests for Blazor components.

Listing 8-2. bUnit Projects

```
<Project Sdk="Microsoft.NET.Sdk.Razor">
```

Write Your First Unit Test

Now that we have everything in place, we can write our first unit test. We will start by writing a simple unit test and see how this works with Visual Studio and Code.

Writing Good Unit Test Methods

Every unit test will consist of three phases: *Arrange*, *Act*, and *Assert*, also known as the *triple A of unit testing*. The Arrange phase will set up the unit test by creating the *subject under test* (SUT), by which I mean the class we want to test and its dependencies. The Act phase will perform the call on the method we want to test, and the Assert will verify if the outcome is successful.

Add a new class called Utils to the Shared project as in Listing 8-3. The Square method should return the square of a number (and it has a bug).

Listing 8-3. A Simple Utils Class

```
namespace Testing.Shared
{
  public class Utils
  {
    public int Square(int i)
    {
      return i;
    }
  }
}
```

Let us write a simple unit test for this method, as in Listing 8-4. With xUnit, a unit test is a *public* method with the [Fact] attribute on it. As this attribute says, the result of the test should be a fact! In the Arrange phase, we set up the subject under test which I like to call sut. This way, it is easy for me to identify the instance that I want to test (just a convention, name it as you like). Then in the Arrange phase, we call the Square

295

method, storing the result in the `actual` variable. Next comes the Assert phase, where I am using the `Assert` class from xUnit, to verify if the result matches the expected result. The `Assert` class has a whole range of methods to check if the outcome of the test is the expected outcome. Here, we are using the `Equals` method to see if the outcome equals 9, which should be the square of 3.

Listing 8-4. Testing the Square Method

```
using Testing.Shared;
using Xunit;

namespace Testing.ComponentTests
{
  public class SquareShould
  {
    [Fact]
    public void Return9For3()
    {
      // Arrange
      var sut = new Utils();
      // Act
      var actual = sut.Square(3);
      // Assert
      Assert.Equal(expected: 9, actual: actual);
    }
  }
}
```

Running Your Tests

With Visual Studio, open the Test Explorer window (Test ➤ Test Explorer) as in Figure 8-2. With Visual Studio, Test Explorer is the place to run unit tests and review the results. After opening Test Explorer, it will scan your solution for unit tests and list them. Now click the left green arrow in this window to run all your tests.

Figure 8-2. *The Test Explorer*

The test will run and fail as shown in Figure 8-3.

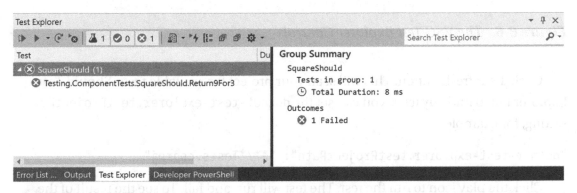

Figure 8-3. *The Test Fails*

You can also run unit tests from Visual Studio Code, but you will have to install the .NET Core Test Explorer extension as shown in Figure 8-4.

Figure 8-4. *The .NET Core Test Explorer Extension*

Now you can run your tests by clicking the Test Explorer icon in the left side of VSC as shown in Figure 8-5.

Figure 8-5. *Test Explorer in VSC*

VSC Test Explorer will display a couple of buttons as shown in Figure 8-6. From left to right, you have a button to run the tests, refresh the list of available tests, stop test execution, and show the log with the test results.

Figure 8-6. *The VSC Test Explorer Controls*

Click the refresh button. This will scan your project for available tests. Should Test Explorer fail to find any tests, you can set the `dotnet-test-explorer.testProjectPath` setting, for example:

```
"dotnet-test-explorer.testProjectPath": "**/*Tests.csproj"
```

Click the play icon to run the test. The test will run and fail. To see the result of the test, click the log button and then check out the PROBLEMS tab as shown in Figure 8-7.

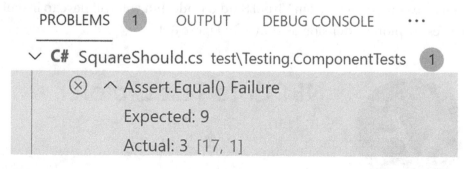

Figure 8-7. *Reviewing Failed Tests*

Making Your Test Pass

Why did the test fail? If you put a breakpoint in the Square method and click the arrow in Test Explorer again, you will see that Visual Studio does not stop on the breakpoint. Same thing for VSC. Why? Debugging needs some special setup, and this takes time. Remember that we want our tests to complete as short as possible? With Visual Studio, you can enable the debugger as follows. Right-click the test in the Test Explorer window and select Debug (similar in VSC). Now the debugger will stop on your breakpoint. When you step in the Square method, you should see the bug (duh!). Fix it as in Listing 8-5.

Listing 8-5. The Corrected Square Method

```
namespace Testing.Shared
{
  public class Utils
  {
    public int Square(int i)
    {
      return i*i;
    }
  }
}
```

Now run the test again (with or without the debugger). Now it should pass as in Figures 8-8 and 8-9.

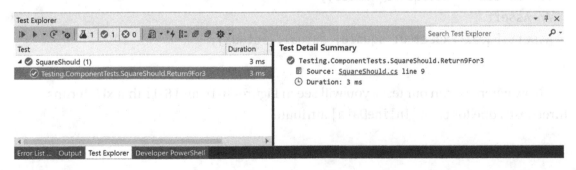

Figure 8-8. *The Test Passes in VS*

Figure 8-9. *The Test Passes in VSC*

Using Facts and Theories

But what about other values? With xUnit, we can write a whole series of tests without having to copy-paste a ton of them (copy-pasting to duplicate code is generally bad, also known as *Don't Repeat Yourself* (DRY)). Add another unit test to the SquareShould class as in Listing 8-6. Here, we are using the [Theory] attribute to tell xUnit to run this with different arguments. And we use the [InlineData] attribute to pass the arguments to the test method.

Listing 8-6. Using Theories

```
[Theory]
[InlineData(1,1)]
[InlineData(2,4)]
[InlineData(-1,1)]
public void ReturnSquareOfNumber(int number, int square)
{
  // Arrange
  var sut = new Utils();
  // Act
  var actual = sut.Square(number);
  // Assert
  Assert.Equal(expected: square, actual: actual);
}
```

Now when we run our tests, you will see in Figures 8-10 and 8-11 that xUnit runs three tests, one for each [InlineData] attribute.

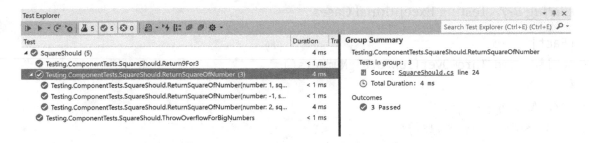

Figure 8-10. *VS Test Results with Theories*

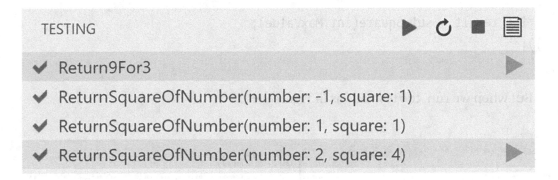

Figure 8-11. *VSC Test Results with Theories*

Checking Your Sanity

Have you ever had a piece of code that did things differently than what you expected? Personally, I start to doubt my sanity then, like "Am I going crazy?" Or have you used someone's method that was badly documented and did not do as it should? With unit testing, you can set up checks to see if a method does what you think it should do. And if it does not, maybe you need to talk to the author and see what makes more sense. When you have a unit test, you can attach it to a bug report, making it easy for the author to reproduce the bug. Let us look at an example again. Now I want to see if the Square method throws an error when we pass a big integer to it (and not every squared integer is another integer because it is limited in range). Add another test method like in Listing 8-7. So here we call Square with the largest int possible. The result can never fit into an int, so we expect this to throw an OverflowException.

Listing 8-7. Testing Exceptional Cases

```
[Fact]
public void ThrowOverflowForBigNumbers()
{
  // Arrange
  var sut = new Utils();
  // Act & Assert
  Assert.Throws<OverflowException>(() =>
  {
    int result = sut.Square(int.MaxValue);
  });
}
```

But when we run, the test fails as in Figure 8-12.

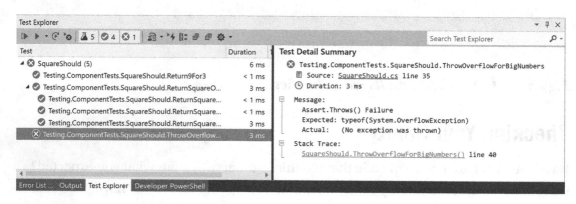

Figure 8-12. *Sanity Check Please?*

Why does this fail? Let us put a breakpoint on the Square method. Maybe we are doing something wrong here? Run the test with the debugger. When the debugger stops, look at the value of the argument: 2147483647. This is the largest signed int. Now step out of the method until after the result is set. What is its value? It is 1. Now 2147483647*2147483647 is not 1! So again, what is happening? It turns out that C# works like C++ and C. These programming languages do not throw exceptions by default when a calculation overflows! They even use this to create hashing and encryption algorithms. So how can we fix this? You can turn on overflow checking using the C# checked keyword as in Listing 8-8.

Listing 8-8. Enabling Overflow Checking

```
namespace Testing.Shared
{
  public class Utils
  {
    public int Square(int i)
    {
      checked
      {
        return i * i;
      }
    }
  }
}
```

Run your test again. Now it passes. Whew! This was actually normal behavior.

Unit testing is great to discover these weird behaviors and allows you to catch modifications that cause bugs later.

Write a bUnit Tests with C#

We have seen how we can write unit tests for .NET classes and their methods. Here, we will look at how we can write tests for Blazor components on top of xUnit.

Note   All tests written here use xUnit, but you can also use NUnit or MSTest. All of these are test frameworks that apply the same principles. You can even mix these frameworks so you don't have to rewrite old tests when moving to another test framework.

Understanding bUnit?

bUnit is a testing library for Blazor components, written by Egil Hansen, and the sources can be found in GitHub at `https://github.com/bUnit-dev/bUnit`. With bUnit, you can easily write unit tests for Blazor components. Why should we write unit tests for Blazor components? Same reason you write unit tests for regular classes: to ensure they work as expected and that they keep on working in case some dependency gets updated. Of course, most of your testing should be on the service classes that implement business logic. For example, you want to make sure your Blazor component calls a certain method on a service when the user interacts with that component. With bUnit, we can automate that so no user has to actually click a button! And we can run these tests continuously so we will know when we break a component minutes after the change.

Part of testing a Blazor component is to render and examine the output of a component. But it goes way beyond this. You can interact with the component and see the changes, replace dependencies, etc.

Let us start with the Counter component, as in Listing 8-9. This now familiar component displays a currentCount field which is initially 0. So a very simple unit test would be to see if the component's output matches the expected output.

Listing 8-9. The Counter Component

```
@page "/counter"

<h1>Counter</h1>

<p>Current count: @currentCount</p>

<button class="btn btn-primary" @onclick="IncrementCount">
  Click me
</button>
@code {
    private int currentCount = 0;

    private void IncrementCount()
    {
        currentCount++;
    }
}
```

Add a new class called CounterShould to the unit test project. You can name this class anything you want, but I like the naming convention where I use the method or component name and then the word "Should". Derive this class from the TestContext base class, which will give you access to all the handy methods from bUnit. We will be using these methods as we go along, and by deriving your test class from

TestContext, they become available through inheritance. Implement the first unit test RenderCorrectlyWithInitialZero as in Listing 8-10.

Listing 8-10. The CounterShould Class

```
using Bunit;
using Testing.Client.Pages;
using Xunit;

namespace Testing.ComponentTests
{
  public class CounterShould : TestContext
  {
    [Fact]
    public void RenderCorrectlyWithInitialZero()
    {
      var cut = RenderComponent<Counter>();
      Assert.Equal(@"
        <h1>Counter</h1>
        <p>Current count: 0</p>
        <button class=""btn btn-primary"" >
          Click me
        </button>
        ", cut.Markup);
    }
  }
}
```

Here, we are using *xUnit* together with bUnit, so our unit test has the [Fact] attribute. First, we do the Arrange phase, where we create the *component under test* (which I name cut, similar to sut) by calling the RenderComponent<Counter> method. This will create the component and render it in one go. So this also takes care of the Act phase. Next, we do the Assert phase, where we want to see if the component generated the right kind of output.

This test will fail. Why? Just run the test, and look at the test output as in Figure 8-13. Look again at the Assert statement in Listing 8-10. Here, we expect the markup of our component to match the literal string. And it does match in a way, except for whitespace and newlines. We could now do the work and update our string to the real output, but this is too sensitive to little changes we might make later to our component.

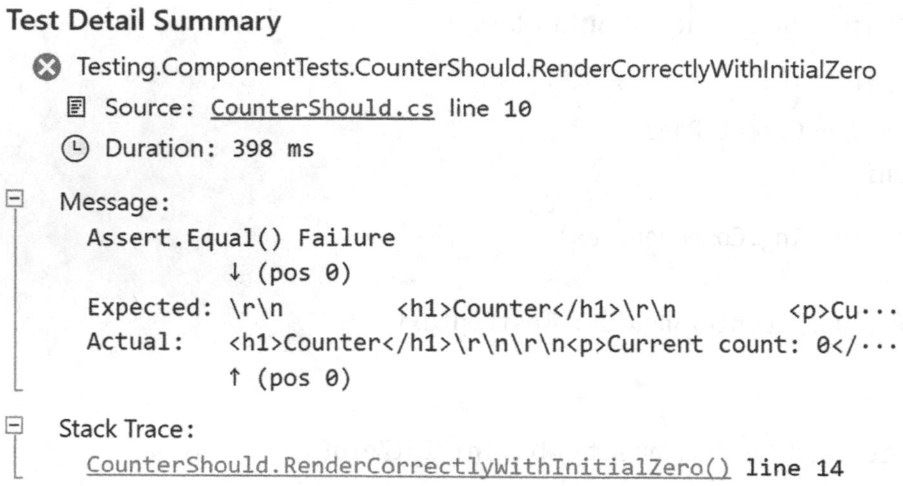

Test Detail Summary

❌ Testing.ComponentTests.CounterShould.RenderCorrectlyWithInitialZero

　　📄 Source: <u>CounterShould.cs</u> line 10

　　🕐 Duration: 398 ms

⊟　Message:
　　Assert.Equal() Failure
　　　　　↓ (pos 0)
　　Expected: \r\n　　　　　<h1>Counter</h1>\r\n　　　　　<p>Cu···
　　Actual:　　<h1>Counter</h1>\r\n\r\n<p>Current count: 0</···
　　　　　↑ (pos 0)

⊟　Stack Trace:
　　<u>CounterShould.RenderCorrectlyWithInitialZero()</u> line 14

Figure 8-13. *Our Test Fails*

Let us improve the test as in Listing 8-11. Now we are using the `MarkupMatches` method, which will perform a *semantic comparison* between the component's markup and our string. This will ignore whitespace, newlines, comments, and other irrelevant things during the comparison, and now we should see the test pass! Now our test will no longer break when we add a newline or a comment in the component that changes the markup's formatting!

Listing 8-11. Improving Our Unit Test with Semantic Comparison

```
using Bunit;
using Testing.Client.Pages;
using Xunit;

namespace Testing.ComponentTests
{
  public class CounterShould : TestContext
  {
    [Fact]
    public void RenderCorrectlyWithInitialZero()
    {
```

```
        var cut = RenderComponent<Counter>();
        cut.MarkupMatches(@"
          <h1>Counter</h1>
          <p>Current count: 0</p>
          <button class=""btn btn-primary"" >
            Click me
          </button>
          ");
      }
    }
}
```

We can even do better and focus on the relevant part of the component. We know that our Counter component uses a <p> element to render the currentCount variable, but how do we access this part of the render tree? The bUnit library has a Find method that takes a *CSS selector* and returns the result of the query. Add another test method to the ShouldRender class as in Listing 8-12. We Find the <p> element, and we can see if it matches the expected output using the MarkupMatches method, which ignores whitespace.

Listing 8-12. Using the Find Method

```
[Fact]
public void RenderParagraphCorrectlyWithInitialZero()
{
  var cut = RenderComponent<Counter>();

  cut.Find(cssSelector: "p")
    .MarkupMatches("<p>Current count: 0</p>");
}
```

Run your tests and see if they pass, which they should.

What happens when the test fails?

In the RenderParagraphCorrectlyWithInitialZero method, replace the 0 with a 1. Run the test. It fails! Select the test and you should see the following output as in Figure 8-14. This output shows us what is wrong, and now we can change the component (or the test) until the test passes. Fix the test.

Test Detail Summary

❌ Testing.ComponentTests.CounterShould.RenderParagraphCorrectlyWithInitialZero

  🗐 Source: <u>CounterShould.cs</u> line 32

  🕒 Duration: 480 ms

⊟ Message:

```
Bunit.HtmlEqualException : HTML comparison failed.

The following errors were found:
  1: The expected text at p(0) > #text(0) and the actual text at p(1) > #text(0) is different.

Actual HTML:
<p>Current count: 0</p>

Expected HTML:
<p>Current count: 1</p>
```

Figure 8-14. Our bUnit Test Fails

Testing Component Interaction

Our Counter component has a button, and when you click the button, it should increment the currentCount by 1 and render the new value. Let us look at how we can perform a test on a Blazor component by interacting with it and see if the component was updated correctly. Add a new unit test to the ShouldRender class as in Listing 8-13. The second line in the test uses the Find method to retrieve the button and then uses the Click method to perform the @onclick event on it. This should have the expected side effect, which we test on the next line to see if the component re-rendered with the expected value. Run the test, which should pass. Hey, this was easy!

Listing 8-13. Interacting with the Counter Component

```
[Fact]
public void IncrementCounterWhenButtonIsClicked()
{
  var cut = RenderComponent<Counter>();
  cut.Find(cssSelector: "button")
    .Click();
  cut.Find(cssSelector: "p")
    .MarkupMatches(@"<p>Current count: 1</p>");
}
```

The bUnit library comes with many dispatch methods that make it possible to trigger events on your component. Retrieve the element in the component using the Find method, and then call the appropriate dispatch method on it, for example, Click. These dispatch methods also allow you to pass event arguments. So let us look at an example.

Start by adding a new component to your Blazor project called MouseTracker with markup from Listing 8-14.

Listing 8-14. The MouseTracker Component's Markup

```
<div style="width: 300px; height: 300px;
            background: green; margin:50px"
    @onmousemove="MouseMove">
  @pos
</div>
```

This component has a MouseMove event handler as shown in Listing 8-15.

Listing 8-15. The MouseTracker Component's Code

```
using Microsoft.AspNetCore.Components.Web;

namespace Testing.Client.Pages
{
  public partial class MouseTracker
  {
    private string pos = "";

    private void MouseMove(MouseEventArgs e)
      => pos = $"Mouse at {e.ClientX}x{e.ClientY}";
  }
}
```

In the unit test project, add a new class called MouseTrackerShould with a single unit test as in Listing 8-16. During the Arrange phase of the bUnit test, we create an instance of MouseEventArgs with ClientX and ClientY set to some value. We then create an instance of the MouseTracker component using the TestContext's RenderComponent method. Now we Find the div from the component and store it in the theDiv reference.

Now we can perform the Act phase of the test by triggering the `MouseMove` event, passing the `MouseMoveEventArgs` instance we created before. This will re-render the component, so we are ready for the Assert phase where we check if the `theDiv` has the expected content using the `MarkupMatches` method. Do note that we use semantic comparison again, and here we can tell the compare to also ignore the style attribute using the `style:ignore` attribute. We will talk more about this in a later section of this chapter.

Listing 8-16. The MouseTrackerShould Unit Test

```
using Bunit;
using Microsoft.AspNetCore.Components.Web;
using System;
using System.Collections.Generic;
using System.Linq;
using System.Net.Http.Headers;
using System.Text;
using System.Threading.Tasks;
using Testing.Client.Pages;
using Xunit;

namespace Testing.ComponentTests
{
  public class MouseTrackerShould : TestContext
  {
    [Fact]
    public void ShowCorrectMousePosition()
    {
      var eventArgs = new MouseEventArgs()
      {
        ClientX = 100,
        ClientY = 200
      };
      var cut = RenderComponent<MouseTracker>();

      var theDiv = cut.Find(cssSelector: "div");
      theDiv.MouseMove(eventArgs);
```

```
theDiv.MarkupMatches($"<div style:ignore>Mouse at {eventArgs.ClientX}
x{eventArgs.ClientY}");
    }
  }
}
```

Run the test; it should pass.

Passing Parameters to Our Component

With data binding, we can pass parameters from the parent component to a child
component. How do we pass parameters with bUnit? Start by copying the Counter
component in the Blazor project, rename it to TwoWayCounter, and change it to look like
Listing 8-17. This TwoWayCounter component has a couple of parameters, including the
CurrentCount and the Increment parameter.

Listing 8-17. The TwoWayCounter Component

```
<h1>Counter</h1>

<p>Current count: @CurrentCount</p>

<button class="btn btn-primary" @onclick="IncrementCount">Click me</button>

@code {
    private int currentCount = 0;

    [Parameter]
    public int CurrentCount
    {
        get => currentCount;
        set
        {
            if (value != currentCount)
            {
                currentCount = value;
```

```
                CurrentCountChanged.InvokeAsync(currentCount);
        }
    }
}

private int increment = 1;

[Parameter]
public int Increment {
    get => increment;
    set
    {
        if( value != increment)
        {
            increment = value;
            IncrementChanged.InvokeAsync(increment);
        }
    }
}

[Parameter]
public EventCallback<int> CurrentCountChanged { get; set; }

[Parameter]
public EventCallback<int> IncrementChanged { get; set; }

private void IncrementCount()
{
    CurrentCount+=Increment;
}
}
```

Add another unit test to the test project called TwoWayCounterShould, and add the first bUnit test as in Listing 8-18. We want to pass two parameters to this component, and we can do this by using an overload of the RenderComponent method as shown in Listing 8-18. This takes a delegate which has a parameters argument of type ComponentParameterColle ctionBuilder<TComponent>. This class has an Add method with two arguments: expression where you pass the name of the parameter and the value for the parameter.

Listing 8-18. The TwoWayCounterShould Test Class

```
using Bunit;
using Testing.Client.Pages;
using Xunit;

namespace Testing.ComponentTests
{
  public class TwoWayCounterShould : TestContext
  {
    [Fact]
    public void IncrementCounterWhenClicked()
    {
      var cut = RenderComponent<TwoWayCounter>(
        parameters =>
            parameters.Add(counter => counter.CurrentCount, 0)
                    .Add(counter => counter.Increment, 1)
          );
      cut.Find("button").Click();
      cut.Find("p")
        .MarkupMatches("<p>Current count: 1</p>");
    }
  }
}
```

This way of passing parameters to a component is very convenient, since we can use *IntelliSense* to choose the parameter's name. There are other ways to pass the parameters, as shown in Listing 8-19. Here, we use xUnit's Theory to pass different parameters to the component, and each parameter is passed as a ValueTuple, containing the name and value of each parameter (that is why these are wrapped in an opening and closing parenthesis).

However, I personally don't like this way of working, because now we are passing the argument's name as a string. The compiler will not check the contents of a string to see if it is actually the name of a parameter. What happens when you make a mistake (or you decide later to rename the parameter)? The compiler will not complain, and you will get a failing test with the following message:

```
Message:
    System.InvalidOperationException : Object of type 'Testing.Client.Pages.
    TwoWayCounter' does not have a property matching the name 'CurrentCuont'.
```

Using hard-coded strings in code that contain names of classes, properties, and other code constructs is an anti-pattern which I call "string-based programming" and should be avoided.

Listing 8-19. Using a Theory to Test Different Cases

```
[Theory]
[InlineData(3)]
[InlineData(-3)]
public void IncrementCounterWithIncrementWhenClicked(int increment)
{
  var cut = RenderComponent<TwoWayCounter>(
        ("CurrentCount", 0),
        ("Increment", increment)
      );

  cut.Find("button").Click();

  cut.Find("p")
     .MarkupMatches($"<p>Current count: {increment}</p>");
}
```

Of course, with modern C#, we can fix this and still use this style as in Listing 8-20. Here, we use the nameof operator, which takes the name of a property and returns the string representation of that property. You can also use nameof with classes, methods, and other things.

Listing 8-20. Using nameof to Pass Property Names

```
[Theory]
[InlineData(3)]
[InlineData(-3)]
public void IncrementCounterWithIncrementWhenClickedWithNameOf(
  int increment)
{
  var cut = RenderComponent<TwoWayCounter>(
        (nameof(TwoWayCounter.CurrentCount), 0),
        (nameof(TwoWayCounter.Increment), increment)
      );
  cut.Find("button").Click();
  cut.Find("p")
    .MarkupMatches($"<p>Current count: {increment}</p>");
}
```

Testing Two-Way Data Binding and Events

Our TwoWayCounter has parameters to implement two-way data binding. Let us see if this component implements this correctly. We can use the same technique as before to pass handlers to the CurrentCountChanged and IncrementChanged parameters. But before we do this, add the FluentAssertions package to your test project. FluentAssertions allows you to write your assert statements in a more readable and concise way, and we will use it here (although this is not required). You can find out more about fluent assertions at https://fluentassertions.com.

Look at the bUnit test from Listing 8-21. We are adding four parameters, where two of them are of type EventCallback<int>. We assign a value to the EventCallback<int> using a delegate, and this delegate increments a local variable. This way, we count the number of invocations of the CurrentCountChanged and IncrementChanged event callback.

Note   You can also use this technique to test regular delegates like Action and Func.

After clicking the button, we expect the CurrentCountChanged to have been invoked, and we test this using the FluentAssertions Should().Be(1) method call. But we also want to test the Increment property's changed handler, and we can do this by accessing the component using the cut.Instance property and directly assigning a new value to Increment. Should your compiler issue a warning on this statement, that is normal because you are normally not allowed to access a component's parameters directly from code.

Listing 8-21. Testing Two-Way Changed Handlers

```
[Fact]
public void TriggerChangedEventForCurrentCounter()
{
  int nrOfCurrentCountChanged = 0;
  int nrOfIncrementChanged = 0;

  var cut = RenderComponent<TwoWayCounter>(parameters =>
        parameters.Add(counter => counter.CurrentCount, 0)
                .Add(counter => counter.Increment, 1)
                .Add(counter => counter.CurrentCountChanged,
                  () => nrOfCurrentCountChanged++)
                .Add(counter => counter.IncrementChanged,
                  () => nrOfIncrementChanged++)
                );
  cut.Find("button").Click();
  cut.Instance.Increment = 2;
  nrOfCurrentCountChanged.Should().Be(1);
  nrOfIncrementChanged.Should().Be(1);
}
```

You can also change a parameter value after the first render of your component. Look for an example in Listing 8-22, where we use the SetParametersAndRender method to modify the value of the Increment parameter.

Listing 8-22. Modifying the Value of a Parameter

```
[Fact]
public void TriggerChangedEventForCurrentCounter2()
{
  int nrOfIncrementChanged = 0;
  var cut = RenderComponent<TwoWayCounter>(parameters =>
        parameters.Add(counter => counter.CurrentCount, 0)
              .Add(counter => counter.Increment, 1)
              .Add(counter => counter.IncrementChanged,
                () => nrOfIncrementChanged++)
              );
  cut.SetParametersAndRender(parameters =>
    parameters.Add(counter => counter.Increment, 2));
  nrOfIncrementChanged.Should().Be(1);
}
```

Testing Components that Use RenderFragment

What about components that use RenderFragment such as ChildContent and templated components? RenderFragment is a special Blazor type, so it needs some special care. Start by adding an Alert component to your Blazor project, such as Listing 8-23.

Listing 8-23. The Alert Component

```
<div class="alert alert-secondary mt-4" role="alert">
  @ChildContent
</div>

@code {
  [Parameter]
  public RenderFragment ChildContent { get; set; } = default!;
}
```

Now add the AlertShould class from Listing 8-24 to your test project. As you can see, the ChildContent is just another parameter but comes with some convenience methods to make it easy to add.

Listing 8-24. The AlertShould Test Class

```
using Bunit;
using Testing.Client.Pages;
using Xunit;

namespace Testing.ComponentTests
{
  public class AlertShould : TestContext
  {
    [Fact]
    public void RenderSimpleChildContent()
    {
      var cut = RenderComponent<Alert>(parameters =>
      parameters.AddChildContent("<p>Hello world!</p>"));
      cut.MarkupMatches(@"
        <div class=""alert alert-secondary mt-4"" role=""alert"">
           <p>Hello world!</p>
        </ div >
      ");
    }
  }
}
```

Should the Alert component have additional parameters, we can pass the just like in Listing 8-18.

In Listing 8-24, we pass some simple HTML as the ChildContent, but we can do more complex things. For example, in Listing 8-25, we pass the Counter as the ChildContent.

Listing 8-25. Passing a Counter As ChildContent

```
[Fact]
public void RenderCounterAsChildContent()
{
  var cut = RenderComponent<Alert>(parameters =>
    parameters.AddChildContent<Counter>());
```

```
    var p = cut.Find("p");
    p.MarkupMatches("<p>Current count: 0</p>");
}
```

We can even pass parameters to the ChildContent, for example, when using the TwoWayCounter as in Listing 8-26.

Listing 8-26. Passing the TwoWayCounter As ChildContent

```
[Fact]
public void RenderTwoWayCounterWithParametersAsChildContent()
{
    var cut = RenderComponent<Alert>(parameters =>
        parameters.AddChildContent<TwoWayCounter>(parameters =>
        parameters.Add(counter=>counter.CurrentCount, 3)));
    var p = cut.Find("p");
    p.MarkupMatches("<p>Current count: 3</p>");
}
```

You can even call AddChildContent multiple times to add more than one fragment. Listing 8-27 illustrates this where we add both an HTML string and a Counter. Also note the use of a const string so we don't need to sync the content used in the AddChildContent and MarkupMatches methods (*Don't Repeat Yourself Principle* (DRY)).

Listing 8-27. Calling AddChildContent Multiple Times

```
[Fact]
public void RenderTitleAndCounterAsChildContent()
{
    const string header = "<h1>This is a counter</h1>";
    var cut = RenderComponent<Alert>(parameters =>
        parameters.AddChildContent(header)
                .AddChildContent<Counter>());
    var h1 = cut.Find("h1");
    h1.MarkupMatches(header);
    var p = cut.Find("p");
    p.MarkupMatches("<p>Current count: 0</p>");
}
```

What about templated components? Start by adding (or copy from the provided code download with this book) the templated component from Listings 8-28 and 8-29 (markup and code). This templated component uses two RenderFragments and one RenderFragment<TItem>. It also has a parameter to pass a Loader which is a function that grabs the items for this component. First, we will look at the RenderFragment and then the RenderFragment<TItem>.

Listing 8-28. The TemplatedList Component's Markup

```
@typeparam TItem

@if (items is null)
{
    @LoadingContent
}
else if (items.Count() == 0)
{
    @EmptyContent
}
else
{
    <div class="list-group @ListGroupClass">
        @foreach (var item in items)
        {
            <div class="list-group-item">
                @ItemContent(item)
            </div>
        }
    </div>
}
```

Listing 8-29. The TemplatedList Component's Code

```
using Microsoft.AspNetCore.Components;
using System;
using System.Collections.Generic;
using System.Diagnostics.CodeAnalysis;
```

```
using System.Threading.Tasks;

namespace Testing.Client.Pages
{
  public partial class TemplatedList<TItem>
  {
    IEnumerable<TItem>? items;

    [Parameter]
    public Func<ValueTask<IEnumerable<TItem>>>? Loader { get; set; }

    [Parameter]
    public RenderFragment LoadingContent { get; set; } = default!;

    [Parameter]
    public RenderFragment? EmptyContent { get; set; } = default!;

    [Parameter]
    public RenderFragment<TItem> ItemContent { get; set; } = default!;

    [Parameter]
    public string ListGroupClass { get; set; } = string.Empty;

    protected override async Task OnParametersSetAsync()
    {
      if (Loader is not null)
      {
        items = await Loader();
      }
    }
  }
}
```

Now add the TemplatedListShould class to your test project from Listing 8-30. Here, we add two parameters, one for the Loader parameter and one for the LoadingContent template. As you can see, we can use the same Add method, just like normal parameters.

Listing 8-30. Using a RenderFragment in a Test

```
using Bunit;
using System;
using System.Collections.Generic;
using System.Linq;
using System.Threading.Tasks;
using Testing.Client.Pages;
using Xunit;

namespace Testing.ComponentTests
{
  public class TemplatedListShould : TestContext
  {
    [Fact]
    public void RenderLoadingTemplateWhenItemsIsNull()
    {
      const string loading =
        "<div class=\"loader\">Loading...</div>";
      Func<ValueTask<IEnumerable<string>?>> loader =
        () => new ValueTask<IEnumerable<string>?>(result:null);

      var cut = RenderComponent<TemplatedList<string>>(
        parameters =>
          parameters.Add(tl => tl.Loader, loader)
                    .Add(tl => tl.LoadingContent, loading)
      );
      cut.Find("div.loader")
         .MarkupMatches(loading);
    }
  }
}
```

But what about the ItemContent parameter which uses the more complex RenderFragment<TItem>? Add a new unit test as in Listing 8-31. Here, we will pass five strings using the loader Func<ValueTask<IEnumerable<string>>>. Do note the use of the Enumerable.Repeat method to create a collection of elements. We pass the loader as a parameter to the TemplatedList<string> component, and we also pass the ItemContent, which is a RenderFragment<string>. Since this takes an argument, we use a Func<string, string> delegate which will return a RenderFragment<string> (because the Add method takes care of this).

Now we want to check if it has used the ItemContent for each item from our collection (of five "A" strings). There is a FindAll method taking a CSS selector that will return all elements that match the selector. The ItemContent RenderFragment uses a p, so we use this as the CSS selector. First, we check if the number of paragraph matches the number of items, and then we iterate over each of these and check if the markup matches the expected output.

Listing 8-31. Passing a RenderFragment<T>

```
[Fact]
public void RenderItemsCorrectly()
{
  const int count = 5;
  Func<ValueTask<IEnumerable<string>>> loader =
    () => new ValueTask<IEnumerable<string>>(
      Enumerable.Repeat("A", count));
  var cut = RenderComponent<TemplatedList<string>>(
    parameters =>
      parameters.Add(tl => tl.Loader, loader)
                .Add(tl => tl.ItemContent,
                    (context) => $"<p>{context}</p>"));
  var ps = cut.FindAll("p");
  ps.Should().NotBeEmpty();
  foreach (var p in ps)
  {
    p.MarkupMatches("<p>A</p>");
  }
}
```

Run this test; it should normally pass. And if it does not, we will discuss this in the section "Handling Asynchronous Re-renders," so keep reading.

One final example. Let us use another component as the ItemContent and pass the context as a parameter. Add a new component called ListItem from Listing 8-32 (which is a copy-paste of the ItemContent from Listing 8-31).

Listing 8-32. The ListItem Component

```
<p>@Item</p>

@code {
  [Parameter]
  public string Item { get; set; } = default!;
}
```

Now copy and paste the RenderItemsCorrectly method, renaming it as in Listing 8-33. The only other part of this listing that needs some modification is where we pass the ItemContent parameter. If you want to use a component to pass as a RenderFragment<TItem>, you need to use the Add<ComponentType, TItem> overload, where the first generic argument is the type of the component to use and the second is the type of the generic argument for RenderFragment<TItem>. So in this specific case, the ComponentType is ListItem, and the TItem is string (because we pass an IEnumerable<string> to the TemplatedList).

Listing 8-33. Passing a Component As a RenderFragment<TItem>

```
[Fact]
public void RenderItemsWithListItemCorrectly()
{
  const int count = 5;
  Func<ValueTask<IEnumerable<string>?>> loader =
    () => new ValueTask<IEnumerable<string>?>(
      Enumerable.Repeat("A", count));
  var cut = RenderComponent<TemplatedList<string>>(
    parameters =>
      parameters.Add(tl => tl.Loader, loader)
                /*component*//*TItem*/
                .Add<ListItem, string>(tl => tl.ItemContent,
                  context => itemParams
                          => itemParams.Add(p => p.Item,
```

```
                                    context)
                    ));
  var ps = cut.FindAll("p");
  ps.Should().NotBeEmpty();
  foreach (var p in ps)
  {
    p.MarkupMatches("<p>A</p>");
  }
}
```

This Add<ListItem, string> overload takes two expressions: the first returns the parameter to set (ItemContent), and the second expression needs some deeper explanation. Let us have a look at this somewhat hard to read piece of code:

```
Add<ListItem, string>(
  tl => tl.ItemContent,
  context => itemParams
          => itemParams.Add(p => p.Item, context)
));
```

So the first argument is tl => tl.ItemContent which returns the parameter to set. The second argument is a lambda function, which takes the value for TItem (so in our case, a string), and returns another lambda function which takes a ComponentParameterCollectionBuilder<TComponent>. Does this sound familiar? Yes. It is the same type we have used to pass parameters to a component from the beginning of this section (Listing 8-18 example). Here, we add parameters to the ListItem component by calling Add.

Run this test (and the others if you like). All tests should pass. Phew!

Using Cascading Parameters

Some components use one or more cascading parameters, so to test these components, we will need to pass a value for the cascading parameter. Start by making a copy of the Counter component, and rename it to CounterWithCV. Add an Increment cascading parameter as in Listing 8-34.

Listing 8-34. The CounterWithVC Component

```
@page "/counter"

<h1>Counter</h1>

<p>Current count: @currentCount</p>

<button class="btn btn-primary" @onclick="IncrementCount">
    Click me
</button>

@code {
    [CascadingParameter]
    public int Increment { get; set; }

    private int currentCount = 0;

    private void IncrementCount()
    {
        currentCount += Increment;
    }
}
```

Add a new test class called CounterWithCVShould and implement the test as in
Listing 8-35. As you can see, since cascading properties are identified through their type,
you only need to pass the value.

Listing 8-35. Testing a Component with a Cascading Parameter

```
using Bunit;
using System;
using System.Collections.Generic;
using System.Linq;
using System.Text;
using System.Threading.Tasks;
using Testing.Client.Pages;
using Xunit;
```

```
namespace Testing.ComponentTests
{
  public class CounterWithVCShould : TestContext
  {
    [Fact]
    public void ShouldUseCascadingIncrement()
    {
      var cut = RenderComponent<CounterWithCV>(parameters =>
        parameters.AddCascadingValue(3));
      cut.Find(cssSelector: "button")
          .Click();
      cut.Find(cssSelector: "p")
          .MarkupMatches(@"<p>Current count: 3</p>");
    }
  }
}
```

You can also have named cascading values, so try this: First name the Increment cascading parameter, as in Listing 8-36, and update the test as in Listing 8-37.

Listing 8-36. Using a Named Cascading Parameter

```
[CascadingParameter(Name = "Increment")]
public int Increment { get; set; }
```

Listing 8-37. Passing a Named Cascading Parameter

```
var cut = RenderComponent<CounterWithCV>(parameters =>
  parameters.AddCascadingValue("Increment", 3));
```

Using MOQ to Create Fake Implementations

We have seen that components should do one thing very well (the single responsibility principle) and that we should use services to implement logic, such as retrieving data using REST, or to implement business logic. We pass these services to the component using dependency injection. Here, we will look at how to pass dependencies to components using bUnit and how to replace your services with fake implementations to better drive your unit tests.

Injecting Dependencies with bUnit

Let us start by reviewing the `FetchData` component from Listing 8-38. This component takes one dependency, an `IWeatherService`.

Listing 8-38. The FetchData Component

```
@page "/fetchdata"
@using Testing.Shared
@inject IWeatherService WeatherService

<h1>Weather forecast</h1>

<p>This component demonstrates fetching data from the server.</p>

@if (forecasts == null)
{
  <p><em>Loading...</em></p>
}
else
{
  <table class="table">
    <thead>
      <tr>
        <th>Date</th>
        <th>Temp. (C)</th>
        <th>Temp. (F)</th>
        <th>Summary</th>
      </tr>
    </thead>
    <tbody>
      @foreach (var forecast in forecasts)
      {
        <tr>
          <td>@forecast.Date.ToShortDateString()</td>
          <td>@forecast.TemperatureC</td>
          <td>@forecast.TemperatureF</td>
```

```
        <td>@forecast.Summary</td>
      </tr>
    }
  </tbody>
</table>
}
@code {
  private IEnumerable<WeatherForecast>? forecasts;

  protected override async Task OnInitializedAsync()
  {
    forecasts = await WeatherService.GetForecasts();
  }
}
```

When you use this component in a Blazor application, the Blazor runtime will take care of injecting this dependency. When you use the component in a bUnit test, the bUnit runtime will take care of injecting the dependency. The only thing we need to tell is which class to use to instantiate the instance.

Add a new test class to the test project, call it FetchDataShould, and complete it as in Listing 8-39. To configure dependency injection in a bUnit test, you add your dependencies to the Services property, using the same methods as regular dependency injection, AddSingleton, AddTransient, and AddScoped.

Listing 8-39. Testing the FetchData Component

```
using Bunit;
using FluentAssertions;
using Microsoft.Extensions.DependencyInjection;
using Testing.Client.Pages;
using Testing.Shared;
using Xunit;

namespace Testing.ComponentTests
{
  public class FetchDataShould : TestContext
  {
```

```
[Fact]
public void UseWeatherService()
{
  // Use Services for dependency injection
  Services.AddSingleton<IWeatherService,
    Testing.Shared.WeatherService>();
  var cut = RenderComponent<FetchData>();
  var rows = cut.FindAll("tbody tr");
  rows.Count.Should().Be(5);
  }
 }
}
```

Try running this test. It fails? Look at the output of the failed test. As it turns out, the WeatherService from the shared project has a dependency of its own, an ILogger. Should we add another dependency? In this case, we should build a class implementing the ILogger interface or find an existing one. We won't. Let us talk about fake objects.

Message:

```
    System.InvalidOperationException : Unable to resolve service for type
'Microsoft.Extensions.Logging.ILogger`1[Testing.Shared.WeatherService]'
while attempting to activate 'Testing.Shared.WeatherService'.
```

Replacing Dependencies with Fake Objects

When you are testing a component, you want full control over dependencies. This means in many cases that you cannot use the real dependency. First of all, remember that tests should be fast and automatic? If the real dependency uses a database or a REST call to fetch data, this will make your test slow. Networks, disks, and databases are several factors slower than accessing data from memory. So we want to avoid these things. Also, databases and disks have memory, so when a test makes modifications to the data, the next time the test runs, it is using different data and will probably fail. So we don't want to use the real dependency (we are testing the component, not the dependency!). So we will use a *fake* implementation of the dependency, and that is why it is so important to have your dependencies implement an interface. Building another class with the same interface is easy and practical.

And there are different kinds of fake objects. Let us discuss stubs and mocks as shown in Figure 8-15. As you can see, both stubs and mocks are special cases of fake objects. The terminology (stub, mock, fake) used here unfortunately is not consistent in the testing community. Some people classify fake object using different names, and some people even use taxonomies containing seven different kinds of stubs!

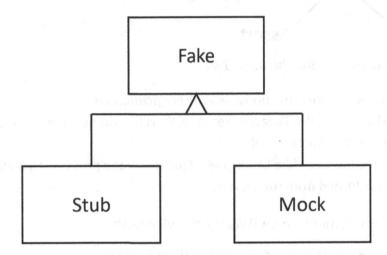

Figure 8-15. *Fake, Stub, and Mock Objects for Testing*

Using Stubs

Let us start with stubs. A *stub* is a fake implementation of a dependency that is just there to assist in a test. Our FetchData component will fetch a couple of forecasts from the IWeatherService dependency. But how many forecasts will this return? If we use the real service, this might depend on a bunch of things which are out of our control. So we use a stub implementation of the IWeatherService where we have full control. The stub is just there to assist in the test, and we will perform our Assert phase on the subject under test, not the stub. Let me use another example. Imagine you work for a car company, and you want to test your new type of car for safety. You want to run this car into a wall and see if it will explode (like in the movies). Will you run the car into a real wall? Someone's house? No. You will have someone build a fake wall in a controlled environment so no one will risk getting hurt. You drive the car into the wall, and then the wall has served its purpose. You will examine the car to see the outcome of the test; the wall is no longer important. This is illustrated in Figure 8-16.

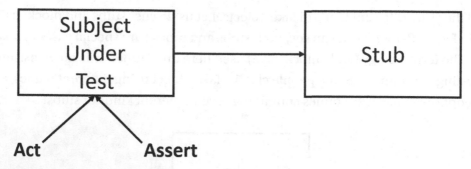

Figure 8-16. *Using a Stub During a Test*

Tests that use stubs are also known as *state verification tests*.

Let us build a stub for the `IWeatherService`. Start by adding a new class called `WeatherServiceStub` to the test project.

Implement the interface like Listing 8-40. Our stub has a property that will hold the data that will be returned from the service.

Listing 8-40. Implementing an IWeatherService Stub

```
private class WeatherServiceStub : IWeatherService
{
  public IEnumerable<WeatherForecast> FakeForecasts { get; set; }
    = default!;

  public ValueTask<IEnumerable<WeatherForecast>> GetForecasts()
    => new ValueTask<IEnumerable<WeatherForecast>>(
        FakeForecasts);
}
```

Now update the `UseWeatherService` test as in Listing 8-41. We create an instance of the stub, initialize it with the data we want, and then pass it to dependency injection as a singleton. When the `FetchData` component gets initialized, we will use the stub, and we are sure that our service returns five rows of data (or a different number; that is why I use a `const` for easy update).

Listing 8-41. Testing the FetchData Component with a Stub

```
[Fact]
public void UseWeatherService()
{
  const int nrOfForecasts = 5;
  var stub = new WeatherServiceStub
  {
    FakeForecasts = Enumerable.Repeat(new WeatherForecast(),
                                      nrOfForecasts)
  };
  Services.AddSingleton<IWeatherService>(stub);
  var cut = RenderComponent<FetchData>();
  var rows = cut.FindAll("tbody tr");
  rows.Count.Should().Be(nrOfForecasts);
}
```

Run the test. It should pass.

Using Mocks

So what is a mock? A *mock* is a fake implementation where we want to verify if the subject under test called certain methods and properties on the mock. A mock therefore works a little like a data recorder, remembering which methods were called, even recording the values of the arguments in the method call. It should not come as a surprise that building a mock is a lot more work! When you use a mock in a test, you will do your Assert phase through the mock, with questions like "Did the subject under test call this method?" Let us use the car example again. Now we want to see if the driver of the car gets hurt in a frontal crash into a wall. We already have a wall, but now we need a driver. Any volunteers? No? Of course, not. We will mimic the driver (a mock object) using a crash test dummy. These dummies look a lot like a human (if you are Homer Simpson) and are crammed full of sensors. You let the car crash into the wall. After the crash, you are not interested in the wall, neither the car. You will ask the dummy (the mock remember) where it hurts. Again, this is illustrated in Figure 8-17.

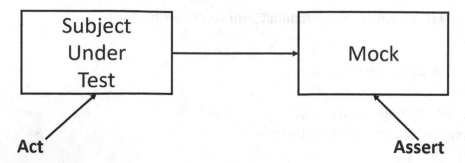

Figure 8-17. *Using a Mock During Testing*

Tests like these are known as *object interaction tests*.

Let us update the FetchData component to perform some logging, so add an @inject for an ILogger, and use it in the OnInitializedAsync as in Listing 8-42.

Listing 8-42. Update the FetchData Component to Use Logging

```
@page "/fetchdata"
@using Microsoft.Extensions.Logging
@using Testing.Shared
@inject IWeatherService WeatherService
@inject ILogger logger

...

    protected override async Task OnInitializedAsync()
    {
        logger.LogInformation("Fetching forecasts");
        forecasts = await WeatherService.GetForecasts();
    }
}
```

So we want to test if the ILogger is used during the OnInitializedAsync. We need a mock implementation because we don't want to have to parse log files. Add a new class to your test project called LoggerMock as in Listing 8-43. Implementing this class alone takes some work! We will next look at how we can make this easier. Our mock logger simply records a couple of arguments in the Journal list.

Listing 8-43. Implementing an ILogger Mock

```
private class LoggerMock : ILogger
{
  public List<(LogLevel logLevel, object? state)> Journal
    { get; set; } = new List<(LogLevel,object?)>();

  public IDisposable BeginScope<TState>(TState state)
    => throw new NotImplementedException();
  public bool IsEnabled(LogLevel logLevel)
    => true;
  public void Log<TState>(LogLevel logLevel, EventId eventId,
                          TState state, Exception? exception,
                    Func<TState, Exception?, string> formatter)
  {
    Journal.Add((logLevel, state));
  }
}
```

Add a new unit test to the FetchDataShould class like in Listing 8-44.

Listing 8-44. Testing the FetchData Component Using a Mock

```
[Fact]
public void UseProperLogging()
{
  const int nrOfForecasts = 5;
  var stub = new WeatherServiceStub
  {
    FakeForecasts = Enumerable.Repeat(new WeatherForecast(),
                                        nrOfForecasts)
  };
  Services.AddSingleton<IWeatherService>(stub);

  LoggerMock logger = new LoggerMock();
  Services.AddSingleton<ILogger>(logger);
  var cut = RenderComponent<FetchData>();
```

```
logger.Journal.Count.Should().Be(1);
logger.Journal.First().state.Should().NotBeNull();
logger.Journal.First().state!.ToString().Should().Contain("Fetching
forecasts");
}
```

So we create a stub for the IWeatherService, a mock for the ILogger, and then we render the component. Now we want to check the Journal of the LoggerMock. There should be one call to the logger, so we check the length of the Journal. Then we check the entry's state to see if it contains the message. All straight forward but a lot of work!

Run all your tests. The UseWeatherService test breaks! Why? Because we introduced another dependency, so we need to dependency inject a logger in this test too. I will leave the fixing in your capable hands.

Implementing Stubs and Mocks with MOQ

How can we implement stubs and mocks with a lot less work? Other people have been asking the same question, and some of them built libraries that make this possible. Generally, these libraries are known as *isolation frameworks*. Isolation frameworks allow you to quickly generate stubs and mocks for classes and interfaces, where you implement just the methods you need for the test, and verify if the subject under test invoked methods with certain arguments a certain number of times. Here, we will look at *MOQ* which is currently one of the most popular in the testing community. We will cover a lot of features of MOQ here, but if you want to learn more, you can visit https://documentation.help/Moq.

Start by adding the MOQ NuGet package to the test project. Now copy the UseWeatherServices method and rename it to UseWeatherServicesMOQ. Change its implementation like Listing 8-45. First, we create the forecasts data we want the IWeatherService to return. Next, we create an instance of Mock<IWeatherService> which is a class from MOQ. This class allows us to Setup methods from the interface and Returns a certain result. It is that simple to provide a stub implementation. But MOQ allows you to go further and makes the method return different results, depending on the arguments, for example.

Next, we configure bUnit's dependency injection to inject a singleton instance, passing the stub.Object, which is an instance implementing the IWeatherService interface. No need to build our own class to create a stub.

Our FetchData component also needs a logger, but here we are not interested in the interaction between the component and the logger, so we create another stub. The rest of the test remains unchanged.

Listing 8-45. Implementing a Stub with MOQ

```
[Fact]
public void UseWeatherServiceMOQ()
{
  const int nrOfForecasts = 5;
  var forecasts = Enumerable.Repeat(new WeatherForecast(), nrOfForecasts);
  Mock<IWeatherService> stub = new Mock<IWeatherService>();
  stub.Setup(s => s.GetForecasts())
      .Returns(new ValueTask<IEnumerable<WeatherForecast>>(forecasts));
  Services.AddSingleton<IWeatherService>(stub.Object);

  Mock<ILogger> loggerStub = new Mock<ILogger>();
  Services.AddSingleton<ILogger>(loggerStub.Object);

  var cut = RenderComponent<FetchData>();
  var rows = cut.FindAll("tbody tr");
  rows.Count.Should().Be(nrOfForecasts);
}
```

Run the test; it should pass.

Now it is time to implement a mock, where we want to see if the FetchData component will invoke the logger. Copy the UseProperLogging method and name it UseProperLoggingMOQ as in Listing 8-46. Here, you should focus on the Verify method. Here, we verify if the Log method got called, and we can state how many times. You can choose between Never, Once, AtLeast, AtMost, Exactly, and more. The Log method takes a bunch of arguments, and the way this Log method works is somewhat awkward. The first argument is of type LogLevel, which we check if the LogLevel.Information value was used with

```
It.Is<LogLevel>(l => l == LogLevel.Information)
```

Each argument is represented with a check of the arguments' value. You can also ignore the value of the argument with It.IsAny<T>, specifying the type of the argument. This type of argument is needed to disambiguate overloading. Other arguments work in a similar way, even generic arguments. For example, if an argument is of type List<T> and you cannot know T, you use It.Is<List<It.IsAnyType>>. We need to use that here because of specific implementation details of ILogger.

Listing 8-46. Implementing a Mock Using MOQ

```
[Fact]
public void UseProperLoggingMOQ()
{
  const int nrOfForecasts = 5;
  var forecasts = Enumerable.Repeat(new WeatherForecast(), nrOfForecasts);
  Mock<IWeatherService> stub = new Mock<IWeatherService>();
  stub.Setup(s => s.GetForecasts())
      .Returns(new ValueTask<IEnumerable<WeatherForecast>>(forecasts));
  Services.AddSingleton<IWeatherService>(stub.Object);

  Mock<ILogger> loggerMock = new Mock<ILogger>();
  Services.AddSingleton<ILogger>(loggerMock.Object);

  var cut = RenderComponent<FetchData>();

  loggerMock.Verify(
    l => l.Log(
      It.Is<LogLevel>(l => l == LogLevel.Information),
      It.IsAny<EventId>(),
      It.Is<It.IsAnyType>(
        (msg,t) => msg.ToString()!
                     .Contains("Fetching forecasts")),
      It.IsAny<Exception>(),
      It.Is<Func<It.IsAnyType, Exception?, string>>(
        (v,t)=>true))
    , Times.Once);
}
```

Run the test. It should pass.

Writing bUnit Tests in Razor

When you build unit tests with bUnit, you sometimes end up with long tests because of all the markup that gets generated. Also, the MarkupMatches method takes a string, and if your markup uses HTML attributes, you need to escape your quotes with \. For these kinds of tests, we can also use razor to author tests. Writing unit tests with razor requires two things: the project needs to reference the razor SDK, meaning your test project should set the SDK type to razor:

```
<Project Sdk="Microsoft.NET.Sdk.Razor">
```

Second, you should add an _Imports.razor file to the test project for easy reference, as in Listing 8-47.

Listing 8-47. The _Imports.razor File for Test Projects

```
@using Microsoft.AspNetCore.Components.Forms
@using Microsoft.AspNetCore.Components.Routing
@using Microsoft.AspNetCore.Components.Web
@using Microsoft.JSInterop
@using Microsoft.Extensions.DependencyInjection
@using AngleSharp.Dom
@using Bunit
@using Bunit.TestDoubles
@using Xunit
```

I do advise to add your project's namespaces here too.

The First Razor Test

In your test project, add a new razor component called RCounterShould as in Listing 8-48. Here, I will prefix the razor unit tests with an R, so we don't get a name conflict with our other CounterShould test class. We will make the test inherit from TestContext, just like our test classes written in C#. Then we add a @code section and put our xUnit test method in there. Because this is a razor file, we can write the test's markup using razor inside the Render method.

And inside the MarkupMatches method, we can also write the markup using plain razor. This makes writing tests like these simpler and agreeable.

Listing 8-48. Writing a Simple Unit Test with Razor

```
@inherits Bunit.TestContext

@code {
  [Fact]
  public void RenderCorrectlyWithInitialZero()
  {
    var cut = Render(@<Counter />);
    cut.Find("p")
       .MarkupMatches(@<p>Current count: 0</p>);
  }

  [Fact]
  public void IncrementCounterWhenButtonIsClicked()
  {
    var cut = RenderComponent<Counter>();
    cut.Find(cssSelector: "button")
       .Click();
    cut.Find(cssSelector: "p")
       .MarkupMatches(@"<p>Current count: 1</p>");
  }
}
```

What about passing parameters? Add a new component called RTwoWayCounterShould like in Listing 8-49. Since we can render our component using plain razor, we can pass parameters inside the razor syntax as shown in the first test method! The second test method illustrates how we can test two-way data binding, again using the same familiar razor syntax.

Listing 8-49. Passing Parameters in a Razor Test

```
@inherits Bunit.TestContext

@code {
  [Fact]
  public void IncrementCounterWhenButtonIsClicked()
  {
    var cut = Render(@<TwoWayCounter CurrentCount="1" Increment="2"/>);
    cut.Find("button").Click();
```

```
  cut.Find("p")
      .MarkupMatches(@<p>Current count: 3</p>
);
}

[Fact]
public void TriggerChangedEventForCurrentCounter2()
{
  int currentCount = 1;
  var cut = Render(@<TwoWayCounter
                      @bind-CurrentCount="currentCount"
                      Increment="2"/>
  );
  cut.Find(cssSelector: "button")
      .Click();
  currentCount.Should().Be(3);
}
}
```

Let us look at an example that uses ChildContent. Add a new razor component called RAlertShould to the test project as in Listing 8-50. The Alert component uses ChildContent, and we can pass this by nesting the child content inside the Alert markup. And to see if the component gets rendered as expected, we can use simple HTML markup inside the MarkupMatches method.

Listing 8-50. Testing a Component with ChildContent

```
@inherits Bunit.TestContext

@code {
  [Fact]
  public void RenderSimpleChildContent()
  {
    var cut = Render(
      @<Alert>
        <h1>Hello world!</h1>
      </Alert>
    );
```

```
  cut.MarkupMatches(
    @<div class="alert alert-secondary mt-4" role="alert">
      <h1>Hello world!</h1>
    </div>
  );
  }
}
```

Add another razor component, called RTemplatedListShould from Listing 8-51. Again, we want to see if the component displays the loading RenderFragment when the items are null. Passing a RenderFragment is again done using razor.

Listing 8-51. Using a Razor Test for a Templated Component

```
@inherits Bunit.TestContext

@code {
  [Fact]
  public void RenderLoadingTemplateWhenItemsIsNull()
  {
    RenderFragment loading =
      @<div class="loader">Loading...</div>;

    Func<ValueTask<IEnumerable<string>?>> loader =
      () => new ValueTask<IEnumerable<string>?>(
            result: null);

    var cut = Render(
      @<TemplatedList Loader="@loader">
        <LoadingContent>
          <div class="loader">Loading...</div>
        </LoadingContent>
      </TemplatedList>
    );
    cut.Find("div.loader")
      .MarkupMatches(loading);
  }
}
```

Handling Asynchronous Re-renders

When you build a component that overrides OnInitializedAsync or
OnParametersSetAsync, your component will at least render itself twice – first, when
the component gets created and after completion of the OnInitializedAsync and again
after completion of each OnParametersSetAsync.

Inside a bUnit test, this can give you issues. Let us look at an example.

Add the following unit test from Listing 8-52 to the RTemplatedListShould class. In
this test, we make the loader really asynchronous using the TaskCompletionSource<T>
class. Instances of this class have a Task<T> which will continue execution by calling the
SetResult method. Until then the Task will block any awaiter. This allows us to render
the component, see the loading UI, then make the Task complete by calling SetResult,
and then see if the items get rendered.

Listing 8-52. Testing Asynchronous Re-renders

```
[Fact]
public void RenderItemsAftersItemsLoadedAsyncCorrectly()
{
  const int count = 5;

  var tcs = new TaskCompletionSource<IEnumerable<string>?>();

  Func<ValueTask<IEnumerable<string>?>> loader =
    () => new ValueTask<IEnumerable<string>?>(tcs.Task);

  var cut = Render(
    @<TemplatedList Loader="@loader">
      <LoadingContent>
        <div class="loader">Loading...</div>
      </LoadingContent>
      <ItemContent Context="item">
        <ListItem Item="@item" />
      </ItemContent>
    </TemplatedList>
  );

  cut.Find("div.loader")
```

```
    .MarkupMatches(@<div class="loader">Loading...</div>);

// Complete the loader task,
// this should rerender the component asynchronously
tcs.SetResult(Enumerable.Repeat("A", count));

var ps = cut.FindAll("p");
ps.Should().NotBeEmpty();
foreach (var p in ps)
{
  p.MarkupMatches(@<p>A</p>);
}
}
```

Run the test. It will fail! Why? Because our component will render the UI on another thread, and the test will check the UI before rendering completes. So we need to wait a bit till the UI rendering completes. How can we do this? Add this line of code after the SetResult call, with the complete method in Listing 8-53.

```
cut.WaitForState(() => cut.FindAll("p").Any());
```

The WaitForState method will wait till the condition returns true. We know that the UI will render a bunch of paragraphs, so we wait till we see them. The WaitForState also has a parameter (not shown here) to set the timeout, which has a default value of 1 second. If the cut does not pass the condition within the timeout, the test will fail with the WaitForFailedException.

Listing 8-53. Testing Asynchronous Re-renders

```
[Fact]
public void RenderItemsAftersItemsLoadedAsyncCorrectly()
{
  const int count = 5;

  var tcs = new TaskCompletionSource<IEnumerable<string>?>();

  Func<ValueTask<IEnumerable<string>?>> loader =
    () => new ValueTask<IEnumerable<string>?>(tcs.Task);

  var cut = Render(
```

```
@<TemplatedList Loader="@loader">
  <LoadingContent>
    <div class="loader">Loading...</div>
  </LoadingContent>
  <ItemContent Context="item">
    <ListItem Item="@item" />
  </ItemContent>
</TemplatedList>
);

cut.Find("div.loader")
  .MarkupMatches(@<div class="loader">Loading...</div>);

// Complete the loader task,
// this should rerender the component asynchronously
tcs.SetResult(Enumerable.Repeat("A", count));

// Wait for rendering to complete
cut.WaitForState(() => cut.FindAll("p").Any());

var ps = cut.FindAll("p");
ps.Should().NotBeEmpty();
foreach (var p in ps)
{
  p.MarkupMatches(@<p>A</p>);
}
}
```

Configuring Semantic Comparison

The bUnit testing library uses the *AngleSharp Diffing library* to compare the generated markup with the expected markup in the MarkupMatches method. You can find AngleSharp on GitHub at https://github.com/AngleSharp/AngleSharp.Diffing. To make your tests more robust, you can configure how the semantic comparison works; for example, we can tell it to ignore certain HTML attributes and elements.

Why Do We Need Semantic Comparison?

Using strings to compare markup is too sensitive to small changes in the markup. For example, formatting your code might add some whitespace, and since string comparison will compare each character, a working test will suddenly fail. And there are many more innocent changes that will break a test, for example, changing the order of attributes, or reordering the classes in the class attribute, or adding comments. Semantic comparison will ignore all of these changes, resulting in tests that will not break because of a simple change.

Customizing Semantic Comparison

Remember one of our previous tests, where we told the MarkupMatches method to ignore the attribute (Listing 8-16). The AngleSharp Diffing library allows us to use special attributes to ignore certain elements and attributes; for example, `<div style:ignore>` will ignore the style attribute's contents. We can also make it ignore certain HTML elements; for example, add the test from Listing 8-54 to the AlertShould class.

Listing 8-54. Ignoring an Element with Semantic Comparison

```
[Fact]
public void RenderCorrectly()
{
  var cut = RenderComponent<Alert>(parameters =>
  parameters.AddChildContent("<p>Hello world!</p>"));
  cut.MarkupMatches(@"
    <div class=""alert alert-secondary mt-4"" role=""alert"">
        <p diff:ignore></p>
    </div>
  ");
}
```

We can do the same with razor tests, for example, Listing 8-55, which should be added to the RAlertShould razor file.

Listing 8-55. Ignoring an Element with a Razor Test

```
[Fact]
public void RenderCorrectly()
{
  var cut = Render(
    @<Alert>
      <h1>Hello world!</h1>
    </Alert>
    );
  cut.MarkupMatches(
    @<div class="alert alert-secondary mt-4" role="alert">
      <h1 diff:ignore></h1>
    </div>
    );
}
```

By default, semantic comparison will ignore whitespace, but in some cases, you want to verify if the component actually renders some whitespace. Do this with diff:whitespace="preserve".

You can also tell semantic comparison to ignore case or use a regular expression for your comparison.

Note   Regular expressions allow you to test for complex patterns in strings with a concise syntax. Regular expressions were invented in 1951, and we are still using them. What else was invented more than half a century ago that we are still using in IT? Learning regular expressions is something worthwhile investing in for your future in IT!

Let us test the simple Card component from Listing 8-56.

Listing 8-56. A Simple Card Component

```
<h3 id="card-@Id">Card @Id</h3>

@code {
    [Parameter]
    public int Id { get; set; }
}
```

A unit test that will check if the id attribute matches card- followed by one to four digits and the content matches Card with one to four digits looks like Listing 8-57. We also want the test to ignore the casing on the card's contents.

Listing 8-57. Ignore Casing and Using Regular Expressions

```
using Bunit;
using Testing.Client.Pages;
using Xunit;

namespace Testing.ComponentTests
{
  public class CardShould : TestContext
  {
    [Fact]
    public void RenderCorrectlyWithProperId()
    {
      var cut = RenderComponent<Card>();
      cut.MarkupMatches(@"<h3 diff:ignorecase diff:regex id:regex=""card-
      \d{1,4}"">card \d{1,4}</h3>");
    }
  }
}
```

Summary

In this chapter, we had a look at unit testing. With unit testing, you can see if your code and components behave as expected, and also it allows you to test if they continue behaving, so small changes that cause bugs are found as fast as possible. Good unit tests are fast, consistent, repeatable, and automatic. We have seen that testing Blazor components becomes very practical with bUnit, and we can author tests using C# or Razor. And with MOQ, we can quickly generate stubs and mocks to replace dependencies in our tests.

CHAPTER 9

Single-Page Applications and Routing

Blazor is a .NET framework you use for building *Single-Page Applications* (SPA), just like you can use popular JavaScript frameworks, such as Angular, React, and Vue.js. But what is a *SPA*? In this chapter, you will use routing to jump between different sections of a SPA and send data between different components.

What Is a Single-Page Application?

At the beginning of the Web, there were only static pages. A *static page* is an HTML file somewhere on the server that gets sent back to the browser upon request. Here, the server is really nothing but a file server, returning HTML pages to the browser. The browser renders the HTML. The only interaction with the browser then was that you could click a link (the anchor <a> HTML element) to get another page from the server.

Later came the rise of dynamic pages. When a browser requests a *dynamic page*, the server runs a program to build the HTML in memory and sends the HTML back to the browser (this HTML never gets stored to disk; of course, the server can store the generated HTML in its cache for fast retrieval later, also known as *output caching*). Dynamic pages are flexible in the way that the same code can generate thousands of different pages by retrieving data from a database and using it to construct the page. Lots of commercial websites like amazon.com use this. But there is still a usability problem. Every time your user clicks a link, the server must generate the next page from scratch and send it to the browser for rendering. This results in a noticeable wait period, and of course, the browser re-renders the whole page.

In 1995, *Brendan Eich* invented *JavaScript* (today known as ECMAScript) to allow simple interactions in the browser. Web pages started to use JavaScript to retrieve parts of the page when the user interacts with the UI. One of the first examples of this technique

351

© Peter Himschoot 2022
P. Himschoot, *Microsoft Blazor*, https://doi.org/10.1007/978-1-4842-7845-1_9

was Microsoft's *Outlook Web Application*. This web application looks and feels like Outlook, a desktop application, with support for all user interactions you expect from a desktop application. Google's Gmail is another example. They are now known as Single-Page Applications. SPAs contain sections of the web page that are replaced at runtime depending on the user's interaction. If you click an email, the main section of the page is replaced by the email's view. If you click your inbox, the main section gets replaced by a list of emails; etc.

Single-Page Applications

A SPA is a web application that replaces certain parts of the UI without reloading the complete page. SPAs use JavaScript to implement this manipulation of the browser's control tree, also known as the Document Object Model (DOM), and most of them consist of a fixed UI and a placeholder element where the contents are overwritten depending on where the user clicks. One of the main advantages of using a SPA is that you can make a SPA stateful. This means that you can keep information loaded by the application in memory, just like when you build a desktop application. You will look at an example of a SPA, built with Blazor, in this chapter.

Layout Components

Let's start with the fixed part of a SPA. Every web application contains UI elements that you can find on every page, such as a header, footer, copyright, menu, etc. Copy-pasting these elements to every page would be a lot of work and would require updating every page if one of these elements needed to change. Developers don't like to do that, so every framework for building websites has had a solution for this. For example, ASP.NET WebForms uses master pages, and ASP.NET MVC has layout pages. Blazor also has a mechanism for this called *layout components*.

Using Blazor Layout Components

Layout components are Blazor components. Anything you can do with a regular component you can do with a layout component, like dependency injection, data binding, and nesting other components. The only difference is that they must inherit from the `LayoutComponentBase` class.

The `LayoutComponentBase` class adds a `Body` property to `ComponentBase` as in Listing 9-1.

Listing 9-1. The LayoutComponentBase Class (Simplified)

```
namespace Microsoft.AspNetCore.Components
{  public abstract class LayoutComponentBase : ComponentBase
   {
     [Parameter]
     public RenderFragment? Body { get; set; }
   }
}
```

As you can see from Listing 9-1, the LayoutComponentBase class inherits from the ComponentBase class. This is why you can do the same thing as with normal components.

Let's look at an example of a layout component. Open the SinglePageApplications solution from the code provided with this chapter. Now, look at the MainLayout.razor component in the SPA.Client's Shared folder, which you'll find in Listing 9-2. Since layout components are used by more than one component, it makes sense to place your layout components in the Shared folder, although there is not technical requirement to do so.

Listing 9-2. MainLayout.razor from the Template

```
@inherits LayoutComponentBase

<div class="page">
  <div class="sidebar">
    <NavMenu />
  </div>

  <div class="main">
    <div class="top-row px-4">
      <a href="http://blazor.net" target="_blank"
         class="ml-md-auto">About</a>
    </div>

    <div class="content px-4">
      @Body
    </div>
  </div>
</div>
```

353

On the first line, the MainLayout component declares that it inherits from LayoutComponentBase. Then you see a `sidebar` and `main` `<div>` element, with the `main` element data binding to the inherited Body property. Any component that uses this layout component will end up where the @Body property is, so inside the `<div class="content px-4">`.

In Figure 9-1, you can see the sidebar on the left side (containing links to the different components of this Single-Page Application) and the main area on the right side with the @Body emphasized with a black rectangle (which I added to the figure). Clicking the Home, Counter, or Fetch Data link in the sidebar will replace the Body property with the selected component, updating the UI without reloading the whole page.

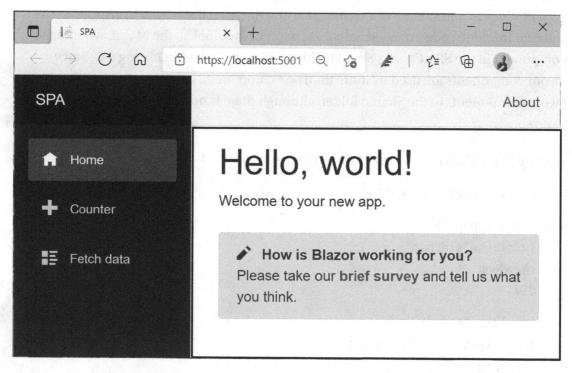

Figure 9-1. *The MainLayout Component*

You can find the CSS style used by this layout component in the MainLayout.razor. css file.

Configuring the Default Layout Component

So how does a component know which layout component to use? A component can change the layout component for itself, and an application can set a default layout component which will be used for all components that do not explicitly set their layout. Let us start with the application. Open the App.razor file as in Listing 9-3. The first thing to notice here is the RouteView component, which has a DefaultLayout property of type Type. This is where the default layout for this application is set. Any component selected by this RouteView component will use the MainLayout by default. And should no suitable component be found to display, the App component uses a LayoutView to display an error message. Again, this LayoutView uses the MainLayout, but of course you can change this to any layout you like.

Listing 9-3. The App.razor Component

```
<Router AppAssembly="@typeof(Program).Assembly">
  <Found Context="routeData">
    <RouteView RouteData="@routeData"
               DefaultLayout="@typeof(MainLayout)" />
  </Found>
  <NotFound>
    <LayoutView Layout="@typeof(MainLayout)">
      <p>Sorry, there's nothing at this address.</p>
    </LayoutView>
  </NotFound>
</Router>
```

Internally, the RouteView component uses the LayoutView component to select the appropriate layout component. LayoutView allows you to change the layout component for any part of your component.

Let us create a simple error layout component, which will display the error horizontally centered. Start by adding a new razor component called ErrorLayout with markup from Listing 9-4 to the Shared folder.

Listing 9-4. The ErrorLayout Component

```
@inherits LayoutComponentBase

<div class="error">
  @Body
</div>
```

Now add a CSS file called ErrorLayout.razor.css from Listing 9-5 to the Shared folder. This tells the error layout to place the body centered in the browser's window.

Listing 9-5. The ErrorLayout Style

```
.error {
  position: relative;
  display: flex;
  justify-content: center;
  align-items: center;
  height: 100vh;
}
```

Now replace the LayoutView's Layout property from App.razor with Listing 9-6.

Listing 9-6. The Updated App.razor File

```
<Router AppAssembly="@typeof(Program).Assembly">
  <Found Context="routeData">
    <RouteView RouteData="@routeData"
               DefaultLayout="@typeof(MainLayout)" />
  </Found>
  <NotFound>
    <LayoutView Layout="@typeof(ErrorLayout)">
      <p>Sorry, there's nothing at this address.</p>
    </LayoutView>
  </NotFound>
</Router>
```

Run the Blazor application and manually change the browser's URL by appending /x. Because there is nothing associated with this URL, the error layout will be used to display the error, as shown in Figure 9-2.

Selecting a Layout Component

Every component can select which layout to use by stating the name of the layout component with the @layout razor directive. For example, start by copying the MainLayout.razor file to MainLayoutRight.razor (this should also make a copy of the CSS file). This will generate a new layout component called MainLayoutRight, inferred from the filename (you might need to rebuild the project to force this). Inside the CSS file for this component, change both flex-direction properties to their reverse counterpart as shown in Listing 9-7.

Figure 9-2. *The ErrorLayout in Action*

Listing 9-7. A Second Layout Component

```
.page {
    position: relative;
    display: flex;
    flex-direction: column-reverse;
}
...
```

```
@media (min-width: 641px) {
    .page {
        flex-direction: row-reverse;
    }
...
}
```

Now open the Counter component and add a @layout razor directive as in Listing 9-8.

Listing 9-8. Choosing a Different Layout with @layout

```
@page "/counter"
@layout MainLayoutRight

<h1>Counter</h1>

<p>Current count: @currentCount</p>

<button class="btn btn-primary" @onclick="IncrementCount">Click me</button>

@code {
  private int currentCount = 0;

  private void IncrementCount()
  {
    currentCount++;
  }
}
```

Run the application and watch the layout change as you alternate between Home and Counter.

Note   You can also use the LayoutAttribute if you're building your component completely in code.

Most components will use the same layout. Instead of copying the same @layout razor directive to every page, you can also add a _Imports.razor file to the same folder as your components. Open the Pages folder from the SPA.Client project and add a new _Imports.razor file. Replace its content with Listing 9-9.

Listing 9-9. _Imports.razor

```
@layout MainLayoutRight
```

Any component in this folder (or subfolder) that does not explicitly declare a @layout component will use the `MainLayoutRight` layout component.

Nesting Layouts

Layout components can also be nested. You could define the MainLayout to contain all the UI that is shared between all components and then define a nested layout to be used by a subset of these components. For example, add a new razor view called NestedLayout.razor to the Shared folder and replace its contents with Listing 9-10.

Listing 9-10. A Simple Nested Layout

```
@inherits LayoutComponentBase
@layout MainLayout

<div class="paper">
  @Body
</div>
```

To build a nested layout, you `@inherit` from `LayoutComponentBase` and set its @layout to another layout, for example, MainLayout. Our nested layout uses a paper class, so add a NestedLayout.razor.css file next to the component and add Listing 9-11.

Listing 9-11. The NestedLayout Component's Style

```
.paper {
  background-image: url("images/paper.jpg");
  padding: 1em;
}
```

This style uses the paper.jpg background from the images folder.

Now add a layout directive to the _Imports.razer file within the Pages folder as in Listing 9-12.

Listing 9-12. Nested Layout

```
@layout NestedLayout
```

Run your application; now you have the Index component inside the nested layout which is inside the main layout, as shown in Figure 9-3.

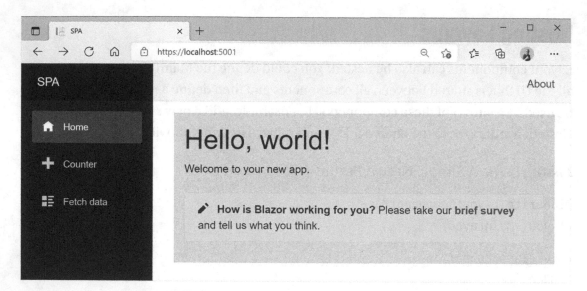

Figure 9-3. *The Index Component Using the Nested Layout*

Blazor Routing

Single-Page Applications use routing to select which component gets picked to fill in the layout component's Body property. Routing is the process of matching the browser's URI to a collection of *route templates* and is used to select the component to be shown on screen. That is why every component in as Blazor SPA uses a @page directive to define the route template to tell the router which component to pick.

Installing the Router

When you create a Blazor solution from scratch, the router is already installed, but let's have a look at how this is done. Open App.razor. This App component only has one component, the Router component, as shown in Listing 9-13.

Listing 9-13. The App Component Containing the Router

```
<Router AppAssembly="@typeof(Program).Assembly">
  <Found Context="routeData">
    <RouteView RouteData="@routeData"
               DefaultLayout="@typeof(MainLayout)" />
  </Found>
  <NotFound>
    <LayoutView Layout="@typeof(ErrorLayout)">
      <p>Sorry, there's nothing at this address.</p>
    </LayoutView>
  </NotFound>
</Router>
```

The Router component is a *templated component* with two templates. The Found template is used for known routes, and the NotFound is shown when the URI does not match any of the known routes. You can replace the contents of the last to show a nice error page to the user.

The Found template uses a RouteView component which will render the selected component with its layout (or default layout). When the Router component gets instantiated, it will search its AppAssembly property for all components that have the RouteAttribute (the @page razor directive gets compiled into a RouteAttribute) and pick the component that matches the current browser's URI. For example, the Counter component has the @page "/counter" razor directive, and when the URL in the browser matches /counter, it will display the Counter component in the MainLayout component.

The NavMenu Component

Review the MainLayout component from Listing 9-2. On the fourth line, you will see the *NavMenu* component. This component contains the links to navigate between components. This component comes with the template; feel free to use another component for navigation. We will use this component here to explore some of the concepts. Open the SPA.Client project and look for the NavMenu component in the Shared folder, which is repeated in Listing 9-14.

Listing 9-14. The NavMenu Component

```
<div class="top-row pl-4 navbar navbar-dark">
  <a class="navbar-brand" href="">SPA</a>
  <button class="navbar-toggler" @onclick="ToggleNavMenu">
    <span class="navbar-toggler-icon"></span>
  </button>
</div>

<div class="@NavMenuCssClass" @onclick="ToggleNavMenu">
  <ul class="nav flex-column">
    <li class="nav-item px-3">
      <NavLink class="nav-link" href="" Match="NavLinkMatch.All">
        <span class="oi oi-home" aria-hidden="true"></span>
        Home
      </NavLink>
    </li>
    <li class="nav-item px-3">
      <NavLink class="nav-link" href="counter">
        <span class="oi oi-plus" aria-hidden="true"></span>
        Counter
      </NavLink>
    </li>
    <li class="nav-item px-3">
      <NavLink class="nav-link" href="fetchdata">
        <span class="oi oi-list-rich" aria-hidden="true"></span>
        Fetch data
      </NavLink>
    </li>
  </ul>
</div>

@code {
  private bool collapseNavMenu = true;

  private string NavMenuCssClass
    => collapseNavMenu ? "collapse" : null;
```

```
private void ToggleNavMenu()
{
  collapseNavMenu = !collapseNavMenu;
}
}
```

The first part of Listing 9-14 contains the Toggle button which allows you to hide and show the navigation menu. This button is only visible on displays with a narrow width (e.g., mobile displays). If you want to look at it, run your application and make the browser width smaller until you see the *hamburger button* in the top right corner, as in Figure 9-4. Click the button to show the navigation menu and click it again to hide the menu again.

Figure 9-4. *Your Application on a Narrow Display Shows the Toggle Button*

The remaining markup contains the navigation menu, which consists of NavLink components. Let's look at the NavLink component.

The *NavLink* component is a specialized version of an anchor element <a/> used for creating navigation links, also known as hyperlinks. When the browser's URI matches the href property of the NavLink, it applies a CSS style (the active CSS class if you want to customize it) to itself to let you know it is the current route. For example, look at Listing 9-15.

Listing 9-15. The Counter Route's NavLink

```
<NavLink class="nav-link" href="counter">
  <span class="oi oi-plus" aria-hidden="true"></span> Counter
</NavLink>
```

When the browser's URI ends with /counter (ignoring things like query strings), this NavLink will apply the active style. Let's look at another one in Listing 9-16.

Listing 9-16. The Default Route's NavLink

```
<NavLink class="nav-link" href="" Match="NavLinkMatch.All">
  <span class="oi oi-home" aria-hidden="true"></span> Home
</NavLink>
```

When the browser's URI is empty (except for the site's URL), the NavLink from Listing 9-16 will be active. But here you have a special case. Normally, NavLink components only match the end of the URI. For example, /counter matches the NavLink from Listing 9-15. But with an empty URI, this would match everything! This is why in the special case of an empty URI you need to tell the NavLink to match the whole URI. You do this with the Match property, which by default is set to NavLinkMatch.Prefix. If you want to match the whole URI, use NavLinkMatch.All as in Listing 9-16.

Setting the Route Template

The Routing component from Blazor examines the browser's URI and searches for a component's route template to match. But how do you set a component's route template? Open the Counter component shown in Listing 9-8. At the top of this file is the @page "/counter" razor directive. It defines the route template. A route template is a string matching a URI, and that can contain parameters, which you can then use in your component.

You can change what gets displayed in the component by passing parameters in the route. You could pass the id of a product, look up the product's details with the id, and use it to display the product's details. Let's look at an example. Change the Counter component to look like Listing 9-17 by adding another route template which will set the CurrentCount parameter. This listing illustrates a couple of things. First, you can have multiple @page razor directives, so the /counter and /counter/55 will both route to the Counter component. The second @page directive will set the CurrentCount parameter property from routing, and the name of the parameter is case-insensitive in the @page directive. Of course, parameters need to be encased in curly brackets so the router can identify it.

Listing 9-17. Defining a Route Template with a Parameter

```
@page "/counter"
@page "/counter/{currentCount:int?}"
@layout MainLayoutRight

<h1>Counter</h1>

<p>Current count: @CurrentCount</p>

<button class="btn btn-primary" @onclick="IncrementCount">Click me</button>

@code {
  [Parameter]
  public int CurrentCount { get; set; }

  private void IncrementCount()
  {
    CurrentCount++;
  }
}
```

Just like routes in ASP.NET MVC Core, you can use *route constraints* to limit the type of parameter to match. For example, if you were to use the /counter/Blazor URI, the route template would not match because the parameter does not hold an integer value and the router would not find any component to match.

Constraints are even mandatory if you're not using string typed parameters; otherwise, the router does not cast the parameter to the proper type. You specify the constraint by appending it using a colon, for example, @page "/counter/{currentCount:int}". You can also make the parameter optional by appending a question mark after the constraint as shown in Listing 9-17.

A list of other routing constraints can be found in Table 9-1. Each of these maps to the corresponding .NET type.

Table 9-1. *Routing Constraints*

Route Constraints
bool
datetime
decimal
double
float
guid
int
long

If you are building your components as pure C# components, apply the `RouteAttribute` to your class with the route template as an argument. This is what the `@page` directive gets compiled into.

Redirecting to Other Pages

How do you navigate to another component using routing? You have three choices: use a standard anchor element, use the NavLink component, and use code. Let's start with the normal anchor tag.

Using an anchor (the `<a/>` HTML element) is effortless if you use a relative `href`. For example, add Listing 9-18 below the button of Listing 9-17.

Listing 9-18. Navigation Using an Anchor Tag

```
<a class="btn btn-primary" href="/">Home</a>
```

This link has been styled as a button using Bootstrap 4. Run your application and navigate to the Counter component. Click the Home button to navigate to the Index component whose route template matches "/".

The NavLink component uses an underlying anchor, so its usage is similar. The only difference is that a NavLink component applies the `active` class when it matches the route. Generally, you only use a NavLink in the NavMenu component, but you are free to use it instead of anchors.

Navigating in code is also possible, but you will need an instance of the *NavigationManager* class through dependency injection. This instance allows you to examine the page's URI and has a helpful `NavigateTo` method. This method takes a string that will become the browser's new URI.

Let's try an example. Modify the Counter component to look like Listing 9-19.

Listing 9-19. Using the NavigationManager

```
@page "/counter"
@page "/counter/{currentCount:int?}"
@layout MainLayoutRight

@inject NavigationManager navigationManager

<h1>Counter</h1>

<p>Current count: @CurrentCount</p>

<button class="btn btn-primary" @onclick="IncrementCount">Click me</button>

<a class="btn btn-primary" href="/">Home</a>

<button class="btn btn-primary" @onclick="StartFrom50">Start from 50</button>

@code {
  [Parameter]
  public int CurrentCount { get; set; }

  private void IncrementCount()
  {
    CurrentCount++;
  }

  private void StartFrom50()
  {
    navigationManager.NavigateTo("/counter/50");
  }
}
```

You tell dependency injection with the @inject razor directive to give you an instance of the NavigationManager and put it in the navigationManager field. The NavigationManager is one of the types that Blazor provides out of the box through dependency injection. Then you add a button that calls the StartFrom50 method when clicked. This method uses the NavigationManager to navigate to another URI by calling the NavigateTo method. Run your application and click the "Start from 50" button. You should navigate to /counter/50.

Understanding the Base Tag

Please don't use absolute URIs when navigating. Why? Because when you deploy your application on the Internet, the base URI will change. Instead, Blazor uses the <base/> HTML element and all relative URIs will be combined with this <base/> tag. Where is the <base/> tag? With Blazor WebAssembly, open the wwwroot folder of your Blazor project and open index.html, shown in Listing 9-20.

Listing 9-20. index.html

```
<!DOCTYPE html>
<html>

<head>
    <meta charset="utf-8" />
    <meta name="viewport" content="width=device-width, initial-scale=1.0,
    maximum-scale=1.0, user-scalable=no" />
    <title>SPA</title>
    <base href="/" />
    <link href="css/bootstrap/bootstrap.min.css" rel="stylesheet" />
    <link href="css/app.css" rel="stylesheet" />
    <link href="SPA.Client.styles.css" rel="stylesheet" />
</head>

<body>
    <div id="app">Loading...</div>

    <div id="blazor-error-ui">
        An unhandled error has occurred.
        <a href="" class="reload">Reload</a>
```

```
        <a class="dismiss">✕</a>
    </div>
    <script src="_framework/blazor.webassembly.js"></script>
</body>

</html>
```

If you are using Blazor Server, the base tag can be found in _Host.cshtml.

When you deploy in production, all you need to do is to update the base tag. For example, you might deploy your application to `https://online.u2u.be/selfassessment`. In this case, you would update the base element to `<base href="/selfassessment" />`. So why do you need to do this? If you deploy to `https://online.u2u.be/selfassement`, the Counter component's URI becomes `https://online.u2u.be/selfassessment/counter`. Routing will ignore the base URI so it will match the counter as expected. You only need to specify the base URI once, as shown in Listing 9-20.

You can also access the base URI (with a trailing slash) using the `NavigationManager BaseUri` property. This can be useful for passing absolute URIs, for example, to certain JavaScript libraries. We will discuss JavaScript interoperability in the next chapter.

Lazy Loading with Routing

Some components in your Blazor application might not be used frequently. But even then, Blazor will need to load these components into the browser before running your application. For large applications, this can mean that your application will take even longer to load. However, with Blazor, we can load components the moment we need them. This is called lazy loading.

Lazy Loading Component Libraries

Lazy loading works by moving your infrequently used components into one or more component libraries, and then download right before you need them. We discussed building component libraries in Chapters 3 and 4. But let us start with a project, move these components and their dependencies into libraries, and then lazy load them. In the book's download, you should find a solution called lazy loading. Open it. This project should look familiar. You should be able to build and run this application. Now, for the sake of the example, assume that the Counter and FetchData components are components we want to lazy load.

Let us start with the Counter component. Create a Razor Class Library project called LazyLoading.Library. Move the Counter component to this library. Now add a project reference to this library in the client project, and add a @using directive to the _Imports. razor (the one in the client project).

Build and run your solution. Click the Counter link. Hmm. No Counter has been found. Why?

When the Router component gets initialized, it searches the assembly from its AppAssembly parameter for components that have a @page razor directive. Before we moved the Counter component to the razor library, the Counter was part of this assembly. But now we have moved it to the razor library. So we need to tell the Router component to search this library for routable components. We can easily do this by setting the router's AdditionalAssemblies parameter. Open App.razor and update it as in Listing 9-21. Here, we set the AdditionalAssemblies parameter to a List<Assembly>, which contains the Assembly for the Counter component. Now the application should show the Counter component.

Listing 9-21. Using AdditionalAssemblies

```
@using System.Reflection

<Router AppAssembly="@typeof(Program).Assembly"
        AdditionalAssemblies="@additionalAssemblies">
    <Found Context="routeData">
        <RouteView RouteData="@routeData"
                   DefaultLayout="@typeof(MainLayout)" />
    </Found>
    <NotFound>
        <LayoutView Layout="@typeof(MainLayout)">
            <p>Sorry, there's nothing at this address.</p>
        </LayoutView>
    </NotFound>
</Router>
```

```
@code {
    private List<Assembly> additionalAssemblies =
      new List<Assembly>
      {
        typeof(Counter).Assembly
      };
}
```

We moved the Counter component to a razor library, but we still load the Counter component when the application is loaded. Time to enable lazy loading for the razor library.

First, we will tell the runtime not to load the assembly automatically, and then we will load it when needed.

Marking an Assembly for Lazy Loading

Open the client project file using the editor and add the `BlazorWebAssemblyLazyLoad` element as in Listing 9-22. This tells the runtime not to load the `LazyLoading.Library.dll` automatically.

Listing 9-22. Turning on Lazy Loading

```
<Project Sdk="Microsoft.NET.Sdk.BlazorWebAssembly">

  <PropertyGroup>
    <TargetFramework>net6.0</TargetFramework>
  </PropertyGroup>
  <ItemGroup>
    ...
  </ItemGroup>
  <ItemGroup>
    <BlazorWebAssemblyLazyLoad
      Include="LazyLoading.Library.dll" />
  </ItemGroup>
</Project>
```

If you would try to run the application, you will get a runtime error:

```
Could not load file or assembly 'LazyLoading.Library, Version=1.0.0.0,
Culture=neutral, PublicKeyToken=null' or one of its dependencies.
```

Dynamically Loading an Assembly

Now we need to load this assembly when needed. When do we load this assembly? When we navigate to a component that needs components from this assembly. How do we know we are navigating? The Router component has an event for this called OnNavigateAsync, and we will use it to detect when we navigate to a component that uses a lazy loaded component. Then we will download the assembly using the LazyAssemblyLoader so it is ready for use.

Update App.razor as in Listing 9-23. First, we get an instance of the LazyAssemblyLoader using dependency injection. Then we implement the OnNavigateAsync event using the OnNavigate method. This method receives a NavigationContext instance, and we check the Path if we are navigating to the Counter component. If so, we load the assembly for the Counter component (LazyLoading.Library.dll), and we add it to the additionalAssemblies collection, so the Router component can scan it for route templates.

Listing 9-23. Loading an Assembly when Needed

```
@using System.Reflection
@using Microsoft.AspNetCore.Components.WebAssembly.Services

@inject LazyAssemblyLoader assemblyLoader

<Router AppAssembly="@typeof(Program).Assembly"
        AdditionalAssemblies="@additionalAssemblies"
        OnNavigateAsync="OnNavigate">
    <Found Context="routeData">
        <RouteView RouteData="@routeData" DefaultLayout="@typeof
        (MainLayout)" />
    </Found>
    <NotFound>
        <LayoutView Layout="@typeof(MainLayout)">
```

```
        <p>Sorry, there's nothing at this address.</p>
      </LayoutView>
    </NotFound>
  </Router>

@code {
    private List<Assembly> additionalAssemblies =
      new List<Assembly>
      {
      };

    private async Task OnNavigate(NavigationContext context)
    {
      if( context.Path == "counter")
      {
        var assembliesToLoad = new List<string>
        {
          "LazyLoading.Library.dll"
        };
        var assemblies = await assemblyLoader.LoadAssembliesAsync
        (assembliesToLoad);
        additionalAssemblies.AddRange(assemblies);
      }
    }
}
```

Before we can run, we need to configure dependency injection

```
builder.Services.AddScoped<LazyAssemblyLoader>();
```

Build and run the application. It should start, and when we click Counter, the browser will download it and then render it.

What if we are on a slow network? Maybe we want to show some loading UI while the assembly downloads? The router has a `Navigating RenderFragment` which it shows while loading. So update the App.razor file again as in Listing 9-24, adding the Navigating UI.

Listing 9-24. Showing a Navigating UI

```
<Router AppAssembly="@typeof(Program).Assembly"
        AdditionalAssemblies="@additionalAssemblies"
        OnNavigateAsync="OnNavigate">
  <Found Context="routeData">
    <RouteView RouteData="@routeData" DefaultLayout="@typeof
    (MainLayout)" />
  </Found>
  <NotFound>
    <LayoutView Layout="@typeof(MainLayout)">
      <p>Sorry, there's nothing at this address.</p>
    </LayoutView>
  </NotFound>
  <Navigating>
    Loading additional components...
  </Navigating>
</Router>
```

Lazy Loading and Dependencies

Let us now try to lazy load the FetchData component. This component uses an IWeatherService instance, implemented by the WeatherService class (the one in the Blazor project). We will move both into the component library.

Start moving the FetchData component and WeatherService class to the component library. Add a project reference to the library project for the shared project since the WeatherService uses the Shared project's IWeatherService.

Your library project should compile now.

Update the OnNavigate method from App.razor to check for the FetchData URI as in Listing 9-25.

Listing 9-25. The OnNavigate Method for FetchData

```
private async Task OnNavigate(NavigationContext context)
{
  if (context.Path == "counter" || context.Path == "fetchdata")
  {
```

```
    var assembliesToLoad = new List<string>
    {
        "LazyLoading.Library.dll"
      };
    var assemblies = await assemblyLoader
      .LoadAssembliesAsync(assembliesToLoad);
    additionalAssemblies.AddRange(assemblies);
  }
}
```

After fixing a couple of namespaces in C#, the project should build. But running will fail. Why? In Program.cs, you are adding the WeatherService class from the lazy loaded library, but that has not been loaded (because you told the runtime not to load it).

Maybe we could postpone registering the WeatherService? Sorry, that will not work. After initialization, dependency injection becomes immutable so you cannot add dependencies later. Of course, we could keep the WeatherService in the Blazor client project, but let us pretend it is worth our while to lazy load it. Time to introduce a little layer. We will use a factory method to create the dependency, and we will use dependency injection to inject the factory method. This will require a couple of changes.

Note   A *factory* is a class that has a method that will create an instance of some class, hiding the creation process. For example, a factory could create an instance, where the class of the instance depends on some business rule. Of course, all instances returned should have some common base class or interface. Actually, IServiceProvider used by dependency injection is also a factory, but we cannot use it here because it does not know about the existence of the WeatherService. Use your favorite search engine and search "Factory Pattern in C#" to learn more about this.

Both the component library and Blazor client application will need to share the factory interface, so add the IWeatherServiceFactory to the Shared project as in Listing 9-26.

Listing 9-26. The IWeatherServiceFactory Interface

```
namespace LazyLoading.Shared
{
  public interface IWeatherServiceFactory
  {
    IWeatherService Create();
  }
}
```

Update the FetchData component to use the IWeatherService factory to create the IWeatherService instance as in Listing 9-27.

Listing 9-27. Update the FetchData Component

```
@page "/fetchdata"
@using LazyLoading.Shared
@inject IWeatherServiceFactory weatherServiceFactory

...

@code {
  private IEnumerable<WeatherForecast> forecasts;

  protected override async Task OnInitializedAsync()
  {
    IWeatherService weatherService = weatherServiceFactory.Create();
    forecasts = await weatherService.GetForecasts();
  }
}
```

Finally, we will implement the IWeatherServiceFactory interface in the client project as in Listing 9-28 to create the actual WeatherService. Because we only need WeatherService implementation when we use the factory, this will work because the library containing the WeatherService will be loaded through lazy loading. However, the WeatherService has its own dependencies, so we will request these in the factory and pass them to the actual service. The factory is a tiny class, and when the actual service with its dependencies is large, this technique becomes interesting.

Listing 9-28. Implementing the IWeatherServiceFactory

```
using LazyLoading.Library.Services;
using LazyLoading.Shared;
using System.Net.Http;

namespace LazyLoading.Client
{
  public class WeatherServiceFactory : IWeatherServiceFactory
  {
    private readonly HttpClient httpClient;

    public WeatherServiceFactory(HttpClient httpClient)
    {
      this.httpClient = httpClient;
    }

    public IWeatherService Create() => new WeatherService(httpClient);
  }
}
```

Adding Another Page to PizzaPlace

Let us add a detail page to the PizzaPlace application. This will allow the customer to check the ingredients and nutritional information about pizzas.

When you navigate between different Blazor components with routing, you will probably encounter the need to send information from one component to another. One way to accomplish this is by setting a parameter in the destination component by passing it in the URI. For example, you could navigate to /pizzadetail/5 to tell the destination component to display information about the pizza with id 5. The destination component can then use a service to load the information about pizza #5 and then display this information. But in Blazor, there are other ways to pass information from one component to another. If both components share a common parent component, we can use data binding. Otherwise, we can use a *State* class (most developers call this State, but this is just a convention and you can call it anything you want; State just makes sense) and then use dependency injection to give every component the same instance of this class. This single State class contains the information that components need. We have seen this before in Chapter 5: this is known as the *singleton pattern*. Our PizzaPlace application is already using a State class, so it should not be too much work to use this pattern.

Start by opening the PizzaPlace solution. Open the Index component from the Pages folder (in the PizzaPlace.Client project) and look for the private State field. Remove this field (I've made it a comment) and replace it with an @inject directive as in Listing 9-29.

Listing 9-29. Using Dependency Injection to Get the State Singleton Instance

```
@page "/"
@inject IMenuService MenuService
@inject IOrderService orderService
@inject State State

...

@code {
  // private State State { get; } = new State();

  ...
}
```

Now configure dependency injection in Program.cs to inject the State instance as a singleton, as in Listing 9-30.

Listing 9-30. Configuring Dependency Injection for the State Singleton

```
using Microsoft.AspNetCore.Components.WebAssembly.Hosting;
using Microsoft.Extensions.DependencyInjection;
using PizzaPlace.Client.Services;
using PizzaPlace.Shared;
using System;
using System.Net.Http;
using System.Threading.Tasks;

namespace PizzaPlace.Client
{
  public class Program
  {
```

```
public static async Task Main(string[] args)
{
  var builder = WebAssemblyHostBuilder.CreateDefault(args);
  builder.RootComponents.Add<App>("#app");

  builder.Services.AddScoped(sp => new HttpClient
  {
    BaseAddress = new Uri(builder.HostEnvironment
                                 .BaseAddress)
  });

  builder.Services.AddTransient<IMenuService,
                                MenuService>();
  builder.Services.AddTransient<IOrderService,
                                 OrderService>();
  builder.Services.AddSingleton<State>();

  await builder.Build().RunAsync();
  }
 }
}
```

Run the application. Everything should still work! What you've done is to use the *singleton pattern* to inject the State singleton into the Index component. Let's add another component that will use the same State instance.

You want to display more information about a pizza using a new component, but before you do this, you need to update the State class. Add a new property called CurrentPizza to the State class, as shown in Listing 9-31.

Listing 9-31. Adding a CurrentPizza Property to the State Class

```
using System.Linq;

namespace PizzaPlace.Shared
{
  public class State
  {
    public Menu Menu { get; } = new Menu();
```

```
    public ShoppingBasket Basket { get; } = new ShoppingBasket();

    public UI UI { get; set; } = new UI();

    public Pizza? CurrentPizza { get; set; }

    public decimal TotalPrice
        => Basket.Orders.Sum(id => Menu.GetPizza(id)!.Price);
    }
}
```

Now when someone clicks a pizza on the menu, it will display the pizza's information. Update the PizzaItem component by wrapping the pizza name in an anchor, like in Listing 9-32. In the PizzaItem class from Listing 9-33, we add a new ShowPizzaInformation parameter, and if this is non-null, we wrap it in an anchor which invokes the ShowPizzaInformation action.

Listing 9-32. Adding an Anchor to Display the Pizza's Information

```
<div class="row">
  <div class="col">
    @if (ShowPizzaInformation is not null)
    {
      <a href=""
         @onclick="@(() => ShowPizzaInformation?.Invoke(Pizza))">
        @Pizza.Name
      </a>
    }
    else
    {
      @Pizza.Name
    }
  </div>
  <div class="col text-right">
    @($"{Pizza.Price:0.00}")
  </div>
  <div class="col"></div>
  <div class="col">
```

```
  <img src="@SpicinessImage(Pizza.Spiciness)"
       alt="@Pizza.Spiciness" />
</div>
<div class="col">
  <button class="@ButtonClass"
          @onclick="@(() => Selected.InvokeAsync(Pizza))">
    @ButtonTitle
  </button>
</div>
</div>
```

Listing 9-33. Add the ShowPizzaInformation Parameter

```
using Microsoft.AspNetCore.Components;
using PizzaPlace.Shared;
using System;

namespace PizzaPlace.Client.Pages
{
  public partial class PizzaItem
  {
    [Parameter]
    public Pizza Pizza { get; set; } = default!;

    [Parameter]
    public string ButtonTitle { get; set; } = default!;

    [Parameter]
    public string ButtonClass { get; set; } = default!;

    [Parameter]
    public EventCallback<Pizza> Selected { get; set; }

    [Parameter]
    public Action<Pizza>? ShowPizzaInformation { get; set; }

    private string SpicinessImage(Spiciness spiciness)
        => $"images/{spiciness.ToString().ToLower()}.png";
  }
}
```

Update the PizzaList component to set the PizzaItem component's ShowPizzaInformation parameter as in Listings 9-34 and 9-35.

When someone clicks this link, it should set the State instance's CurrentPizza property. But you don't have access to the State object. One way to solve this would be by injecting the State instance in the PizzaItem component. But you don't want to overburden this component, so you add a ShowPizzaInformation callback delegate to tell the containing PizzaList component that you want to display more information about the pizza. Clicking the pizza name link simply invokes this callback without knowing what should happen.

You are applying a pattern here known as *"Dumb and Smart Components."* A dumb component is a component that knows nothing about the global picture of the application. Because it doesn't know anything about the rest of the application, a dumb component is easier to reuse. A smart component knows about the other parts of the application (such as which service to use to talk to the database) and will use dumb components to display its information. In our example, the PizzaList and PizzaItem are dumb components because they receive all their data through data binding, while the Index component is a smart component which talks to services.

Listing 9-34. Adding a PizzaInformation Callback to the PizzaList Component

```
<ItemList Items="@Items">
  <Loading>
    <div class="spinner-border text-danger" role="status">
      <span class="visually-hidden">Loading...</span>
    </div>
  </Loading>
  <Header>
    <h1>@Title</h1>
  </Header>
  <RowTemplate Context="pizza">
    <PizzaItem Pizza="@pizza"
               ButtonClass="@ButtonClass"
               ButtonTitle="@ButtonTitle"
               Selected="@Selected"
               ShowPizzaInformation="@ShowPizzaInformation"/>
  </RowTemplate>
</ItemList>
```

Listing 9-35. Add the ShowPizzaInformation Callback Parameter

```
using Microsoft.AspNetCore.Components;
using PizzaPlace.Shared;
using System;
using System.Collections.Generic;

namespace PizzaPlace.Client.Pages
{
  public partial class PizzaList
  {
    [Parameter]
    public string Title { get; set; } = default!;

    [Parameter]
    public IEnumerable<Pizza> Items { get; set; } = default!;

    [Parameter]
    public string ButtonClass { get; set; } = default!;

    [Parameter]
    public string ButtonTitle { get; set; } = default!;

    [Parameter]
    public EventCallback<Pizza> Selected { get; set; }

    [Parameter]
    public Action<Pizza>? ShowPizzaInformation { get; set; }
  }
}
```

You added a ShowPizzaInformation callback to the PizzaList component, and you simply pass it to the PizzaItem component. The Index component will set this callback, and the PizzaList will pass it to the PizzaItem component.

Update the Index component to set the State instance's CurrentPizza and navigate to the PizzaInfo component, as shown in Listing 9-36. The Index component tells the PizzaList component to call the ShowPizzaInformation method when someone clicks the information link from the PizzaItem component. The ShowPizzaInformation

method then sets the State's CurrentPizza property (which we need in the PizzaInfo
component) and navigates using the NavigationManager's NavigateTo method to
the /PizzaInfo route.

   If you call NavigateTo as part of a callback, Blazor returns to the original route. That
is why I use a background Task so Blazor will navigate after the callback.

Listing 9-36. The Index Component Navigates to the PizzaInfo Component

```
@page "/"
@inject IMenuService MenuService
@inject IOrderService orderService
@inject State State
@inject NavigationManager NavigationManager

@if (State.Menu.Pizzas.Any())
{
  <!-- Menu -->

  <PizzaList Title="Our Selection of Pizzas"
             Items="@State.Menu.Pizzas"
             ButtonTitle="Order"
             ButtonClass="btn btn-success pl-4 pr-4"
             Selected="@AddToBasket"
             ShowPizzaInformation="@ShowPizzaInformation"/>

  <!-- End menu -->
  <!-- Shopping Basket -->

  ...

@code {
  ...

  private void ShowPizzaInformation(Pizza selected)
  {
    this.State.CurrentPizza = selected;
    Task.Run(() => this.NavigationManager.NavigateTo("/pizzainfo"));
  }
}
```

Right-click the Pages folder and add a new razor component called PizzaInfo, as shown in Listings 9-37 and 9-38 (to save you some time and to keep things simple, you can copy most of the PizzaItem component). The PizzaInfo component shows information about the State's CurrentPizza. This works because you share the same State instance between these components. The Index component will set the CurrentPizza property in State, which is then displayed by the PizzaInfo component. Because State's CurrentPizza property can be null, I also added a helper property to the PizzaInfo component that always returns a non-nullable CurrentPizza (using the null-forgiving operator) to avoid compiler warnings.

Listing 9-37. Adding a PizzaInfo Component

```
@page "/PizzaInfo"

<h2>Pizza @CurrentPizza.Name Details</h2>

<div class="row">
  <div class="col">
    @CurrentPizza.Name
  </div>
  <div class="col">
    @CurrentPizza.Price
  </div>
  <div class="col">
    <img src="@SpicinessImage(CurrentPizza.Spiciness)"
         alt="@CurrentPizza.Spiciness" />
  </div>
</div>
<div class="row">
  <div class="col">
    <a class="btn btn-primary" href="/">Back to Menu</a>
  </div>
</div>
```

Listing 9-38. The PizzaInfo Class

```
using Microsoft.AspNetCore.Components;
using PizzaPlace.Shared;

namespace PizzaPlace.Client.Pages
{
  public partial class PizzaInfo
  {
    [Inject]
    public State State { get; set; } = default!;

    public Pizza CurrentPizza
      => State.CurrentPizza!;

    private string SpicinessImage(Spiciness spiciness)
    => $"images/{spiciness.ToString().ToLower()}.png";
  }
}
```

At the bottom of the markup, you add an anchor (and made it look like a button using bootstrap styling) to return to the menu. It's an example of changing the route with anchors. Of course, in a real-life application, you would show the ingredients of the pizza, a nice picture, and nutritional information. I leave this as an exercise for you.

Summary

In this chapter, we looked at Single-Page Applications, layouts, routing, and lazy loading components. Single-Page Applications avoid navigating to another URLs because the browser will wipe its memory before loading the next page. By staying on the same page, we can keep data in memory, and to update the UI, we use code to replace part of the page. Layouts allow you to avoid replicating markup in your application and help keep your applications look consistent. We also saw that layouts can be nested. Routing is an important part of building Single-Page Applications and takes care of picking the component to show based on the browser's URI. You define route templates using the @page syntax where you use route parameters and constraints. Navigation in your Single-Page Application can be done using anchor tags and from code using the

`NavigationManager` class. We also saw that you can lazy load components by moving them into a component library and then dynamically load the library just when you need it. Finally, we modified the PizzaPlace application to show how to share information between different routes in a Blazor application.

CHAPTER 10

JavaScript Interoperability

Sometimes there is just no escape from using *JavaScript*. For example, Blazor itself uses JavaScript to update the browser's *DOM* from your Blazor components. In this chapter, you will look at interoperability with JavaScript and, as an example, you will build a Blazor component library to display a map using a popular open source JavaScript library. This chapter does require you to have some basic JavaScript knowledge.

Calling JavaScript from C#

Browsers have a lot of capabilities you might want to use in your Blazor website. For example, you might want to use the Browser's *local storage* to keep track of some data. Thanks to Blazor's JavaScript interoperability, this is easy.

Providing a Glue Function

To call JavaScript functionality, you start by building a glue function in JavaScript. I like to call these functions glue functions (my own naming convention) because they become the glue between .NET and JavaScript.

Glue functions are regular JavaScript functions. A JavaScript glue function can take any number of arguments, on the condition that they are *JSON serializable* (meaning that you can only use types that are convertible to JSON, including classes whose properties are JSON serializable). This is required because the arguments and return type are sent as JSON between .NET and JavaScript runtimes.

You then add this function to the JavaScript *global scope* object, which in the browser is the *window* object. You will look at an example a little later, so keep reading. You can then call this JavaScript glue function from your Blazor component.

P. Himschoot, *Microsoft Blazor*, https://doi.org/10.1007/978-1-4842-7845-1_10

Using IJSRuntime to Call the Glue Function

Back to .NET land. To invoke your JavaScript glue function from C#, you use the .NET *IJSRuntime* instance provided through dependency injection. This instance has the InvokeAsync<T> generic method, which takes the name of the glue function and its arguments and returns a value of type T, which is the .NET return type of the glue function. If your JavaScript method returns nothing, there is also the InvokeVoidAsync method. If this sounds confusing, you will look at an example right away.

The InvokeAsync method is asynchronous to support all asynchronous scenarios, and this is the recommended way of calling JavaScript. If you need to call the glue function synchronously, you can downcast the IJSRuntime instance to IJSInProcessRuntime and call its synchronous Invoke<T> method. This method takes the same arguments as InvokeAsync<T> with the same constraints.

Using synchronous calls for JavaScript interop is not recommended! Server-side Blazor requires the use of asynchronous calls because the calls will be serialized over SignalR to the client.

Storing Data in the Browser with Interop

It's time to look at an example and you will start with the JavaScript glue function. Open the provided JSInterop solution (or you can create a new Blazor WebAssembly project from scratch). Open the wwwroot folder from the JSInterop project and add a new subfolder called scripts. Add a new JavaScript file to the scripts folder called interop. js and add the glue functions from Listing 10-1. This will add the blazorLocalStorage object to the global window object, containing three glue functions. These glue functions allow you to access the localStorage object from the browser, which allows you to store data on the client's computer so you can access it later, even after the user has restarted the browser or computer.

Listing 10-1. The blazorLocalStorage Glue Functions

```
window.blazorLocalStorage = {
  get: key => key in localStorage ? JSON.parse(localStorage[key]) : null,
  set: (key, value) => { localStorage[key] = JSON.stringify(value); },
  delete: key => { delete localStorage[key]; },
};
```

Your Blazor website needs to include this script, so open the index.html file from the wwwroot folder and add a script reference after the Blazor script, as shown in Listing 10-2.

Visual Studio Tip   You can drag and drop the interop.js file from Solution Explorer into the index.html file, and Visual Studio will do the rest.

Listing 10-2. Including the Script Reference in Your HTML Page

```html
<!DOCTYPE html>
<html>

<head>
  <meta charset="utf-8" />
  <meta name="viewport" content="width=device-width, initial-scale=1.0,
  maximum-scale=1.0, user-scalable=no" />
  <title>JSInterop</title>
  <base href="/" />
  <link href="css/bootstrap/bootstrap.min.css" rel="stylesheet" />
  <link href="css/app.css" rel="stylesheet" />
  <link href="JSInterop.styles.css" rel="stylesheet" />
</head>

<body>
  <div id="app">Loading...</div>

  <div id="blazor-error-ui">
    An unhandled error has occurred.
    <a href="" class="reload">Reload</a>
    <a class="dismiss">✖</a>
  </div>
  <script src="_framework/blazor.webassembly.js"></script>
  <script src="scripts/interop.js"></script>
</body>

</html>
```

Now let's look at how to call these set/get/delete glue functions. Open the Counter. razor Blazor component and modify it to look like Listing 10-3. The Counter component now will use local storage to remember the last value of the counter. Even restarting your browser will not lose the value of the counter because local storage is permanent. To do this, you use a CurrentCount property, which invokes your glue functions in the property setter to store the last value. The Counter component overrides the OnInitializedAsync method to retrieve the last stored value from local storage using the window.blazorLocalStorage.get glue function. It is possible that there is no value yet, and that is why we need to catch the exception that gets thrown in this case. I tried using a nullable int, but the IJSRuntime throws an error when converting a JavaScript null to a value type.

Listing 10-3. Invoking the Glue Functions from a Blazor Component

```
@page "/counter"
@inject IJSRuntime js

<h1>Counter</h1>

<p>Current count: @CurrentCount</p>

<button class="btn btn-primary" @onclick="IncrementCount">Click me</button>

@code {
  private int currentCount = 0;

  public int CurrentCount
  {
    get => currentCount;
    set
    {
      if (currentCount != value)
      {
        currentCount = value;
        js.InvokeVoidAsync("blazorLocalStorage.set",
          nameof(CurrentCount), currentCount);
      }
    }
  }
```

```
private void IncrementCount()
{
  CurrentCount++;
}

protected override async Task OnInitializedAsync()
{
  try
  {
    int c = await js.InvokeAsync<int>(
      "blazorLocalStorage.get", nameof(CurrentCount));
    currentCount = c;
  }
  catch { }
}
}
```

Run the solution and modify the Counter's value. Now when you refresh your browser, you will see the last value of Counter. The Counter is now persisted between sessions! You can exit your browser and open it again, and you will see the Counter again with the last value.

Passing a Reference to JavaScript

Sometimes your JavaScript needs to access one of your HTML elements. You can do this by storing the element in an `ElementReference` and then pass this `ElementReference` to the glue function.

Note   Never use JavaScript interop to modify the DOM because this will interfere with the Blazor rendering process! If you need to modify the browser's DOM, use a Blazor component.

You should use this `ElementReference` as an opaque handle, meaning you can only pass it to a JavaScript glue function, which will receive it as a JavaScript reference to the element. You cannot even pass the ElementReference to another component. This is by design, because each component gets rendered independently, and this might make the ElementReference point to a DOM element that is no longer there.

Let's look at an example by setting the focus on an input element using interop. To be honest, there is a built-in method in Blazor to do this, but I want to use this as a simple example. Keep on reading; I will show you how to focus an input element without interop.

Start by adding a property of type ElementReference to the @code area in the Counter component as in Listing 10-4.

Listing 10-4. Adding an ElementReference Property

```
private ElementReference? inputElement;
```

Then add an input element with a @ref attribute to set the inputElement field as in Listing 10-5. We have seen this @ref syntax before; you can use it to get a reference to a Blazor component and also to an HTML element.

Listing 10-5. Setting the inputElement

```
<div>
  <input @ref="inputElement" @bind="@CurrentCount" />
</div>
```

Now add another JavaScript file focus.js with the glue function from Listing 10-6. Don't forget to add the script reference to index.html.

Listing 10-6. Adding the blazorFocus.set Glue Function

```
window.blazorFocus = {
  set: (element) => { element.focus(); }
}
```

Now comes the "tricky" part. Blazor will create your component and then call the life cycle methods, such as OnInitializedAsync. If you invoke the blazorFocus.set glue function in OnInitializedAsync, the DOM has not been updated with the input element so this will result in a runtime error because the glue function will receive a null reference. You need to wait for the DOM to be updated, which means that you should only pass the ElementReference to your glue function in the OnAfterRender/OnAfter RenderAsync method!

Override the `OnAfterRenderAsync` method as in Listing 10-7. Since rendering is complete, we can expect the `inputElement` to be set, and we call the `blazorFocus.set` glue function. But just to be on the safe side, I check if `inputElement` is not null.

Listing 10-7. Passing the ElementReference in OnAfterRenderAsync

```
protected override async Task OnAfterRenderAsync(bool firstRender)
{
  if (inputElement is not null)
  {
    await js.InvokeVoidAsync("blazorFocus.set", inputElement);
  }
}
```

Run your solution, and you should see that the input element receives focus automatically, as in Figure 10-1.

Counter

Current count: 1

1|

Click me

Figure 10-1. *The Counter Input Element Receives Focus Automatically*

Calling .NET Methods from JavaScript

You can also call .NET methods from JavaScript. For example, your JavaScript might want to tell your component that something interesting has happened, like the user clicking something in the browser. Or your JavaScript might want to ask the Blazor component about some data it needs. You can call a .NET method, but with a couple of conditions. First, your .NET method's arguments and return value need to be *JSON serializable*, the method must be public, and you need to add the `JSInvokable` attribute to the method. The method can be a static or instance method.

To invoke a static method, you use the JavaScript `DotNet.invokeMethodAsync` or `DotNet.invokeMethod` function, passing the name of the assembly, the name of the method, and its arguments. To call an instance method, you pass the instance wrapped as a `DotNetObjectRef` to a JavaScript glue function, which can then invoke the .NET method using the `DotNetObjectRef`'s `invokeMethodAsync` or `invokeMethod` function, passing the name of the .NET method and its arguments. If you want your component to work in Blazor Server, you need to use the asynchronous functions.

Adding a Glue Function Taking a .NET Instance

Let's continue with the previous example. When you make a change to local storage, the storage triggers a JavaScript storage event, passing the old and new value (and more). This allows you to register for changes in other browser tabs or windows and use it to update the page with the latest data in localStorage.

Open interop.js from the previous example and add a watch function, as in Listing 10-8. The `watch` function takes a reference to a `DotNetObjectRef` instance and invokes the `UpdateCounter` method on this instance when storage changes. You can detect changes in storage by registering for the JavaScript `storage` event.

Listing 10-8. The watch Function Allows You to Register for Local Storage Changes

```
window.blazorLocalStorage = {
  get: key => key in localStorage ? JSON.parse(localStorage[key]) : null,
  set: (key, value) => { localStorage[key] = JSON.stringify(value); },
  delete: key => { delete localStorage[key]; },
  watch: async (instance) => {
    window.addEventListener('storage', (e) => {
      instance.invokeMethodAsync('UpdateCounter');
    });
  }
};
```

When anyone or anything changes the local storage for this web page, the browser will trigger the `storage` event, and our JavaScript interop will invoke the `UpdateCounter` method (which we will implement next) in our C# Blazor component.

Time to add the UpdateCounter method. Open Counter.razor and add the UpdateCounter method to the @code area, as shown in Listing 10-9.

Listing 10-9. The UpdateCounter Method

```
[JSInvokable]
public async Task UpdateCounter()
{
  int c = await js.InvokeAsync<int>("blazorLocalStorage.get",
nameof(CurrentCount));
  currentCount = c;
  this.StateHasChanged();
}
```

This method triggers the UI to update with the latest value of CurrentCounter. Please note that this method follows the .NET *async pattern* returning a Task instance because the JavaScript interop will call this asynchronously using the invokeMethodAsync function from Listing 10-8. To complete the example, add the OnAfterRenderAsync life cycle method shown in Listing 10-10. The OnAfterRenderAsync method wraps the Counter component's this reference in a DotNetObjectRef and passes it to the blazorLocalStorage.watch glue function.

Listing 10-10. The OnAfterRenderAsync Method

```
protected override async Task OnAfterRenderAsync(
  bool firstRender)
{
  if (inputElement is not null)
  {
    await js.InvokeVoidAsync("blazorFocus.set", inputElement);
  }
  var objRef = DotNetObjectReference.Create(this);
  await js.InvokeVoidAsync("blazorLocalStorage.watch", objRef);
}
```

To see this in action, open two browser tabs side by side on your website. When you change the value in one tab, you should see the other tab update to the same value automatically! You can use this to communicate between two tabs in the same browser like we do here.

Using Services for Interop

The previous example is not the way I would recommend doing interop with JavaScript because our components are tightly coupled to the IJSRuntime. There is a better way, and that is encapsulating the IJSRuntime code in a *service*. This will hide all the dirty details of interacting with JavaScript and allow for easier maintenance. In future generations of Blazor, some of this functionality might just be included, and then we only need to update the service implementation. Services can also easily be replaced during unit testing.

Building the LocalStorage Service

Add a new Services folder to the client project. Add a new interface inside this folder, name it ILocalStorage, and add the three methods from Listing 10-11 to it.

Listing 10-11. Building the ILocalStorage Service Interface

```
using System.Threading.Tasks;

namespace JSInterop.Services
{
  public interface ILocalStorage
  {
    ValueTask<T> GetProperty<T>(string propName);
    ValueTask SetProperty<T>(string propName, T value);
    ValueTask WatchAsync<T>(T instance) where T : class;
  }
}
```

These methods correspond with the glue functions from interop.js.

Now add a new class to the same Services folder and name it LocalStorage. This class should implement the ILocalStorage interface as in Listing 10-12. See how this class hides away all the details of performing JavaScript interop? And this is a simple case!

Listing 10-12. Implementing the LocalStorage Service Class

```
using Microsoft.AspNetCore.Components;
using Microsoft.JSInterop;
using System.Threading.Tasks;

namespace JSInterop.Services
{
  public class LocalStorage : ILocalStorage
  {
    private readonly IJSRuntime js;

    public LocalStorage(IJSRuntime js)
    {
      this.js = js;
    }

    public ValueTask<T> GetProperty<T>(string propName)
      => js.InvokeAsync<T>("blazorLocalStorage.get", propName);

    public ValueTask SetProperty<T>(string propName, T value)
      => js.InvokeVoidAsync("blazorLocalStorage.set", propName, value);

    public ValueTask WatchAsync<T>(T instance) where T : class
      => js.InvokeVoidAsync("blazorLocalStorage.watch",
                            DotNetObjectReference.Create(instance));
  }
}
```

Components will receive this service through *dependency injection*, so add it as a *singleton* as in Listing 10-13.

Listing 10-13. Registering the LocalStorage Service in Dependency Injection

```
using JSInterop.Services;
using Microsoft.AspNetCore.Components.WebAssembly.Hosting;
using Microsoft.Extensions.Configuration;
using Microsoft.Extensions.DependencyInjection;
using Microsoft.Extensions.Logging;
using System;
using System.Collections.Generic;
using System.Net.Http;
using System.Text;
using System.Threading.Tasks;

namespace JSInterop
{
  public class Program
  {
    public static async Task Main(string[] args)
    {
      var builder = WebAssemblyHostBuilder.CreateDefault(args);
      builder.RootComponents.Add<App>("#app");

      builder.Services
            .AddScoped(sp => new HttpClient
            {
              BaseAddress =
                new Uri(builder.HostEnvironment.BaseAddress)
            });
      builder.Services
            .AddSingleton<ILocalStorage, LocalStorage>();

      await builder.Build().RunAsync();
    }
  }
}
```

Go back to the Counter component and replace each call of IJSRuntime using blazorLocalStorage with the LocalStorage service. Start by adding the inject directive for the ILocalStorage service as in Listing 10-14.

Listing 10-14. Injecting the ILocalStorage Service into the Counter Component

```
@page "/counter"
@inject JSInterop.Services.ILocalStorage localStorage
```

Now onto the OnInitialiazedAsync method, where we retrieve the value from local storage. Replace the IJSRuntime calls with LocalStorage calls, as in Listing 10-15.

Listing 10-15. Implementing OnInitializedAsync

```
protected override async Task OnInitializedAsync()
{
  try
  {
    await localStorage.WatchAsync(this);

    int c = await localStorage
      .GetProperty<int>(nameof(CurrentCount));
    currentCount = c;
  }
  catch { }
}
```

Do the same for the UpdateCounter method from Listing 10-16.

Listing 10-16. The UpdateCounter Method Using the LocalStorage Service

```
[JSInvokable]
public async Task UpdateCounter()
{
  int c = await localStorage
    .GetProperty<int>(nameof(CurrentCount));
  currentCount = c;
  this.StateHasChanged();
}
```

Update the setter for the CurrentCount property as in Listing 10-17.

Listing 10-17. Remembering the Counter's Value

```
private int currentCount = 0;

public int CurrentCount
{
  get => currentCount;
  set
  {
    if (currentCount != value)
    {
      currentCount = value;
      localStorage
        .SetProperty<int>(nameof(CurrentCount), currentCount);
    }
  }
}
```

And finally, update the OnAfterRenderAsync method as in Listing 10-18. This method now also uses the built-in FocusAsync method to set the focus on the input. No need for JavaScript interop. This method does require you to add a @using statement because FocusAsync is an extension method:

```
@using Microsoft.AspNetCore.Components
```

Listing 10-18. The Counter's OnAfterRenderAsync Method

```
private ElementReference inputElement = default!;

protected override async Task OnAfterRenderAsync(bool firstRender)
{
  if (firstRender)
  {
    await inputElement.FocusAsync();
  }
}
```

This was not so hard, was it?

Dynamically Loading JavaScript with Modules

Our application has added some JavaScript to the application, and we have added this to the index.html page. This means that our JavaScript gets downloaded, even if we don't use it (because no one clicked the Counter link). This is not so good. Also, our JavaScript is adding yet another identifier to the JavaScript window object. Again not so good, because another component might accidentally pick the same name. Here, we will examine how we can download JavaScript dynamically using modules, so only when we need it.

Using JavaScript Modules

Early use of JavaScript was for small and straightforward functionality. Then JavaScript usage started to explode making programs complex and hard to maintain. Since then, there have been attempts at introducing "libraries" in JavaScript which could be included in your program. Today, JavaScript has a module mechanism that we can use in Blazor. You can compare a JavaScript module like a .NET library, which you can load dynamically. In the current JSInterop Blazor application we have been building, copy the interop.js file, name it localstorage.js, and modify it to look like Listing 10-19. Instead of adding the get, set, and watch functions to the global window object, we export these functions (similar to the C# public keyword being used to make classes available outside the library) using a JavaScript module. A module also acts like a namespace, making the get, set, and watch functions relative to the module and not contaminating the global JavaScript window object.

Listing 10-19. The localStorage JavaScript Module

```
let get = key => key in localStorage ? JSON.
parse(localStorage[key]) : null;
let set = (key, value) => { localStorage[key] = JSON.stringify(value); };
let watch = async (instance) => {
  window.addEventListener('storage', (e) => {
    instance.invokeMethodAsync('UpdateCounter');
  });
};

export { get, set, watch };
```

Loading the Module into a Blazor Service

Once the module is ready, we can import it into a Blazor component or a service using the IJSRuntime instance. It works just like any other JavaScript interop by using the InvokeAsync<T> method, but now we use the IJSObjectReference type for T, calling the import function which is provided by Blazor.

First, add an Init method to the ILocalStorage interface as in Listing 10-20.

Listing 10-20. The Updated ILocalStorage Interface

```
using System.Threading.Tasks;

namespace JSInterop.Services
{
  public interface ILocalStorage
  {
    ValueTask Init();
    ValueTask<T> GetProperty<T>(string propName);
    ValueTask SetProperty<T>(string propName, T value);
    ValueTask WatchAsync<T>(T instance) where T : class;
  }
}
```

Implement this method in the LocalStorage class as in Listing 10-21. This method does absolutely nothing here, but we will implement it in another class.

Listing 10-21. LocalStorage's Init Method

```
public ValueTask Init() => new ValueTask();
```

Create a copy of the LocalStorage.cs service, and name it LocalStorageWithModule. cs. Modify it to look like Listing 10-22. Most of this class is similar to the implementation of the LocalStorage class, but note the Init method. Here, we invoke the "import" method, passing the path to the JavaScript module. Blazor dynamically loads it and returns an IJSObjectReference, which we use to invoke the get, set, and watch JavaScript functions. Why not do this in the constructor? Because InvokeAsync<T> is an asynchronous method, and we should not call these in the constructor.

Listing 10-22. Loading a JavaScript Module

```
using Microsoft.AspNetCore.Components;
using Microsoft.JSInterop;
using System.Threading.Tasks;

namespace JSInterop.Services
{
  public class LocalStorageWithModule : ILocalStorage
  {
    private readonly IJSRuntime js;
    private IJSObjectReference? module;

    public LocalStorageWithModule(IJSRuntime js)
    {
      this.js = js;
    }

    public async ValueTask Init()
    {
      module = module ?? await js.InvokeAsync<IJSObjectReference>
        ("import", "./scripts/localstorage.js");
    }

    public ValueTask<T> GetProperty<T>(string propName)
      => module!.InvokeAsync<T>("get", propName);

    public ValueTask SetProperty<T>(string propName, T value)
      => module!.InvokeVoidAsync("set", propName, value);

    public ValueTask WatchAsync<T>(T instance) where T : class
      => module!.InvokeVoidAsync("watch",
                DotNetObjectReference.Create(instance));
  }
}
```

Use this new class in the Counter component as shown in Listing 10-23. Actually, the
only thing we need to change is to call the Init method on the localStorage service.

Listing 10-23. The Counter Component Using the JavaScript Module

```
protected override async Task OnInitializedAsync()
{
  try
  {
    await localStorage.Init();
    await localStorage.WatchAsync(this);

    int c = await localStorage.GetProperty<int>(nameof(CurrentCount));
    currentCount = c;
  }
  catch { }
}
```

Build and run; everything should still work. The big advantage is that we don't need to add the JavaScript to the index.html page. This becomes even more interesting for component libraries.

Adding a Map to PizzaPlace

Many physical businesses use a map to show to people where they are located. Wouldn't it be nice to embellish the PizzaPlace application with a map, showing where you are and where the PizzaPlace restaurant is? That is what we will do next.

Choosing the Map JavaScript Library

Which map library will we use? There are many JavaScript libraries to choose from, for example, Google maps, Bing maps, etc. Author's prerogative is to choose the maps library, and I have chosen the Leaflet open source library, which is lightweight, has many customization options, and is used by some of the leading companies such as GitHub, Flickr, Etsy, and Facebook. You can find the library's website at `https://leafletjs.com`.

Adding the Leaflet Library

Open the index.html page, and add the Leaflet styling and JavaScript script to it as in
Listing 10-24. The easiest way to do this is by copying this from the Leaflet QuickStart
page at `https://leafletjs.com/examples/quick-start/`. This will also ensure you use
the latest version (at the risk of breaking changes).

Listing 10-24. Adding the Leaflet Library

```
<!DOCTYPE html>
<html>

<head>
  <meta charset="utf-8" />
  <meta name="viewport" content="width=device-width, initial-scale=1.0,
  maximum-scale=1.0, user-scalable=no" />
  <title>PizzaPlace</title>
  <base href="/" />
  <link href="css/bootstrap/bootstrap.min.css" rel="stylesheet" />
  <link href="css/app.css" rel="stylesheet" />
  <link href="PizzaPlace.Client.styles.css" rel="stylesheet" />
  <link rel="stylesheet" href="https://unpkg.com/leaflet@1.7.1/dist/
  leaflet.css"
        integrity="sha512-xodZBNTC5n17Xt2atTPuE1HxjVMSvLVW9ocqUKLsCC5CXdbqC
        mblAshOMAS6/keqq/sMZMZ19scR4PsZChSR7A=="
        crossorigin="" />
</head>

<body>
  <div id="app">Loading...</div>

  <div id="blazor-error-ui">
    An unhandled error has occurred.
    <a href="" class="reload">Reload</a>
    <a class="dismiss">✖</a>
  </div>
  <script src="_framework/blazor.webassembly.js"></script>
  <script src="https://unpkg.com/leaflet@1.7.1/dist/leaflet.js"
```

407

```
            integrity="sha512-XQoYMqMTK8LvdxXYG3nZ448hOEQiglfqkJs1NOQV44cWnUr
            Bc8PkAOcXy2OwOvlaXaVUearIOBhiXZ5V3ynxwA=="
            crossorigin=""></script>
</body>

</html>
```

Note   We use *SubResource Integrity (SRI) Checking* to download this library to
ensure we are using the correct library. Recently, British Airways (BA) got hacked
(`https://gbhackers.com/british-airways-hacked/`), and more than
380,000 payment cards got compromised. So how could this have happened?
Imagine that BA uses some external JavaScript library. If a hacker can change this
external source and add his/her own code to the library, it is a piece of cake to
steal any information that the user enters on the website. So how can you avoid
this hack? *SubResource Integrity (SRI) Checking* adds a hash value (a checksum of
the file) to the `<script>` tag, so if the external source gets modified, the browser
will refuse to load and execute it.

Building the Leaflet Map Razor Library

You can use a map in many applications, so I think it makes a lot of sense to build this as
a razor library. You can find Blazor component libraries that give you a Map component
(e.g., `https://github.com/fis-sst/BlazorMaps`), but here we will build one as an
exercise. Add a new Razor Class Library to your solution and name it Leaflet.Map.

Remove all the files from this project except the _Imports.razor file and wwwroot
folder. Add a new map.js JavaScript file as in Listing 10-25 inside wwwroot. To save on
typing (and typos), I suggest you copy this from the provided sources.

Listing 10-25. The Map JavaScript Module

```
let showOrUpdate = (elementId, zoom, markers) => {
  let elem = document.getElementById(elementId);
  if (!elem) {
    throw new Error('No element with ID ' + elementId);
  }
```

```
  // Initialize map if needed
  if (!elem.map) {
    elem.map = L.map(elementId).setView([50.88022, 4.29660], zoom);

    L.tileLayer('https://api.mapbox.com/styles/v1/{id}/tiles/{z}/{x}/
{y}?access_token=***ACCESSTOKEN***', {
        attribution: 'Map data &copy; <a href="https://www.openstreetmap.org/
copyright">OpenStreetMap</a> contributors, Imagery © <a href="https://www.
mapbox.com/">Mapbox</a>',
        maxZoom: 18,
        id: 'mapbox/streets-v11',
        tileSize: 512,
        zoomOffset: -1,
        accessToken: '***ACCESSTOKEN***'
    }).addTo(elem.map);
  }
}

export { showOrUpdate };
```

There is one more thing we need to do to complete Listing 10-25. This is the
ACCESSTOKEN placeholder which you need to replace with your own token, which
we will do next.

Registering with the Map Provider

Leaflet will download its maps from a map provider, and here, we will use *MapBox*
which you can use for free for development. You can find their site at www.mapbox.com/
maps. You will need to sign up with this site to get your access token. So after signing up,
you should go to your account and create an access token. Copy this token and replace
ACCESSTOKEN with your token in Listing 10-25 (twice).

Creating the Map Component

Now add a new razor component to the Leaflet.Map library project and call it Map.
Implement the component as shown in Listing 10-26. This component uses a div, which
Leaflet will replace with the map. This div needs a unique id, which we generate using

the Guid type from .NET, and we set its style to fill the parent element. The JavaScript module from Listing 10-25 uses the id to retrieve the div from the DOM:

```
let elem = document.getElementById(elementId);
```

The Map component then loads the map.js module using a path to the static map.js resource from wwwroot. We only need to do this once, so we do this in the OnInitializedAsync method.

Finally, when the Map component has been rendered, we call the Leaflet library using our module in the OnAfterRenderAsync method. However, since the OnInitializedAsync method has not completed yet, we need to check if the module has been loaded. When the OnInitializedAsync method completes, the component will render again, and then the showOrUpdate JavaScript method will get invoked.

Listing 10-26. The Map Component

```
@using Microsoft.JSInterop

@inject IJSRuntime JSRuntime

<div id="@elementId" style="height: 100%; width: 100%;"></div>

@code {
  string elementId = $"map-{Guid.NewGuid().ToString("D")}";

  [Parameter] public double Zoom { get; set; } = 17.0;

  private IJSObjectReference leaflet;

  protected override async Task OnInitializedAsync()
  {
    leaflet = await JSRuntime.InvokeAsync<IJSObjectReference>
            ("import", "./_content/Leaflet.Map/map.js");
  }

  protected async override void OnAfterRender(bool firstRender)
  {
    if (leaflet is not null)
    {
      await leaflet.InvokeVoidAsync(
```

```
        "showOrUpdate",
        elementId, Zoom/*, Markers*/);
    }
  }
}
```

Consuming the Map Component

In the PizzaPlace.Client project, add a project reference to the Leaflet.Map component library.

Add a @using Leaflet.Map to your PizzaPlace.Client project's _Imports.razor file as in Listing 10-27. This will facilitate using the library.

Listing 10-27. Add a @using to _Imports.razor

```
@using System.Net.Http
@using System.Net.Http.Json
@using Microsoft.AspNetCore.Components.Forms
@using Microsoft.AspNetCore.Components.Routing
@using Microsoft.AspNetCore.Components.Web
@using Microsoft.AspNetCore.Components.Web.Virtualization
@using Microsoft.AspNetCore.Components.WebAssembly.Http
@using Microsoft.JSInterop
@using PizzaPlace.Client
@using PizzaPlace.Client.Shared

@using PizzaPlace.Shared
@using Leaflet.Map
```

Open Index.razor, and below the CustomerEntry component, add the Map component as in Listing 10-28. We also need to set the Zoom parameter, and I have found that Zoom 17 will show the location in sufficient detail to see roads. You can experiment with this parameter if you like.

Listing 10-28. Adding the Map Component

```
<!-- End customer entry -->

<!-- Map -->
<div class="map">
  <Map Zoom="17" />
</div>
<!-- End Map -->
```

Add a new file called Index.razor.css to the client project in the Pages folder and add the map class as in Listing 10-29.

Listing 10-29. Styling the map Container

```
.map {
  width: 550px;
  height: 550px;
}
```

Run the PizzaPlace application. You should see a map like in Figure 10-2. As you can see, the map shows the location of where I work. If you like, you can change the coordinates in Listing 10-25 to suit where you live or work.

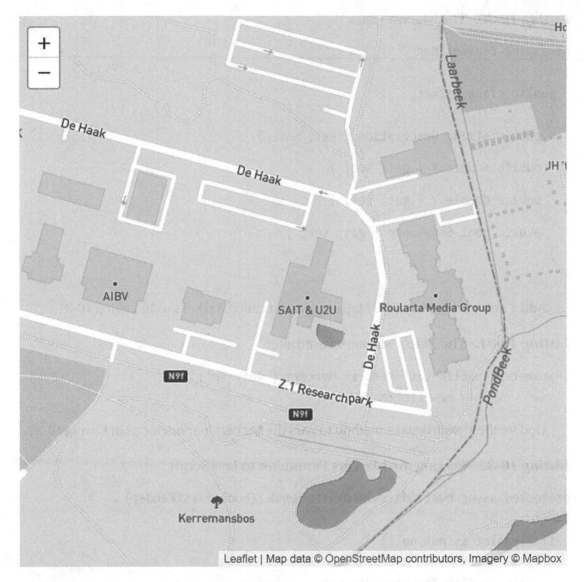

Figure 10-2. *The Map Showing a Location*

Adding Markers to the Map

Showing just a map is not enough. Let us add some markers to show the PizzaPlace location and your location. First, add a new class Marker to the Leaflet.Map project as in Listing 10-30. The class will serialize to a JavaScript object used by the Leaflet library. On the Leaflet library website, you can find more information to add circles, polygons, and popups. We will not do that since this is very similar to markers.

Listing 10-30. The Marker Class

```
namespace Leaflet.Map
{
  public class Marker
  {
    public string Description { get; set; }

    public double X { get; set; }

    public double Y { get; set; }

    public bool ShowPopup { get; set; }
  }
}
```

Add a new parameter to the Map component called `Markers` as in Listing 10-31.

Listing 10-31. The Map's Markers Parameter

```
[Parameter] public List<Marker> Markers { get; set; }
            = new List<Marker>();
```

Update the `showOrUpdate` method to pass the `Markers` parameter as in Listing 10-32.

Listing 10-32. Passing the Markers Parameter to JavaScript

```
protected async override void OnAfterRender(bool firstRender)
{
  if (leaflet is not null)
  {
    await leaflet.InvokeVoidAsync(
        "showOrUpdate",
        elementId, Zoom, Markers);
  }
}
```

Our JavaScript is not doing anything with these markers yet, so we will have to update the JavaScript module. Update map.js as in Listing 10-33. This is a lot to type, so you may want to copy this from the provided sources. Don't forget to update the ***ACCESSTOKEN*** placeholder.

Listing 10-33. The Updated map.js Module

```javascript
let showOrUpdate = (elementId, zoom, markers) => {
  let elem = document.getElementById(elementId);
  if (!elem) {
    throw new Error('No element with ID ' + elementId);
  }

  // Initialize map if needed
  if (!elem.map) {
    elem.map = L.map(elementId).setView([50.88022, 4.29660], zoom);
    elem.map.addedMarkers = [];

    L.tileLayer('https://api.mapbox.com/styles/v1/{id}/tiles/{z}/{x}/
{y}?access_token=***ACCESSTOKEN***', {
      attribution: 'Map data &copy; <a href="https://www.openstreetmap.org/
copyright">OpenStreetMap</a> contributors, Imagery © <a href="https://www.
mapbox.com/">Mapbox</a>',
      maxZoom: 18,
      id: 'mapbox/streets-v11',
      tileSize: 512,
      zoomOffset: -1,
      accessToken: '***ACCESSTOKEN***'
    }).addTo(elem.map);
  }

  // Add markers
  let map = elem.map;
  if (map.addedMarkers.length !== markers.length) {
    // Markers have changed, so reset
    map.addedMarkers.forEach(marker => marker.removeFrom(map));
    map.addedMarkers = markers.map(m => {
      return L.marker([m.y, m.x]).bindPopup(m.description).addTo(map);
    });

    // Auto-fit the view
    var markersGroup = new L.featureGroup(map.addedMarkers);
    map.fitBounds(markersGroup.getBounds().pad(0.3));
```

```javascript
      // Show applicable popups. Can't do this until after the view was
      auto-fitted.
      markers.forEach((marker, index) => {
        if (marker.showPopup) {
          map.addedMarkers[index].openPopup();
        }
      });
    } else {
      // Same number of markers, so update positions/text without changing
      view bounds
      markers.forEach((marker, index) => {
        animateMarkerMove(
          map.addedMarkers[index].setPopupContent(marker.description),
          marker,
          4000);
      });
    }
};

let animateMarkerMove = (marker, coords, durationMs) => {
  if (marker.existingAnimation) {
    cancelAnimationFrame(marker.existingAnimation.callbackHandle);
  }

  marker.existingAnimation = {
    startTime: new Date(),
    durationMs: durationMs,
    startCoords: { x: marker.getLatLng().lng, y: marker.getLatLng().lat },
    endCoords: coords,
    callbackHandle: window.requestAnimationFrame(() => animateMarker
    MoveFrame(marker))
  };
}

let animateMarkerMoveFrame = (marker) => {
  var anim = marker.existingAnimation;
```

```javascript
  var proportionCompleted = (new Date().valueOf() - anim.startTime.
  valueOf()) / anim.durationMs;
  var coordsNow = {
    x: anim.startCoords.x + (anim.endCoords.x - anim.startCoords.x) *
    proportionCompleted,
    y: anim.startCoords.y + (anim.endCoords.y - anim.startCoords.y) *
    proportionCompleted
  };

  marker.setLatLng([coordsNow.y, coordsNow.x]);

  if (proportionCompleted < 1) {
    marker.existingAnimation.callbackHandle = window.requestAnimationFrame(
      () => animateMarkerMoveFrame(marker));
  }
}

export { showOrUpdate };
```

Now let us add some markers to our PizzaPlace application. Add a new to the Index. razor component as in Listing 10-34. Feel free to update the coordinates to a place near you.

Listing 10-34. Adding Some Markers

```csharp
private List<Marker> Markers = new List<Marker> {
 new Marker {
   X = 4.29660,
   Y = 50.88022,
   Description = "Pizza Place" },
 new Marker {
   X = 4.27638,
   Y = 50.87136,
   Description = "You",
   ShowPopup = true },
};
```

Data bind this to the Map component's Markers parameter as in Listing 10-35.

417

Listing 10-35. Passing the Markers to the Map Component

```
<!-- Map -->
<div class="map">
  <Map Zoom="17" Markers="@Markers"/>
</div>
<!-- End Map -->
```

Build and run the PizzaPlace application. You should now see markers on the map as in Figure 10-3. When you click the marker, it will show a popup.

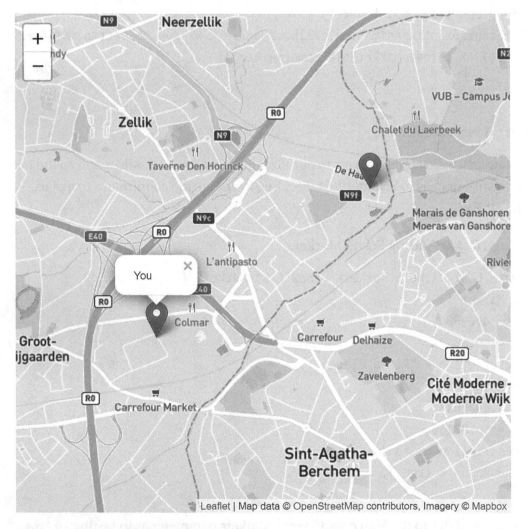

Figure 10-3. *The Map Showing Markers*

Summary

In this chapter, you saw how you can call JavaScript from your Blazor components using the `IJSRuntime.InvokeAsync<T>` method. This requires you to register a JavaScript glue function by adding this function to the browser's window global object. Or you can expose a JavaScript module and then load this module dynamically.

You can call your .NET static or instance method from JavaScript. Start by adding the `JSInvokable` attribute to the .NET method. If the method is static, you use the JavaScript `DotNet.invokeMethodAsync` function (or `DotNet.invokeMethod` if the call is synchronous), passing the name of the assembly, the name of the method, and its arguments. If the method is an instance method, you pass the .NET instance wrapped in a `DotNetObjectRef` to the glue function, which can then use the `invokeMethodAsync` function to call the method, passing the name of the method and its arguments.

Finally, you applied this knowledge by adding a map to the PizzaPlace application. You built a Blazor component library which uses a JavaScript module to call the Leaflet library and added a class to pass markers to the map.

When should we use JavaScript interop? Whenever you need to use a feature of the browser, such as local storage or the geolocation API, which is not supported by WebAssembly, you will have to resort to JavaScript interop. There are a lot of nice people out there who already did the work and provide their implementation as a Blazor component library, saving you a lot of time. So google around a bit first!

CHAPTER 11

Blazor State Management

Blazor is used to build Single-Page Applications and has a stateful programming model, meaning that a Blazor application keeps its state in memory, as long as the user does not refresh the browser. Refreshing the browser will restart your Blazor application, losing all state in memory. How can you keep the application's state? In this chapter, we will look at how your application can manage its state and pass data between pages, browser tabs, and even different browsers. Some of these techniques we have been using before, and we will also look at building complex Blazor applications using the redux pattern.

Examining Component State

This chapter comes with a prepared demo, because it reviews some of the techniques we have seen before. So start Visual Studio and open the StateManagement demo solution. Now start the StateManagementWASM project. Your browser should open. Navigate to the Counter page by clicking the Counter link in the navigation column of the application. A familiar component should render.

Click the button a couple of times and then refresh your browser. The Counter goes back to 0! The same thing happens when you click another link in the navigation menu. Imagine that this is your application and the user just spent a couple of minutes entering their data. Your user clicks another page, maybe to look at some references the user needs, the user comes back, and all the painstakingly entered data is gone! Should I encounter an application like this, I will most likely vow to never use this application again!

In a Blazor WebAssembly application, your component is running in the browser, and data gets stored in the memory of the browser. With Blazor Server, all the work is done on the server with a thin SignalR connection to update the DOM. The application's data gets stored in a circuit, which is the way Blazor Server differentiates between data of different users. Data in a circuit gets stored in the server's memory. But when the browser refreshed, the Blazor runtime creates a new circuit, losing all data stored in the original circuit.

421

© Peter Himschoot 2022
P. Himschoot, *Microsoft Blazor*, https://doi.org/10.1007/978-1-4842-7845-1_11

All of this means that you should do some extra things to keep your user's data. What kind of data does Blazor store in the browser's memory/circuit?

- **Render tree**: Each time Blazor renders your components, it stores this in the render tree, which is an in-memory representation of all the HTML markup. This allows Blazor to calculate the difference between the previous render tree, so it only updates the DOM with the changes.

- **Component's fields and properties**.

- **Dependency injection instances**.

- **JavaScript interop data**.

Where can we store data so it does not get lost, even after a browser refresh? Options are not to store the data, use local storage, use a server, or use the URL.

What Not to Store

First of all, I would like to note that you only need to save the data that is being created by the user. All other data can easily be reconstructed; for example, it is useless to store the render tree yourself. Blazor can always recreate this from scratch, provided your components still have their state. Data retrieved using a service, for example, the weather forecasts, can also be retrieved by revisiting the server. You only need to store changes made by the application user, for example, shopping carts, registration information for new users, etc.

Local Storage

All modern browsers allow you to persist data in the browser. You can choose between local storage and session storage, and their use is similar. The main difference is that local storage is kept even when you shut down your machine, while session storage will be lost when you close the application's browser tab or the browser. Another advantage of local storage is that you can easily share data between browser tabs.

With the StateManagementWASM application running, click the Local Storage link in the navigation menu. Click the button to increment the counter. Now navigate to the Counter page, and back to the Local Storage page. Your counter keeps its value! Refresh your browser. Again, the counter keeps its value. You can even restart the browser.

How does this work? In Chapter 10, we built a local storage service which uses JavaScript interop to store values in local storage. Let us review this again.

Start with the service, which you can find in Listing 11-1. Here, we use the IJSRuntime to load the JavaScript module from Listing 11-2. It has methods to store values in local storage.

Listing 11-1. The LocalStorage Service

```
using Microsoft.JSInterop;
using System.Threading.Tasks;

namespace JSInterop.Services
{
  public class LocalStorageWithModule : ILocalStorage
  {
    private readonly IJSRuntime js;
    private IJSObjectReference? module;

    public LocalStorageWithModule(IJSRuntime js)
      => this.js = js;

    public async ValueTask Init()
      => this.module = this.module ?? await this.js.InvokeAsync<IJSObject
        Reference>
        ("import", "./scripts/localstorage.js");

    public ValueTask<T> GetProperty<T>(string propName)
      => this.module!.InvokeAsync<T>("get", propName);

    public ValueTask SetProperty<T>(string propName, T value)
      => this.module!.InvokeVoidAsync("set", propName, value);

    public ValueTask WatchAsync<T>(T instance) where T : class
      => this.module!.InvokeVoidAsync("watch",
                          DotNetObjectReference.Create(instance));
  }
}
```

Listing 11-2. The JavaScript LocalStorage Module

```
let get = key => key in localStorage ? JSON.
parse(localStorage[key]) : null;
let set = (key, value) => { localStorage[key] = JSON.stringify(value); };
let watch = async (instance) => {
  window.addEventListener('storage', (e) => {
    instance.invokeMethodAsync('UpdateCounter');
  });
};

export { get, set, watch };
```

The CounterLocalStorage component from Listing 11-3 uses the local storage service to get the value when it initializes and again to store the value whenever the user changes it by clicking the button.

Listing 11-3. The CounterLocalStorage Component

```
@page "/localStorage"
@inject JSInterop.Services.ILocalStorage localStorage
@using Microsoft.AspNetCore.Components

<h1>Counter With Local Storage</h1>

<p>Current count: @CurrentCount</p>

<button class="btn btn-primary" @onclick="IncrementCount">
  Click me
</button>

@code {

  public int CurrentCount { get; set; }

  private void IncrementCount()
  {
    CurrentCount++;
    localStorage.SetProperty<int>(nameof(CurrentCount), CurrentCount);
  }
```

```
protected override async Task OnInitializedAsync()
{
  try
  {
    await localStorage.Init();
    await localStorage.WatchAsync(this);

    int c =
      await localStorage.GetProperty<int>(nameof(CurrentCount));
    CurrentCount = c;
  }
  catch { }
}

[JSInvokable]
public async Task UpdateCounter()
{
  int c =
    await localStorage.GetProperty<int>(nameof(CurrentCount));
  CurrentCount = c;
  this.StateHasChanged();
}
}
```

You do need to be careful with the value retrieved from local storage. When this value gets corrupted, it might crash the component, and since this value is persisted, the user cannot simply restart the application to fix the problem. That is why there is a try-catch block around this code. Worst case, the counter will start from 0 again. That is why in some cases using session storage is a better alternative, because this will clear once the user closes the tab in the browser.

You can use the browser's debugger to examine data stored in local and session storage. Open the browser's debugger and open the debugger's application tab. Select Local Storage, and click the application's URL (e.g., https://localhost:5001). This will display all the local storage keys and values as in Figure 11-1. You might have other keys here, especially when developing because other applications you are building might have data stored here.

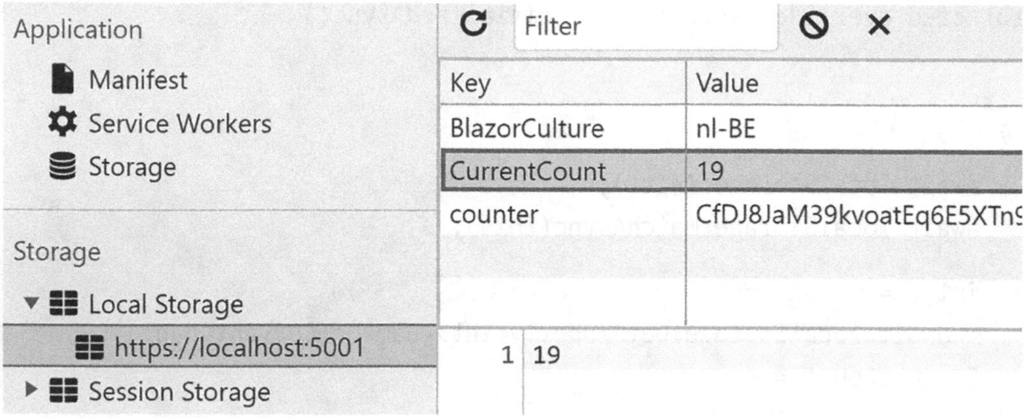

Figure 11-1. *The Browser's Local Storage*

One disadvantage of this is that tech savvy users can open local storage in the browser debugger and see or modify the value. So do not store secrets here! With Blazor Server, you can use protected storage, which we discuss later in this chapter.

Local storage can also be used to communicate between two or more tabs in your browser. With the Local Storage page open, copy the URL and open a new tab to it. Select the Local Storage page, and increment the counter. You will see the counter update in the other tab! Every time a value in local storage is modified, the browser will trigger the `storage` event, and you can register for this using the `WatchAsync` method from the local storage service. This will invoke the `UpdateCounter` method from the component, as in Listing 11-3.

The Server

What if the user decides to switch to another browser? Local storage does not work across browsers, so in that case, you will need to store your state on a server. The server can then decide where to persist this data, for example, in a database.

The demo solution has a StateService project, which you will need to run before running the StateManagementWASM project. Use the command line and set your current folder to the StateService project's folder. Then type `dotnet run`. This should start the server (I have kept this server as minimal as possible, so it only keeps the data in memory, but with a little work, you can store the data wherever you want). It does mean that restarting the server will reset all of its data.

Start the StateManagementWASM project and now select the State Service page from the navigation menu. Increment the counter a couple of times. Now open the page from another browser (or use another tab). You will now see that this other application will use the counter's value you set in the first browser!

So how does this work? Open the StateService project, and look for the `StateService` class in the Services folder, as in Listing 11-4. This generic class allows you to store and retrieve a state using a key (`user`). Why user? Because this state service can and will be used by everyone, so we need to have some user identifying property. Since we will look at identifying the user in Chapter 16 later, I decided to simply hard-code the user in the client application, but you can substitute this easily with a string identifying the user obtained through authentication.

Listing 11-4. The StateService Class

```
using System.Collections.Generic;

namespace StateService.Services
{
  public class StateService<T>
  {
    private readonly Dictionary<string, T> counters
      = new Dictionary<string, T>();

    public T? GetState(string user)
    {
      if (this.counters.TryGetValue(user, out T? state))
      {
        return state;
      }
      return default;
    }

    public void SetState(string user, T state)
      => this.counters[user] = state;
  }
}
```

The StateService instance is exposed using the StateController from Listing 11-5. Nothing new here, except the [FromRoute] and [FromBody] attributes. With Web API, the controller tries to insert the correct value for its arguments, and it will look at the route, query strings, the body, and other places. Using the [FromRoute] and [FromBody] attribute on arguments will limit where the data comes from. For example, the user argument should always come from routing, so we use [FromRoute]. We will post the new state value in the body of the request, so we tell the controller to only accept this value from the body of the request. You can find more information at https://docs. microsoft.com/aspnet/core/mvc/models/model-binding.

Listing 11-5. The StateController Class

```
using Microsoft.AspNetCore.Mvc;
using StateService.Services;

namespace StateService.Controllers
{
  [ApiController]
  public class StateController : ControllerBase
  {
    private readonly StateService<int> stateService;

    public StateController(StateService<int> stateService)
      => this.stateService = stateService;

    [HttpGet("state/{user}")]
    public ActionResult<int> Get([FromRoute] string user)
      => Ok(this.stateService.GetState(user));

    [HttpPost("state/{user}")]
    public void Post([FromRoute] string user, [FromBody] int state)
      => this.stateService.SetState(user, state);
  }
}
```

One more thing, our service will run on another URL than the application (we could host the state service and our application using the same ASP.NET project, but I want to show you something important), and in that case, we need to configure *Cross-Origin*

Requests (CORS). Browsers do not allow you to access services that run on another URL (Cross-Origin) without some extra work. This is a security feature, known as *same-origin policy*, and prevents a malicious site from reading data from another site.

Servers can enable browsers to access their data from another origin (so from another URL), but then we need to enable this explicitly on the server using CORS. You can learn more about CORS at `https://docs.microsoft.com/aspnet/core/security/cors`.

Open the `Startup` class and examine the `ConfigureServices` method as in Listing 11-6. Here, we add a CORS policy that allows `localhost:5001` (our Blazor application) to access this service. We also need to enable the `content-type` header (used with REST) and the HTTP methods we need.

Listing 11-6. The ConfigureServices Method

```
public void ConfigureServices(IServiceCollection services)
{
  services.AddCors(options =>
  {
    options.AddPolicy(name: "CORS",
                builder =>
                {
                  builder.WithOrigins("https://localhost:5001");
                  builder.WithHeaders("content-type");
                  builder.WithMethods("GET", "POST");
                });
  });

  services.AddControllers();

  services.AddSingleton<StateService<int>>();
}
```

Finally, we enable the CORS middleware in the `Startup` class's `Configure` method as in Listing 11-7 that will allow the browser to query our service about CORS. Documentation states that we need to put the `UseCors` method between the `UseRouting` and `UseEndpoints` methods. We pass the policy name with the `UseCors` call.

Listing 11-7. The Configure Method

```
app.UseRouting();

app.UseCors("CORS");

app.UseAuthorization();

app.UseEndpoints(endpoints =>
{
  endpoints.MapControllers();
});
```

This concludes our discussion about the state service. Time to look at the implementation in the Blazor application.

We are using a service in the Blazor WASM application to talk to the server as in Listing 11-8. This service uses the HttpClient to talk to the StateService server.

Listing 11-8. The Client's StateService Class

```
using System.Net.Http;
using System.Net.Http.Json;
using System.Threading.Tasks;

namespace StateManagementWASM.Services
{
  public class StateService<T>
  {
    private readonly HttpClient httpClient;

    public StateService(HttpClient httpClient)
    {
      this.httpClient = httpClient;
    }

    public async Task<int?> GetState(string user)
      => await httpClient.GetFromJsonAsync<int>($"state/{user}");

    public async Task SetState(string user, T state)
      => await httpClient.PostAsJsonAsync($"state/{user}", state);
  }
}
```

The CounterState component in Listing 11-9 uses this service to retrieve the state's value in its OnInitializedAsync method and updates the state in the IncrementCount method. Almost identical to the local storage case.

Listing 11-9. The CounterState Component

```
using Microsoft.AspNetCore.Components;
using StateManagementWASM.Services;
using System.Threading.Tasks;

namespace StateManagementWASM.Pages
{
  public partial class CounterState
  {
    [Inject]
    public StateService<int> counterStateService { get; set; }
      = default!;

    public int CurrentCount { get; set; }

    private async Task IncrementCount()
    {
      CurrentCount++;
      await counterStateService.SetState("peter", CurrentCount);
    }

    protected override async Task OnInitializedAsync()
    {
      int? state = await counterStateService.GetState("peter");
      if (state.HasValue)
      {
        CurrentCount = state.Value;
      }
    }
  }
}
```

URL

In some cases, it might make a lot of sense to store your navigation data, for example, the step count in a wizard, or the product ID being shown, in the URL of the page. This has the advantage that users can add this page to their favorites, and data stored in the URL will survive a browser refresh and work across different browsers. Let us look at an example.

Using the StateManagementWASM demo, click the URL link in the navigation column. This will show the counterURL component. Now increment the counter using the button and watch the URL. This is where we store the current value of the counter.

Look at the counterURL component in Listing 11-10. Here, we use routing to put the value of the CurrentCount in the parameter with the same name. I have also used the int? constraint to make this parameter an optional integer. When the button gets clicked, we use the NavigationManager to navigate to the same URL, but with an incremented value. That's it.

Listing 11-10. The counterURL Component

```
@page "/counterURL/{CurrentCount:int?}"
@inject NavigationManager navigationManager

<h1>Counter in URL</h1>

<p>Current count: @CurrentCount</p>

<button class="btn btn-primary"
        @onclick="IncrementCount">
  Click me
</button>

@code {

  [Parameter]
  public int CurrentCount { get; set; }

  private void IncrementCount()
  {
    navigationManager.NavigateTo($"/counterURL/{CurrentCount + 1}");
  }
}
```

Using Protected Browser Storage

You can use the same techniques to store your state with Blazor Server, but there is one more possibility. We can have our data stored in local or session storage, but now using encryption. This uses the ASP.NET Core Data Protection API which will encrypt your data on the server which will then store the encrypted data in the browser's local storage (or session storage). This only works with Blazor Server because the data protection API requires the server to provide encryption.

In the demo solution, you can find the StateManagementServer project. Run this project and click the Local Storage navigation link. Increment the counter and now open the browser's debugger. Choose the application tab, and click the application's URL in local storage. Look at the counter key (again, other keys might show up from other projects since every project uses localhost:5001 by default). The counter key is clearly encrypted here (containing some integer value).

Let us look at the CounterProtectedStorage component as in Listing 11-11. To use protected storage, you use the `ProtectedLocalStorage` (or `ProtectedSessionStorage`) instance which you request using dependency injection. This instance allows you to get, set, and delete a key asynchronously.

In the `OnInitializedAsync` method, use the `GetAsync` method to retrieve the value. This might not succeed, so this method returns a `ProtectedBrowserStorageResult`, which has a `Success` property. When this property is `true`, you can access the value using the `Value` property.

When the button gets clicked, use the `SetAsync` method to update the value.

Listing 11-11. The CounterProtectedStorage Component

```
@page "/localStorage"

@inject ProtectedLocalStorage localStorage

<h1>Counter With Protected Local Storage</h1>

<p>Current count: @currentCount</p>

<button class="btn btn-primary" @onclick="IncrementCount">Click me</button>

@code {
  private int currentCount = 0;
```

```
private async Task IncrementCount()
{
  currentCount++;
  await localStorage.SetAsync("counter", currentCount);
}

protected override async Task OnInitializedAsync()
{
  var state = await localStorage.GetAsync<int>("counter");
  if (state.Success)
  {
      currentCount = state.Value;
  }
}
}
```

The Redux Pattern

Building complex applications with Blazor can become challenging. Single-Page Applications have to manage a lot more state than traditional web pages because some of this state is shared among different pages. Sometimes customers might also want advanced features, such as undo/redo functionality. *Redux* is a pattern used to reduce an application's complexity. With redux, we will apply a couple of principles which are based on a minimal API and giving us predictable behavior using immutability. With redux, state mutability becomes predictable. Let us start with a couple of building blocks in redux.

The Big Picture

With redux, we have an application store which we modify through actions and reducers. When the user interacts with the application, we *dispatch* an action which holds the changes we need to apply. Then the *reducer* applies these changes to the *store*, resulting in a new store instance. Our components (the *view*) will then update themselves from the store. This process then repeats itself, as illustrated in Figure 11-2. Note the *unidirectional flow of changes.*

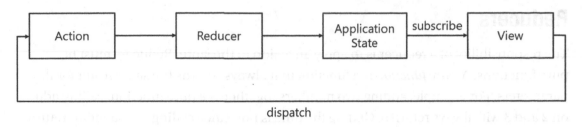

Figure 11-2. *Redux Overview*

The Application Store

With redux, we will store all our state in a single object hierarchy, known as the application store. We will consider this store to be the "Single Source of Truth." To keep things manageable, the store is immutable, meaning that every change to the store will result in a new instance. Please realize that this does not mean that we will create a deep clone of the store instance after every change; no, a single object in the hierarchy will be replaced with a new instance when it needs a change. For example, with the PizzaPlace application, the store would contain three pieces of data, the menu, the shopping basket, and the customer information. When we add something to the shopping basket, we will get a new store instance, with the same menu and customer; only the shopping basket will be replaced with a new instance. Note that this allows us to keep track of each state change and easily undo this, opening up features like undo/redo. To undo a change, we simply restore the previous state from our tracked states! The application store allows the views (Blazor components) to access its data and uses reducers to modify it (by creating new immutable fragments).

There is another pattern called *flux*; the only difference between these two is that with flux we have multiple stores, while redux chooses to put everything in a single store.

Actions

Whenever the application wants to trigger a state change, for example, because of the user clicking a button, a timer expiring, etc., we dispatch an action. The action contains the data needed so the dispatcher knows what to do. For example, with the Counter component, we can have an `IncrementCounterAction` class, which does not contain any data because the `Type` of the instance is enough for the dispatcher to handle it. Should we want to set the Counter to a specific value, we can have the `UpdateCounterAction` which would contain the desired value. Actions describe what happened in the application and are used by the dispatcher to apply the desired change.

Reducers

The responsibility of a reducer is to apply an action to the store. Reducers must be pure functions. A *pure function* is a function that always returns the same result for its parameters. For example, adding two numbers together is a pure function, calling add on 2 and 3 will always return 5. Getting the time is not, since calling this function returns a different value at different points in time.

Views

Views (in our case, Blazor components) access the store to render the data and subscribe for changes in the store so they can update themselves when the data has been changed through a reducer.

Using Fluxor

Time to look at an actual implementation using the redux pattern. We will use *Fluxor*, which was written by Peter Morris and the GitHub community and which is an amazing implementation of the flux pattern (of which redux is a special case).

Start by creating a new hosted Blazor WebAssembly project; call it UsingRedux. Do enable the nullable reference type C# option in the shared project as in Listing 11-12.

Listing 11-12. Enabling Nullable Reference Types

```
<Project Sdk="Microsoft.NET.Sdk">

  <PropertyGroup>
    <TargetFramework>net6.0</TargetFramework>
    <Nullable>enable</Nullable>
  </PropertyGroup>

  <ItemGroup>
    <SupportedPlatform Include="browser" />
  </ItemGroup>
</Project>
```

Let us first implement the Counter component using the Fluxor library, so add the NuGet package Fluxor to the UsingRedux.Shared project. I like putting the store, actions, and reducers in a shared library, which makes it easy to use with other application types.

Creating the Store

Add a new folder called Stores to the shared project.

Add a new class called AppStore as in Listing 11-13. Here, I am using the new C# record type, which is a very practical way to build an immutable reference type. With its convenient syntax, we can create the AppStore type and add three immutable properties. Because of that, the parameters of the AppStore type use *Pascal casing*. These parameters will get compiled into public read-only properties on the AppStore type, so we should use the naming convention for properties. You can learn more about record types at https://docs.microsoft.com/dotnet/csharp/whats-new/tutorials/records. The ClickCounter property holds the Counter's data, and the IsLoading and Forecasts properties hold the data used by the FetchData component.

Listing 11-13. Our Application's Store

```
namespace UsingRedux.Shared.Stores
{
  // AppStore is an immutable reference type!
  public record AppStore(
    int ClickCounter,
    bool IsLoading,
    WeatherForecast[]? Forecasts
    );
}
```

The AppStore instance will be initialized using the generic Feature<T> type that comes with the Fluxor library. Add a new folder called Features to the shared project, and add the AppFeature class as in Listing 11-14. The AppFeature will initialize our AppStore instance, since Fluxor will call the GetInitialState method and use the result as the initial store's value.

Listing 11-14. The AppFeature Class

```
using Fluxor;
using System;
using UsingRedux.Shared.Stores;

namespace UsingRedux.Shared.Features
{
  public class AppFeature : Feature<AppStore>
  {
    public override string GetName()
      => nameof(AppStore);

    protected override AppStore GetInitialState()
      => new AppStore(
          ClickCounter: 0,
          IsLoading: false,
          Forecasts: Array.Empty<WeatherForecast>()
        );
  }
}
```

Using the Store in Our Blazor Application

Now enable nullable reference types in the UsingRedux.Client project and add the Fluxor.Blazor.Web NuGet package to it. We also need to add some JavaScript, so open your index.html page and add the <script> tag from Listing 11-15 to the end of the <head> section.

Listing 11-15. The Fluxor Script

```
<script src="_content/Fluxor.Blazor.Web/scripts/index.js">
</script>
```

Open Program.cs and add support for Fluxor by configuring dependency injection as in Listing 11-16. Fluxor uses dependency injection to find our redux classes, such as the reducers. Since these are defined in the shared project, we use the AppStore class to retrieve the appropriate assembly.

Listing 11-16. Enabling Fluxor in Blazor

```
using Fluxor;
using Microsoft.AspNetCore.Components.WebAssembly.Hosting;
using Microsoft.Extensions.DependencyInjection;
using System;
using System.Net.Http;
using System.Reflection;
using System.Threading.Tasks;
using UsingRedux.Shared.Stores;

namespace UsingRedux.Client
{
  public class Program
  {
    public static async Task Main(string[] args)
    {
      var builder = WebAssemblyHostBuilder.CreateDefault(args);
      builder.RootComponents.Add<App>("#app");

      builder.Services.AddScoped(sp => new HttpClient
      {
        BaseAddress =
          new Uri(builder.HostEnvironment.BaseAddress) });

      Assembly storeAssembly = typeof(AppStore).Assembly;
      builder.Services
        .AddFluxor(options =>
          options.ScanAssemblies(storeAssembly));

      await builder.Build().RunAsync();
    }
  }
}
```

Open the App.razor class and add the StoreInitializer component to the top as in Listing 11-17. This component will initialize the store for the current user using the AppFeature class.

Listing 11-17. Adding the Store Initializer

```
<Fluxor.Blazor.Web.StoreInitializer/>
```

Add a new file called Counter.razor.cs to the Pages folder of the client project. Implement this class as in Listing 11-18. Our counter needs access to the store, so we use dependency injection to retrieve an instance of IState<AppStore>. This interface wraps our AppState and can be retrieved using the Value property. To simplify access, I have also added a helper property AppStore.

Listing 11-18. The Counter's Code

```csharp
using Fluxor;
using Microsoft.AspNetCore.Components;
using UsingRedux.Shared.Stores;

namespace UsingRedux.Client.Pages
{
  public partial class Counter
  {
    [Inject]
    public IState<AppStore> State { get; set; } = default!;

    public AppStore AppStore => State.Value;
  }
}
```

Now update the Counter.razor file as in Listing 11-19. Each component that uses the store should subscribe to changes in the store. The FluxorComponent takes care of that so we need to derive our component from this base class. Our counter needs to display a counter, which is in the store so we use the @AppStore.ClickCounter to display its value.

Listing 11-19. The Counter's Markup

```razor
@inherits Fluxor.Blazor.Web.Components.FluxorComponent
@page "/counter"

<h1>Counter</h1>

<p>Current count: @AppStore.ClickCounter</p>

<button class="btn btn-primary">Click me</button>
```

Build and run the application. Select the Counter link. You get a Counter with initial value 0, but the button does not do anything yet. Time to add an action and reducer.

Adding an Action

In the shared project, add a folder called Actions and add the IncrementCounterAction class from Listing 11-20. Again, I use a record type, since the action should not be mutable (and I like the conciseness). This action does not need any data, since the type of the action is enough to allow the reducer to do its work.

Listing 11-20. The IncrementCounterAction

```
namespace UsingRedux.Shared.Actions
{
  public record IncrementCounterAction;
}
```

We will add more actions later in this chapter, so let us proceed to the reducer.

Implementing the Reducer

Add a new folder called Reducers to the shared project and add the AppReducer class to it from Listing 11-21. Reducers should be pure functions, so calling a reducer with the same arguments should result in the same result. I know I am repeating myself, but this is very important. Since reducers should be pure, they normally do not require any data except what they can find in the AppStore and Action class. So not to be tempted, I advise you make reducer methods static, and you add it to a static class. This should not limit the testability of your reducers. Fluxor also requires you to add the [ReducerMethod] attribute to the method, enabling it to detect reducers with reflection. In general, using reflection is slow, but if you just do reflection once, especially during the initialization of your application, this is no problem. So don't worry about this. This reducer should return a new AppStore instance, with the ClickCounter incremented by 1. Again, C# records are very practical for this because we can make a full copy (a shallow clone) of the AppStore using the *with syntax* and listing the properties that need to change. This syntax will return new instance of the store, with new values for the listed properties.

Listing 11-21. The AppReducer Static Class

```
using Fluxor;
using UsingRedux.Shared.Actions;
using UsingRedux.Shared.Stores;

namespace UsingRedux.Shared.Reducers
{
  public static class AppReducer
  {
    [ReducerMethod]
    public static AppStore ReduceIncrementCounterAction
      (AppStore state, IncrementCounterAction action)
    => state with { ClickCounter = state.ClickCounter + 1 };
  }
}
```

We have an action and a reducer, so now we can update the Counter component to make the button work.

First update the Counter's code as in Listing 11-22. We need a dispatcher so we ask dependency injection to supply one. And in the `IncrementCounter` method, we create the `IncrementCounterAction` and use the `Dispatcher` to dispatch it. That is all! With redux, your component knows the action, but not how this will be implemented, again keeping this logic out of your component!

Listing 11-22. The Counter's Code with Action and Dispatch

```
using Fluxor;
using Microsoft.AspNetCore.Components;
using UsingRedux.Shared.Actions;
using UsingRedux.Shared.Stores;

namespace UsingRedux.Client.Pages
{
  public partial class Counter
  {
    [Inject]
    public IState<AppStore> State { get; set; } = default!;
```

```
[Inject]
public IDispatcher Dispatcher { get; set; } = default!;

public AppStore AppStore => State.Value;

public void IncrementCounter()
{
    var action = new IncrementCounterAction();
    Dispatcher.Dispatch(action);
}
}
}
```

Update the Counter so the button calls the IncrementCounter method when clicked as in Listing 11-23.

Listing 11-23. Making the Counter Button Work

```
@inherits Fluxor.Blazor.Web.Components.FluxorComponent
@page "/counter"

<h1>Counter</h1>

<p>Current count: @AppStore.ClickCounter</p>

<button class="btn btn-primary" @onclick="IncrementCounter">
  Click me
</button>
```

Run the application and click the button on the Counter component. It should increment!

Redux Effects

What if we need to call an asynchronous method? Do we call it in the reducer? No! Since reducers are synchronous, calling the asynchronous method would either block the reducer or return without the required result. To solve this, redux uses effects, which are asynchronous and function through use of actions and reducers. With effects, we will use two actions, one to start the effect asynchronously, and when the effect is done, it uses another action to dispatch the result. The best way to understand effects is with an example, so let us implement the FetchData component with redux.

Adding the First Action

Start by adding another action which will initiate the asynchronous call to fetch the weather forecasts. Inside the Actions folder of the shared project, add the FetchDataAction record from Listing 11-24.

Listing 11-24. The FetchDataAction Record

```
namespace UsingRedux.Shared.Actions
{
  public record FetchDataAction;
}
```

Add a new FetchData.razor.cs file to the Pages folder of the client project to implement the FetchData component as in Listing 11-25. Again, we inject the store and dispatcher, and we dispatch the FetchDataAction in the OnInitialized life cycle method. Don't forget to call the base class's OnInitialized method!

Listing 11-25. The FetchData Component's Code

```
using Fluxor;
using Microsoft.AspNetCore.Components;
using UsingRedux.Shared.Actions;
using UsingRedux.Shared.Stores;

namespace UsingRedux.Client.Pages
{
  public partial class FetchData
  {
    [Inject]
    public IState<AppStore> State { get; set; } = default!;

    [Inject]
    public IDispatcher Dispatcher { get; set; } = default!;

    public AppStore AppStore => State.Value;
```

```
  protected override void OnInitialized()
  {
    Dispatcher.Dispatch(new FetchDataAction());
    base.OnInitialized();
  }
 }
}
```

Update the FetchData.razor file to inherit from FluxorComponent and use the store instance as in Listing 11-26. We don't need the HttpClient (or service) here, so please remove it. We also check the store's IsLoading property to show the loading UI while we are fetching the data. Finally, we will iterate over the Forecasts property to show the weather forecasts.

Listing 11-26. The FetchData Component's Markup

```
@inherits Fluxor.Blazor.Web.Components.FluxorComponent
@page "/fetchdata"
@using UsingRedux.Shared

<h1>Weather forecast</h1>

<p>This component demonstrates fetching data from the server.</p>

@if (AppStore.IsLoading)
{
  <p><em>Loading...</em></p>
}
else
{
  <table class="table">
    <thead>
      <tr>
        <th>Date</th>
        <th>Temp. (C)</th>
        <th>Temp. (F)</th>
        <th>Summary</th>
      </tr>
    </thead>
```

```
  <tbody>
    @foreach (var forecast in AppStore.Forecasts!)
    {
      <tr>
        <td>@forecast.Date.ToShortDateString()</td>
        <td>@forecast.TemperatureC</td>
        <td>@forecast.TemperatureF</td>
        <td>@forecast.Summary</td>
      </tr>
    }
  </tbody>
</table>
}
```

We also need to add a reducer for this action, so add the ReduceFetchDataAction method to the AppReducer static class from Listing 11-27. This will simply set the IsLoading property on our store, so the FetchData component will show the loading UI.

Listing 11-27. The ReduceFetchDataAction Reducer Method

```
[ReducerMethod]
public static AppStore ReduceFetchDataAction
  (AppStore state, FetchDataAction action)
=> state with { IsLoading = true };
```

Adding the Second Action and Effect

Add another action called FetchDataResultAction to the Actions folder of the shared project as in Listing 11-28. This type has one property holding the forecasts which we will use in the reducer.

Listing 11-28. The FetchDataResultAction Record

```
namespace UsingRedux.Shared.Actions
{
  public record FetchDataResultAction(WeatherForecast[]? Forecasts);
}
```

Add a new Effects folder to the Shared project and also add the System.Net.Http.
Json package. We need this package to access the HttpClient class and its extension
methods.

Now implement the effect as in Listing 11-29. Our effect needs to inherit from the
Effect<T> base class, where T is the action that will trigger the effect. So when the
FetchData component dispatches the FetchDataAction, this effect gets instantiated
and the HandleAsync method will be invoked by Fluxor. When your effect needs some
dependency, it can just ask using the effect's constructor. Dependency injection will
provide! Inside the HandleAsync method, we call the asynchronous method, in this
case, the GetFromJsonAsync, and when that returns, we dispatch the result using the
FetchDataResultAction.

Listing 11-29. The FetchDataActionEffect Class

```
using Fluxor;
using System.Net.Http;
using System.Net.Http.Json;
using System.Threading.Tasks;
using UsingRedux.Shared.Actions;

namespace UsingRedux.Shared.Effects
{
  public class FetchDataActionEffect : Effect<FetchDataAction>
  {
    private readonly HttpClient httpClient;

    public FetchDataActionEffect(HttpClient http)
      => this.httpClient = http;

    public override async Task HandleAsync
      (FetchDataAction action,
        IDispatcher dispatcher)
```

```
  {
    WeatherForecast[]? forecasts =
      await this.httpClient
        .GetFromJsonAsync<WeatherForecast[]>("WeatherForecast");
      dispatcher.Dispatch(new FetchDataResultAction(forecasts));
    }
  }
}
```

Now we need another reducer, so add the method to the AppReducer class as in Listing 11-30. This will set the store's IsLoading to false and sets our Forecasts store property to the forecasts that were fetched by the effect.

Listing 11-30. The ReduceFetchDataResultAction Reducer

```
[ReducerMethod]
public static AppStore ReduceFetchDataResultAction
  (AppStore state, FetchDataResultAction action)
  => state with { IsLoading = false, Forecasts = action.Forecasts };
```

Build and run. You should be able to fetch the forecasts now!

Think of effects as an interception mechanism that gets triggered by dispatching a certain action.

Summary

In this chapter, we looked at state management, so how do we keep state around even when the user refreshes the browser? We can store our application state in local storage, the server, and the URL. Then we looked at the redux pattern, which is used to build complex applications. Redux makes this easier by applying a couple of principles. Components data bind to the Store object, which you mutate by dispatching actions that contain the required change. Then a reducer applies this change to the store which will trigger an update of your components, completing the circle. Redux and flux have the advantage that you end up with a lot of little classes which are easier to maintain, applying the single responsibility principle.

CHAPTER 12

Building Real-Time Applications with Blazor and SignalR

What if your application needs some real-time communication between client and server and even between clients? In this case, you can use SignalR. In this chapter, we will explore how we can use SignalR in Blazor to build real-time applications.

What Is SignalR?

SignalR is a library that allows you to build real-time applications and allows the server and clients to send messages to each other. You can use SignalR in desktop applications, mobile applications, and of course websites. There is an implementation for .NET and also one for JavaScript. A typical application that should use SignalR is a chat application, where clients communicate with each other over a server. When the server receives a chat message from the client, it can send this message back to the other clients. SignalR is especially useful for applications that need high-frequency updates, such as multi-player games, social networks, auctions, etc.

How Does SignalR Work?

SignalR uses WebSockets, which, unlike HTTP, use a full-duplex connection between client and server, meaning that clients and server keep the TCP connection open and thus can send messages to each other without the classic model where the client has to start the conversation. To implement this, WebSockets set up a TCP connection

P. Himschoot, *Microsoft Blazor*, https://doi.org/10.1007/978-1-4842-7845-1_12

between client and server over the existing HTTP connection, which is way more efficient to send small messages. All modern browsers support WebSockets, as shown on `https://caniuse.com/?search=websockets` and in Figure 12-1.

IE	Edge	Firefox	Chrome	Safari	Safari on iOS*	Opera Mini*	Chrome for Android	UC Browser for Android	Samsung Internet
					13.7				
		89	90	14	14.4				
11	91	90	91	14.1	14.7	all	91	12.12	14.0
		91	92	15					
		92	93	TP					
			94						

Figure 12-1. Supporting Browsers

SignalR takes care of the connection and allows you to send messages to all clients simultaneously or to specific groups of clients or even to a single specific client.

Building a WhiteBoard Application

Let us build a WhiteBoard application, in which you will have a white board (such as you can find in many offices) on which you can draw. After this, we will add SignalR so all users can interact with the white board and can see what others are drawing in real time.

Creating the WhiteBoard Solution

Start by creating a new server-hosted Blazor WebAssembly solution, and name it WhiteBoard. Remove all Blazor components from the Pages and Shared folder. We don't need these. Also remove all contents of the App component. Finally, remove the `@using WhiteBoard.Client` statement from _Imports.razor.

Start by adding a new C# struct called `LineSegment` from Listing 12-1 to the shared project. We will use this struct in both the server and the client to represent the drawing, segment by segment.

Listing 12-1. The LineSegment Class

```
using System.Drawing;

namespace WhiteBoard.Shared
{
  public struct LineSegment
  {
    public LineSegment(PointF start, PointF end)
    {
      Start = start;
      End = end;
    }
    public PointF Start { get; set; }
    public PointF End { get; set; }
  }
}
```

Add a new component to the Pages folder and name it Board. Complete the markup as in Listing 12-2. Our Board component will use an HTML <canvas> element to show the drawing and handle the user interaction with the board.

Listing 12-2. The Board Component

```
<canvas width="600" height="600"
        @onmousedown="MouseDown"
        @onmouseup="MouseUp"
        @onmousemove="MouseMove"
        @ref="board">
</canvas>
```

Add a new C# file called Board.razor.cs as in Listing 12-3. For the moment, this class does not do a lot of useful stuff, except making the project compile, but we will get to this next.

Listing 12-3. The Board Component's Implementation

```
using Microsoft.AspNetCore.Components;
using Microsoft.AspNetCore.Components.Web;
using Microsoft.JSInterop;
using System;
using System.Collections.Generic;
using System.Drawing;
using System.Threading.Tasks;
using WhiteBoard.Shared;

namespace WhiteBoard.Client.Pages
{
  public partial class Board
  {
    [Parameter]
    public List<LineSegment> LineSegments { get; set; }
      = default!;

    [Parameter]
    public Func<LineSegment, Task> AddSegment { get; set; }
      = default!;

    public ElementReference board = default!;

    private void MouseDown(MouseEventArgs e)
    {
    }

    private void MouseUp(MouseEventArgs e)
    {
    }

    private void MouseMove(MouseEventArgs e)
    {
    }
  }
}
```

Now update the App component's markup from Listing 12-4 with code behind from Listing 12-5. The App component will keep track of the line segments, so it passes the segments as an argument and passes the `AddLineSegment` callback to the board.

Listing 12-4. The App Component

```
<Board LineSegments="@LineSegments"
       AddSegment="@AddLineSegment" />
```

Listing 12-5. The App Component's Implementation

```
using System.Collections.Generic;
using System.Threading.Tasks;
using WhiteBoard.Shared;

namespace WhiteBoard.Client
{
  public partial class App
  {
    private readonly List<LineSegment> LineSegments
      = new List<LineSegment>();

    private Task AddLineSegment(LineSegment segment)
    {
      List<LineSegment> segments =
        new List<LineSegment>() { segment };
      this.LineSegments.Add(segment);
      return Task.CompletedTask;
    }
  }
}
```

Implementing the Mouse Handling Logic

Now we can implement the Board component's mouse handling logic. When the user clicks and drags the mouse, we will add a new segment. Start by adding the `MouseButton` enumeration next to the Board class as shown in Listing 12-6. This abstracts the numbers used for mouse buttons by the mouse events (I hate using "mystery" numbers in code).

Listing 12-6. The MouseButton Enumeration

```
public enum MouseButton
{
  Left, Middle, Right
}
```

Now update the Board's mouse handling methods as in Listing 12-7. The trackMouse field is used to track whether the left mouse button is down. It is set to true in the MouseDown event handling method and back to false in the MouseUp event handling method.

The MouseMove event handling method calls the AddSegment callback when the trackMouse field is true. But we need another thing. Mouse events can easily trigger tens of times per second, so we need to throttle these events. That is why the lastEvent field tracks the difference between the mouse moves and will only call the AddSegment callback with at least 200 milliseconds between them. Of course, we need to know the mouse position, and for that, this implementation uses the lastPos field. We initialize this to the current mouse position in the MouseDown method when the left mouse button is pressed. We then use this field to invoke the AddSegment callback with lastPos and currentPos. Finally, we reset the lastPos to the current mouse position because this will become the starting point for the next segment.

Listing 12-7. Implementing Mouse Tracking

```
private PointF lastPos = new PointF(0, 0);
private DateTime lastEvent;
private bool trackMouse = false;

private void MouseDown(MouseEventArgs e)
{
  if (e.Button == (int)MouseButton.Left)
  {
    this.trackMouse = true;
    this.lastPos =
      new PointF((float)e.ClientX, (float)e.ClientY);
  }
}
```

```
private void MouseUp(MouseEventArgs e)
  => this.trackMouse = false;

private void MouseMove(MouseEventArgs e)
{
  var currentPos =
    new PointF((float)e.ClientX, (float)e.ClientY);
  DateTime currentEvent = DateTime.Now;
  TimeSpan time = currentEvent - this.lastEvent;
  if (this.trackMouse && time.TotalMilliseconds > 200)
  {
    AddSegment.Invoke(new LineSegment(this.lastPos, currentPos));
    this.lastEvent = currentEvent;
    this.lastPos = currentPos;
  }
}
```

Painting the Segments on the Board

Running the application will not yield the proper result. We need to paint the segments. And since we are using a <canvas> element, we need some JavaScript.

Add a new scripts folder below the wwwroot folder, and add a new JavaScript file called canvas.js as in Listing 12-8. This JavaScript module exports a single drawLines function, which draws each line segment on the canvas.

To draw on a canvas, we need a reference to it, so we pass the ElementReference as the first argument and the segments as the second argument. Next, we ask the canvas element to give us a 2D content by calling the getContext method. Then we iterate over each segment, calling the drawLine method. This method then uses the 2D context to draw the line.

Listing 12-8. JavaScript to Draw on Canvas

```
let drawLine = (context, x1, y1, x2, y2, strokeStyle) => {
  context.beginPath();
  context.moveTo(x1, y1);
  context.lineTo(x2, y2);
  context.strokeStyle = strokeStyle || "black";
```

```
    context.stroke();
    context.closePath();
}
let drawLines = (board, segments) => {
    let context = board.getContext('2d');
    for (let i = 0; i < segments.length; i += 1) {
        let segment = segments[i];
        drawLine(context, segment.start.x, segment.start.y,
                          segment.end.x, segment.end.y)
    }
}

export { drawLines };
```

We now should import this module in our Blazor component. Use dependency injection to get a reference to the IJSRuntime instance as in Listing 12-9.

Listing 12-9. Use the Inject Attribute to Inject the JSRuntime

```
public partial class Board
{
    [Inject]
    public IJSRuntime JSRuntime { get; set; } = default!;
```

Override the `OnInitializedAsync` method as in Listing 12-10. This code should be familiar from Chapter 10, and it loads a JavaScript module into an `IJSObjectReference`.

Listing 12-10. Importing the JavaScript Module

```
private IJSObjectReference? canvas = default;

protected override async Task OnInitializedAsync()
{
    this.canvas =
        await JSRuntime.InvokeAsync<IJSObjectReference>
        ("import", "./scripts/canvas.js");
    await base.OnInitializedAsync();
}
```

Where should we call the JavaScript module? We can only do this after the Blazor runtime has updated the browser's DOM, so we should override the `OnAfterRenderAsync` method from Listing 12-11 as described in Chapter 3. There is one more problem. We are loading the JavaScript module in `OnInitializedAsync`, and because this is an asynchronous method, the module will not be loaded in the first call to `OnAfterRenderAsync`, so we need to check if the `canvas` field has been set.

Listing 12-11. Calling the drawLines JavaScript Function

```
protected override async Task OnAfterRenderAsync(bool firstRender)
{
  if (this.canvas is not null)
  {
    await this.canvas
      .InvokeVoidAsync("drawLines", this.board, LineSegments);
  }
}
```

Build and run. Now you can make some abstract art like I did in Figure 12-2.

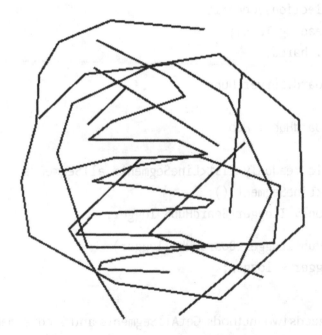

Figure 12-2. *The WhiteBoard Application in Action*

Adding a SignalR Hub on the Server

Our WhiteBoard application is currently single user. Let us make this an application where everyone can draw on the same white board using SignalR.

With SignalR, we need to create a Hub on the server, which will have methods we can call from the clients. On the client, we will implement methods that we will invoke from the hub. A hub sits at the heart of SignalR and runs on the server. The clients will send messages to the central hub, which can then notify the other clients. So we need a hub.

Implementing the BoardHub Class

In the server project, add a new Hubs folder and add the BoardHub class from Listing 12-12. We need to derive this class from the Hub base class (or strongly typed Hub<T> class). Currently, it has the allSegments list, containing the segments of the Board.

Listing 12-12. The BoardHub Class

```
using Microsoft.AspNetCore.SignalR;
using Microsoft.Extensions.Logging;
using System.Collections.Generic;
using System.Threading.Tasks;
using WhiteBoard.Shared;

namespace WhiteBoard.Server.Hubs
{
  public class BoardHub : Hub
  {
    private static readonly List<LineSegment> allSegments
      = new List<LineSegment>();
    private readonly ILogger<BoardHub> logger;

    public BoardHub(ILogger<BoardHub> logger)
      => this.logger = logger;
}
```

Our BoardHub needs two methods, GetAllSegments and SendSegments. The GetAllSegments method from Listing 12-13 is used by a new client to retrieve the already present segments from other clients. So how does the server know who the clients are?

The Hub base class has a Clients property of type IHubCallerClients. This interface has three properties: All, Caller, and Others. The All property gives you access to all the clients connected to the Hub, the Caller property returns the client calling the BoardHub, and the Others returns all clients except the caller. Since the GetAllSegments method needs to return its allSegments collection to the client, we use Clients.Caller and call the client's InitSegments method. This method also performs some server-side logging using the ILogger.

Listing 12-13. The BoardHub's GetAllSegments Method

```
public async Task GetAllSegments()
{
  this.logger.LogInformation(
    $"{nameof(GetAllSegments)} - {allSegments.Count}");
  await Clients.Caller.SendAsync("InitSegments", allSegments);
}
```

The SendSegments method from Listing 12-14 is used by a client to notify the other clients. Here, the server adds the client's segments to its collection and notifies the other clients by calling their AddSegments method.

Listing 12-14. The SendSegments Method

```
public async Task SendSegments(IEnumerable<LineSegment> segments)
{
  this.logger.LogInformation(nameof(SendSegments));
  allSegments.AddRange(segments);
  await Clients.Others.SendAsync("AddSegments", segments);
}
```

Configuring the Server

Open Startup.cs on the server project and update the ConfigureServices method in Listing 12-15 to configure dependency injection for SignalR. To really make the SignalR messages as small as possible, we also add the response compression middleware.

Listing 12-15. Adding the Required SignalR Dependencies

```
public void ConfigureServices(IServiceCollection services)
{

  services.AddControllersWithViews();
  services.AddRazorPages();
  services.AddSignalR();
  services.AddResponseCompression(opts =>
  {
    opts.MimeTypes = ResponseCompressionDefaults.MimeTypes
      .Concat(new[] { "application/octet-stream" });
  });
}
```

Update Startup's Configure method as in Listing 12-16. The response compression middleware should come first, and we need to add our BoardHub to the server's endpoints. Our BoardHub can now receive messages from clients using the /board URL.

Listing 12-16. Adding SignalR Middleware

```
public void Configure(IApplicationBuilder app, IWebHostEnvironment env)
{
  app.UseResponseCompression();

  ...

  app.UseEndpoints(endpoints =>
  {
    endpoints.MapRazorPages();
    endpoints.MapControllers();
    endpoints.MapHub<BoardHub>("/board");
    endpoints.MapFallbackToFile("index.html");
  });
}
```

Implementing the SignalR Client

Start by adding the `Microsoft.AspNetCore.SignalR.Client` package to the client project.

Our `Board` component does not need to know we are using SignalR, so we will add the SignalR logic to the `App` component.

Making the SignalR Hub Connection

Start by adding the `NavigationManager` through dependency injection and a `HubConnection` field as in Listing 12-17.

Listing 12-17. Adding Some Dependencies

```
public partial class App
{
  [Inject]
  public NavigationManager navigationManager { get; set; } = default!;

  private HubConnection hubConnection = default!;
```

We need to create the `HubConnection` in the `OnInitializedAsync` method as in Listing 12-18. First, we use the `HubConnectionBuilder` to create the `HubConnection`, passing the URL of our server's SignalR endpoint. To retrieve the SignalR server's URL, we use the `navigationManager.ToAbsoluteUri` method.

Then we define the `AddSegments` method (which the server will call) which simply adds the segments to the App component's segments. Since this call is asynchronous, we need to call `StateHasChanged` so the App component will perform change detection and render itself.

We also add the `InitSegments` method, which by some weird coincidence does the same as the `AddSegments` method (but this may change in the future).

Now our `hubConnection` is ready, so we call `StartAsync`, and when this returns, the connection has been made, and we ask the server to send its segments (which could have been modified by other clients) using the `GetAllSegments` method.

461

Listing 12-18.   Creating the HubConnection

```
protected override async Task OnInitializedAsync()
{
  this.hubConnection = new HubConnectionBuilder()
    .WithUrl(navigationManager.ToAbsoluteUri("/board"))
    .Build();

  this.hubConnection.On<IEnumerable<LineSegment>>("AddSegments",
    segments =>
    {
      this.LineSegments.AddRange(segments);
      StateHasChanged();
    });

  this.hubConnection.On<List<LineSegment>>("InitSegments",
    allSegments =>
    {
      this.LineSegments.AddRange(allSegments);
      StateHasChanged();
    });

  await this.hubConnection.StartAsync();

  await this.hubConnection.SendAsync("GetAllSegments");
}
```

Notifying the Hub from the Client

Our App component should notify the server when the user added a segment, so we call
the hubConnection's SendSegments method, passing the extra segment. This will update
any other client out there. Add the AddLineSegment method from Listing 12-19.

Listing 12-19. Updated AddLineSegment Method

```
private async Task AddLineSegment(LineSegment segment)
{
  List<LineSegment> segments =
    new List<LineSegment>() { segment };
  await this.hubConnection.SendAsync("SendSegments", segments);
  this.LineSegments.Add(segment);
}
```

Cleaning Up the Hub Connection

Finally, we should not forget to notify the server that we are not interested in other messages.

Start by declaring the IAsyncDisposable interface on the App component as in Listing 12-20.

Listing 12-20. Declaring the IAsyncDisposable Interface

```
public partial class App : IAsyncDisposable
```

Implement the DisposeAsync method in the App component as in Listing 12-21. Here, we call DisposeAsync on the hubConnection, which will unregister this client with the server's hub.

Listing 12-21. Implementing IAsyncDisposable

```
public async ValueTask DisposeAsync()
{
  if (this.hubConnection is not null)
  {
    await this.hubConnection.DisposeAsync();
  }
}
```

Build and run. Open another browser tab on the same URL (or another browser). Drawing in one tab will automatically draw in another tab. Again, open another tab or browser; the current drawing should be shown as in Figure 12-3.

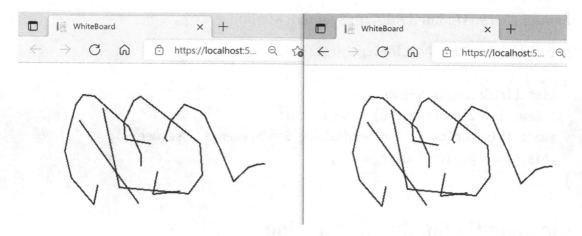

Figure 12-3. *The WhiteBoard Application in Action*

Summary

In this chapter, we looked at using SignalR for building real-time applications. Who is using SignalR out there? First of all, Blazor Server uses SignalR to set up the two-way communication between the server and the browser. Microsoft Azure also uses SignalR. It is also used by lots of companies. Any time you need real-time communication, SignalR is the choice to make. We could integrate SignalR in our PizzaPlace application to notify the customers when their pizza enters the oven, then when it is put in the pizza box, and when delivery is estimated to arrive. They could even see where delivery is in traffic!

You start by adding a Hub to the server, and then you make clients connected to this hub using a HubConnection. Once this connection has been established, both client and server can send messages to each other. We only scratched the surface of what is possible with SignalR, but as we have seen, using SignalR is easy!

CHAPTER 13

Efficient Communication with gRPC

Blazor WebAssembly applications that have the need to exchange large amounts of data will probably run into communication overhead when using REST. With *gRPC*, you can use a more efficient way to exchange data with the back end.

What Is gRPC?

Before we were using SOAP and REST, developers were using *Remote Procedure Calls* (*RPC*) to invoke methods in another process. We've seen how to communicate with REST APIs between two applications, but the serialization to and from JSON causes some overhead. This is mostly done to make messages human-readable. If the communication only needs to happen between applications and there is no need to have a human-readable form, we can use gRPC. Because the serialized data does not have to be readable by humans, it can be more compact and efficient and thus more performant.

Pros and Cons of RPC

With RPC, you can expose a method in another process and call it just like a normal method, using the same syntax. Behind the scenes, the client method serializes the method call itself with its arguments and sends it to another process, for example, using a network stack. The other process would then call the actual server method and return the return value back over the network, after which the client method deserializes the return value and returns it. With RPC, developers at the client end do not see the difference between a normal method call and a remote call. This is of course quite convenient but comes at a price. Imagine you are talking to some other person directly, or you would have to talk to someone using a fax machine (remember?) or good old

465

© Peter Himschoot 2022
P. Himschoot, *Microsoft Blazor*, https://doi.org/10.1007/978-1-4842-7845-1_13

mail. Talking directly to another person allows for a **chatty interface** where small messages get exchanged, like "How are you?" and "Good, and you?", while using a letter over mail or fax would use a **chunky interface**, where you would write down everything at once because you know the answer will take a long time. Just ask your parents 😊. The dream of RPC was that you would not be able to see the difference. But making calls over a network for a computer has the same efficiency as using a fax machine or mail for us. So designing RPC calls requires some thought and should use chunky interfaces.

Understanding gRPC

What is gRPC? This framework gives us a modern and highly efficient way to communicate with the same principles of RPC. It works for languages, such as C#, Java, JavaScript, Go, Swift, C++, Python, Node.js, and other languages. It provides interoperability between different languages through the use of an *Interface Definition Language* (*IDL*) described in *.proto* files. These files are then used to generate the necessary code used by both server and client.

Using gRPC is highly performant and very lightweight. A gRPC call can be up to eight times faster than the equivalent REST call. Because it uses binary serialization, messages can be 60 to 80 percent smaller than JSON. Some of you might be familiar with *Windows Communication Foundation* (WCF). In that case, think of gRPC as the equivalent of using the `NetTcpBinding` in WCF.

Protocol Buffers

The gRPC framework uses an open source technology called *Protocol Buffers* which was created by Google. With Protocol Buffers, we use an IDL specified in a text-based .proto file to allow us to communicate with other languages. With this IDL, you create service contracts, each containing one or more RPC methods, and each method takes a request and a response message.

Describing Your Network Interchange with Proto Files

Let us update an existing application that currently uses REST to use gRPC. The source code that comes with this book contains a starter solution called BlazorWithgRPC. Starter. Open this solution. You can run it if you like, but to keep things simple and familiar, it uses the same components from before. Here, the FetchData component uses a WeatherService to request a list of WeatherForecast instances using REST. We will make this use gRPC now.

Let us now describe the contract between the server and client. Since we are using Blazor, we can use the Shared project to generate the code for both.

Installing the gRPC Tooling

The first thing that we should do to use gRPC is to add a couple of packages to the Shared project (take the latest stable version of each):

- Google.Protobuf

- Grpc.Net.Client

- Grpc.Net.Client.Web

- Grpc.Tools

Now add a new text file called WeatherForecast.proto. When you are using Visual Studio, you should set the Build Action to Protobuf compiler as in Figure 13-1.

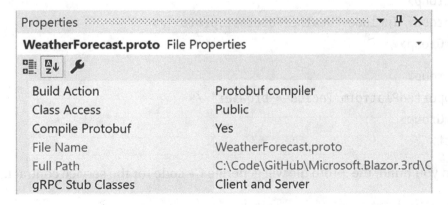

Figure 13-1. *Proto File Settings*

When you are using another tool like Visual Studio Code, you can directly set the build action in the project file as in Listing 13-1.

Listing 13-1. Setting the Build Action in the Project File

```
<Project Sdk="Microsoft.NET.Sdk">

  <PropertyGroup>
    <TargetFramework>net6.0</TargetFramework>
    <Nullable>enable</Nullable>
  </PropertyGroup>

  <ItemGroup>
    <PackageReference Include="Google.Protobuf" Version="3.17.3" />
    <PackageReference Include="Grpc.Net.Client" Version="2.38.0" />
    <PackageReference Include="Grpc.Net.Client.Web" Version="2.38.0" />
    <PackageReference Include="Grpc.Tools" Version="2.38.1">
      <PrivateAssets>all</PrivateAssets>
      <IncludeAssets>runtime; build; native; contentfiles; analyzers;
      buildtransitive</IncludeAssets>
    </PackageReference>
  </ItemGroup>

  <ItemGroup>
    <None Remove="WeatherForecast.proto" />
  </ItemGroup>

  <ItemGroup>
    <Protobuf Include="WeatherForecast.proto" />
  </ItemGroup>

  <ItemGroup>
    <SupportedPlatform Include="browser" />
  </ItemGroup>
</Project>
```

When you build, the .proto file will generate C# code for the service contract.

Adding the Service Contract

Update the .proto file as in Listing 13-2. First, we choose the syntax to be proto3 syntax. Then we tell it which C# namespace we want the generated code to use.

Listing 13-2. The Initial Proto File

```
syntax = "proto3";

option csharp_namespace = "BlazorWithgRPC.Shared.Protos";
```

So what should the service contract look like? A service contract consists of at least one method, a mandatory request message and mandatory response message. When declaring a contract, you should focus on the messages first, so let us think about the request message. We don't have any arguments for the getForecasts method, but we still need to declare the request message with zero parts as in Listing 13-3. Should we decide later that we need an extra argument, we can easily add it to this message.

Listing 13-3. Declaring the Request Message

```
message getForecastsRequest {
}
```

The response message does contain data: a list of weatherForecast instances. First, we declare the weatherForecast message as in Listing 13-4. This message has four fields: the date using the google.protobuf.Timestamp type – kind of like DateTime, the temperatureC using the int32 type, a summary of string type, and finally the image which is of bytes type, representing a collection of byte. As you can see, the types used in the proto IDL kind of match with .NET types (but other language mappings such as Java exist too).

Listing 13-4. The WeatherForecast Message IDL

```
message weatherForecast {
  google.protobuf.Timestamp date = 1;
  int32 temperatureC = 2;
  string summary = 3;
  bytes image = 4;
}
```

To use the google.protobuf.Timestamp type, we do need to import this as in Listing 13-5.

Listing 13-5. Using the Timestamp Type

```
import "google/protobuf/timestamp.proto";
```

As Listing 13-4 illustrates, each field also has a unique number which is used to identify the field during serialization and deserialization. With JSON and REST, each field is identified through its name; with Protobuf, the unique number is used which results in faster and more compact serialization.

The getForecastResponse message from Listing 13-6 is declared as a list of weatherForecast instances, using the repeated keyword. In C#, this will generate a Google.Protobuf.Collections.RepeatedField<T> type which implements IList<T>.

Listing 13-6. The getForecastResponse Message

```
message getForecastsResponse {
  repeated weatherForecast forecasts = 1;
}
```

Now that we have the request and response message, we can create the service contract as in Listing 13-7. Here, we define the protoWeatherForecasts service with just one getForecasts method. Of course, you can add more than one RPC method here.

Listing 13-7. The Service Contract

```
service protoWeatherForecasts {
  rpc getForecasts(getForecastsRequest) returns (getForecastsResponse);
}
```

Listing 13-8 contains the whole .proto file just to allow you to check on the order of each statement.

Listing 13-8. The Whole Proto File

```
syntax = "proto3";

option csharp_namespace = "BlazorWithgRPC.Shared.Protos";
```

```
import "google/protobuf/timestamp.proto";

service protoWeatherForecasts {
  rpc getForecasts(getForecastsRequest) returns (getForecastsResponse);
}

message getForecastsRequest {
}

message getForecastsResponse {
  repeated weatherForecast forecasts = 1;
}

message weatherForecast {
  google.protobuf.Timestamp date = 1;
  int32 temperatureC = 2;
  string summary = 3;
  bytes image = 4;
}
```

Build the Shared project; this should compile without errors.

If you are interested, you can look at the generated C# code inside the obj/Debug/net6.0 folder. Look for the protoWeatherForecastsBase and protoWeatherForecastsClient classes inside the WeatherForecastGrpc.cs file.

Implementing gRPC on the Server

With the Shared project ready, we can implement the server side of the gRPC service. Start by adding the following packages to the BlazorWithgRPC.Server project (take the last stable version for each):

- Grpc.AspNetCore
- Grpc.AspNetCore.Web

Implementing the Service

Inside the Services folder, add a new WeatherForecastProtoService class as in Listing 13-9 which inherits from the generated protoWeatherForecasts. protoWeatherForecastsBase class.

Listing 13-9. The WeatherForecastProtoService Class

```
using BlazorWithgRPC.Shared.Protos;

namespace BlazorWithgRPC.Server.Services
{
  public class WeatherForecastProtoService
    : protoWeatherForecasts.protoWeatherForecastsBase
  {
  }
}
```

Our service needs the ImageService through dependency injection, so add a constructor as in Listing 13-10. We also need some Summaries.

Listing 13-10. Adding Dependencies

```
public class WeatherForecastProtoService
  : protoWeatherForecasts.protoWeatherForecastsBase
{
  private static readonly string[] Summaries = new[]
  {
    "Freezing", "Cool", "Warm", "Hot", "Sweltering", "Scorching"
  };
  private readonly ImageService imageService;
  public WeatherForecastProtoService(ImageService imageService)
    => this.imageService = imageService;
```

We also need to implement the service; this is done by overriding the getForecasts method from the base class as in Listing 13-11. This implementation will generate a couple of random forecasts.

Listing 13-11. Implementing the getForecasts Service Method

```
public override Task<getForecastsResponse> getForecasts(
  getForecastsRequest request, ServerCallContext context)
{
  IEnumerable<weatherForecast>? forecasts =
  Enumerable.Range(1, 5).Select(index => new weatherForecast
  {
    Date = Timestamp.FromDateTime(
      DateTime.UtcNow.AddDays(index)),
    TemperatureC = Random.Shared.Next(-20, 55),
    Summary = Summaries[Random.Shared.Next(Summaries.Length)],
    Image = ByteString.CopyFrom(this.imageService.RandomImage())
  });

  var response = new getForecastsResponse();
  response.Forecasts.AddRange(forecasts);

  return Task.FromResult(response);
}
```

A couple of remarks about this implementation. Protobuf uses the `Timestamp` type, so we need to convert our `DateTime` using the `FromDateTime` method. The `Timestamp` type is provided through the `Google.Protobuf.WellKnownTypes` namespace from the Google.Protobuf NuGet package. The `Image` property is of type `ByteString`, and we can use the `ByteString.CopyFrom` method to convert from a `byte[]`. The base class's `getForecasts` method is asynchronous, so we need to return the result as a `Task` using the `Task.FromResult` method. In real life, this service would read the data from a database, so it makes a lot of sense that this method is asynchronous.

Adding gRPC

With the service implemented, all that rests (some pun here!) is to add gRPC support to the server. Start by configuring dependency injection as in Listing 13-12.

473

Listing 13-12. Configuring Dependency Injection in Startup

```
public void ConfigureServices(IServiceCollection services)
{
  services.AddControllersWithViews();
  services.AddRazorPages();
  services.AddSingleton<ImageService>();
  services.AddGrpc();
}
```

Then add the gRPC middleware to the `Configure` method as in Listing 13-13. Because Blazor uses the JavaScript library for gRPC, we need to use GrpcWeb implementation instead of regular gRPC. Because gRPC uses the HTTP/2 stack in a way that is not supported by browsers, we need to use a proxy to take care of the proper message format, and that is what gRPC Web does. Regular gRPC clients can still talk to our service, so using gRPC Web does not break regular gRPC.

Listing 13-13. Adding the gRPC Middleware

```
public void Configure(IApplicationBuilder app, IWebHostEnvironment env)
{
  if (env.IsDevelopment())
  {
    app.UseDeveloperExceptionPage();
    app.UseWebAssemblyDebugging();
  }
  else
  {
    app.UseExceptionHandler("/Error");
    app.UseHsts();
  }

  app.UseHttpsRedirection();
  app.UseBlazorFrameworkFiles();
  app.UseStaticFiles();

  app.UseRouting();
  app.UseGrpcWeb();
```

```
app.UseEndpoints(endpoints =>
{
  endpoints.MapGrpcService<WeatherForecastProtoService>()
          .EnableGrpcWeb();
  endpoints.MapRazorPages();
  endpoints.MapControllers();
  endpoints.MapFallbackToFile("index.html");
});
}
```

Build the server project.

Think about this. What you had to do was quite simple: inherit from a base class, override the base method, and use Protobuf types with some conversions. No need to think about headers, deserialization, etc.

Building a gRPC Client in Blazor

Now we can add gRPC support to the client project. First, we need to install these packages (take the last stable version for each):

- Google.Protobuf

- Grpc.Net.Client

- Grpc.Net.Client.Web

- Grpc.Tools

Creating the ForecastGrpcService

Now add a new class called ForecastGrpcService to the Services folder as in Listing 13-14. To use gRPC, we first need a GrpcChannel which we request through dependency injection. Inside the getForecasts method, we create the gRPC protoWeatherForecastsClient client (generated from the .proto file) passing it the GrpcChannel instance. Then we create the request message and invoke the getForecastsAsync method. This returns a getForecastsResponse instance containing a RepeatedField<weatherForecast>. Now we need to convert these to the regular WeatherForecast instances our FetchData component uses which we do using a LINQ Select.

Listing 13-14. The ForecastGrpcService Class

```
using BlazorWithgRPC.Shared;
using BlazorWithgRPC.Shared.Protos;
using Grpc.Net.Client;
using System;
using System.Collections.Generic;
using System.Linq;
using System.Threading.Tasks;

namespace BlazorWithgRPC.Client.Services
{
  public class ForecastGrpcService
  {
    private readonly GrpcChannel grpcChannel;

    public ForecastGrpcService(GrpcChannel grpcChannel)
      => this.grpcChannel = grpcChannel;

    public async Task<IEnumerable<WeatherForecast>?> GetForecasts()
    {
      var client =
        new protoWeatherForecasts
         .protoWeatherForecastsClient(this.grpcChannel);

      var request = new getForecastsRequest();

      getForecastsResponse? response =
        await client.getForecastsAsync(request);

      return response.Forecasts.Select(f =>
        new WeatherForecast
        {
          Date = f.Date.ToDateTime(),
          TemperatureC = f.TemperatureC,
```

```
        Summary = f.Summary,
        Image = f.Image.ToByteArray()
    });
  }
 }
}
```

Enabling gRPC on the Client

Now we need to configure dependency injection for the GrpcChannel instance. This
instance requires a URL to talk to the server, and we will put this in configuration. Add
a new appsettings.json file to the client project's wwwroot folder and complete it as in
Listing 13-15.

Listing 13-15. The GrpcChannel Configuration

```
{
  "gRPC": {
    "weatherServices": "https://localhost:5001"
  }
}
```

Now we can read configuration while instructing dependency injection how to create
a valid GrpcChannel as in Listing 13-16. First, we add a scoped ForecastGrpcService.
Then we add a scoped GrpcChannel using a lambda function which reads the
configuration and creates a GrpcChannel using the ForAddress method. Because we are
using gRPC Web, we need to tell the GrpcChannel to use the GrpcWebHandler.

Listing 13-16. Configuring Dependency Injection

```
builder.Services.AddScoped<ForecastGrpcService>();

builder.Services
  . AddScoped(services =>
  {
    IConfiguration config =
      services.GetRequiredService<IConfiguration>();
    string backEndUrl = config["gRPC:weatherServices"];
```

```
var httpHandler =
    new GrpcWebHandler(GrpcWebMode.GrpcWebText,
                        new HttpClientHandler());
    return GrpcChannel.ForAddress(backEndUrl,
        new GrpcChannelOptions { HttpHandler = httpHandler });
});
```

Updating the FetchData Component

One more thing before we can try this. Update the FetchData component to use the ForecastGrpcService as in Listing 13-17.

Listing 13-17. Updating the FetchData Component

```
@page "/fetchdata"
@inject ForecastGrpcService forecastService
```

Build and run. Choose the Fetch data link. You should get forecasts like in Figure 13-2.

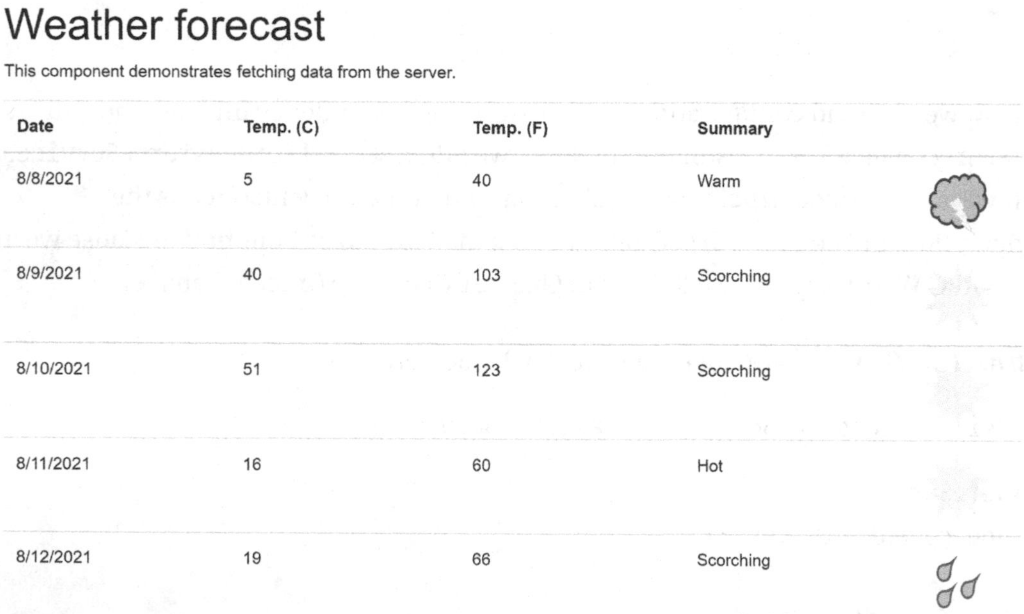

Weather forecast

This component demonstrates fetching data from the server.

Date	Temp. (C)	Temp. (F)	Summary
8/8/2021	5	40	Warm
8/9/2021	40	103	Scorching
8/10/2021	51	123	Scorching
8/11/2021	16	60	Hot
8/12/2021	19	66	Scorching

Figure 13-2. *Displaying Forecasts*

Comparing REST with gRPC

Let us see how REST compares to gRPC. Let us try REST first, so restore the WeatherService in the FetchData component as in Listing 13-18.

Listing 13-18. Updating the FetchData Component

```
@page "/fetchdata"
@inject ForecastService forecastService
```

In the server project, update the WeatherForecastController as in Listing 13-19 to return 250 rows instead of 5.

Listing 13-19. Returning 250 Forecasts

```
[HttpGet]
public IEnumerable<WeatherForecast> Get()
  => Enumerable.Range(1, 250)
  .Select(index => new WeatherForecast
  {
    Date = DateTime.Now.AddDays(index),
    TemperatureC = Random.Shared.Next(-20, 55),
    Summary = Summaries[Random.Shared.Next(Summaries.Length)],
    Image = this.imageService.RandomImage()
  })
  .ToArray();
```

Run the application and open the browser's debugger on the Network tab. Now select the Fetch data link. This will make the REST call, and the Network tab should display the amount of data sent and how long this took. Figure 13-3 displays what I got.

Name	Status	Type	Initiator	Size	Time	Waterfall
☐ WeatherForecast	200	fetch	dotnet.6,...	2.1 MB	86 ms	▮

Figure 13-3. *Using a REST Call*

You can click the request row to see what the serialized data looks like, for example, Figure 13-4.

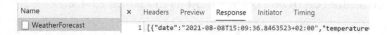

Figure 13-4. *REST Using JSON*

Restore Listing 13-17 and update the WeatherForecastProtoService to also return 250 rows as in Listing 13-20.

Listing 13-20. Returning 250 Rows Using gRPC

```
public override Task<getForecastsResponse> getForecasts(
  getForecastsRequest request, ServerCallContext context)
{
  IEnumerable<weatherForecast>? forecasts =
    Enumerable.Range(1, 250)
  .Select(index => new weatherForecast
  {
    Date = Timestamp.FromDateTime(
      DateTime.UtcNow.AddDays(index)),
    TemperatureC = Random.Shared.Next(-20, 55),
    Summary = Summaries[Random.Shared.Next(Summaries.Length)],
    Image = ByteString.CopyFrom(this.imageService.RandomImage())
  });

  var response = new getForecastsResponse();
  response.Forecasts.AddRange(forecasts);

  return Task.FromResult(response);
}
```

Run again and use the browser's debugger to capture the network traffic when visiting the Fetch data link. Figure 13-5 shows what I got.

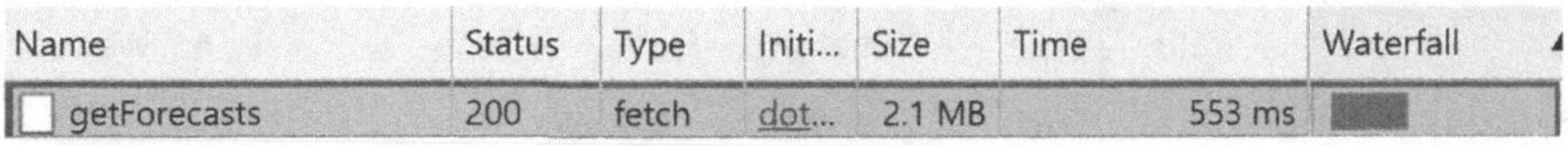

Name	Status	Type	Initi...	Size	Time	Waterfall	
☐ getForecasts	200	fetch	dot...	2.1 MB	553 ms	▬▬	

Figure 13-5. *Using gRPC with Text Encoding*

Not the expected result. This is slower!?! Why? Let us look at the response of the getForecasts request as in Figure 13-6. This is clearly not using binary encoding.

Name		×	Headers	Preview	Response	Initiator	Timing
☐ getForecasts				1	AAAXdNYKhjMKDAi4r7+IBhCc+M3CAhAHGghGcmVlemluZyLpMolQT		

Figure 13-6. *The Base-64 Encoded Response*

OK. Time to fix this. We need to use gRPC Web with binary encoding. Modify the client's program to use GrpcWebMode.GrpcWeb as in Listing 13-21.

Listing 13-21. Using Binary Encoding

```
builder.Services
  .AddSingleton(services =>
  {
    IConfiguration config =
      services.GetRequiredService<IConfiguration>();
    string backEndUrl = config["gRPC:weatherServices"];
    var httpHandler =
      new GrpcWebHandler(GrpcWebMode.GrpcWeb,
        new HttpClientHandler());
    return GrpcChannel.ForAddress(backEndUrl,
      new GrpcChannelOptions
      {
        HttpHandler = httpHandler,
        MaxReceiveMessageSize = null
      });
  });
```

Run the application again. Now we can see a nice decrease in network traffic size and time as in Figure 13-7. Compare this to Figure 13-3.

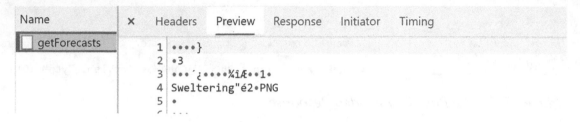

Name	Status	Type	Initiator	Size	Time	▲	Waterfall
☐ getForecasts	200	fetch	dotnet.6....	1.6 MB	32 ms		☐ ▬▬

Figure 13-7. *Using gRPC with Binary Encoding*

We can also see that we are using binary encoding as in Figure 13-8.

Figure 13-8. *The Binary Encoded Response*

Summary

In this chapter, we looked at using gRPC with Blazor. We started with a discussion what RPC means and that gRPC is a modern implementation of RPC. We then created our service contract using a .proto file and generated the code for the messages and service contract. Implementation of the server is easy because we can derive from the generated server base class and override the service contract method. Client side allows us to call the server using again the generated code; we only need to supply the configured GrpcChannel. We then verified if performance was actually better, and we changed encoding to use binary encoding getting the promised performance increase.

CHAPTER 14

Supporting Multiple Languages in Your Blazor Application

The Web is a big place. So your Blazor application will probably be used by people who speak different languages. I live in Belgium, where people speak Dutch, French, and German, and even if you live in a country where there is one official language, there are no borders on the Web. So if you want to enlarge your application's reach and be more inclusive, you should consider supporting multiple languages. So how do you do this?

Understanding Internationalization, Globalization, and Localization

Let us first get a couple of definitions cleared out. *Internationalization* is the process of making an application support a range of languages. This means changing your application to support different languages but also taking into consideration things like decimal points and data formats. When users enter numbers and dates, you will have to take special support, for example, giving people a data picker. Internationalization is often abbreviated as *I18n*. Expect internalization to take a certain amount of time and effort. It is actually better to implement this as soon as possible.

After internationalizing your application, you can start localization. *Localization* is the process (probably repeated several times) to make the application support a specific language or locale. Localization is often abbreviated as *L10n*. The difference between a language and a *locale* is the country where a certain language is spoken. For example, in French as spoken in France, people use "petit déjeuner" to mean breakfast, while in

483

© Peter Himschoot 2022
P. Himschoot, *Microsoft Blazor*, https://doi.org/10.1007/978-1-4842-7845-1_14

French-speaking Belgium, the same word "déjeuner" is used. You have to take this into account, because some words have a completely different meaning. Dutch-speaking people may know what I am talking about!

Globalization, abbreviated as *g11n*, is the combination of internationalization and localization.

Note   If you have experience with globalization in ASP.NET Core, you will see that the concepts and implementation are very similar.

Representing the User's Locale

In .NET programs, the user's locale is stored in an instance of the CultureInfo class. You can create a CultureInfo instance passing the locale string in the constructor. A locale string uses two lowercase characters to represent the language, a hyphen, and two/three uppercase characters to represent the country. For example, American English uses "en-US", while Canadian English used "en-CA". You can also create a CultureInfo instance by just passing the two-character language as a string. CultureInfo has all kinds of capabilities; for example, you can ask what Monday means in the current locale or what the decimal separator is.

Create a new console application called UserLocales, and complete it as in Listing 14-1. Here, we create two CultureInfo instances, one for American English and one for Belgian Dutch (you can change this to your locale if you like). Then we print the localized name for Monday and the decimal separator.

Listing 14-1. Using CultureInfo

```
using System;
using System.Globalization;

namespace UserLocales
{
  internal class Program
  {
    private static void Main(string[] args)
    {
```

```
    var enUS = new CultureInfo("en-US");
    Console.WriteLine(enUS.DateTimeFormat
      .GetDayName(DayOfWeek.Monday));
    Console.WriteLine(enUS.NumberFormat
      .NumberDecimalSeparator);

    var nlBE = new CultureInfo("nl-BE");
    Console.WriteLine(nlBE.DateTimeFormat
      .GetDayName(DayOfWeek.Monday));
    Console.WriteLine(nlBE.NumberFormat
      .NumberDecimalSeparator);
  }
 }
}
```

The program's output will look something like the following. It prints out "Monday" as the name of the English Monday and a "." as the decimal separator. For Belgian Dutch, it prints "maandag" and a "," as the decimal separator.

```
Monday
.
maandag
,
```

Some .NET methods allow you to pass a `CultureInfo`, especially the `DateTime.class`'s `ToString` method. Update the UserLocales application by adding Listing 14-2 to the end. This will print out today's date in Belgian Dutch.

Listing 14-2. Print the Localized Date

```
Console.WriteLine(DateTime.Now.ToString("D", nlBE));
```

A lot of people like to use C#'s string interpolation. If you want this to use a certain locale, you need to set `CultureInfo.CurrentCulture` to the appropriate `CultureInfo` as in Listing 14-3.

Listing 14-3. Using String Interpolation with Another CultureInfo

```
CultureInfo.CurrentCulture = nlBE;
Console.WriteLine($"{DateTime.Now:D}");
```

This will again print today's date as a localized string:

```
zaterdag 17 juli 2021
```

You can set the current `CultureInfo` explicitly, but you can have your Blazor application automatically detect the user's language as we will see shortly.

CurrentCulture vs. CurrentUICulture

You will see that the `CultureInfo` class has two static properties, `CurrentCulture` and `CurrentUICulture`, to represent the current `CultureInfo`. What is the difference between these? The `CurrentCulture` property is used as the default for formatting values as we just saw in Listing 14-3. The `CurrentUICulture` is used by the runtime to look up the values from resource files which we will discuss in depth when we look at localization. Most of the time, you will keep both properties set to the same `CultureInfo`. But when you want to display numbers and dates in a different language than the UI, you would set these to different cultures.

Enabling Multiple Languages

Internationalizing your Blazor application is different between using Blazor WebAssembly and Blazor Server. Luckily, most concepts stay the same, so we will start with Blazor Server and continue with Blazor WebAssembly by internationalizing the PizzaPlace application.

Using Request Localization

Create a new Blazor Server application and name it `L10nBlazorServer`.

Open `appsettings.json` and add the "Cultures" configuration as in Listing 14-4. These are the languages our application will support. You can of course choose to hard-code the supported languages in your application, but I like the flexibility of putting the supported languages in configuration. I have put in this configuration a series of cultures (some of which are region independent) because some browsers do not allow me to set a region for certain languages, and Dutch is one of them. Feel free to replace these cultures with your own, which will make a lot more sense when you don't understand Dutch or French.

Listing 14-4. Configuring the Supported Languages

```
{
  "Logging": {
    "LogLevel": {
      "Default": "Information",
      "Microsoft": "Warning",
      "Microsoft.Hosting.Lifetime": "Information"
    }
  },
  "AllowedHosts": "*",
  "Cultures": {
    "en-US": "English",
    "nl-BE": "Nederlands (BE)",
    "nl": "Nederlands",
    "fr-BE": "Français (BE)",
    "fr": "Francais"
  }
}
```

Add a new folder called Globalization to your project (next to Pages) and add the ConfigurationExtensions class to it from Listing 14-5. This class contains a single GetCulturesSection extension method which will hide how configuration looks like by creating a Dictionary<string,string>.

Listing 14-5. The ConfigurationExtensions Class

```
using Microsoft.Extensions.Configuration;
using System.Collections.Generic;
using System.Linq;

namespace L10nBlazorServer.Globalization
{
  public static class ConfigurationExtensions
```

```
{
  public static Dictionary<string, string> GetCulturesSection
    (this IConfiguration configuration)
    => configuration.GetSection("Cultures")
      .GetChildren()
      .ToDictionary(k => k.Key, v => v.Value);
}
}
```

We will use this method in the Startup class to retrieve our configuration
and convert it into a RequestLocalizationOptions. We need this to configure
the request localization middleware which will set the current culture. Add a new
GetLocalizationOptions method from Listing 14-6 to the Startup class. Here, we do a
couple of things. We need to set the supported cultures, and we need to set the culture
which everything will default to in case someone visits with an unsupported culture.

Listing 14-6. Retrieving the RequestLocalizationOptions

```
private RequestLocalizationOptions GetLocalizationOptions()
{
  // This site gets the list of supported languages
  // from configuration. Open appsettings.json to add more...

  Dictionary<string, string> cultures =
    Configuration.GetCulturesSection();
  string[] supportedCultures =
    cultures.Keys.ToArray();
  RequestLocalizationOptions localizationOptions =
    new RequestLocalizationOptions()
    .SetDefaultCulture(supportedCultures[0])
    .AddSupportedCultures(supportedCultures)
    .AddSupportedUICultures(supportedCultures);

  localizationOptions.RequestCultureProviders.Clear();
  localizationOptions.RequestCultureProviders
    .Add(new AcceptLanguageHeaderRequestCultureProvider());

  return localizationOptions;
}
```

How does our Blazor Server application determine what language the user speaks? We could ask the user what language they prefer upon first use, use a cookie, or use the query string, or we could use the IP address to figure out the country the user is visiting our site from. There is a better option in my humble opinion. Most people use a localized version of Windows. I cannot imagine my parents using an English Windows; no, they use a Dutch Windows. Same thing for the browser. Browsers actually send the language of the browser to the server using the `Accept-Language` header. For example, when I start the Blazor Server application and the browser opens the page, I can use the browser's debugger to look at this header, which displays on my machine as

```
accept-language:
en-US,en;q=0.9,nl-BE;q=0.8,nl;q=0.7,fr-BE;q=0.6,fr;q=0.5
```

I prefer English (I am a developer), and I configured my browser to also support Dutch and French because I am from Belgium, so this header lists these locales in order of preference. This means we can simply look at this header to figure out the user's preferred language. And in .NET, there is the request localization middleware that does exactly this!

To choose the `Accept-Language` header for localization, we need to configure the `RequestCultureProviders`. Initially, there will be three configured providers, one using the query string from the URL, one using cookies, and one using the `Accept-Language` header. As shown at the end of Listing 14-6, since we only want to use the last, we clear the list of providers and add the required `AcceptLanguageHeaderRequestCultureProvider` provider.

Open the `Startup` class, and update the `ConfigureServices` method by adding the `services.AddLocalization` method call as in Listing 14-7.

Listing 14-7. Enabling Request Localization

```
public void ConfigureServices(IServiceCollection services)
{
  services.AddRazorPages();
  services.AddServerSideBlazor();
  services.AddSingleton<WeatherForecastService>();
  services.AddLocalization();
}
```

Now add the request localization middleware to your ASP.NET pipeline by calling the UseRequestLocalization method in the Configure method as in Listing 14-8. This method requires a RequestLocalizationOptions instance which we retrieve from configuration (containing the list of supported cultures).

Listing 14-8. Enable the Request Localization Middleware

```
public void Configure(IApplicationBuilder app,
                      IWebHostEnvironment env)
{
  if (env.IsDevelopment())
  {
    app.UseDeveloperExceptionPage();
  }
  else
  {
    app.UseExceptionHandler("/Error");
    app.UseHsts();
  }

  app.UseHttpsRedirection();
  app.UseStaticFiles();

  // This middleware uses a couple of approaches to determine
  // the language used. More in documentation.
  app.UseRequestLocalization(GetLocalizationOptions());

  app.UseRouting();

  app.UseEndpoints(endpoints =>
  {
    endpoints.MapBlazorHub();
    endpoints.MapFallbackToPage("/_Host");
  });
}
```

Time to see if all of this works. Open the Index.razor page and update it to display the current culture as in Listing 14-9.

Listing 14-9. Displaying the Current Culture

```
@page "/"

<h1>Hello, world!</h1>

Welcome to your new app.

Current culture : @CultureInfo.CurrentCulture.Name

<SurveyPrompt Title="How is Blazor working for you?" />
```

Running this should show the current culture as in Figure 14-1. Of course, depending on your browser's settings, the culture might be different.

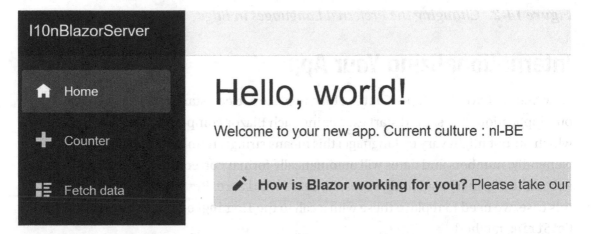

Figure 14-1. *Testing Request Localization*

When I want to test my application's localization, I change the Accept-Language header from the browser. I want to show you how to do this using Edge; other browsers like Chrome and Firefox have similar settings.

Open Settings and search for the Languages tab. You can add additional languages by clicking the Add languages button, and you can reorder the languages using the ellipsis (…) buttons as in Figure 14-2.

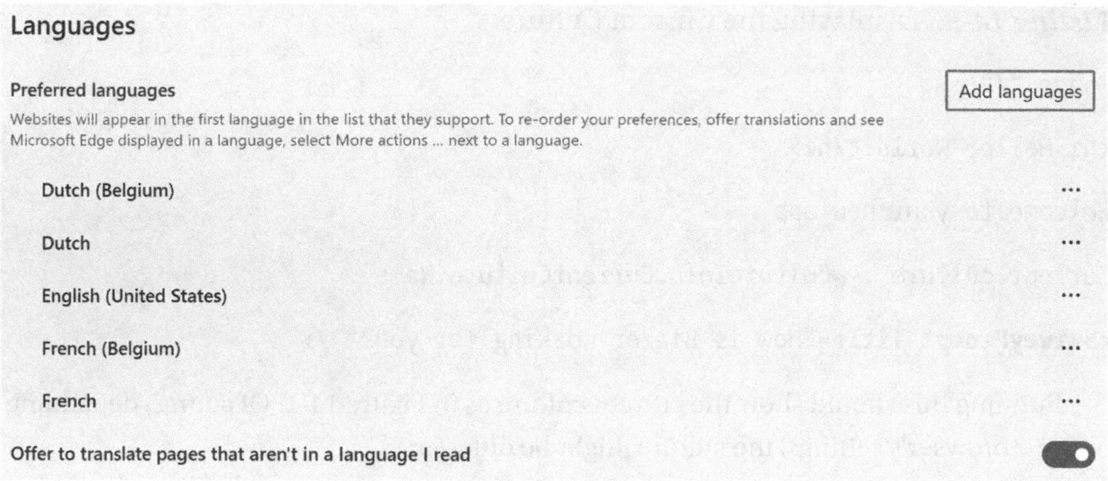

Languages

Preferred languages   Add languages

Websites will appear in the first language in the list that they support. To re-order your preferences, offer translations and see
Microsoft Edge displayed in a language, select More actions ... next to a language.

   Dutch (Belgium)   ...

   Dutch   ...

   English (United States)   ...

   French (Belgium)   ...

   French   ...

Offer to translate pages that aren't in a language I read

Figure 14-2. Changing the Preferred Languages in Edge

Internationalizing Your App

Now that we have the proper `CultureInfo` in place, we can start to internationalize
our application. You should start examining each Blazor component and determine
which output might vary by language; this means strings, numbers, and dates.
Generally, numbers and dates will automatically format correctly when you use APIs
such as string interpolation that uses the `CurrentCulture`. But what about strings? In
this case, we need to replace these with a call to the `IStringLocalizer<T>` interface's
`GetString` method.

Start by adding the `Microsoft.Extensions.Localization` namespace to
your _Imports.razor file as shown in Listing 14-10.

Listing 14-10. Enabling the Microsoft.Extensions.Localization Namespace

```
@using System.Net.Http
@using Microsoft.AspNetCore.Authorization
@using Microsoft.AspNetCore.Components.Authorization
@using Microsoft.AspNetCore.Components.Forms
@using Microsoft.AspNetCore.Components.Routing
@using Microsoft.AspNetCore.Components.Web
@using Microsoft.AspNetCore.Components.Web.Virtualization
@using Microsoft.JSInterop
```

```
@using L10nBlazorServer
@using L10nBlazorServer.Shared
@using System.Globalization
@using Microsoft.Extensions.Localization
```

Now update the Index.razor file as in Listing 14-11. As you can see, we use dependency injection to get an instance for the `IStringLocalizer<Index>` interface, and then we call the `localizer.GetString` method, passing the string we want to localize. You can also use the indexer property of this interface instead of `GetString`. Both work the same way, so the choice is a matter of taste.

Listing 14-11. Using the IStringLocalizer<T> Interface

```
@page "/"
@inject IStringLocalizer<Index> localizer

<h1>@localizer.GetString("Hello, world!")</h1>
<p>@localizer["Welcome to your new app."]</p>
<p>@localizer["Current culture :"] @CultureInfo.CurrentCulture.Name</p>
<p>Pi = @Math.PI</p>
<p>@localizer["Today's date is"] @DateTime.Now.ToLongDateString()</p>

<SurveyPrompt Title="@localizer["How is Blazor working for you?"]" />
```

The `IStringLocalizer<T>` interface allows you to internationalize your application without any translation effort on your parts. Hey, you are still busy developing things, so putting effort in translations is way too early. This interface will simply return the string passed as an argument when there is no translation available yet!

Running an application will render as in Figure 14-3. Again, this might vary depending on the culture you use. Both PI and today's date are rendered according to the `CultureInfo.CurrentCulture`, and the strings returned are the strings we passed to the localizer since we still have to localize these.

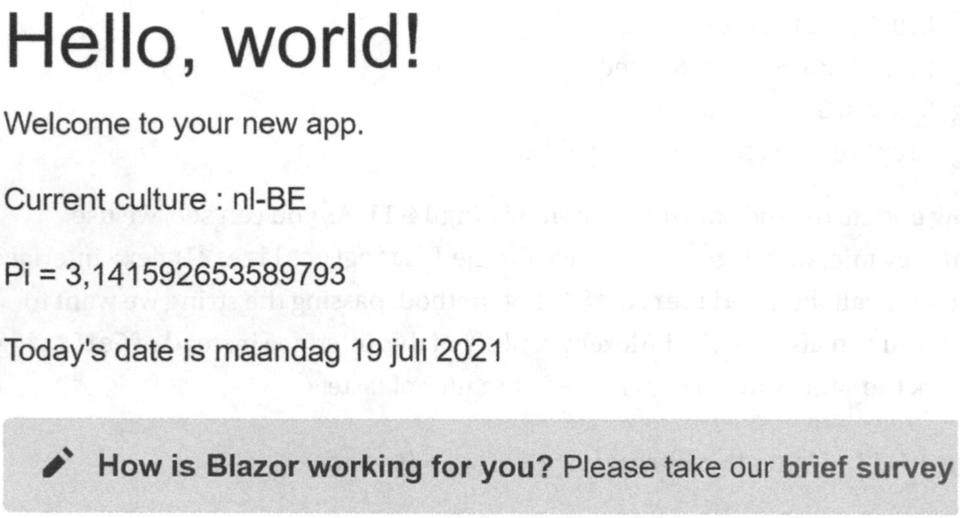

Hello, world!

Welcome to your new app.

Current culture : nl-BE

Pi = 3,141592653589793

Today's date is maandag 19 juli 2021

✎   **How is Blazor working for you?** Please take our **brief survey**

Figure 14-3. *The Index Component with the nl-BE Culture*

Localizing Your App

The IStringLocalizer<T> interface will try to find a localized version of each string by searching the resources for that component. Resources are stored in a .resx file, and if you have localized other applications, this will be familiar because Blazor uses the same mechanism used in .NET.

Adding Your First Resource File

Right-click the Pages folder and select Add ➤ New Item…. Search for the Resources File item as in Figure 14-4. Fill in Index.nl-BE.resx as the name (you might want to replace nl-BE with your locale) and click Add.

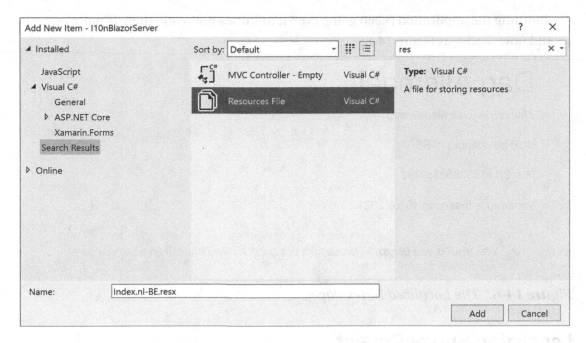

Figure 14-4. *Add a New Resource*

This will open the resource editor. Now copy each string from the localizer as the key, and translate it into the locale as in Figure 14-5. The comment is used to give more meaning to the translator, which is real life is probably not you.

Name	Value	Comment
Current culture :	Huidige cultuur :	Current culture label
Hello, world!	Dag Allemaal!	Greeting used as title for the page
How is Blazor working for you?	Wat vind u van Blazor?	Ask the user about Blazor
Today's date is	Vandaag is	Today's date label
Welcome to your new app.	Welkom in jouw nieuwe app	Greeting below title
String1		

Figure 14-5. *The Localized Resource for nl-BE*

Tip   Modern Windows allows you to copy a series of strings which it puts on a clipboard ring. You can then paste items from this clipboard ring using Windows key-V, instead of Ctrl-V.

Running the application (keep going even if this does not work; there is more) should now render as Figure 14-6.

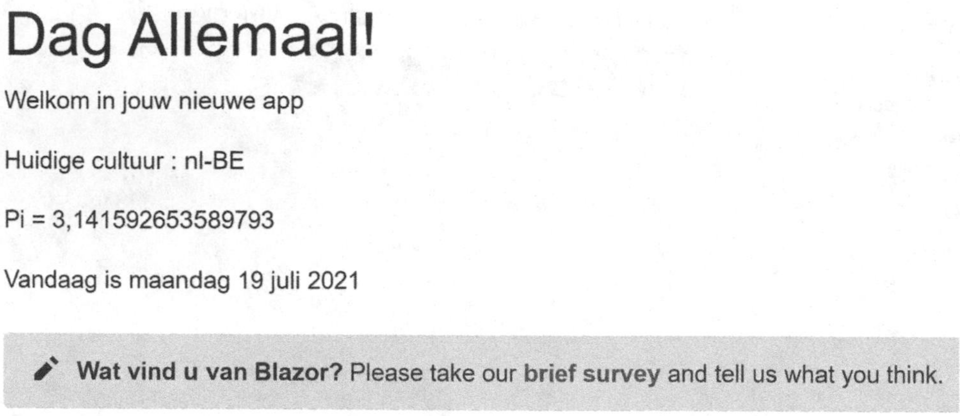

Dag Allemaal!

Welkom in jouw nieuwe app

Huidige cultuur : nl-BE

Pi = 3,141592653589793

Vandaag is maandag 19 juli 2021

> ✏ **Wat vind u van Blazor?** Please take our **brief survey** and tell us what you think.

Figure 14-6. *The Localized Index Page*

Localizing SurveyPrompt

Why does the survey from Figure 14-6 still contain English? Because this is a different component of course! You should also internationalize and then localize this component too! However, the SurveyPrompt brings some challenges: It uses a couple of strings to build the prompt. Do not be tempted to internationalize each string individually because the structure of sentences (grammar) is different for different languages, and you don't want to end up using Yoda (assuming you know *Star Wars* here) sentences!

First, we need to update the SurveyPrompt component as in Listing 14-12. Instead of using two string segments with an anchor in the middle, we should use a single string with a placeholder for the anchor. That is why we use a `Prompt` property, which will use `string.Format` to place the anchor somewhere as our translation will require. And the anchor also contains some text, so we should also internationalize the anchor, again using the same technique.

One other important thing. The `Prompt` property cannot return a string, because Blazor will HTML encode this string, replacing characters like "<" with "<". With ASP. NET, you could use `Html.Raw`, but Blazor uses the `MarkupString` type to indicate that no HTML encoding is required. Bypassing HTML encoding is dangerous, so only use it where you are sure what the output will be like; otherwise, you may open your site for hacks like cross-site scripting!

Listing 14-12. The Internationalized SurveyPrompt

```
@inject IStringLocalizer<SurveyPrompt> localizer

<div class="alert alert-secondary mt-4">
  <span class="oi oi-pencil mr-2" aria-hidden="true"></span>
  <strong>@Title</strong>

  <span class="text-nowrap">
      @Prompt
  </span>
</div>

@code {
  // Demonstrates how a parent component can supply parameters
  [Parameter]
  public string Title { get; set; }

  private const string anchor =
  "<a target=\"_blank\" class=\"font-weight-bold\" href=\"https://
go.microsoft.com/fwlink/?linkid=2149017\">{0}</a>";

  private string Anchor
  => string.Format(anchor, localizer["brief survey"]);

  private MarkupString Prompt
  => (MarkupString)string.Format(
      localizer["Please take our {0} and tell us what you think."],
      Anchor
    );
}
```

Add the SurveyPrompt.nl-BE.resx resource file (or use your own locale) to the Shared folder, and complete it as in Figure 14-7.

abc Strings ▾	🗋 Add Resource ▾	✕ Remove Resource	🔲 ▾	Access Modifier:	No code ger ▾

	Name		Value	Comment
▶	brief survey		korte enquete	
	Please take our {0} and tell us what you think.		Neem aub onze {0} en laat ons weten wat	
*				

***Figure 14-7.** Localizing the SurveyPrompt Component*

Running the application should now give you a completely localized Index component. The other components are left as an exercise because this is just repeating what we have learned.

Understanding Resource Lookup

When I run the application in Edge, everything looks fine, but when I open this with Firefox, I still get English! Why? Because Firefox does not support my locale – it only supports Dutch, not Belgian Dutch. So the Accept-Language header contains the following contents:

```
Accept-Language nl,en-US;q=0.7,en;q=0.3
```

This means that the Dutch CultureInfo instance will be installed for this browser, and Blazor will not find my nl-BE resource. What happens when the IStringLocalizer<Index> searches for localized content? It will start with the CurrentUICulture and look for a resource for it, so when the current culture is nl-BE, it will find the Index.nl-BE.resx resource. But now the culture is just nl, and I don't have a resource file for that! Let us fix this. Copy the Index.nl-BE.resx file and rename it to Index.nl.resx. When I run the application, it displays Dutch again. So did we fix it? Yes, but at a price. Now we have two copies of each string in our application; what a waste! Twice as much to maintain… Is there a way to reuse the nl.resx file for the nl-BE locale? Yes! IStringLocalizer<Index> uses a resource lookup mechanism that will first search the nl-BE.resx file, and if it cannot find it, it will look for the language resource file, this time nl.resx. And if it cannot find it there, it will look for a .resx file. This means that we can remove any duplicates from the more specific nl-BE resource file. Remove all strings except the "Hello World!" key as in Figure 14-8. Why? As it turns out this greeting is different for people living in the Netherlands and this is the Dutch localization for Belgium.

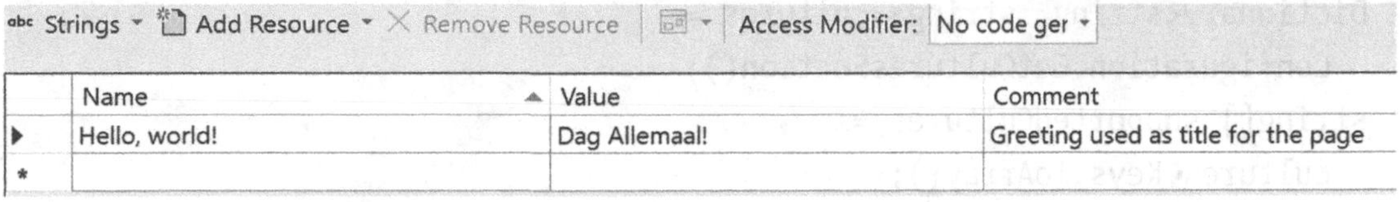

	Name	Value	Comment
▶	Hello, world!	Dag Allemaal!	Greeting used as title for the page
*			

abc Strings ▾ 🗋 Add Resource ▾ ✕ Remove Resource   🖾 ▾   Access Modifier: No code ger ▾

Figure 14-8. *The nl-BE Resource File*

Update the nl resource file as in Figure 14-9 (the "Hello World!" key).

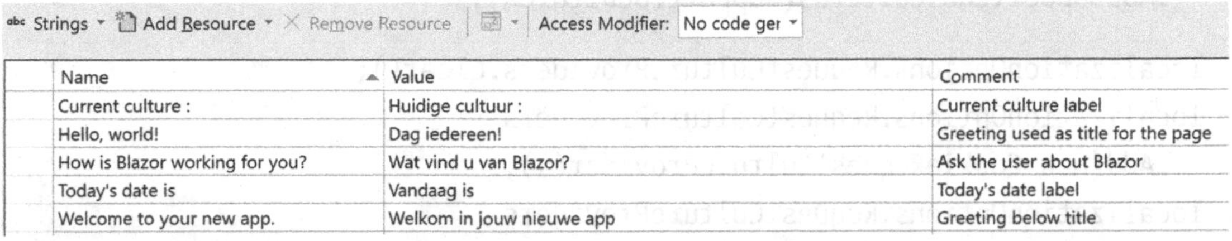

abc Strings ▾ 🗋 Add Resource ▾ ✕ Remove Resource   🖾 ▾   Access Modifier: No code ger ▾

Name	Value	Comment
Current culture :	Huidige cultuur :	Current culture label
Hello, world!	Dag iedereen!	Greeting used as title for the page
How is Blazor working for you?	Wat vind u van Blazor?	Ask the user about Blazor
Today's date is	Vandaag is	Today's date label
Welcome to your new app.	Welkom in jouw nieuwe app	Greeting below title

Figure 14-9. *The nl Resource File*

Running the app in Edge will now give me the Belgian greeting, and running it in Firefox will give me the greeting for the Netherlands. Mission accomplished!

Adding a Language Picker in Blazor Server

Many professional applications allow the user to pick the language for the UI in case the `Accept-Language` header is wrong, so let us do that. Of course, we will also need a way for the browser to remember that choice, and since all our logic is running on the server (we are still discussing Blazor Server), we will use a cookie to store the culture. This requires us to add another localization provider: the `CookieRequestCultureProvider`.

Open the `Startup` class and add this provider with code from Listing 14-13.

Listing 14-13. Adding the CookieRequestCultureProvider

```
private RequestLocalizationOptions GetLocalizationOptions()
{
  // This site gets the list of supported languages
  // from configuration. Open appsettings.json to add more...
```

```
    Dictionary<string, string> cultures =
      Configuration.GetCulturesSection();
    string[] supportedCultures =
      cultures.Keys.ToArray();
    RequestLocalizationOptions localizationOptions =
      new RequestLocalizationOptions()
      .SetDefaultCulture(supportedCultures[0])
      .AddSupportedCultures(supportedCultures)
      .AddSupportedUICultures(supportedCultures);

    localizationOptions.RequestCultureProviders.Clear();
    localizationOptions.RequestCultureProviders
      .Add(new CookieRequestCultureProvider());
    localizationOptions.RequestCultureProviders
      .Add(new AcceptLanguageHeaderRequestCultureProvider());

    return localizationOptions;
}
```

Now add a new Blazor component called LanguagePicker with markup from Listing 14-14 to the Shared folder. This will show a drop-down with the different available locales which we will read from configuration.

Listing 14-14. The LanguagePicker Component's Markup

```
@if (cultures != null)
{
  <form class="form-inline">
    <select class="form-control mr-2" @bind="selectedCulture">
      <option>@Localizer.GetString("Select...")</option>
      @foreach(var culture in cultures)
      {
        <option value="@culture.Key">@culture.Value</option>
      }
    </select>
    <button class="btn btn-outline-primary"
      @onclick="RequestCultureChange">
```

```
      @Localizer.GetString("Change")
    </button>
  </form>
}
```

Also add a new LanguagePicker class as code-beside as in Listing 14-15. This will read the cultures from Configuration in the OnInitialized method and redirects to a CultureController when the user clicks the button, passing the component's URI to it.

Listing 14-15. The LanguagePicker Class

```csharp
using L10nBlazorServer.Globalization;
using Microsoft.AspNetCore.Components;
using Microsoft.Extensions.Configuration;
using Microsoft.Extensions.Localization;
using System;
using System.Collections.Generic;
using System.Globalization;

namespace L10nBlazorServer.Shared
{
  public partial class LanguagePicker
  {
    [Inject]
    public IConfiguration Configuration
    { get; set; }

    [Inject]
    public IStringLocalizer<LanguagePicker> Localizer
    { get; set; }

    [Inject]
    public NavigationManager NavigationManager
    { get; set; }

    private string selectedCulture =
      CultureInfo.CurrentUICulture.Name;

    private Dictionary<string, string> cultures;
```

501

```
    protected override void OnInitialized()
      => this.cultures = Configuration.GetCulturesSection();

    // Navigate to the CultureController,
    // passing new culture and redirecturi back to this page
    private void RequestCultureChange()
    {
      if (string.IsNullOrWhiteSpace(this.selectedCulture))
      {
        return;
      }
      string uri = new Uri(NavigationManager.Uri)
        .GetComponents(UriComponents.PathAndQuery,
                       UriFormat.Unescaped);
      string query = $"?culture={Uri.EscapeDataString(this.
      selectedCulture)}
  &redirectUri={Uri.EscapeDataString(uri)}";
      NavigationManager
        .NavigateTo($"/Culture/SetCulture/{query}",
                    forceLoad: true);
    }
  }
}
```

Now add a new Controllers folder to your project and inside it add the
CultureController class from Listing 14-16 to it. This controller will set
the cookie holding the selected culture, which gets picked up again by the
CookieRequestCultureProvider and which will set the CurrentCulture and
CurrentUICulture.

Listing 14-16. The CultureController Class

```
using Microsoft.AspNetCore.Localization;
using Microsoft.AspNetCore.Mvc;

namespace L10nBlazorServer.Controllers
{
  public class CultureController : Controller
```

```
{
  // This action sets the culture cookie used by the
  // UseRequestLocalization middleware

  [HttpGet("/Culture/SetCulture")]
  public IActionResult SetCulture(string culture, string redirectUri)
  {
    if (culture != null)
    {
      HttpContext
        .Response
        .Cookies
        .Append(CookieRequestCultureProvider.DefaultCookieName,
                CookieRequestCultureProvider.MakeCookieValue(
                  new RequestCulture(culture)));
    }

    return LocalRedirect(redirectUri);
  }

}
}
```

Our Blazor project does not support controllers yet, so update Startup's
ConfigureServices method as in Listing 14-17 and the Configure method as in
Listing 14-18.

Listing 14-17. Enabling Support for Controllers

```
public void ConfigureServices(IServiceCollection services)
{
  services.AddRazorPages();
  services.AddServerSideBlazor();
  services.AddSingleton<WeatherForecastService>();
  services.AddLocalization();
  services.AddControllers();
}
```

Listing 14-18. Adding Endpoint Routing for Controllers

```
public void Configure(IApplicationBuilder app,
                      IWebHostEnvironment env)
{
  ...

  app.UseRouting();

  app.UseEndpoints(endpoints =>
  {
    endpoints.MapControllers();
    endpoints.MapBlazorHub();
    endpoints.MapFallbackToPage("/_Host");
  });
}
```

To complete the application, we need to add the LanguagePicker to our layout page, so update MainLayout as in Listing 14-19.

Listing 14-19. Adding the LanguagePicker to the Layout Page

```
@inherits LayoutComponentBase
@inject IStringLocalizer<MainLayout> Localizer

<div class="page">
  <div class="sidebar">
    <NavMenu />
  </div>

  <main>
    <div class="top-row px-4">
      <span class="pr-2 ml-md-auto">@Localizer.GetString
      ("SiteLanguage")</span>
      <LanguagePicker />
      <a href="https://docs.microsoft.com/aspnet/" target="_blank">
      About</a>
    </div>
```

```
  <article class="content px-4">
    @Body
  </article>
 </main>
</div>
```

Both `LanguagePicker` and `MainLayout` use an `IStringLocalizer`, so we need to add resource files for both of them. Add a new resource file called MainLayout.nl.resx with contents matching Figure 14-10. Or even better, use your own language (except when you are English speaking 😊).

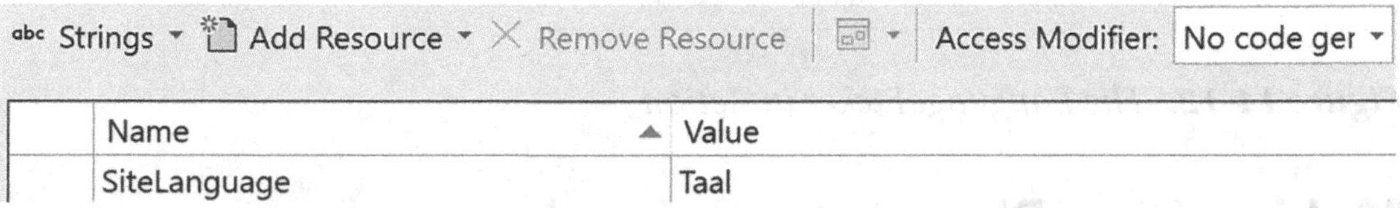

abc Strings ▾ 🗂 Add Resource ▾ ✕ Remove Resource	🔲 ▾	Access Modifier:	No code ger ▾

Name	▲	Value
SiteLanguage		Taal

Figure 14-10. *The MainLayout Resource*

And another resource called LanguagePicker.nl.resx as in Figure 14-11.

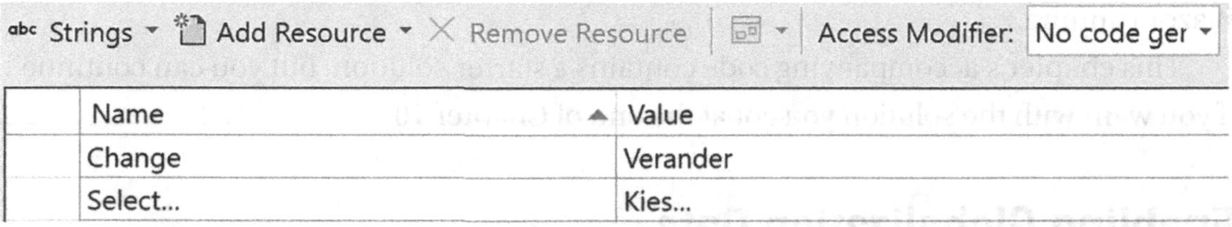

abc Strings ▾ 🗂 Add Resource ▾ ✕ Remove Resource	🔲 ▾	Access Modifier:	No code ger ▾

Name	▲	Value
Change		Verander
Select...		Kies...

Figure 14-11. *The LanguagePicker Resource*

Run the application. The user can now select their preferred language from the drop-down as in Figure 14-12. When the user clicks the change button, the page will reload with the new language in place. And when they revisit the page, this choice will remain as long as the user does not clear the cookies. Our application now works in English and Dutch, and to support French, we need to provide additional resource files, for example, Index.fr.resx and Index.fr-BE.resx.

Figure 14-12. The LanguagePicker in Action

Making PizzaPlace International

Now it is time to look at Blazor WebAssembly. Most of the things we have seen will still work, but we do need to change our approach. For example, we can read the CultureInfo directly from the browser, and this is actually automatically done by the Blazor runtime.

This chapter's accompanying code contains a starter solution, but you can continue if you want with the solution you got at the end of Chapter 10.

Enabling Globalization Data

To keep things small during the initial loading of your application, Blazor does not fully support globalization. But with a globalized application, we need these additional resources. Please add the BlazorWebAssemblyLoadAllGlobalizationData element from Listing 14-20 to the client project.

Note Be careful to place everything in the BlazorWebAssemblyLoadAll GlobalizationData element on one single line; otherwise, you will receive compile errors (own experience).

Listing 14-20. Enabling Globalization Data

```
<PropertyGroup>
  <BlazorWebAssemblyLoadAllGlobalizationData>True</BlazorWebAssemblyLoad
  AllGlobalizationData>
</PropertyGroup>
```

You also need to add the `Microsoft.Extensions.Localization` package to the client project. This adds about 0.2 MB to the initial download.

Globalizing Your Components

Let us examine each PizzaPlace component and see if it needs globalization. Start with the `PizzaItem` component as repeated in Listing 14-21. This component has no strings, so we don't need to add the `IStringLocalizer<T>` interface. And the price for the pizza will automatically be localized by the runtime.

Listing 14-21. The PizzaItem Component

```
<div class="row">
  <div class="col">
    @if (ShowPizzaInformation is not null)
    {
      <a href=""
         @onclick="@(() => ShowPizzaInformation?.Invoke(Pizza))">
        @Pizza.Name
      </a>
    }
    else
    {
      @Pizza.Name
    }
  </div>
  <div class="col text-right">
    @($"{Pizza.Price:0.00}")
  </div>
  <div class="col"></div>
```

```
<div class="col">
  <img src="@SpicinessImage(Pizza.Spiciness)"
      alt="@Pizza.Spiciness" />
</div>
<div class="col">
  <button class="@ButtonClass"
          @onclick="@(() => Selected.InvokeAsync(Pizza))">
    @ButtonTitle
  </button>
</div>
</div>
```

The ItemList templated component from Listing 14-22 also does not have any localization needs.

Listing 14-22. The ItemList Component

```
@typeparam TItem

@if (Header is not null)
{
  @Header
}
@foreach (TItem item in Items)
{
  @RowTemplate(item)
}
@if (Footer is not null)
{
  @Footer
}
```

The ItemList component from Listing 14-23 does show a loading UI which we can localize.

Listing 14-23. The PizzaList Component

```
<ItemList Items="@Items">
  <Loading>
    <div class="spinner-border text-danger" role="status">
      <span class="visually-hidden">Loading...</span>
    </div>
  </Loading>
  <Header>
    <h1>@Title</h1>
  </Header>
  <RowTemplate Context="pizza">
    <PizzaItem Pizza="@pizza"
               ButtonClass="@ButtonClass"
               ButtonTitle="@ButtonTitle"
               Selected="@Selected"
               ShowPizzaInformation="@ShowPizzaInformation"/>
  </RowTemplate>
</ItemList>
```

First, add the Microsoft.Extensions.Localization namespace to your _Imports. razor file as in Listing 14-24. This way, we don't have to place a @using statement for each localized component.

Listing 14-24. Updating _Imports.razor

```
@using Microsoft.Extensions.Localization
```

Add an IStringLocalizer<PizzaList> and use it in the loading UI, as in Listing 14-25.

Listing 14-25. Internationalizing the PizzaList Component

```
@inject IStringLocalizer<PizzaList> localizer

<ItemList Items="@Items">
  <Loading>
    <div class="spinner-border text-danger" role="status">
```

509

```
  <span class="visually-hidden">
    @localizer["Loading..."]
  </span>
</div>
</Loading>
```

Add a new resource file PizzaList.nl.resx next in the same folder as the PizzaList component with contents from Figure 14-13. This resource file here is provided as an example; feel free to replace this with a language you know.

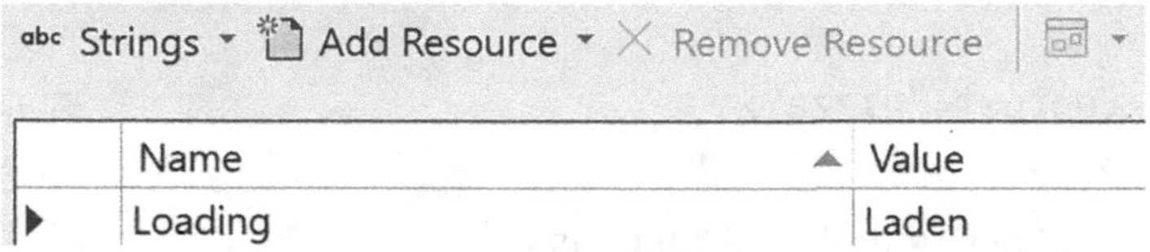

abc Strings ▾ 🗋 Add Resource ▾ ✕ Remove Resource   🗔 ▾

Name	Value
▶	Loading	Laden

Figure 14-13. *The PizzaList Resource*

We should configure dependency injection to provide the IStringLocalizer<T> instances, so add the last line of Listing 14-26 to Program.cs.

Listing 14-26. Configure Dependency Injection

```
builder.Services.AddTransient<IMenuService, MenuService>();
builder.Services.AddTransient<IOrderService, OrderService>();
builder.Services.AddSingleton<State>();
builder.Services.AddLocalization();
```

Next is the ShoppingBasket component. Update this component as in Listing 14-27.

Listing 14-27. The ShoppingBasket Component

```
@inject IStringLocalizer<ShoppingBasket> localizer

@if (Pizzas.Any())
{
  <ItemList Items="@Pizzas">
    <Header>
      <h1>@localizer["Your current order"]</h1>
    </Header>
```

```
    <RowTemplate Context="tuple">
      <PizzaItem Pizza="@tuple.pizza"
                 ButtonClass="btn btn-danger"
                 ButtonTitle="@localizer["Remove"]"
                 Selected="@(() => Selected.InvokeAsync(tuple.pos))" />
    </RowTemplate>
    <Footer>
      <div class="row">
        <div class="col"></div>
        <div class="col"><hr /></div>
        <div class="col"> </div>
        <div class="col"> </div>
      </div>
      <div class="row">
        <div class="col"> @localizer["Total"]:</div>
        <div class="col text-right font-weight-bold">
          @($"{TotalPrice:0.00}")
        </div>
        <div class="col"> </div>
        <div class="col"> </div>
        <div class="col"> </div>
      </div>
    </Footer>
  </ItemList>
}
```

Add a new ShoppingBasket.nl.resx resource file and update as in Figure 14-14.

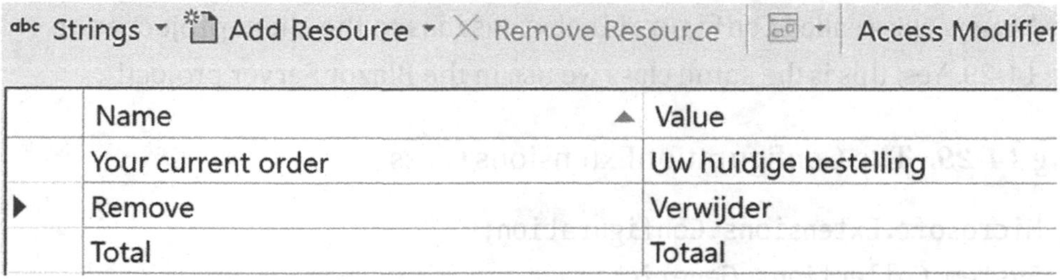

abc Strings ▾ 🗋 Add Resource ▾ ✕ Remove Resource   🖼 ▾   Access Modifier

Name	Value
Your current order	Uw huidige bestelling
▸ Remove	Verwijder
Total	Totaal

Figure 14-14. *The ShoppingBasket Resource*

For the other components, you are on your own. Update the three labels in the CustomerEntry component to use the localizer and build a resource file for these. The Index component has a couple of titles in it, so replace this with the localizer. Again, provide a resource file.

You should be ready to run the application, but first ensure your browser has been set to the language you have been using for the resource files before running. Your PizzaPlace should now support another language!

Adding a Language Picker in Blazor WebAssembly

Just like in the "Enabling Globalization Data" section, we will add a language picker so users can select the language they prefer. Except now we will not use a cookie to store the user's choice. Instead, we will store it in local storage.

Let us start with configuration. With Blazor WebAssembly, we need to store our client-side configuration in the wwwroot folder, so add new App Settings file to the wwwroot folder and complete it as in Listing 14-28.

Listing 14-28. The appsettings.json File

```
{
  "Cultures": {
    "en-US": "English",
    "nl-BE": "Nederlands (BE)",
    "nl": "Nederlands",
    "fr-BE": "Francais (BE)",
    "fr": "Francais"
  }
}
```

Add a new class called ConfigurationExtensions to the client project as in Listing 14-29. Yes, this is the same class we use in the Blazor Server project!

Listing 14-29. The ConfigurationExtensions Class

```
using Microsoft.Extensions.Configuration;
using System.Collections.Generic;
using System.Linq;
```

```
namespace PizzaPlace.Client
{
  public static class ConfigurationExtensions
  {
    public static Dictionary<string, string> GetCulturesSection(
      this IConfiguration configuration)
      => configuration.GetSection("Cultures")
        .GetChildren()
        .ToDictionary(k => k.Key, v => v.Value);
  }
}
```

We will store the user's choice in local storage, so add the script element from Listing 14-30 to the bottom of index.html.

Listing 14-30. Storing the CultureInfo in localStorage

```
<script>
  window.blazorCulture = {
    get: () => localStorage['BlazorCulture'],
    set: (value) => localStorage['BlazorCulture'] = value
  };
</script>
```

When the PizzaPlace application starts, we will attempt to read the culture from local storage, so add a new class called WebAssemblyHostExtension from Listing 14-31.

Listing 14-31. Reading the Culture from Local Storage

```
using Microsoft.AspNetCore.Components.WebAssembly.Hosting;
using Microsoft.Extensions.DependencyInjection;
using Microsoft.JSInterop;
using System.Globalization;
using System.Threading.Tasks;

namespace PizzaPlace.Client
{
  public static class WebAssemblyHostExtension
  {
```

```
  public static async Task SetDefaultCulture(this WebAssemblyHost host)
  {
    IJSRuntime? jsInterop =
      host.Services.GetRequiredService<IJSRuntime>();
    string? result =
      await jsInterop.InvokeAsync<string>("blazorCulture.get");

    CultureInfo culture;

    if (result != null)
    {
      culture = new CultureInfo(result);
      CultureInfo.DefaultThreadCurrentCulture = culture;
      CultureInfo.DefaultThreadCurrentUICulture = culture;
    }
  }
}
```

We now need to update our Program class to use this extension method when the application starts, so replace the last line in Program.cs with Listing 14-32.

Listing 14-32. Modifying Program

```
WebAssemblyHost? host = builder.Build();
await host.SetDefaultCulture();
await host.RunAsync();
```

Now we are ready to create the LanguagePicker component. Add a new component called LanguagePicker with markup from Listing 14-33 and code-beside class from Listing 14-34. This will display a drop-down for the language, and when the user changes the selected language, we update local storage and install the correct culture. Then we use the NavigationManager to reload the page, which is necessary to update the page with the correct resource.

Listing 14-33. The LanguagePicker Component's Markup

```
@if (cultures != null)
{
  <form class="form-inline">
    <select class="form-control mr-2" @bind="Culture">
      @foreach (var culture in cultures)
      {
        <option value="@culture.Key">@culture.Value</option>
      }
    </select>
  </form>
}
```

Listing 14-34. The LanguagePicker Class

```
using Microsoft.AspNetCore.Components;
using Microsoft.Extensions.Configuration;
using Microsoft.JSInterop;
using System.Collections.Generic;
using System.Globalization;

namespace PizzaPlace.Client.Shared
{
  public partial class LanguagePicker
  {
    [Inject]
    public NavigationManager NavManager { get; set; } = default!;

    [Inject]
    public IJSRuntime JSRuntime { get; set; } = default!;

    [Inject]
    public IConfiguration Configuration { get; set; } = default!;

    private Dictionary<string, string>? cultures;

    protected override void OnInitialized()
      => this.cultures = Configuration.GetCulturesSection();
```

```
    private string Culture
    {
      get => CultureInfo.CurrentCulture.Name;
      set
      {
        if (Culture != value)
        {
          var js = (IJSInProcessRuntime)JSRuntime;
          js.InvokeVoid("blazorCulture.set", value);
          var culture = new CultureInfo(value);
          CultureInfo.DefaultThreadCurrentCulture = culture;
          CultureInfo.DefaultThreadCurrentUICulture = culture;
          // Force the page to reload
          NavManager.NavigateTo(NavManager.Uri, forceLoad: true);
        }
      }
    }
  }
}
```

To complete the application, we need to use the LanguagePicker in the MainLayout component. So update the MainLayout component from Listing 14-35.

Listing 14-35. The MainLayout Component

```
@inherits LayoutComponentBase
@inject IStringLocalizer<MainLayout> Localizer

<div class="page">
  <div class="sidebar">
    <NavMenu />
  </div>

  <div class="main">
    <div class="top-row px-4">
      <span class="pr-2 ml-md-auto">
        @Localizer["Language"]
      </span>
```

```
<LanguagePicker />
<a href="http://blazor.net" target="_blank" class="ml-md-auto">
  @Localizer["About"]
</a>
  </div>
  <div class="content px-4">
    @Body
  </div>
 </div>
</div>
```

Finally, we need to add a MainLayout.nl.resx file as in Figure 14-15.

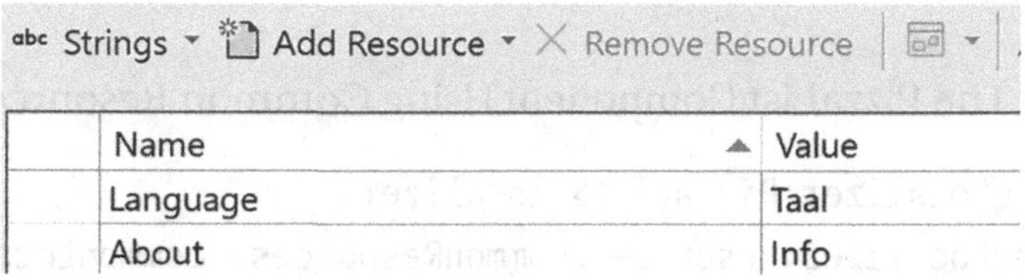

abc Strings ▾ 📄 Add Resource ▾ ✕ Remove Resource	🔲 ▾

Name	▲	Value
Language		Taal
About		Info

Figure 14-15. *The MainLayout Resource*

You should now be able to run the PizzaPlace application and pick the language from the LanguagePicker. Switch between US English and a language you provided the resources for. In Figure 14-16, I switched to Belgian Dutch (Nederlands). The drop-down menu also allows you to select French, but until we provide the proper resources for this language, it will display the default which is English.

	Taal	Nederlands (BE) ˅		Info

Onze selectie van pizzas

Diabolo	9,99		Bestellen
Margarita	7,99		Bestellen
Pepperoni	8,99		Bestellen

Figure 14-16. *Running the PizzaPlace Application in Dutch*

Using Global Resources

You might have noticed something: can we reuse resources? Both Index and PizzaList components need a resource for the loading UI. Could we put this somewhere as a common resource? Yes, we can!

The IStringLocalizer<T> interface will look up resources for a certain type; whether this is a component or a simple class does not differ its behavior. So add a new folder to the PizzaPlace client project called Resources, and add a new class called CommonResources. Leave this class as it is and now add a new resource file called CommonResources.nl.resx. Put the common resources in this file, and now update the PizzaList component to use another IStringLocalizer<CommonResources> as in Listing 14-36. Now you can use the same type for other components that need a common resource.

Listing 14-36. The PizzaList Component Using Common Resources

```
@inject IStringLocalizer<PizzaList> localizer
@inject IStringLocalizer<Resources.CommonResources> commonLocalizer

<ItemList Items="@Items">
  <Loading>
    <div class="spinner-border text-danger" role="status">
      <span class="visually-hidden">@commonLocalizer["Loading"]</span>
    </div>
  </Loading>
  <Header>
    <h1>@Title</h1>
  </Header>
  <RowTemplate Context="pizza">
    <PizzaItem Pizza="@pizza"
               ButtonClass="@ButtonClass"
               ButtonTitle="@ButtonTitle"
               Selected="@Selected"
               ShowPizzaInformation="@ShowPizzaInformation"/>
  </RowTemplate>
</ItemList>
```

Summary

In this chapter, we reviewed terms like internationalization (I18n) and localization (L10n). Then we looked at internationalizing a Blazor Server application using the `IStringLocalizer<T>` interface, and we added the proper resource files (.resx) to localize this application to another language. After this, we proceeded to support multiple languages for our PizzaPlace application, and we built a `LanguagePicker` so users can choose the language from a menu. We also looked at using the same resources in multiple components.

CHAPTER 15

Deploying Your Blazor Application

At a certain point in time, your Blazor application will be ready for the big public. Yeah! But the work is not yet done. We need to take our application and copy it to a server connected to the network so other people can use their browser to admire your work! Let us look at how we can deploy our Blazor application.

Deploying Standalone Blazor WebAssembly

When your Blazor application does not require any server support, you can host the application just like any other static website. In this case, the host just needs to serve the files to the browser since everything is executed on the browser.

Hosting on GitHub

GitHub is a free service that allows you to collaborate with others on a development project. It has support for *git* source control, builds automation, and allows you to host static websites, all free of charge.

Note If you are not familiar with git source control, there is an excellent book available for free digitally at `https://git-scm.com/book/en/v2`.

Here, we will host our Blazor application on GitHub, and the process is similar for other static hosting platforms. There are many other excellent hosting solutions out there, but I had to pick one, and GitHub is widely known in the developer community.

© Peter Himschoot 2022
P. Himschoot, *Microsoft Blazor*, https://doi.org/10.1007/978-1-4842-7845-1_15

Using GitHub requires some knowledge about git. If all of this is familiar, great. If not, the walk-through gives you the git commands you need to execute.

If you don't have a GitHub account, you will need to create one on `https://github.com/`. Because modern websites have the tendency to change how they look, I won't be using screenshots here, but the process should explain itself.

Once you have an account, you should create an organization at `https://github.com/settings/organizations`. GitHub allows you to have multiple organizations, and each can host a static website. Select a unique name for your organization; here, I will use the MicrosoftBlazorBook organization. After creating the organization, select it. Your browser will show the organization's page, for example, `https://github.com/MicrosoftBlazorBook`.

Here, you can find a list of repositories. A repository will host all your sources and their history as you make changes to files using git source control. Since you just created the organization, you will have to create a new repository. Click the New button; give your repository a nice name and description. You should also choose if you want the repository to be public (anyone can see your code) or private. The deployment process is the same for either, so pick one. Complete creating the repository, but don't add any files like README.

After completion, GitHub will show you a page that displays the command-line commands you can use to create the repository locally.

Note   I will be using Windows Terminal here, which has built-in support for PowerShell commands. All commands should work well with Linux and OSX command line.

On your local machine, create a folder where you want your project to go, open a command line on that folder, and execute the commands shown in GitHub there (just use copy-paste). For example, my organization is called `MicrosoftBlazorBook` and the repository is `StandAloneWASM`:

```
echo "# StandAloneWASM" >> README.md
git init
git add README.md
git commit -m "first commit"
git branch -M main
```

```
git remote add origin https://github.com/MicrosoftBlazorBook/
StandAloneWASM.git
git push -u origin main
```

First, this will create a README.md file in the current folder, and then this will create a git repository in the current folder. Next, this adds the README.md file to the repository, creates a new commit with a comment, and finally pushes the repository to the GitHub server. Now we are ready to deploy a static website.

Creating a Simple Website

Add a new index.html file in your folder with some simple content like Listing 15-1.

Listing 15-1. A Basic HTML File

```
<!DOCTYPE html>
<html lang="en">
<head>
  <meta charset="UTF-8">
  <meta http-equiv="X-UA-Compatible" content="IE=edge">
  <meta name="viewport" content="width=device-width, initial-scale=1.0">
  <title>Document</title>
</head>
<body>
  <h1>Hello world!</h1>
</body>
</html>
```

Since we made a change to your site, we will upload these changes into GitHub using git in the command line.

First, you need to add the modifications to git by executing the git add . command. Don't forget the . which will make git add all changes in the current folder and subfolders to the commit when we create it, so make sure you are in the project's folder where the README.md file is.

```
git add .
```

Now we need to take all these changes and group them into a commit with

```
git commit -m "Step 1"
```

A git commit is all the changes grouped with meta-data, including a mandatory message which we set using the -m parameter. And finally, we can send our changes to the GitHub repository using

```
git push
```

When you refresh the GitHub repository page, you should see index.html.

Deploying a Simple Site in GitHub

To host your simple website in GitHub, we need to select a specific branch it should host. Think of a branch like a separate copy of your files with its own history. Branches are normally used so developers can work on new features without bothering other developers. When the feature is complete, we can take the changes and apply it to the main branch where everyone will merge their changes. You can select the branch using the https://github.com/MicrosoftBlazorBook/StandAloneWASM/settings/pages page, but there is another way. If the branch is named gh-pages, then GitHub picks that branch automatically. Run the following commands to create a gh-pages branch locally, choose the gh-pages as the current branch using the checkout command, and push it to the GitHub repository on the server:

```
git branch gh-pages
git checkout gh-pages
git push --set-upstream origin gh-pages
```

After executing these commands, the deployment process will start, and by refreshing the pages page (the preceding URL), you can see the status. Refresh until GitHub tells you it is ready.

Click the link (e.g., https://microsoftblazorbook.github.io/StandAloneWASM/), and you should see your static website in action!

Deploying a Blazor WASM Project

Let us create and deploy a standalone Blazor WASM project now. First, we need to use the main branch:

```
git checkout main
```

Using the command line, create a new Blazor WASM project:

```
dotnet new blazorwasm
```

When we compile our Blazor project, two new folders will be created: obj and bin. We don't need to keep these folders in source control, and an easy way to do this is by telling git to ignore these. Since this is a common scenario, we can use

```
dotnet new gitignore
```

Finally, we don't need the index.html file from the previous part:

```
rm index.html
```

Now we can commit all our changes to GitHub with

```
git add .
git commit -m "Step 2"
git push
```

Now we are ready to publish our project. We will tell dotnet to create a release version using the -c option and put it into a release folder using the -o option. Publishing will optimize our Blazor WASM project by removing all unneeded code and assemblies, making the initial download smaller. This will take longer to build and shorter to load the Blazor site in the browser.

```
dotnet publish -c Release -o release
```

In the next step, we will copy the release folder into the gh-pages branch. Start by moving the release folder to a temporary folder outside our local repository:

```
mv release ../temp
```

Now check out the gh-pages branch:

```
git checkout gh-pages
```

Let us look at the files in our gh-pages branch:

```
ls
```

You will see that we have a bin and obj folder which we don't need:

```
Mode                LastWriteTime         Length Name
----                -------------         ------ ----
d-----        8/21/2021   12:03 PM               bin
d-----        8/21/2021   12:03 PM               obj
-a----        8/21/2021   12:11 PM           285 index.html
-a----        8/21/2021   11:13 AM            38 README.md
```

Remove these folders:

```
rm -r bin
rm -r obj
```

We can now inspect the publish folder using the tree command:

```
tree ../temp /F
```

This will show us all the files that make up our application:

```
Folder PATH listing for volume Local Disk
Volume serial number is 1044-BB65
C:\CODE\GITHUB\MICROSOFT.BLAZOR.3RD\CH15\TEMP
│   web.config
│
└───wwwroot
    │   favicon.ico
    │   icon-192.png
    │   index.html
    │   StandAlone.styles.css
    │
    ├───css
    │   │   app.css
    │   │
    │   ├───bootstrap
    │   │       bootstrap.min.css
```

```
|       |           bootstrap.min.css.map
|       |
|       └────open-iconic
|       |       FONT-LICENSE
|       |       ICON-LICENSE
|       |       README.md
|       |
|       |       └────font
|       |               ├────css
|       |               |       open-iconic-bootstrap.min.css
|       |               |
|       |               └────fonts
|       |                       open-iconic.eot
|       |                       open-iconic.otf
|       |                       open-iconic.svg
|       |                       open-iconic.ttf
|       |                       open-iconic.woff
|       |
├──────sample-data
|       weather.json
|
└─____framework
        blazor.boot.json
        blazor.boot.json.br
        blazor.boot.json.gz
        blazor.webassembly.js
        blazor.webassembly.js.br
        blazor.webassembly.js.gz
        dotnet.6.0.0-preview.7.21377.19.js
        dotnet.6.0.0-preview.7.21377.19.js.br
        dotnet.6.0.0-preview.7.21377.19.js.gz
        dotnet.timezones.blat
        dotnet.timezones.blat.br
        dotnet.timezones.blat.gz
        dotnet.wasm
```

```
dotnet.wasm.br
dotnet.wasm.gz
icudt.dat
icudt.dat.br
icudt.dat.gz
icudt_CJK.dat
icudt_CJK.dat.br
icudt_CJK.dat.gz
icudt_EFIGS.dat
icudt_EFIGS.dat.br
icudt_EFIGS.dat.gz
icudt_no_CJK.dat
icudt_no_CJK.dat.br
icudt_no_CJK.dat.gz
Microsoft.AspNetCore.Components.dll
Microsoft.AspNetCore.Components.dll.br
Microsoft.AspNetCore.Components.dll.gz
Microsoft.AspNetCore.Components.Web.dll
Microsoft.AspNetCore.Components.Web.dll.br
Microsoft.AspNetCore.Components.Web.dll.gz
Microsoft.AspNetCore.Components.WebAssembly.dll
Microsoft.AspNetCore.Components.WebAssembly.dll.br
Microsoft.AspNetCore.Components.WebAssembly.dll.gz
Microsoft.Extensions.Configuration.Abstractions.dll
Microsoft.Extensions.Configuration.Abstractions.dll.br
Microsoft.Extensions.Configuration.Abstractions.dll.gz
Microsoft.Extensions.Configuration.dll
Microsoft.Extensions.Configuration.dll.br
Microsoft.Extensions.Configuration.dll.gz
Microsoft.Extensions.Configuration.Json.dll
Microsoft.Extensions.Configuration.Json.dll.br
Microsoft.Extensions.Configuration.Json.dll.gz
Microsoft.Extensions.DependencyInjection.Abstractions.dll
Microsoft.Extensions.DependencyInjection.Abstractions.dll.br
Microsoft.Extensions.DependencyInjection.Abstractions.dll.gz
```

```
Microsoft.Extensions.DependencyInjection.dll
Microsoft.Extensions.DependencyInjection.dll.br
Microsoft.Extensions.DependencyInjection.dll.gz
Microsoft.Extensions.Logging.Abstractions.dll
Microsoft.Extensions.Logging.Abstractions.dll.br
Microsoft.Extensions.Logging.Abstractions.dll.gz
Microsoft.Extensions.Logging.dll
Microsoft.Extensions.Logging.dll.br
Microsoft.Extensions.Logging.dll.gz
Microsoft.Extensions.Options.dll
Microsoft.Extensions.Options.dll.br
Microsoft.Extensions.Options.dll.gz
Microsoft.Extensions.Primitives.dll
Microsoft.Extensions.Primitives.dll.br
Microsoft.Extensions.Primitives.dll.gz
Microsoft.JSInterop.dll
Microsoft.JSInterop.dll.br
Microsoft.JSInterop.dll.gz
Microsoft.JSInterop.WebAssembly.dll
Microsoft.JSInterop.WebAssembly.dll.br
Microsoft.JSInterop.WebAssembly.dll.gz
StandAlone.dll
StandAlone.dll.br
StandAlone.dll.gz
StandAlone.pdb.gz
System.Collections.Concurrent.dll
System.Collections.Concurrent.dll.br
System.Collections.Concurrent.dll.gz
System.Collections.dll
System.Collections.dll.br
System.Collections.dll.gz
System.ComponentModel.dll
System.ComponentModel.dll.br
System.ComponentModel.dll.gz
System.Linq.dll
```

```
System.Linq.dll.br
System.Linq.dll.gz
System.Memory.dll
System.Memory.dll.br
System.Memory.dll.gz
System.Net.Http.dll
System.Net.Http.dll.br
System.Net.Http.dll.gz
System.Net.Http.Json.dll
System.Net.Http.Json.dll.br
System.Net.Http.Json.dll.gz
System.Net.Primitives.dll
System.Net.Primitives.dll.br
System.Net.Primitives.dll.gz
System.Private.CoreLib.dll
System.Private.CoreLib.dll.br
System.Private.CoreLib.dll.gz
System.Private.Runtime.InteropServices.JavaScript.dll
System.Private.Runtime.InteropServices.JavaScript.dll.br
System.Private.Runtime.InteropServices.JavaScript.dll.gz
System.Private.Uri.dll
System.Private.Uri.dll.br
System.Private.Uri.dll.gz
System.Runtime.CompilerServices.Unsafe.dll
System.Runtime.CompilerServices.Unsafe.dll.br
System.Runtime.CompilerServices.Unsafe.dll.gz
System.Runtime.dll
System.Runtime.dll.br
System.Runtime.dll.gz
System.Text.Encodings.Web.dll
System.Text.Encodings.Web.dll.br
System.Text.Encodings.Web.dll.gz
System.Text.Json.dll
System.Text.Json.dll.br
System.Text.Json.dll.gz
```

The web.config file is used for Internet Information Services (IIS) deployments, but we don't need it for GitHub. We only need the files from the wwwroot folder, so copy this folder in our gh-pages branch:

```
mv ..\temp\wwwroot\*
```

Git works for both Windows- and Unix-based operating systems. However, these use different file endings, and we don't want git to change these. Why? Because the Blazor runtime will check if our files have been changed after deployment, and it will refuse to load these files. We can tell git not to make changes using a .gitattributes file, so add one using the following command:

```
"* binary" >> .gitattributes
```

This tells git to treat all our files as binary so it will not try to fix file endings. Commit these files and push them to the git repository on GitHub:

```
git add .
git commit -m "Step 3"
git push
```

Now you can reload the site (which will not work yet); for example, in my case, this would be https://microsoftblazorbook.github.io/StandAloneWASM/.

This will display Figure 15-1.

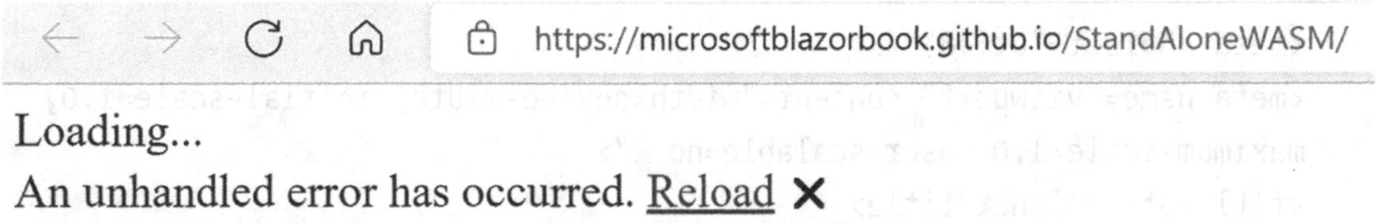

Loading...

An unhandled error has occurred. Reload ✕

Figure 15-1. *Our Blazor Site Does Not Load Correctly (Yet)*

Fix the Base Tag

Why is this not loading correctly? Open the browser debugger's console, as shown in Figure 15-2.

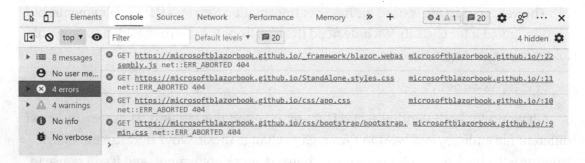

Figure 15-2. *The Browser Debugger's Console*

As you can see, the browser is trying to load the JavaScript and CSS files from the root of `https://microsoftblazorbook.github.io`, but our files are hosted at `https://microsoftblazorbook.github.io/StandAloneWASM/`. What we need to do is to instruct the browser to prefix each file's URL with StandAloneWASM. This is done through the index.html's `base` tag. And if you remember from Chapter 9, routing also used this `base` tag to figure out which component to show! So use your favorite editor to update the `base` tag in index.html to use your repository's name as in Listing 15-2.

Listing 15-2. Update the index.html's Base Tag

```
<!DOCTYPE html>
<html>

<head>
    <meta charset="utf-8" />
    <meta name="viewport" content="width=device-width, initial-scale=1.0,
    maximum-scale=1.0, user-scalable=no" />
    <title>StandAlone</title>
    <!-- Start change, use your repository's name! -->
    <base href="/StandAloneWASM/" />
    <!-- End change -->
    <link href="css/bootstrap/bootstrap.min.css" rel="stylesheet" />
    <link href="css/app.css" rel="stylesheet" />
    <link href="StandAlone.styles.css" rel="stylesheet" />
</head>
```

```
<body>
    <div id="app">Loading...</div>

    <div id="blazor-error-ui">
        An unhandled error has occurred.
        <a href="" class="reload">Reload</a>
        <a class="dismiss">✖</a>
    </div>
    <script src="_framework/blazor.webassembly.js"></script>
</body>

</html>
```

Now we can push our change to GitHub with the following commands:

```
git add .
git commit -m "Fix base tag"
git push
```

Wait for the deployment to complete and refresh your site's page. You can review the deployment process at https://github.com/MicrosoftBlazorBook/StandAloneWASM/ deployments/activity_log?environment=github-pages, replacing your organization and repository name in the URL.

Disabling Jekyll

Still not working. Again, let us look at the browser debugger's console as shown in Figure 15-3. It is loading the JavaScript and CSS files, but it cannot find the _ framework files.

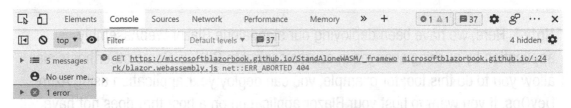

Figure 15-3. *Blazor Does Not Find the _framework Files*

Why? GitHub uses Jekyll (`https://github.com/jekyll`) which is a static site generator. Jekyll stores its files in folders that start with an underscore, and GitHub will not host files inside folders that start with an underscore. We can disable Jekyll by adding an empty `.nojekyll` file in the root folder. So use your favorite editor again to add this file and use the following commands to send this to GitHub:

```
git add .
git commit -m "Fix Jekyll"
git push
```

Wait for the deployment to complete and refresh your site's page. Your Blazor site should work! Great!

Fixing GitHub 404s

There is still one problem we need to fix. Navigate in your Blazor site to the Counter route and make the browser refresh by hitting F5. It will display a 404 page! This is because GitHub will try to load the Counter file from the URL. We can fix this by copying our root index.html file to a 404.html file, which GitHub will then send back to the browser.

First, copy index.html to 404.html using this command:

```
cp index.html 404.html
```

Now we need to push this change back to the GitHub with these commands:

```
git add .
git commit -m "Fix 404 page"
git push
```

Now refreshing the counter route will work.

Note   Here, we have been deploying our standalone Blazor WebAssembly application by pushing changes in source control to GitHub. Some other hosts also allow you to do this too; for example, you can deploy your application using Azure DevOps. If you want to host your Blazor application on a host that does not have source control integration, you will have to upload the publish folder using the host its own tools; this might even be with FTP!

Alternatives for GitHub

There are many alternatives to deploy your Blazor Standalone WebAssembly project; each will have its own little quirks to make it work, but everyone will require you to set the base tag in index.html correctly. For example, you could also deploy your project as an *Azure Static Website*. For more information about deploying your project as an Azure Static Website, visit `https://docs.microsoft.com/azure/static-web-apps/deploy-blazor`.

Deploying Your Site As WebAssembly

With .NET 6, we can now compile our complete solution as a WASM file and run everything as WebAssembly. By default, you will run .NET assemblies in the browser where the WASM .NET runtime will interpret IL instructions. By compiling everything into WASM, you can get significant performance improvements! However, the WASM file is larger than the .NET assembly equivalent, so compiling everything as WASM will come at the cost of a longer initial download. This is also known as *Ahead-Of-Time* (*AOT*) *compilation*. AOT mainly benefits applications that are CPU intensive, so you might not even need this for your application.

To enable AOT compilation, you should add the `RunAOTCompilation` flag to your project as shown in Listing 15-3.

Listing 15-3. Enabling AOT Compilation

```
<PropertyGroup>
  <TargetFramework>net6.0</TargetFramework>
  <Nullable>enable</Nullable>
  <RunAOTCompilation>true</RunAOTCompilation>
</PropertyGroup>
```

Now you can publish your application just like before with the publish command

```
dotnet publish -c Release -o release
```

This will take some time, so grab something to drink. While you are developing, AOT is not used because compiling takes so much longer.

Once deployment is ready, look inside the release/_framework folder and search for dotnet.wasm. This file on my machine is around 12 MB! Without OAT, this file is around 2 MB. Do note that the actual download is a lot smaller due to the compression used by Blazor. You will also find the original .dll files in the release folder. Sometimes your application might use reflection; in that case, the necessary .dll files are still downloaded. So we still need to deploy these.

We can now deploy our AOT compiled release just like before.

Deploying Hosted Applications

For both the hosted Blazor WebAssembly and Blazor Server applications, you will need to deploy to a host that supports executing .NET on the server. You can deploy this to Windows Internet Information Services (IIS) or to Linux Apache.

Understanding the Deployment Models

With ASP.NET Core hosted applications, we have a number of choices for deploying our application.

One option is to use a *framework-dependent deployment*. In this case, the deployment files only contain your application files with their dependencies. No runtime is deployed, so this will only work on a server where the .NET runtime has been deployed before. One advantage of using framework-dependent deployment is that your deployment will work everywhere since portable .NET assemblies are used.

The other option is to use a *self-contained deployment*. In this case, the deployment contains all the files that are needed to run the application, including the runtime. Because of this, you need to specify which platform you want to target, for example, 64-bit Windows, and it will only deploy to that platform. The main advantage of this is that there is no dependency on what has been installed on the server, except for the platform of course. Another advantage is that you can use any version of .NET, even previews. Most commercial hosts will only give you long-term support versions of the .NET runtime.

To create a deployment, you use the dotnet publish command. For example, to create a self-contained deployment for 64-bit Linux, you use

```
dotnet publish -c Release -o release --self-contained --runtime linux-x64
```

And if you want to create a portable framework-dependent deployment:

```
dotnet publish -c Release -o release –no-self-contained
```

Deploying to Microsoft Azure

Most of us don't have a server lying around to deploy to, so here we will deploy to an Azure web app. If you don't have an Azure account, you can get one for free. Open your browser and visit https://azure.microsoft.com/. Here, you can create a free account, and you even get $200 credit.

An Azure web app is a hosting service that makes it very easy to deploy and run your Blazor application.

We will use Visual Studio to create a release and deploy it into Azure. Create a new hosted Blazor WebAssembly project (or Blazor Server, your choice). Before we can deploy to Azure, we need to add our Azure account to Visual Studio. So open File ➤ Account Settings.... Click Add as in Figure 15-4 to add your Azure account.

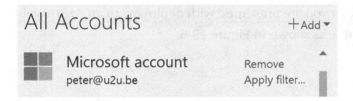

Figure 15-4. *Add Your Azure Account*

Creating the Publishing Profile

Right-click the server project and select Publish... from the drop-down menu. The Publish wizard will open, which gives you the choices of deployment targets. Choose Azure as in Figure 15-5.

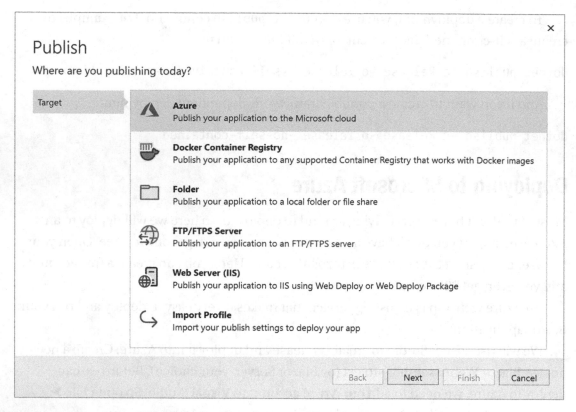

Figure 15-5. *Deploy to Azure*

Click Next. Now you are presented with deploying to an Azure web app, a container, or a virtual machine as shown in Figure 15-6.

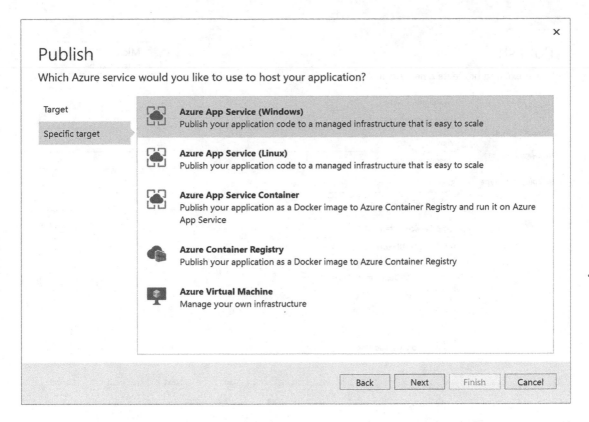

Figure 15-6. *Azure Deployment Choices*

Select Azure App Service (Windows) and click Next. Now the Select existing or create a new Azure App Service dialog from Figure 15-7 appears. You can either select an existing App Service or create a new one.

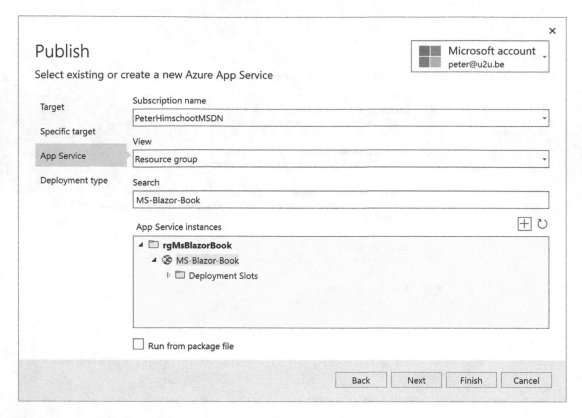

Figure 15-7. *Select Azure App Service*

Click the + button to add a new Azure App Service. Figure 15-8 will be shown. Enter a unique name, select your Azure subscription if you have more than one, and create a new resource group and hosting plan.

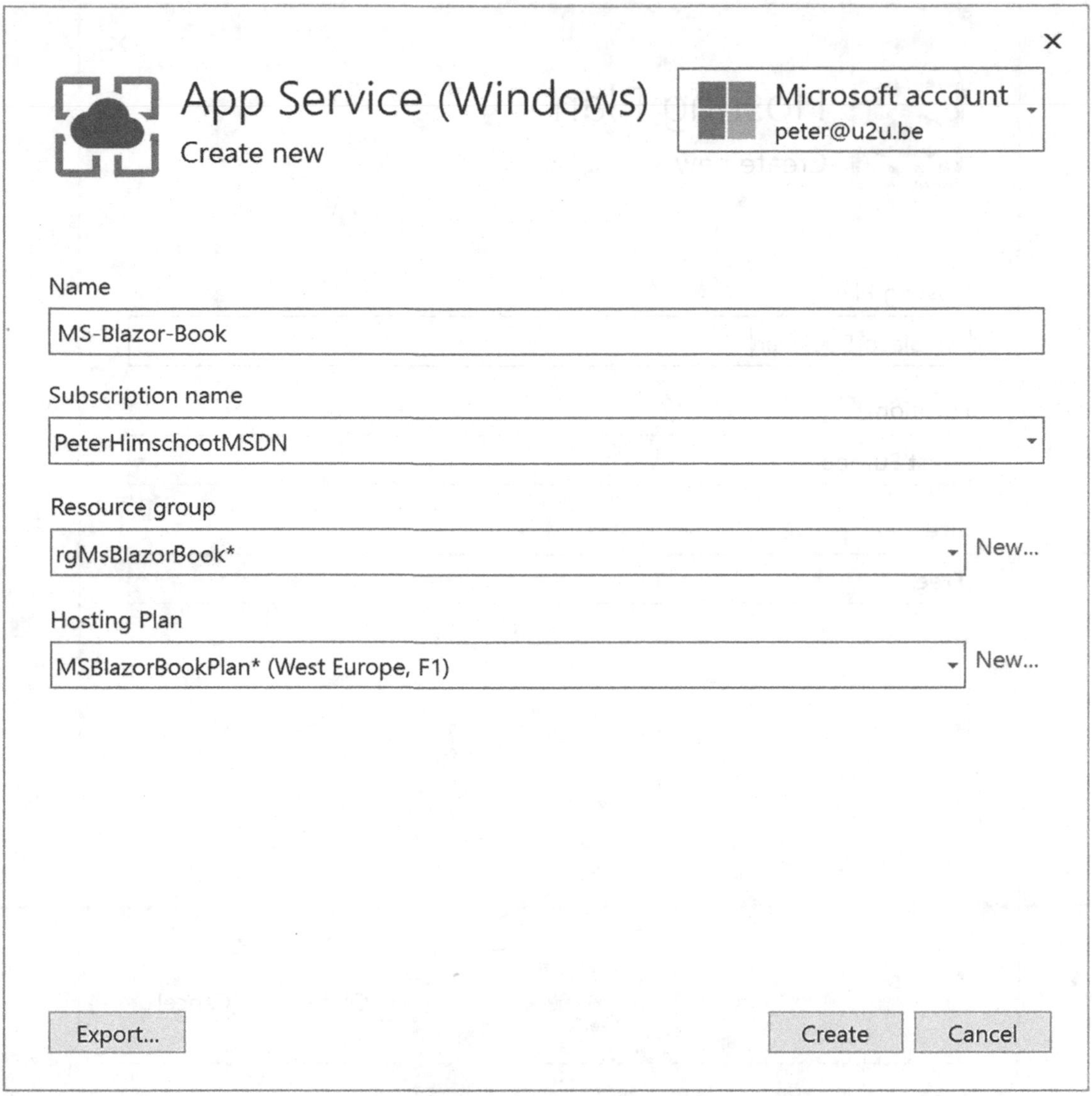

App Service (Windows)
Create new

☒ Microsoft account
peter@u2u.be

×

Name

MS-Blazor-Book

Subscription name

PeterHimschootMSDN

Resource group

rgMsBlazorBook*   New...

Hosting Plan

MSBlazorBookPlan* (West Europe, F1)   New...

Export...   Create   Cancel

Figure 15-8. *Create an App Service Dialog*

A resource group groups together a bunch of Azure resources, such as a web app and its database, and allows you to manage and delete all of them as one. To create a new resource group, click New... and enter a new resource group name.

A hosting plan will select what kind of hardware your site will run on and the data center where the hardware resides. Click New... and enter a name, select a data center near you, and select the Free size (shown here as F1 in Figure 15-8) as in Figure 15-9. You can have up to ten free hosting plans per region for your subscription.

Figure 15-9. *Create a Hosting Plan*

Click Next again and select the Publish option as in Figure 15-10. The other option will set up for you a Continuous Integration and Deployment using *GitHub Actions* which actually is a better option. With GitHub Actions, you can have your site deployed automatically every time you push new features into your repository. If you would like to learn more about GitHub Actions, visit `https://github.com/features/actions`, or if you prefer a book, read `www.apress.com/gp/book/9781484264638`.

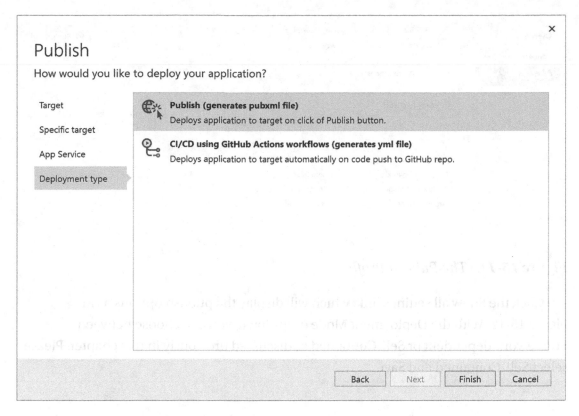

Figure 15-10. *Publish or Use CI/CD*

Select Finish.

Selecting Publishing Options

VS will now display the Publish profile as in Figure 15-11, and you can change some of the deployment options before proceeding.

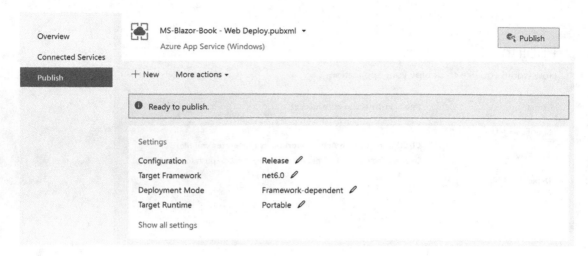

Figure 15-11. *The Publish Profile*

Click the Show all settings link, which will display the publish options as in
Figure 15-12. With the Deployment Mode drop-down, you can choose between
Framework-dependent or Self-Contained as discussed previously in this chapter. Please
select Self-Contained and Save.

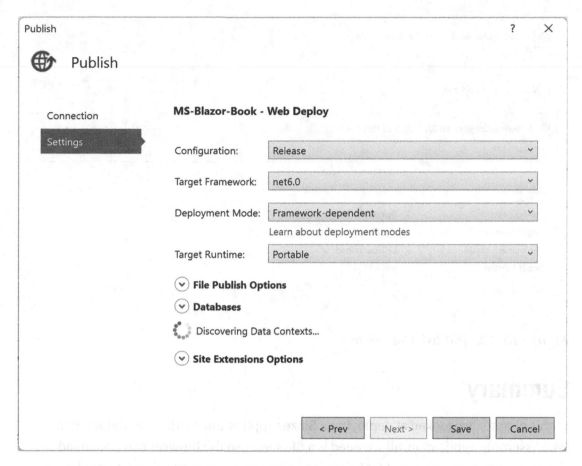

Figure 15-12. *Publish Options*

Publishing the Application

Now you can click the Publish button as shown in the top right corner of Figure 15-11. Visual Studio will build a release version and deploy it to Azure.

When publishing completes, an alert as in Figure 15-13 will be shown. Click the link to look at the result of the publish. Now everyone with an Internet connection can admire your work!

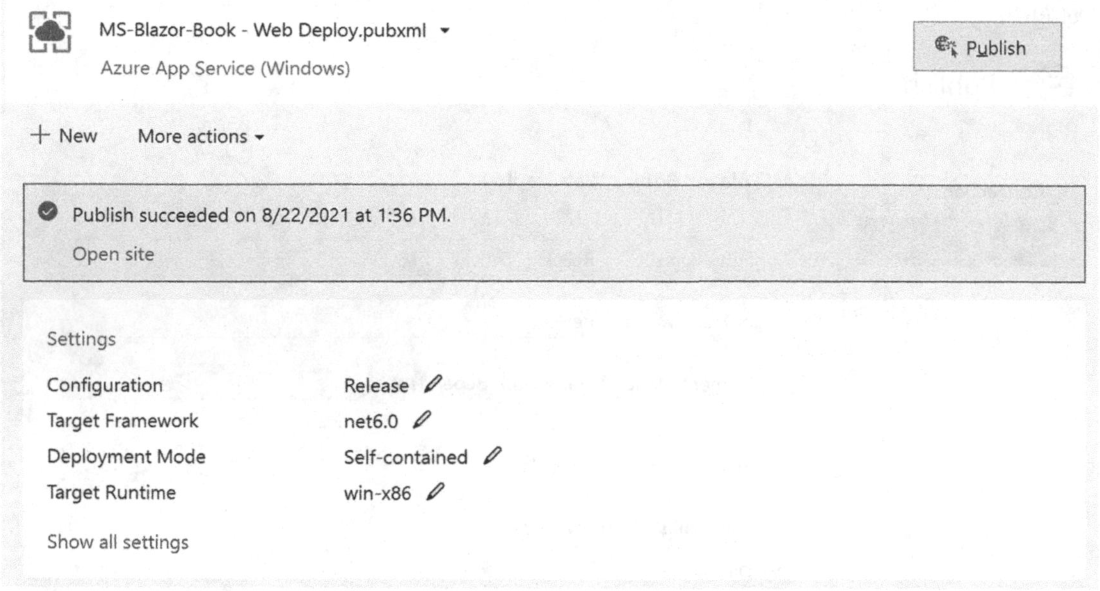

Figure 15-13. *Publish Complete*

Summary

In this chapter, we looked at deploying a Blazor application. With a standalone Blazor WebAssembly application, all we need is a file server so the browser can download the html, CSS, JavaScript, and DLL files. As an example, we used GitHub to deploy to. Remember to set the `base` tag in the html page to match the location where the files are downloaded from.

Deploying a Blazor Server or Blazor WebAssembly hosted project is just like deploying an ASP.NET Core site. As an example, we deployed our application to Azure as a web app. Visual Studio takes care of most of the work. Without Visual Studio, we can still create a deployment using the command line, and then we would need to upload the files onto the server. Each hosting provider has their own specific way of doing this.

CHAPTER 16

Security with OpenId Connect

Many web applications need some way to identify the user, also known as *authentication*. Sometimes this is only to show the user what they were looking at before, so we need an identity to retrieve the user's state from the server. Sometimes we need to protect certain resources, also known as *authorization*, which can be personal information, or contents that the user has paid for, or because of some legal requirement. In this chapter, we will look at *OpenId Connect* and how we can use this to identify the user and decide what the current user can do.

Representing the User

Let us first discuss how we can represent users. You might think that we just need to know the user's name, but this is not true. We will represent the user as a collection of properties about the user, which can include the user's name and also information like age and which department the user works for. We call this *claims-based security*. Some claims can represent things the user can do; these are known as roles. For example, one claim could state that the user has the admin role, allowing our software to check the role instead of the name. Users can move around in an organization, and then you simply change the role claims to give users more or less things they can do with the software.

Using Claims-Based Security

Claims-based security uses a *token* to represent the user, and this token is a collection of *claims* about the user. Claims represent statements about the user; for example, one claim could be that the user's first name is Peter. In real life, we also have tokens; for example, your passport is a nice example of a token, containing claims such as your

© Peter Himschoot 2022
P. Himschoot, *Microsoft Blazor*, https://doi.org/10.1007/978-1-4842-7845-1_16

nationality, name, date of birth, etc. If this was all there about a token, they would be worthless because anyone could create a token. Why does the airport security trust your passport? Because it was issued by a *trusted party*, also known as an *identity provider*. In my case, the airport security trusts the claims on my passport because it was issued by the Belgian government. Passports use all kinds of nifty protections such as holograms to make it hard to create a passable fake passport. Tokens used by computers work in the same manner; they are issued by a trusted party, which uses a digital signature so that the *relying party* (the application) can verify to see if the token was issued by a trusted party known to the application. Of course, the identity provider will need a way to verify who the user actually is. They can use any means they want, a user and password combination, or some smart card you need to insert in a card reader. This whole process is illustrated in Figure 16-1.

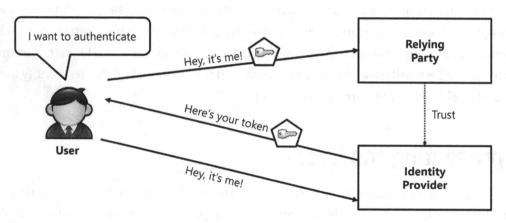

Figure 16-1. *The Authentication Process*

One more aspect about tokens is that once a user has received a token, the user can use it again and again without the need to go back to the identity provider. Of course, there needs to be a limit to this, and that is why tokens have a valid period, and after this period, the user will need to get a new token. My passport was issued to me a couple of years ago, but I can still use it until it expires. Then I will have to go back to city hall and get a new one. Of course, software tokens will not last that long, because it is easy to get a new one over the network.

Understanding Token Serialization

How are tokens serialized over a network? Modern applications using REST use the *JSON Web Token* (*JWT*) open standard. This allows us to transmit tokens in a secure way in the form of a JSON object.

JWT tokens are serialized as a base-64 encoded string, and each token consists of three parts, a header, a payload containing the claims, and a signature. Listing 16-1 shows an example of a serialized token.

Listing 16-1. A Serialized Token

eyJhbGciOiJSUzI1NiIsImtpZCI6InVibTdLa1BjQXZ5Z0NXYlR1djRVQWciLCJoeXAiOiJKV1Q
ifQ.eyJuYmYiOjE2MjY5NTIzMDAsImV4cCI6MTYyNjk1MjYwMCwiaXNzIjoiaHR0cHM6Ly9sb2
NhbGhvc3Q6NTAwMCIsImF1ZCI6ImJsYXpvciIsImlhdCI6MTYyNjk1MjMwMCwiYXRfaGFzaCI6I
k9oMFRJdXExZVh6S2pDaXExdVpKdGciLCJzX2hhc2giOiJOaWwwcmllZzUwdWdlBTdU45TVNnNTl3
Iiwic2lkIjoibXBqODROWkdaNaOlORGtXWgwR0FNQSIsInN1YiI6IjZkOTY4NjIxLTI3ZTAtND
ZkYS1iNzNiLTlkNWNjNjODc4ZGIwYSIsImF1dGhfdGltZSI6MTYyNjk1MjI5OSwiaWRwIjoibG9
jYWwiLCJhbXIiOlsicHdkIl19.fORm_sVFlwc2PnJwFmufrDLY9h1HJ6VnejdouMKhMYOwfyK
LukUa6D3Zum5gRw-4jJQvevaBQe5dGFmZzN24nS8bzTOC3UxSLUTtdNIajiQ5SpHOdkuM5HDO9
AOmdKygy5MizAsXTiClOymXFXun-gS1YfM2mezrvjJbhgY-gRAxCyOnnPaIDs1M6gQ_zMuyb
lwznj5ovo-Hh_tWD3qHE_ttEsDJe6KR9aM1-Qyz87sKn-wL_oo6DKiyCimG_y6qe27hjmuSg-B5
BDOeOUEaHEpSHXwrdJCTuYAY88Jx2k5W_fDnqwWPFx9Yvtkycp-nrBoOlbsOEzByj8QHOCoTBg

This token is not human-readable, but using a tool like https://jwt.io, you can easily inspect the token's content. Doing this reveals that this token contains the following header with the type of the token (JWT) and the signing algorithm:

```
{
  "alg": "RS256",
  "kid": "ubm7KkPcAvygCWbTuv4UAg",
  "typ": "JWT"
}
```

Generally, you should ignore the header, but the payload contains the following claims:

```
{
  "nbf": 1626952300,
  "exp": 1626952600,
  "iss": "https://localhost:5000",
  "aud": "blazor",
  "iat": 1626952300,
  "at_hash": "OhOTIuq1eXzKjCiq1uZJtg",
  "s_hash": "NilOrieg50vPSuN9MSgO9w",
  "sid": "mpj84NZGMkINDkWQhOGAMA",
  "sub": "6d968621-27e0-46da-b73b-9d5cc878db0a",
  "auth_time": 1626952299,
  "idp": "local",
  "amr": [
    "pwd"
  ]
}
```

The **issuer** claim (`iss`) states that this token was issued by my development identity provider with URL `https://localhost:5000`, and the **not before** claim (`nbf`) together with the **expiry** claim (`exp`) gives this token a validity period. The **audience** claim (`aud`) states that this token is intended for the application called Blazor. Finally, the **subject** claim (`sub`) contains a unique identifier for the current user. There are a lot of other official claims you can find in a token, and you can find their meaning on the IANA JSON Web Token Registry's site at `www.iana.org/assignments/jwt/jwt.xhtml`.

The payload of the token is not encrypted, so never include sensitive information in here!

The signature allows our software to check if the token has been modified, and again you should ignore this (but not our software!).

Representing Claims in .NET

So how are claims represented in .NET? From the start, Microsoft has provided us with two interfaces to represent the user, `IPrincipal` and `IIdentity`.

The IPrincipal interface represents the security context for the current user, including the user's identity (the IIdentity interface) and roles. It is implemented by the ClaimsPrincipal class which holds a collection of Claim instances in its Claims property. Our code will use the ClaimsPrincipal instance to see if a user holds a certain claim. For example, we can retrieve the user's name using the implementation from Listing 16-2. Here, we use the AuthenticationState class (more details later) with the User property of type ClaimsPrincipal. The ClaimsPrincipal class has the FindFirst method which will search the collection of Claims and returns the claim with given key or returns a null if there is no claim with the given key. Here, I use the ClaimTypes class which holds the name of most standard claims.

Listing 16-2. Retrieving the Name of the User from ClaimsPrincipal

```
Claim givenNameClaim =
  authState.User.FindFirst(ClaimTypes.GivenName);
```

OpenId Connect

OpenId Connect is a standard protocol that allows us to secure our applications, including websites, mobile applications, server, and desktop applications. Because of differences in application types, OpenId Connect describes a number of flows, such as Resource Owner Password Credential, Client Credential, Implicit, Authorization Code, and Hybrid flows. With Blazor, we will use the Hybrid and Authorization Code flows.

Understanding OpenId Connect Hybrid Flow

In Blazor Server, we will use the *Hybrid flow*, so let us review how this flow works as illustrated in Figure 16-2. Figure 16-2 shows the identity provider, our Blazor Server application, and the user using a browser. When we look at Blazor WebAssembly, we will review Authorization Code flow.

When the not yet authenticated user visits a protected resource (Step 1), the Blazor Server will return an HTTP redirect result (Step 2) which will make the browser visit the identity provider, also known as an authorization server (AS). The URL contains credential information about the client (the ClientId and ClientSecret) together with a redirect URI. The identity provider identifies the client application through its ClientId and verifies if the redirect URI matches its list of registered client redirect URIs. The identity provider will then present the user with some kind of login UI (Step 3), for example, to enter the username and password. The identity provider is free how this login process works, and after a successful login, the identity provider will return an HTTP redirect to the browser (Step 4) so the browser will visit the redirect URI (the Blazor Server application) with the request containing a code and identity token. The redirect URI is then processed by the Blazor application, the identity token is turned into a ClaimsPrincipal, and the user has been authenticated. The Blazor application is also responsible for storing the ClaimsPrincipal, and with Blazor Server, this is done by storing the ClaimsPrincipal in a cookie, so the next request containing that cookie can deserialize it again. For the moment, we don't need the code, but we will use it later.

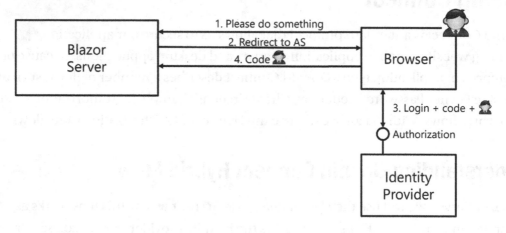

Figure 16-2. *The OpenId Connect Hybrid Flow*

A couple of remarks: an identity provider will only send tokens to known redirect URIs, so these have to be registered with the identity provider. This prevents unknown parties (hackers!) from hijacking requests. When you deploy your application, you should not forget to register the new redirect URI in the identity provider. There can be several registered redirect URIs, so you can keep developing locally and run the application in production using the same identity provider.

Identity Providers

There are many identity providers out there. For example, there is Microsoft Azure Active Directory, Google, Facebook, etc. Each of these identity providers comes with their own UI, but as long as they use OpenID Connect, the implementation works on the same principles.

Here, I want to use IdentityServer4 (`www.identityserver.com/`) which allows you to build your own identity provider for free (however, identity server is not free for commercial use). These people need to eat too!

Implementing the Identity Provider with IdentityServer4

Let us start by creating the project that we will use as our identity provider, using IdentityServer4. Create a new AspNet .NET Core Web App project and name it IdentityProvider.

Modify the ports in launchSettings.json as in Listing 16-3. Our identity provider needs to run on another URI, and changing the port is the easiest way. Here, we will use HTTPS port 5011.

Listing 16-3. Changing the Port

```
{
  ...
  "profiles": {
    "IdentityProvider": {
      "commandName": "Project",
      "dotnetRunMessages": true,
      "launchBrowser": true,
      "applicationUrl": "https://localhost:5011;http://localhost:5010",
      "environmentVariables": {
        "ASPNETCORE_ENVIRONMENT": "Development"
      }
    },
    ...
  }
}
```

Use NuGet to add the latest stable version of *IdentityServer4,* or modify your project directly as in Listing 16-4.

Listing 16-4. Use NuGet to Add IdentityServer4

```
<Project Sdk="Microsoft.NET.Sdk.Web">

  <PropertyGroup>
    <TargetFramework>net6.0</TargetFramework>
  </PropertyGroup>

  <ItemGroup>
    <PackageReference Include="IdentityServer4" Version="4.1.2" />
  </ItemGroup>

</Project>
```

Configure dependency injection for IdentityServer by modifying the `Startup` class's `ConfigureServices` method as in Listing 16-5.

Listing 16-5. Configuring Dependency Injection

```
public void ConfigureServices(IServiceCollection services)
{
  services.AddIdentityServer();
}
```

And use IdentityServer in the ASP.NET pipeline with the `Configure` method as in Listing 16-6.

Listing 16-6. Adding IdentityServer to the Pipeline

```
public void Configure(IApplicationBuilder app,
                      IWebHostEnvironment env)
{
  if (env.IsDevelopment())
  {
    app.UseDeveloperExceptionPage();
  }
  app.UseIdentityServer();
}
```

IdentityServer4 can be configured using a database or an in-memory configuration. We will use the latter because it is easier for learning and experimentation. Add a new class called Config to the project next to Program.cs. This Config class will contain the configuration for IdentityServer4.

First, we need a couple of users, so add the GetUsers method from Listing 16-7. We use IdentityServer's TestUser class which allows us to set the SubjectId unique key, Username, Password, and Claims. We also add a couple of standard identifying claims which belong to the *Profile* scope. *Scopes* are used to group a number of claims and can be requested during the authentication process.

Listing 16-7. Adding Users to IdentityServer

```
public static List<TestUser> GetUsers()
=> new List<TestUser>
{
  new TestUser
  {
    SubjectId = "{223C9865-03BE-4951-8911-740A438FCF9D}",
    Username = "peter@u2u.be",
    Password = "u2u-secret",
    Claims = new List<Claim>
    {
      new Claim("given_name", "Peter"),
      new Claim(JwtClaimTypes.Name, "Peter Himschoot"),
      new Claim("family_name", "Himschoot"),
    }
  },
  new TestUser
  {
    SubjectId = "{34119795-78A6-44C2-B128-30BFBC29139D}",
    Username = "student@u2u.be",
    Password = "u2u-secret",
    Claims = new List<Claim>
    {
      new Claim("given_name", "Student"),
```

```
      new Claim(JwtClaimTypes.Name, "Student Blazor"),
      new Claim("family_name", "Blazor"),
    }
  }
};
```

Next, we need to add a couple of identity resources with the GetIdentityResources method from Listing 16-8. These map to scopes that will give us access to certain claims from configuration. Scopes are used to group claims and provide an easy way to request claims. The OpenId method will give us access to the subject id (sid) which is a unique identifier of the current user, and the Profile method gives us access to claims about the user, such as given_name and family_name.

Listing 16-8. Adding Identity Resources

```
public static IEnumerable<IdentityResource> GetIdentityResources()
=> new List<IdentityResource>
{
  new IdentityResources.OpenId(),
  new IdentityResources.Profile(),
};
```

We will also need to add the client applications that our identity provider will support. For the moment, we will only have one client, so implement the GetClients method as in Listing 16-9. Here, we added the ClientId and ClientSecrets which the client will use to prove itself. We will use the *Hybrid* flow as described before, and we set the RedirectUris to include the client's URI. We also need to configure which scopes our client application will get. The Profile and OpenId scopes are provided by default, but we will add more scopes later, and it does not hurt to be explicit.

Listing 16-9. Adding Clients

```
public static IEnumerable<Client> GetClients()
=> new List<Client>
{
  new Client
  {
    ClientName = "Blazor Server",
```

```
    ClientId = "BlazorServer",
    AllowedGrantTypes = GrantTypes.Hybrid,
    RedirectUris = new List<string>{
      "https://localhost:5001/signin-oidc"
    },
    RequirePkce = false,
    AllowedScopes = {
      IdentityServerConstants.StandardScopes.OpenId,
      IdentityServerConstants.StandardScopes.Profile
    },
    ClientSecrets = { new Secret("u2u-secret".Sha512()) },
    RequireConsent = true
  }
};
```

Now we are ready to complete the configuration as in Listing 16-10. Here, we are adding our users, identity resources, and clients. We also need a valid certificate for signing, and when developing, we can use the AddDeveloperSigningCredentials. When you move to production, you will have to get a valid certificate and use the AddSigningCredentials method.

Listing 16-10. Adding Users, Identity Resources, and Clients

```
public void ConfigureServices(IServiceCollection services)
=> services.AddIdentityServer()
        .AddInMemoryIdentityResources(
          Config.GetIdentityResources())
        .AddTestUsers(Config.GetUsers())
        .AddInMemoryClients(Config.GetClients())
        .AddDeveloperSigningCredential();
```

You can now run your identity provider if you like. However, you will not get any UI until we complete the next step. IdentityServer4 will emit logging in the console, for example:

```
info: IdentityServer4.Startup[0]
    Starting IdentityServer4 version
4.1.2+997a6cdd643e46cd5762b710c4ddc43574cbec2e
info: IdentityServer4.Startup[0]
```

```
       You are using the in-memory version of the persisted grant store.
       This will store consent decisions, authorization codes, refresh
       and reference tokens in memory only. If you are using any of those
       features in production, you want to switch to a different store
       implementation.
info: IdentityServer4.Startup[0]
       Using the default authentication scheme idsrv for IdentityServer
info: Microsoft.Hosting.Lifetime[14]
       Now listening on: https://localhost:5011
info: Microsoft.Hosting.Lifetime[14]
       Now listening on: http://localhost:5010
info: Microsoft.Hosting.Lifetime[0]
       Application started. Press Ctrl+C to shut down.
info: Microsoft.Hosting.Lifetime[0]
       Hosting environment: Development
info: Microsoft.Hosting.Lifetime[0]
       Content root path: C:\Code\GitHub\Microsoft.Blazor.3rd\Ch16\Blazor.
       OpenIdConnect\src\IdentityProvider
```

Adding the Login UI to Our Identity Provider

When our users want to log in to the identity provider, the identity provider will present a login screen to the user. IdentityServer4 comes with a built-in UI, so here we will add this to the IdentityProvider project.

Getting everything installed is pretty easy with dotnet CLI.

You can get all files installed using dotnet CLI using the following command from your project's folder:

```
dotnet new -i identityserver4.templates
dotnet new is4ui
```

This will install two new folders called QuickStart and Views and will also install some CSS and scripts in the wwwroot folder.

Of course, we need to add support for MVC in the IdentityProvider project so it can render the login and consent pages. Add support for controllers and views in the ConfigureServices method as in Listing 16-11.

Listing 16-11. Configure Services for MVC

```
public void ConfigureServices(IServiceCollection services)
{
  services.AddIdentityServer()
          .AddInMemoryIdentityResources(
            Config.GetIdentityResources())
          .AddTestUsers(Config.GetUsers())
          .AddInMemoryClients(Config.GetClients())
          .AddDeveloperSigningCredential();
  services.AddControllersWithViews();
}
```

And use the middleware from Listing 16-12 in the pipeline.

Listing 16-12. Adding MVC Middleware

```
public void Configure(IApplicationBuilder app, IWebHostEnvironment env)
{
  if (env.IsDevelopment())
  {
    app.UseDeveloperExceptionPage();
  }
  app.UseStaticFiles();
  app.UseRouting();
  app.UseIdentityServer();
  app.UseAuthorization();
  app.UseEndpoints(endpoints =>
  {
    endpoints.MapDefaultControllerRoute();
  });
}
```

Running the application will show the UI similar to Figure 16-3.

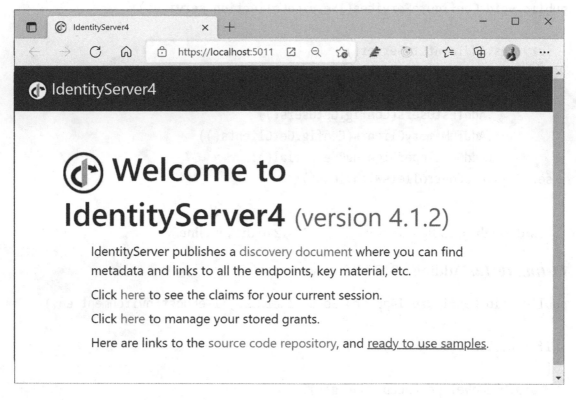

Figure 16-3. *The Identity Server Home Page*

Click the second link (see the claims); you will be asked to log in (with one of our users from Listing 16-7), after which it will display the claims just like Figure 16-4.

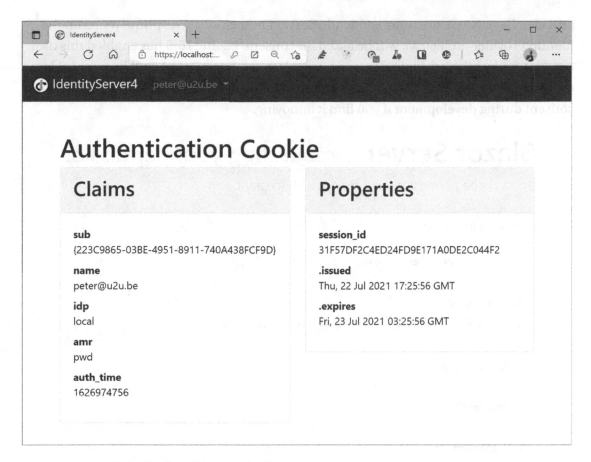

Figure 16-4. *Displaying the User's Claims*

Understanding User Consent

OpenId Connect is used to authenticate users, but it is also used to allow an application to access another application's resources. Facebook, for example, uses this to allow third-party applications to use Facebook's identity provider as an authentication mechanism and then to post things on your Facebook page. When the user logs in for the first time, an identity provider should tell the user which claims will be used by the application, and a user can then decide which claims it will allow. IdentityServer4's default UI will look somewhat like Figure 16-5. This will list the personal information that the application will be able to access and also any APIs that the application can access on the user's behalf. Users can then click the "Yes, Allow" button after optionally unchecking any claims they don't want to share. Next time, the identity provider will not ask this question again because this information is stored by the identity provider. Because we are running IdentityServer4 in memory, every time we rerun the IdentityProvider project, we will be asked for consent. Listing 16-9 has enabled this user consent, and while developing, you can use this to temporarily test stuff by unchecking claims and see how your application reacts to this missing claim. Feel free to disable user consent during development if you find it annoying.

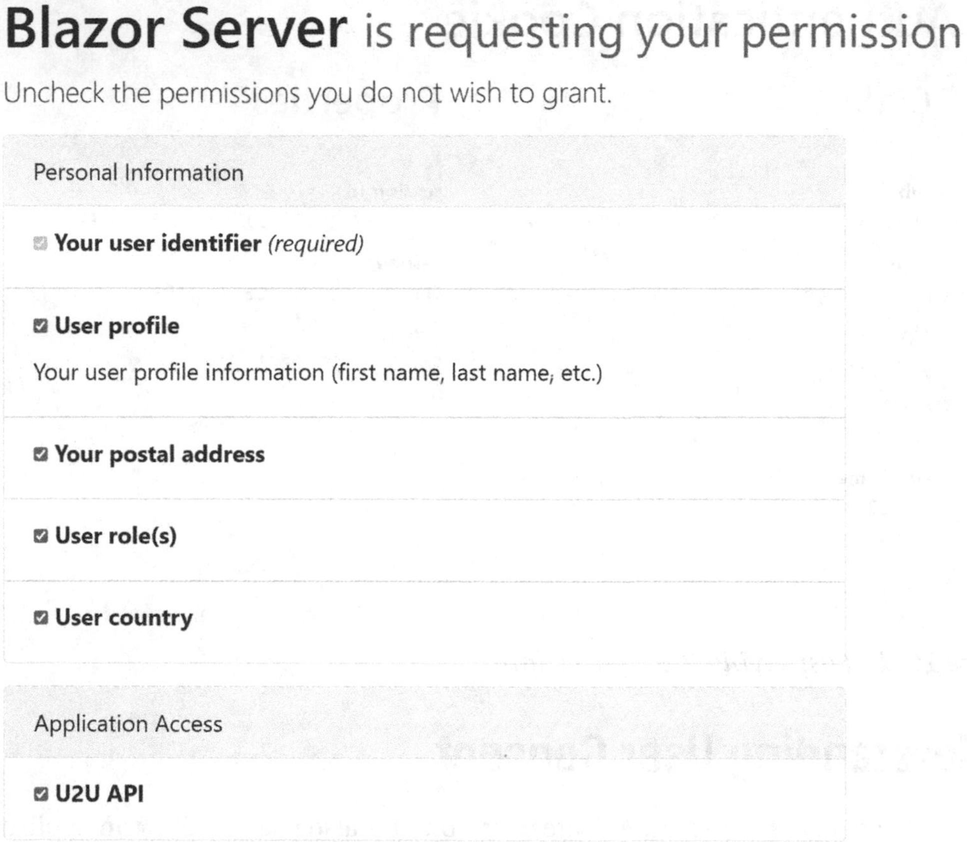

Blazor Server is requesting your permission

Uncheck the permissions you do not wish to grant.

Personal Information

☑ **Your user identifier** *(required)*

☑ **User profile**
Your user profile information (first name, last name, etc.)

☑ **Your postal address**

☑ **User role(s)**

☑ **User country**

Application Access

☑ **U2U API**

Figure 16-5. *The User Consent Screen*

Protecting a Blazor Server Application with Hybrid Flow

Now that we have our own identity provider, we can build a Blazor Server application and secure it. Later, we will do the same for Blazor WebAssembly.

Add a new Blazor Server application to the existing solution and name it Blazor. Server.OpenIdConnect. If you are using Visual Studio, leave the Authentication Type set to None. This will generate the project without any authentication components. In the next chapter on using OpenId Connect with Blazor WebAssembly, you will use a more practical approach that will generate the authentication components for you using the Authentication Type set to Individual Accounts.

Adding OpenId Connect to Blazor Server

Add the `Microsoft.AspNetCore.Authentication.OpenIdConnect` package to the Blazor.Server.OpenIdConnect project.

Now add Listing 16-13 to the `Startup` class's `ConfigureServices` method of your Blazor Server project. This tells authentication to retrieve and store the `ClaimsPrincipal` in a cookie and use it as the `DefaultScheme`. You can also configure the cookie's name and expiry period here, but we will go with the defaults. We are also telling the middleware that when the user is not yet authenticated, it should use OpenId Connect through the `DefaultChallengeScheme` property.

Listing 16-13. Configuring Authentication

```
services.AddAuthentication(options =>
{
  options.DefaultScheme =
    CookieAuthenticationDefaults.AuthenticationScheme;
  options.DefaultChallengeScheme =
    OpenIdConnectDefaults.AuthenticationScheme;
})
.AddCookie(CookieAuthenticationDefaults.AuthenticationScheme);
```

Next, we should add the authentication/authorization middleware in the `Configure` method as shown in Listing 16-14.

Listing 16-14. Add Authentication Middleware

```
app.UseRouting();
app.UseAuthentication();
app.UseAuthorization();
```

We still need to tell the OpenIdConnect middleware where it should go if there is no valid cookie containing the `ClaimsPrincipal`. So add Listing 16-15 to the

563

ConfigureServices method right after the AddCookie method. Here, we set the Authority property to the URL of the identity provider (which runs on port 5011), and we pass the ClientId and ClientSecret of the Client we configured in Listing 16-9. We also tell it to use the Hybrid flow (code id_token) and that it should get the profile claims such as given_name from the userinfo endpoint which will result in a smaller initial id token.

Listing 16-15. Configuring OpenId Connect

```
.AddOpenIdConnect(OpenIdConnectDefaults.AuthenticationScheme,
 options =>
{
  options.SignInScheme =
    CookieAuthenticationDefaults.AuthenticationScheme;
  options.Authority = "https://localhost:5011";
  options.ClientId = "BlazorServer";
  options.ClientSecret = "u2u-secret";

  // When set to code, the middleware will use PKCE protection
  options.ResponseType = "code id_token";

  // It's recommended to always get claims from the
  // UserInfoEndpoint during the flow.
  options.GetClaimsFromUserInfoEndpoint = true;
});
```

Implementing Authorization in Blazor Server

Before running the application, we should also protect one of our resources; otherwise, there is no need to authenticate using the identity provider. But first we need to understand how authentication works in Blazor using the AuthenticationState and AuthenticationStateProvider classes. The AuthenticationState class allows access to the current user's claims with the User property of type ClaimsPrincipal, and the AuthenticationStateProvider abstracts away how we retrieve the current AuthenticationState, because the process is different in Blazor Server and Blazor WebAssembly. So you should always use the AuthenticationStateProvider in your Blazor components if you want these to work in both Blazor Server and Blazor WebAssembly. Listing 16-16 contains a nice example of how you do this.

In Blazor Server, the user's `ClaimsPrincipal` is stored in the `HttpContext.User` property so `AuthenticationStateProvider` retrieves it there.

Let us update the Index component to show the list of claims of the current user. Add a new class called `Index` as the code-beside class (so use the Index.razor.cs filename) and implement it as in Listing 16-16. Here, we use the `AuthenticationStateProvider` received through dependency injection and call its `GetAuthenticationStateAsync` asynchronous method. When we receive a non-null `AuthenticationState` instance, we set the `Claims` and `UserName` properties for use in the component.

Listing 16-16. Using the AuthenticationState in a Component

```csharp
using Microsoft.AspNetCore.Components;
using Microsoft.AspNetCore.Components.Authorization;
using System.Collections.Generic;
using System.Linq;
using System.Security.Claims;
using System.Threading.Tasks;

namespace Blazor.Server.OpenIdConnect.Pages
{
  public partial class Index
  {
    [Inject]
    public AuthenticationStateProvider
      AuthenticationStateProvider { get; set; }

    private IEnumerable<Claim> Claims { get; set; }

    public string UserName { get; set; } = "Unknown";

    protected override async Task OnInitializedAsync()
    {
      AuthenticationState authState =
        await AuthenticationStateProvider
              .GetAuthenticationStateAsync();

      if (authState is not null)
      {
        Claims = authState.User.Claims;
```

565

```
      Claim givenNameClaim =
        authState.User.FindFirst("given_name");
      if( givenNameClaim is not null)
      {
        UserName = givenNameClaim.Value;
      }
    }
   }
  }
 }
}
```

Update the Index component's markup as in Listing 16-17. Here, we display the UserName property, and we iterate over each Claim and display it. We also protect the Index component using the Authorize attribute, so only authenticated users can see it.

Listing 16-17. The Index Component

```
@page "/"
@attribute [Authorize]

<h1>Hello, world!</h1>

Welcome @UserName

@if( Claims is not null )
{
  foreach(Claim claim in Claims)
  {
    <p>@claim.Type - @claim.Value</p>
  }
}
```

But wait, there is more. We need routing to check the Authorize attribute, so we will need to make same changes to routing. In our application, the App component contains the router. When we want to redirect the user to the identity provider so he or she can log in, we need to use the AuthorizeRouteView. This templated component has a NotAuthorized property that allows us to show some UI if the user is not authorized to view the protected component. Update the App component as in Listing 16-18.

First, we wrap the `Router` component in a `CascadingAuthenticationState` component, which provides the current `AuthenticationState` as a cascading parameter. This component is required for the `AuthorizeRouteView`. In the `NotAuthorized` property of the `AuthorizeRouteView`, we first check if the user has been authenticated. If not, we use the `RedirectToLogin` component (to follow) to redirect the user to the identity provider so he or she can log in. Otherwise, it means that the user tried to access a protected resource that this user is not allowed to use, so we show some unauthorized UI.

Listing 16-18. Update App Component

```
<CascadingAuthenticationState>
  <Router AppAssembly="@typeof(Program).Assembly"
    PreferExactMatches="@true">
    <Found Context="routeData">
      <AuthorizeRouteView RouteData="@routeData"
                          DefaultLayout="@typeof(MainLayout)">
        <NotAuthorized>
          @if (!context.User.Identity.IsAuthenticated)
          {
            <RedirectToLogin />
          }
          else
          {
            <p>
              You are not authorized to access this resource.
            </p>
          }
        </NotAuthorized>
      </AuthorizeRouteView>
    </Found>
    <NotFound>
      <LayoutView Layout="@typeof(MainLayout)">
        <p>Sorry, there's nothing at this address.</p>
      </LayoutView>
    </NotFound>
  </Router>
</CascadingAuthenticationState>
```

567

Let us see how we can redirect the user to the identity provider and back. Add a new component called `RedirectToLogin` with contents from Listing 16-19. This Blazor component tells the browser to navigate to the login page. We are running as a Blazor Server application, so we need to tell the ASP.NET application to perform the login, which requires a couple of hoops to jump through.

Listing 16-19. Add RedirectToLogin

```
@inject NavigationManager Navigation
@code {
  protected override void OnInitialized()
  {
    Navigation.NavigateTo(
      $"/login?returnUrl={Uri.EscapeDataString(Navigation.Uri)}");
  }
}
```

Add a new razor page (NOT a razor component!) and name it Login.cshtml. Complete its markup as in Listing 16-20 and model as in Listing 16-21. Its major purpose it to redirect the browser to the identity provider using the OpenId Connect middleware. The way to do this is to return a `Challenge ActionResult`, passing the OpenId Connect option and the redirect URI, so after the user has been successfully authenticated, we end up at the protected component. When the user has been already authenticated, it immediately redirects back to the `redirectUri`.

Listing 16-20. Add the Login.cshtml Razor Page

```
@page
@model Blazor.Server.OpenIdConnect.LoginModel
@{
}
```

Listing 16-21. The Login Page's Model

```
using Microsoft.AspNetCore.Authentication;
using Microsoft.AspNetCore.Authentication.OpenIdConnect;
using Microsoft.AspNetCore.Mvc;
using Microsoft.AspNetCore.Mvc.RazorPages;
```

```
using System.Threading.Tasks;

namespace Blazor.Server.OpenIdConnect
{
  public class LoginModel : PageModel
  {
    public async Task<IActionResult> OnGetAsync(
      string redirectUri)
    {
      // just to remove compiler warning
      await Task.CompletedTask;

      if (string.IsNullOrWhiteSpace(redirectUri))
      {
        redirectUri = Url.Content("~/");
      }
      // If user is already logged in, we can redirect directly...
      if (HttpContext.User.Identity.IsAuthenticated)
      {
        Response.Redirect(redirectUri);
      }

      return Challenge(
          new AuthenticationProperties
          {
            RedirectUri = redirectUri
          },
          OpenIdConnectDefaults.AuthenticationScheme);
    }
  }
}
```

Let us walk through the authentication process step by step. First, start the IdentityProvider project; next, start the Blazor.Server.OpenIdConnect project.

Note   Please do not forget to always start the IdentityProvider project; the easiest way with Visual Studio is to set up multiple startup projects.

On the Browser tab for the localhost:5001 URL, open the browser debugger on the Network tab and navigate to `https://localhost:5001` again to get a fresh network log. You should see Figure 16-6. This shows that visiting the Index page (first line) will redirect to the login page (second line), which will then cause the middleware to redirect to the identity provider (third line), which will show its login page (fourth line). Should your browser immediately show the Index component, you need to clear your cookies and try again.

Name	Status
localhost	302
login?returnUrl=https%3A%2F%2Flocalhost%3A5001%2F	302
authorize?client_id=BlazorServer&redirect_uri=http...lient-SKU=...	302
Login?ReturnUrl=%2Fconnect%2Fauthorize%2Fcallback%...SKU...	200

Figure 16-6. *Redirecting to the Identity Provider*

After completing the login process, you will be redirected to the Blazor Server's signin-oidc URL which will be handled by the OpenId Connect middleware. This middleware will convert the identity token into a `ClaimsPrincipal` and redirect to the original URI that initiated the login process. The Cookie middleware will serialize the `ClaimsPrincipal` into a cookie (actually, it might use multiple cookies because of the limited length of cookies). The browser then will process the original URI and convert the cookie into the `ClaimsPrincipal` and because now the user is authenticated will give access to the Index component.

Select the signin-oidc URL in the browser's debugger and scroll down. You will see that this will return the code and the identity token as in Figure 16-7.

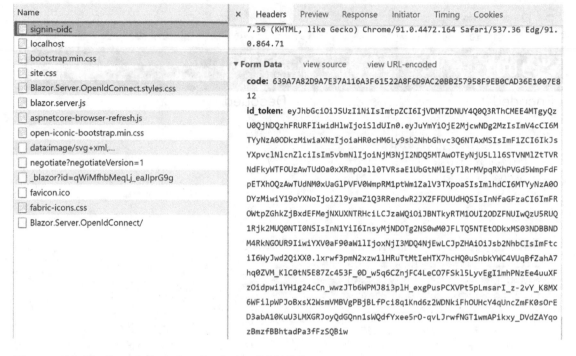

Figure 16-7. *Receiving the Code and Id Token*

You can inspect the id token by copying its value, open another browser tab on https://jwt.io, and paste the value as shown in Figure 16-8.

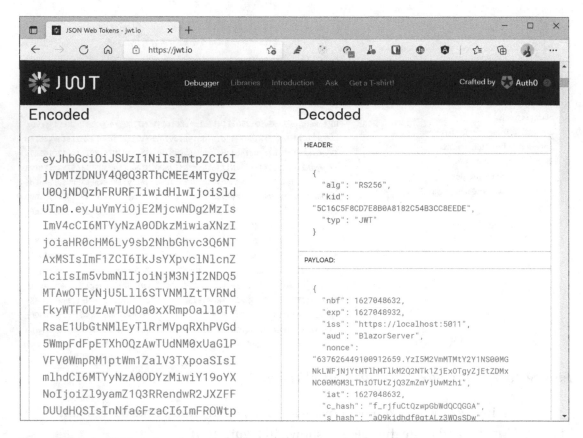

Figure 16-8. *Using jwt.io to Inspect a Token*

Congratulations. You have just added authentication to your Blazor Server application!

Using AuthorizeView

Let us add some UI so the user can log in and log out explicitly. Of course, we should only show the Login link when the user has not yet authenticated and only show the Logout link otherwise. For this, Blazor comes with the AuthorizeView templated component, which has three properties – Authorized, NotAuthorized, and Authorizing – which will render a UI when the user is authorized, not authorized, and in the process of authorizing. We can use this to modify our navigation menu to either show a Login link or the normal page links with an additional Logout link as in Listing 16-22. Do note that the AuthorizeView requires a CascadingAuthenticationState, which we added in the App component.

Listing 16-22. Modifying the NavMenu Component

```
<div class="@NavMenuCssClass" @onclick="ToggleNavMenu">
  <nav class="flex-column">
    <AuthorizeView>
      <Authorized>
        <li class="nav-item px-3">
          <NavLink class="nav-link" href=""
            Match="NavLinkMatch.All">
            <span class="oi oi-home"
                  aria-hidden="true"></span>
            Home
          </NavLink>
        </li>
        <li class="nav-item px-3">
          <NavLink class="nav-link" href="counter">
            <span class="oi oi-plus"
                  aria-hidden="true"></span>
            Counter
          </NavLink>
        </li>
        <li class="nav-item px-3">
          <NavLink class="nav-link" href="fetchdata">
            <span class="oi oi-list-rich"
                  aria-hidden="true"></span>
            Fetch data
          </NavLink>
        </li>
        <li class="nav-item px-3">
          <NavLink class="nav-link" href="logout">
            <span class="oi oi-list-rich"
                  aria-hidden="true"></span>
            Logout
          </NavLink>
        </li>
      </Authorized>
```

```
    <NotAuthorized>
      <li class="nav-item px-3">
        <NavLink class="nav-link" href="login">
          <span class="oi oi-list-rich"
                aria-hidden="true"></span>
          Login
        </NavLink>
      </li>
    </NotAuthorized>
  </AuthorizeView>
  </nav>
</div>
```

We already have a login razor page, but we still need one for logout. Again, add a new razor page (NOT a razor component) and name it Logout.cshtml. Update the LogoutModel as in Listing 16-23. Here, we return a SignOutResult which will cause the middleware to log out. There are two middlewares involved (Cookie and OpenIdConnect), so we need to pass both as the authenticationSchemes parameter.

Listing 16-23. The LogoutModel Class

```
using Microsoft.AspNetCore.Authentication.Cookies;
using Microsoft.AspNetCore.Authentication.OpenIdConnect;
using Microsoft.AspNetCore.Mvc;
using Microsoft.AspNetCore.Mvc.RazorPages;
using System.Threading.Tasks;

namespace Blazor.Server.OpenIdConnect.Pages
{
  public class LogoutModel : PageModel
  {
    public async Task<IActionResult> OnGetAsync()
    {
      // just to remove compiler warning
      await Task.CompletedTask;
      return SignOut(
          OpenIdConnectDefaults.AuthenticationScheme,
```

```
        CookieAuthenticationDefaults.AuthenticationScheme);
    }
  }
}
```

Let us test this, but first comment the Index component's `Authorize` attribute as in Listing 16-24.

Listing 16-24. Remove the Authorize Attribute

```
@page "/"
@*@attribute [Authorize]
*@
<h1>Hello, world!</h1>
```

Run the application, and log in. Then click the Logout link which will take you to the identity server logout page as shown in Figure 16-9.

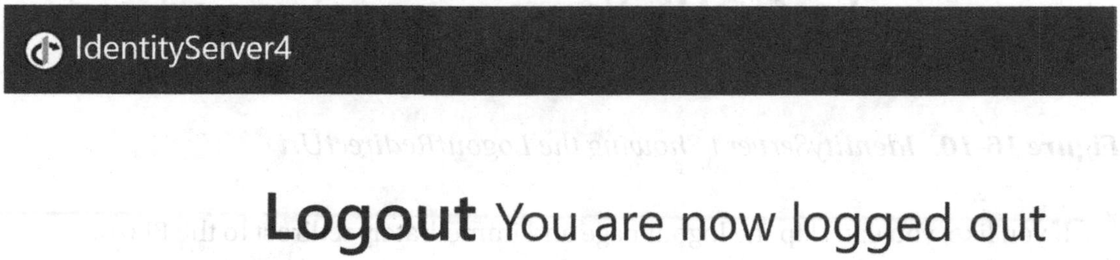

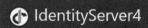

Logout You are now logged out

Figure 16-9. *The Logout Page*

The problem here is that this page will stay put; now the user has to manually navigate to the site in order to log in back again. We can change this by setting the client application's `PostLogoutRedirectUris` property in our identity provider as in Listing 16-25.

Listing 16-25. Setting the PostLogoutRedirectUris Property

```
public static IEnumerable<Client> GetClients()
=> new List<Client>
{
  new Client
  {
```

```
  ...
  RequireConsent = true,
  PostLogoutRedirectUris = new List<string>
  {
    "https://localhost:5001/signout-callback-oidc"
  }
 }
};
```

When this property is set, IdentityServer will add a hyperlink in its logout page as shown in Figure 16-10. Clicking this link will take us back to the Blazor Server site.

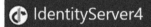

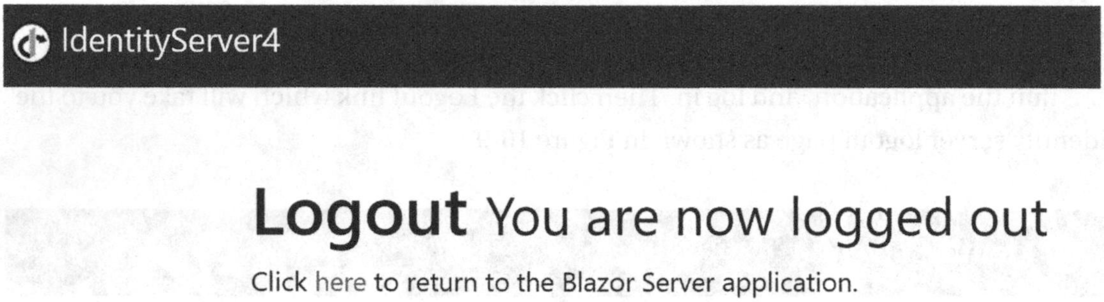

Logout You are now logged out

Click here to return to the Blazor Server application.

Figure 16-10. *IdentityServer4 Showing the LogoutRedirectUri*

If you like, you can skip the logout page and immediately redirect to the Blazor application. Look for the AccountOptions class in the QuickStart folder, and set the AutomaticRedirectAfterSignOut property to true as in Listing 16-26.

Listing 16-26. Enable Automatic Redirect After Signing Out

```
public class AccountOptions
{
  public static bool AllowLocalLogin = true;
  public static bool AllowRememberLogin = true;
  public static TimeSpan RememberMeLoginDuration =
    TimeSpan.FromDays(30);
  public static bool ShowLogoutPrompt = true;
  public static bool AutomaticRedirectAfterSignOut = true;
```

```
public static string InvalidCredentialsErrorMessage =
  "Invalid username or password";
}
```

Adding and Removing Claims

Let us add another claim for our users; let's say we need to know the address of the user. First, we will need to add a scope to the identity provider, and then we will need to request this scope in the client. Start by adding the address claim to each user as in Listing 16-27.

Listing 16-27. Adding an Additional Claim to the Users

```
public static List<TestUser> GetUsers()
=> new List<TestUser>
{
  new TestUser
  {
    SubjectId = "{223C9865-03BE-4951-8911-740A438FCF9D}",
    Username = "peter@u2u.be",
    Password = "u2u-secret",
    Claims = new List<Claim>
    {
      new Claim("given_name", "Peter"),
      new Claim(JwtClaimTypes.Name, "Peter Himschoot"),
      new Claim("family_name", "Himschoot"),
      new Claim("address", "Melle"),
    }
  },
  new TestUser
  {
    SubjectId = "{34119795-78A6-44C2-B128-30BFBC29139D}",
    Username = "student@u2u.be",
    Password = "u2u-secret",
    Claims = new List<Claim>
    {
```

```
    new Claim("given_name", "Student"),
    new Claim(JwtClaimTypes.Name, "Student Blazor"),
    new Claim("family_name", "Blazor"),
    new Claim("address", "Zellik"),
  }
 }
};
```

Now we need to add a new scope (using an IdentityResource) for address to the GetIdentityResources method as in Listing 16-28.

Listing 16-28. Adding an IdentityResource for Address

```
public static IEnumerable<IdentityResource> GetIdentityResources()
=> new List<IdentityResource>
{
  new IdentityResources.OpenId(),
  new IdentityResources.Profile(),
  new IdentityResources.Address(),
};
```

And we should allow this scope for our client application as in Listing 16-29.

Listing 16-29. Allowing the Address Scope for a Client

```
public static IEnumerable<Client> GetClients()
=> new List<Client>
{
  ...
  AllowedScopes = {
     IdentityServerConstants.StandardScopes.OpenId,
     IdentityServerConstants.StandardScopes.Profile,
     IdentityServerConstants.StandardScopes.Address
   },
  ...
};
```

Now we can request this claim in our client application by adding the address scope as in Listing 16-30.

Listing 16-30. Requesting the Address Scope

```
.AddOpenIdConnect(OpenIdConnectDefaults.AuthenticationScheme,
 options =>
{
  ...

  // We should add mappings for additional claims
  // (not openid and profile)
  options.Scope.Add("address");
});
```

Running the application will show that the claim has been returned to the client. We can see this in IdentityServer4's logging (which should be easy to find in the IdentityProvider application's console):

```
info: IdentityServer4.ResponseHandling.UserInfoResponseGenerator[0]
      Profile service returned the following claim types: given_name name
      family_name address
```

However, we will not find the address claim in the Index component. Why? Because we need to explicitly map this additional claim using ClaimActions.

Add Listing 16-31 to your Blazor Server Startup's ConfigureServices. The MapUniqueJsonKey will retrieve the address from the JWT and create the address claim. The DeleteClaims method will remove the sid and s_hash claim.

Listing 16-31. Add and Remove Claims with ClaimActions

```
options.Scope.Add("address");
options.ClaimActions
      .MapUniqueJsonKey("address", "address");
options.ClaimActions
      .DeleteClaims("sid", "s_hash");
```

Running the application and logging in again (!) will show the address claim.

Enabling Role-Based Security

Currently, we have claims that allow us to identify the user. We have the user's name and address. But what if we would like to protect certain parts of our application so only certain users can access it? Should we check a long list of user names? No, in this case, we will define a number of roles, assign these roles to some of our users, and only allow access when the user has a specific role. This is known as *role-based access control* (*RBAC*).

Start by adding some role claims to each user as in Listing 16-32. Here, Peter will have the admin role, while Student will have the tester role.

Listing 16-32. Adding User Roles

```
new TestUser
{
  ...
  Claims = new List<Claim>
  {
    new Claim("given_name", "Peter"),
    new Claim(JwtClaimTypes.Name, "Peter Himschoot"),
    new Claim("family_name", "Himschoot"),
    new Claim("address", "Melle"),
    new Claim("role", "admin"),
  }
},
new TestUser
{
  ...
  Claims = new List<Claim>
  {
    new Claim("given_name", "Student"),
    new Claim(JwtClaimTypes.Name, "Student Blazor"),
    new Claim("family_name", "Blazor"),
    new Claim("address", "Zellik"),
    new Claim("role", "tester"),
  }
}
```

This also means we need to add a roles scope, so update the `GetIdentityResources` method as in Listing 16-33. This also illustrates how we can add a custom `IdentityResource`. The `displayName` property is used during user consent.

Listing 16-33. Adding a Roles Scope

```
public static IEnumerable<IdentityResource> GetIdentityResources()
=> new List<IdentityResource>
{
  new IdentityResources.OpenId(),
  new IdentityResources.Profile(),
  new IdentityResources.Address(),
  new IdentityResource(name: "roles",
    displayName: "User role(s)",
    userClaims: new List<string> { "role" }),
};
```

And in our client configuration, we add the roles scope as in Listing 16-34.

Listing 16-34. Adding the Roles Scope

```
new Client
{
  ClientName = "Blazor Server",
  ...
  AllowedScopes = {
    IdentityServerConstants.StandardScopes.OpenId,
    IdentityServerConstants.StandardScopes.Profile,
    IdentityServerConstants.StandardScopes.Address,
    "roles"
  },
  ...
}
```

All similar to adding the address scope. Guess what we need to do in our Blazor application? Same steps as for address, but with one additional piece of code as in Listing 16-35 that declares the "role" claim to be used for RBAC.

Listing 16-35. Declaring the Roles Scope and Role Claim

```
options.Scope.Add("roles");
options.ClaimActions.MapUniqueJsonKey("role", "role");
options.TokenValidationParameters = new TokenValidationParameters
{
  RoleClaimType = "role"
};
```

Run the application, and log in again; the user's role should be shown.

Now we can protect one of our routes. Add the `Authorize` attribute to the Counter component as in Listing 16-36. With the `Authorize` attribute, we can verify if the user has a certain role.

Listing 16-36. Using the Authorize Attribute for RBAC

```
@page "/counter"

@attribute [Authorize(Roles = "admin")]

<h1>Counter</h1>

<p role="status">Current count: @currentCount</p>

<button class="btn btn-primary" @onclick="IncrementCount">Click me</button>

@code {
    private int currentCount = 0;

    private void IncrementCount()
    {
        currentCount++;
    }
}
```

We can also use the `AuthorizeView` component to show certain content based on a user's role; for example, add Listing 16-37 to the Index component.

Listing 16-37. Using AuthorizeView to Show Additional Content

```
<AuthorizeView Roles="admin">
```

```
<Authorized>
  Hey, you're an admin!
</Authorized>
</AuthorizeView>
```

We can do the same in the NavMenu component as in Listing 16-38 to hide the Counter component when the user does not have the proper role.

Listing 16-38. Hiding NavLinks in the NavMenu

```
<AuthorizeView Roles="admin">
  <Authorized>
    <li class="nav-item px-3">
      <NavLink class="nav-link" href="counter">
        <span class="oi oi-plus" aria-hidden="true"></span>
        Counter
      </NavLink>
    </li>
  </Authorized>
</AuthorizeView>
```

Run and log in with a user who has the admin role; you should see the Counter link in the navigation bar, and it should appear when you click it. Do the same for a user without the admin role; now there should be no Counter link in the navigation bar, and even manually modifying the browser's URL to /counter will show a not authorized screen.

Accessing a Secured API

Where are we? We can use OpenId Connect to implement the authentication for our Blazor Server site, and we can use roles to protect certain sections of our application, either by writing code using the `AuthenticationState` or declaratively using the `Authorize` and `AuthorizeView` classes. This is enough when your Blazor Server accesses data itself. There is one more thing. Your Blazor application might need to access a protected API running in another application. How do we do this? The answer is of course more claims!

Using an Access Token

Access tokens are just ordinary tokens, but they don't contain information about the user; they contain information about the client application and what the current user can do with the API. Because the API is yet another application, both should use the same identity provider. The client application (Blazor) can then use an OpenId Connect flow to request an access token from the identity provider and use it to access the API. Let us look at this process using the OpenId Connect Hybrid flow as shown in Figure 16-11.

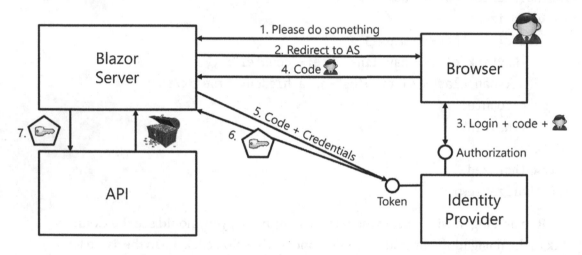

Figure 16-11. *API Authorization with OpenId Connect Hybrid Flow*

Steps 1–4 are the same as before, and our Blazor Server application receives an identity token and a code (which we ignored until now). This code can then be used together with the Blazor Server application's identifying information to retrieve an access token (Step 5) from the identity provider. The identity provider will then use the code to verify which claims it should give to the Blazor Server application (Step 6). Once our application has an access token, it can send it along with the API request (Step 7) using a header to the API application, which can then use the claims in the access token to determine how is should behave.

Let us create an API application and register it with our identity provider. Add a new ASP.NET Core Web API project and name it WeatherServices. Change its launchSettings to run HTTPS at port 5005 as in Listing 16-39.

Listing 16-39. Change the API Project's Port

```
{
  "$schema": "https://json.schemastore.org/launchsettings.json",
  "iisSettings": {
    "windowsAuthentication": false,
    "anonymousAuthentication": true,
    "iisExpress": {
      "applicationUrl": "http://localhost:7628",
      "sslPort": 44310
    }
  },
  "profiles": {
    "WeatherServices": {
      "commandName": "Project",
      "dotnetRunMessages": true,
      "launchBrowser": true,
      "launchUrl": "swagger",
      "applicationUrl": "https://localhost:5005;http://localhost:5004",
      "environmentVariables": {
        "ASPNETCORE_ENVIRONMENT": "Development"
      }
    },
    "IIS Express": {
      "commandName": "IISExpress",
      "launchBrowser": true,
      "launchUrl": "swagger",
      "environmentVariables": {
        "ASPNETCORE_ENVIRONMENT": "Development"
      }
    }
  }
}
```

Run the API project. By default, it will open the browser and show the *Swagger* UI as in Figure 16-12. This will allow you to test the API (which is currently unprotected).

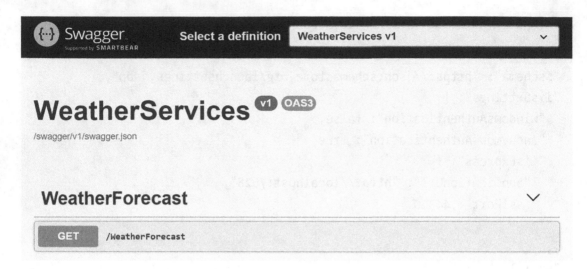

Figure 16-12. *The Swagger UI*

Click the GET button, then click Try It Out, and then Execute. You should see some forecasts.

Since our client will come from another origin, we also need to enable CORS. Add Listing 16-40 to the API's `Startup.ConfigureServices` method. Here, we allow any origin because we will use an access token to protect our services.

Listing 16-40. Creating the CORS Policy

```
public void ConfigureServices(IServiceCollection services)
{
  services.AddControllers();
  services.AddSwaggerGen(c =>
  {
    c.SwaggerDoc("v1", new OpenApiInfo
    {
      Title = "WeatherServices", Version = "v1"
    });
  });
  services.AddCors(options =>
  {
    options.AddPolicy("CorsPolicy",
      builder =>
```

```
            builder.AllowAnyOrigin()
            .AllowAnyMethod()
            .AllowAnyHeader());
    });
}
```

Now add the CORS middleware to the API project's middleware as in Listing 16-41.

Listing 16-41. Adding the CORS Middleware

```
public void Configure(IApplicationBuilder app, IWebHostEnvironment env)
{
  if (env.IsDevelopment())
  {
    app.UseDeveloperExceptionPage();
    app.UseSwagger();
    app.UseSwaggerUI(
      c => c.SwaggerEndpoint("/swagger/v1/swagger.json",
                            "WeatherServices v1"));
  }
  app.UseHttpsRedirection();
  app.UseCors("CorsPolicy");
  app.UseRouting();
  app.UseAuthorization();
  app.UseEndpoints(endpoints =>
  {
    endpoints.MapControllers();
  });
}
```

Registering the API Project with the Identity Provider

Now we are ready to register the WeatherService API client with our identity provider. To do this, we create an APIScope, so add Listing 16-42 after the GetClients method in the identity provider's Config class. This APIScope will be included in the scope claim and is used to verify if the client has access.

Listing 16-42. Adding an APIScope

```
public static IEnumerable<ApiScope> GetApiScopes()
  => new List<ApiScope>
  {
    new ApiScope("u2uApi", "U2U API")
  };
```

We also need to create an `ApiResource`, so add Listing 16-43 below the `GetApiScopes` method.

Listing 16-43. Creating an ApiResource

```
public static IEnumerable<ApiResource> GetApiResources()
  => new List<ApiResource>
  {
    new ApiResource("u2uApi", "U2U API")
    {
        Scopes = { "u2uApi" }
    }
  };
```

We can now grant our Blazor Server application access to this API resource by adding the API scope to the client's `AllowedScopes` as in Listing 16-44.

Listing 16-44. Allowing the Client to Access an API

```
AllowedScopes = {
  IdentityServerConstants.StandardScopes.OpenId,
  IdentityServerConstants.StandardScopes.Profile,
  IdentityServerConstants.StandardScopes.Address,
  "roles",
  "u2uApi"
},
```

Finally, we should invoke the `Config.GetApiScopes` and `Config.GetApiResources` methods as in Listing 16-45.

Listing 16-45. Registering the ApiScopes and ApiResources

```
public void ConfigureServices(IServiceCollection services)
{
  services.AddIdentityServer()
          .AddInMemoryApiScopes(Config.GetApiScopes())
          .AddInMemoryApiResources(Config.GetApiResources())
          .AddInMemoryIdentityResources(
            Config.GetIdentityResources())
          .AddTestUsers(Config.GetUsers())
          .AddInMemoryClients(Config.GetClients())
          .AddDeveloperSigningCredential();
  services.AddControllersWithViews();
}
```

Adding JWT Bearer Token Middleware

A client application will send the access token using an HTTP Authorization Bearer header, and we need our API project to look for this header and install the ClaimsPrincipal from the access token. Use NuGet to install the Microsoft. AspNetCore.Authentication.JwtBearer package in the WeatherServices project.

Now we can register this JWT handling using dependency injection, so add Listing 16-46 to the API project's ConfigureServices method. Authentication will look for the Bearer header, convert the JWT access token into a ClaimsPrincipal, and then process the request. We need to set the Authority property to the trusted identity provider's URL (which in our case uses port 5011), and we use the Audience property, so set the u2uApi scope to use. Do note that we are hard-coding everything here; for a real production application, we should read this from configuration.

Listing 16-46. Adding JWT Authentication

```
services
  .AddAuthentication("Bearer")
  .AddJwtBearer("Bearer", opt =>
  {
    opt.RequireHttpsMetadata = false; // for development purposes, disable
                                      in production!
```

```
    opt.Authority = "https://localhost:5011";
    opt.Audience = "u2uApi";
  });
```

And don't forget to add the Authentication and Authorization middleware as in Listing 16-47.

Listing 16-47. Adding the Authentication Middleware

```
public void Configure(IApplicationBuilder app,
                      IWebHostEnvironment env)
{
  if (env.IsDevelopment())
  {
    app.UseDeveloperExceptionPage();
    app.UseSwagger();
    app.UseSwaggerUI(
      c =>
      c.SwaggerEndpoint("/swagger/v1/swagger.json",
                        "WeatherServices v1"));
  }
  app.UseHttpsRedirection();
  app.UseCors("CorsPolicy");
  app.UseRouting();
  app.UseAuthentication();
  app.UseAuthorization();
  app.UseEndpoints(endpoints =>
  {
    endpoints.MapControllers();
  });
}
```

That's all for the moment for our API.

Enabling the Bearer Token in the Client

Our client application should now use the received code to request an access token from the identity provider and use it in its API requests.

Update the Blazor Server WeatherForecastService as in Listing 16-48. This class uses the IHttpClientFactory interface to create an HttpClient instance. We do this so we can configure it to automatically use the access token.

Listing 16-48. The WeatherForecastService

```
using System;
using System.Net.Http;
using System.Net.Http.Json;
using System.Threading.Tasks;

namespace Blazor.Server.OpenIdConnect.Data
{
  public class WeatherForecastService
  {
    private readonly IHttpClientFactory httpClientFactory;

    public WeatherForecastService(
      IHttpClientFactory httpClientFactory)
    => this.httpClientFactory = httpClientFactory;

    public async ValueTask<WeatherForecast[]> GetForecastAsync(
      DateTime startDate)
    {
      HttpClient httpClient =
        this.httpClientFactory
          .CreateClient(nameof(WeatherForecastService));
      var result =
        await httpClient
          .GetFromJsonAsync<WeatherForecast[]>("weatherforecast");
      return result;
    }
  }
}
```

We also need to configure dependency injection in the Blazor Server project to give us an instance of the IHttpClientFactory. The IHttpClientFactory will give us an HttpClient that will be configured for us to include the access token and which will send it as a Bearer token to the API.

Proceed by adding the new API scope to our list of scopes as in Listing 16-49.

Listing 16-49. Adding the API Scope to the Client

```
options.Scope.Add("u2uApi");
```

Add the IdentityModel.AspNetCore package to the client project. This package will take care of things like exchanging the code for an access token and attaching it to the HttpClient request. Now we can add this to dependency injection, so add Listing 16-50 to the end of the ConfigureServices method of the client project. Now when the WeatherForecastService creates the HttpClient instance for the WeatherForecastService through the IHttpClientFactory, it will be configured with the access token.

Listing 16-50. Add Token Management

```
services.AddAccessTokenManagement();
services.AddUserAccessTokenHttpClient(
  nameof(WeatherForecastService), null, client =>
  {
    client.BaseAddress = new Uri("https://localhost:5005");
  });
```

Start the IdentityProvider project, next the WeatherServices project, and finally the Blazor.Server.OpenIdConnect project. Log out (if you're still logged in) and log in again. This will refresh our tokens.

Now we can use the debugger to inspect the ClaimsPrincipal in the WeatherServices project. Put a breakpoint on the GetForecastAsync method and now use the client to fetch the forecasts. The debugger should stop, and now we can use the watch window to inspect the this.User property as in Figure 16-13.

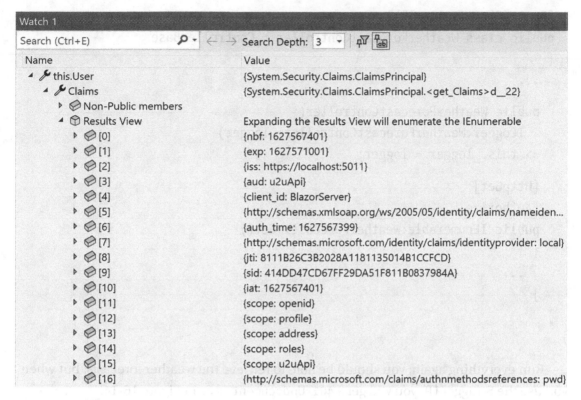

Figure 16-13. The WeatherServices ClaimsPrincipal

If the results view is empty, you will need to review your code because you forgot something. You should see the `scope: u2uApi` claim.

Now we can protect our `WeatherForecastController`'s `Get` method by adding the `Authorize` attribute as in Listing 16-51.

Listing 16-51. Protecting the WeatherForecastController

```
using Microsoft.AspNetCore.Authorization;
using Microsoft.AspNetCore.Mvc;
using Microsoft.Extensions.Logging;
using System;
using System.Collections.Generic;
using System.Linq;

namespace WeatherServices.Controllers
{
  [ApiController]
```

```
[Route("[controller]")]
public class WeatherForecastController : ControllerBase
{
  ...

  public WeatherForecastController(
    ILogger<WeatherForecastController> logger)
  => this._logger = logger;

  [HttpGet]
  [Authorize]
  public IEnumerable<WeatherForecast> Get()
  {
    ...
  }
 }
}
```

Run everything again; you should be able to retrieve the weather forecasts, but when you use the Swagger UI, you will get a 401 Undocumented as in Figure 16-14.

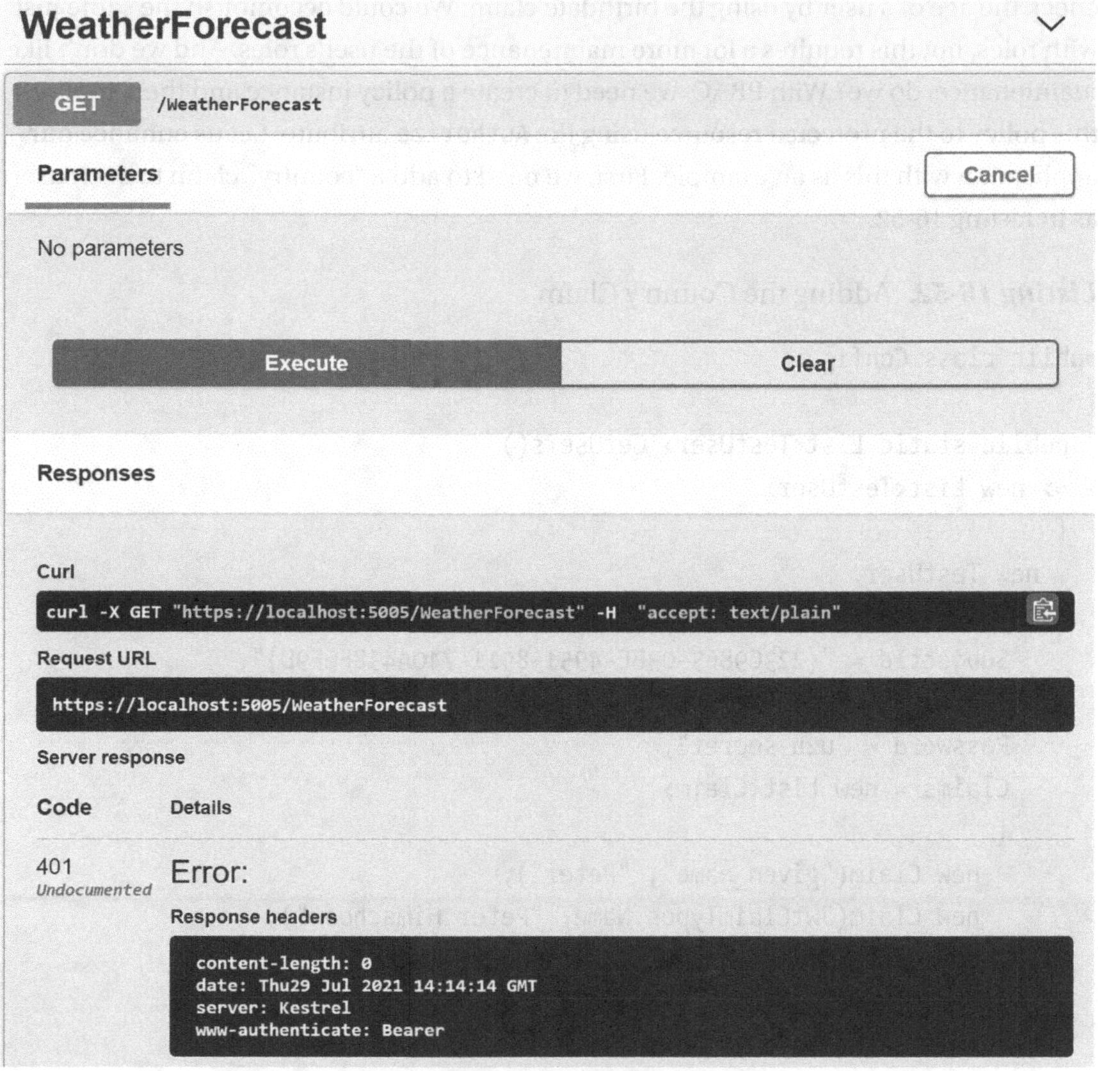

WeatherForecast ⌄

GET	/WeatherForecast

Parameters   Cancel

No parameters

Execute	Clear

Responses

Curl

```
curl -X GET "https://localhost:5005/WeatherForecast" -H  "accept: text/plain"
```

Request URL

```
https://localhost:5005/WeatherForecast
```

Server response

Code	Details
401 Undocumented	**Error:**

Response headers

```
content-length: 0
date: Thu29 Jul 2021 14:14:14 GMT
server: Kestrel
www-authenticate: Bearer
```

Figure 16-14. *Accessing a Protected API with Swagger*

Using Policy-Based Access Control

What if we want to use one or more claims to determine if the user can access a certain resource? For example, we might only want to allow authenticated users that live in Belgium to access the forecasts. In that case, we can use *policy-based access control* (*PBAC*).

Policies allow us to combine claims to determine if the user can access a certain component or API resource. You can even build complex policies that can, for example,

595

check the age of a user by using the birthdate claim. We could accomplish the same just with roles, but this requires a lot more maintenance of the user's roles. And we don't like maintenance, do we? With PBAC, we need to create a policy instance and then apply this policy to the protected resource using the Authorize attribute. Let us enhance our application with this as an example. First, we need to add a "country" claim to each user as in Listing 16-52.

Listing 16-52. Adding the Country Claim

```
public class Config
{
  public static List<TestUser> GetUsers()
  => new List<TestUser>
  {
    new TestUser
    {
      SubjectId = "{223C9865-03BE-4951-8911-740A438FCF9D}",
      Username = "peter@u2u.be",
      Password = "u2u-secret",
      Claims = new List<Claim>
      {
        new Claim("given_name", "Peter"),
        new Claim(JwtClaimTypes.Name, "Peter Himschoot"),
        new Claim("family_name", "Himschoot"),
        new Claim("address", "Melle"),
        new Claim("role", "admin"),
        new Claim("country", "Belgium"),
      }
    },
    new TestUser
    {
      SubjectId = "{34119795-78A6-44C2-B128-30BFBC29139D}",
      Username = "student@u2u.be",
      Password = "u2u-secret",
      Claims = new List<Claim>
      {
```

```
      new Claim("given_name", "Student"),
      new Claim(JwtClaimTypes.Name, "Student Blazor"),
      new Claim("family_name", "Blazor"),
      new Claim("address", "Zellik"),
      new Claim("role", "tester"),
      new Claim("country", "France"),
    }
  }
};
```

Of course, we will also need a scope using an IdentityResource for this as in
Listing 16-53.

Listing 16-53. Adding the Country IdentityResource

```
public static IEnumerable<IdentityResource> GetIdentityResources()
=> new List<IdentityResource>
{
  new IdentityResources.OpenId(),
  new IdentityResources.Profile(),
  new IdentityResources.Address(),
  new IdentityResource(name: "roles",
    displayName: "User role(s)",
    userClaims: new List<string> { "role" }),
  new IdentityResource(name: "country",
    displayName: "User country",
    userClaims: new List<string> { "country" })
};
```

And finally, we make this scope available to our client application as in Listing 16-54.

Listing 16-54. Allowing the Country Scope

```
public static IEnumerable<Client> GetClients()
=> new List<Client>
{
  new Client
  {
```

```
    ...
    AllowedScopes = {
      IdentityServerConstants.StandardScopes.OpenId,
      IdentityServerConstants.StandardScopes.Profile,
      IdentityServerConstants.StandardScopes.Address,
      "roles",
      "u2uApi",
      "country"
    },
    ...
  }
};
```

This completes the identity provider. Now we need to retrieve the country scope in our client application, so add Listing 16-55 to the AddOpenIdConnect method.

Listing 16-55. Requesting the Country Scope in the Client

```
options.Scope.Add("country");
options.ClaimActions.MapUniqueJsonKey("country", "country");
```

Next, we should add the policy configuration to the end of the client's ConfigureServices method as in Listing 16-56. Here, we add a policy named FromBelgium, requiring the user to be authenticated and having the country claim set to BE (which the peter@u2u.be user has).

Listing 16-56. Adding the FromBelgium Policy

```
services.AddAuthorization(options =>
{
  options.AddPolicy("FromBelgium", policyBuilder =>
  {
    policyBuilder.RequireAuthenticatedUser();
    policyBuilder.RequireClaim("country", "Belgium");
  });
});
```

We also need to hide the navigation menu to not show the Fetch link. How can we do this? We have seen the `AuthorizeView` component which allows us to show content when the user has been authenticated or when the user has a certain role. We can also use this to show content when a user passes a certain policy. Modify the NavMenu component as in Listing 16-57 (just move the Fetch data NavLink to the bottom and wrap it into an `AuthorizeView`).

Listing 16-57. Using Policies with the AuthorizeView

```
<div class="top-row pl-4 navbar navbar-dark">
  <a class="navbar-brand" href="">Blazor.Server.OpenIdConnect</a>
  <button title="Navigation menu" class="navbar-toggler"
    @onclick="ToggleNavMenu">
    <span class="navbar-toggler-icon"></span>
  </button>
</div>

<div class="@NavMenuCssClass" @onclick="ToggleNavMenu">
  <nav class="flex-column">
    <AuthorizeView>
      <Authorized>
        <li class="nav-item px-3">
          <NavLink class="nav-link" href=""
            Match="NavLinkMatch.All">
            <span class="oi oi-home" aria-hidden="true"></span>
            Home
          </NavLink>
        </li>
        <li class="nav-item px-3">
          <NavLink class="nav-link" href="logout">
            <span class="oi oi-list-rich"
                  aria-hidden="true"></span>
            Logout
          </NavLink>
        </li>
      </Authorized>
      <NotAuthorized>
```

```
                <li class="nav-item px-3">
                  <NavLink class="nav-link" href="login">
                    <span class="oi oi-list-rich"
                            aria-hidden="true"></span>
                    Login
                  </NavLink>
                </li>
          </NotAuthorized>
        </AuthorizeView>
        <AuthorizeView Roles="admin">
            <Authorized>
              <li class="nav-item px-3">
                <NavLink class="nav-link" href="counter">
                    <span class="oi oi-plus"
                            aria-hidden="true"></span>
                    Counter
                </NavLink>
              </li>
            </Authorized>
        </AuthorizeView>
        <AuthorizeView Policy="FromBelgium">
            <li class="nav-item px-3">
              <NavLink class="nav-link" href="fetchdata">
                <span class="oi oi-list-rich"
                        aria-hidden="true"></span>
                Fetch data
              </NavLink>
            </li>
        </AuthorizeView>
      </nav>
</div>
@code {
  private bool collapseNavMenu = true;

  private string NavMenuCssClass
  => collapseNavMenu ? "collapse" : null;
```

```
private void ToggleNavMenu()
{
    collapseNavMenu = !collapseNavMenu;
}
}
```

Running the application and logging in as student@u2u.be will not show the link because this user is from France, while logging in as peter@u2u.be will show the link since the FromBelgium policy passed. This completes the client.

We want to use this policy with the API project as well, so we could copy this code. Let us do the proper thing and move the policy into a library project so we can use the same policy in our Blazor and API projects.

Start by adding a new library project to the solution called Blazor.Shared. OpenIdConnect. Add the Microsoft.AspNetCore.Authorization package. Now add the Policies class from Listing 16-58. This class will create a new AuthorizationPolicy which will check if the user has been authenticated and is from Belgium.

Listing 16-58. The Policies Class

```
using Microsoft.AspNetCore.Authorization;

namespace Blazor.Shared.OpenIdConnect
{
  public static class Policies
  {
    public const string FromBelgium = "FromBelgium";

    public static AuthorizationPolicy FromBelgiumPolicy()
        => new AuthorizationPolicyBuilder()
        .RequireAuthenticatedUser()
        .RequireClaim("country", "Belgium")
        .Build();
  }
}
```

Add the shared project as a project reference to API project. Now we can add this as an authorization policy in the API project's ConfigureServices method as in Listing 16-59. Now do the same instead of Listing 16-56 for the client project.

Listing 16-59. Enabling the FromBelgium Policy in the API Project

```
services.AddAuthorization(options =>
{
  options.AddPolicy(Policies.FromBelgium,
    Policies.FromBelgiumPolicy());
});
```

In the API project, modify the `Authorize` attribute on the `WeatherForecastController`'s `Get` method to use this policy as in Listing 16-60.

Listing 16-60. Using a Policy to Protect an API

```
[HttpGet]
[Authorize(Policy = Policies.FromBelgium)]
public IEnumerable<WeatherForecast> Get()
```

However, there is one more thing we need to do. The access token will not contain the user's country claim by default, and that is why we need to update the `ApiResource` to include this claim as in Listing 16-61.

Listing 16-61. Including the Country Claim in the Access Token

```
public static IEnumerable<ApiResource> GetApiResources()
  => new List<ApiResource>
  {
    new ApiResource("u2uApi", "U2U API")
    {
        // To use user's country claim we need to add it here
        Scopes = { "u2uApi" }, UserClaims = new [] { "country"}
    },
  };
```

Run all three projects, and log in with the peter@u2u.be user; the Fetch data link should be shown, and when you click the link, you should get a list of forecasts.

Congratulations. You just completed authentication and authorization for Blazor Server applications! Now let us look at Blazor WebAssembly in the next chapter.

Summary

In this chapter, we looked at protecting a Blazor Server application using OpenId Connect. In our modern world, applications use claims to allow applications to identify the current user and to protect resources. We then learned about the OpenId Connect Hybrid flow and used it for authentication, getting an identity token containing user's claims. We then used the `AuthenticationState` class to access these claims. We updated routing to check the `Authorize` attribute and used the `AuthorizeView` component to conditionally render a UI according to the user's claims. After this, we looked at retrieving an access token and used it to protect an API. This allows us to use different applications with the same Web API, each given different levels of access to our API. All of this using IdentityServer4 as the identity provider.

CHAPTER 17

Securing Blazor WebAssembly

In the previous chapter, we looked at securing a Blazor Server application using OpenId Connect with identity and access tokens. Here, we will do the same but for Blazor WebAssembly. This time, we will use another OpenId Connect flow: *Authorization Code flow* with PKCE (pronounced pixie). I do recommend that you read the previous chapter before this one because it builds on top of some of the topics we saw there, and it continues with the code example from that chapter.

Authorization Code Flow with PKCE

When comparing the Authorization Code flow from Figure 17-1 and Hybrid flow, you will see a lot of similarities. The big difference is that the identity token is only returned when the client application sends the code to the identity provider. Since the code is sent using the browser, there is a chance of this code being intercepted by a malicious user using an "Authorization Code Interception Attack," so to protect this code, we will use *Proof Key for Code Exchange* (*PKCE*). This is to prevent another party of using the code to gain an access token.

© Peter Himschoot 2022
P. Himschoot, *Microsoft Blazor*, https://doi.org/10.1007/978-1-4842-7845-1_17

Understanding PKCE

How does PKCE work? It is all about proving ownership. Imagine the user wants to log in. The browser will generate a cryptographically random **code verifier** and then use a **code challenge method** to turn the code verifier into a **code challenge** (Step 1). The code challenge is then sent to the identity provider together with the code challenge method (Step 2). The identity provider will then make the user log in (with optional consent), save the code challenge with code challenge method, and return the code that allows the token retrieval back to the application (Step 3). The application can then use the code with the code verifier (Step 4) to prove that it was the client requesting the code (assuming a third party is unable to retrieve the code verifier from the code challenge – that is why generally a cryptographic hash method is used because it is practically impossible to retrieve reverse a hash). After the identity provider checks that the code verifier and code challenge match by applying the code challenge method to the code verifier and then comparing the results, it returns the requested tokens. Of course, this only works over HTTPS; otherwise, figuring out the code verifier is a piece of cake.

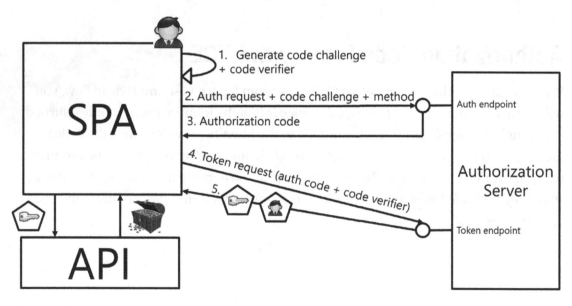

Figure 17-1. *Authorization Code Flow with PKCE*

Registering the WASM Client Application

Let's start by adding authentication to a Blazor WebAssembly application. Start with the solution from the previous chapter (which you can find in the provided sources should you want).

Creating and Examining the Application

Add a new Blazor WebAssembly project called Blazor.Wasm.OpenIdConnect. No need to choose the Hosted option here, but you need to choose the **Individual Accounts** option as in Figure 17-2.

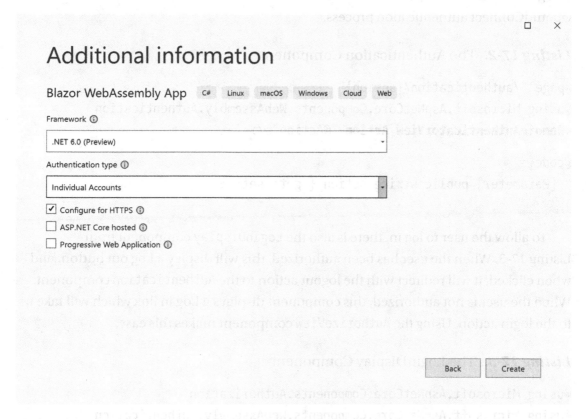

Figure 17-2. *Creating the Blazor WebAssembly Project*

Using the dotnet CLI, you can use the following command:

```
dotnet new blazorwasm -au Individual -o Blazor.Wasm.OpenIdConnect
```

The Individual Accounts option will automatically add the Microsoft.AspNetCore. Components.WebAssembly.Authentication package to your project and will also register a JavaScript library in index.html as in Listing 17-1. This library is used by Blazor to take care of talking to the identity provider.

Listing 17-1. The Authentication JavaScript Library

```
<script src="_content/Microsoft.AspNetCore.Components.WebAssembly.
Authentication/AuthenticationService.js"></script>
```

In the Pages folder, you will also find the Authentication component as in Listing 17-2 which handles the /authentication/{action} URL. This component delegates the action to the RemoteAuthenticatorView which takes care of the OpenIdConnect authentication process.

Listing 17-2. The Authentication Component

```
@page "/authentication/{action}"
@using Microsoft.AspNetCore.Components.WebAssembly.Authentication
<RemoteAuthenticatorView Action="@Action" />

@code{
  [Parameter] public string Action { get; set; }
}
```

To allow the user to log in, there is also the LoginDisplay component from Listing 17-3. When the user has been authorized, this will display a Log out button, and when clicked, it will redirect with the logout action to the Authentication component. When the user is not authorized, this component displays a Log in link which will take us to the login action. Using the AuthorizeView component makes this easy.

Listing 17-3. The LoginDisplay Component

```
@using Microsoft.AspNetCore.Components.Authorization
@using Microsoft.AspNetCore.Components.WebAssembly.Authentication

@inject NavigationManager Navigation
@inject SignOutSessionStateManager SignOutManager

<AuthorizeView>
```

```
<Authorized>
  Hello, @context.User.Identity.Name!
  <button class="nav-link btn btn-link" @onclick="BeginSignOut">Log out
  </button>
</Authorized>
<NotAuthorized>
  <a href="authentication/login">Log in</a>
</NotAuthorized>
</AuthorizeView>

@code{
  private async Task BeginSignOut(MouseEventArgs args)
  {
    await SignOutManager.SetSignOutState();
    Navigation.NavigateTo("authentication/logout");
  }
}
```

The App component is the same as the one in the Blazor Server component which will redirect us to the login page when the user is not yet authenticated.

Update the applicationUrl in the launchSettings.json file as in Listing 17-4 to change the port number to 5003 for HTTPS.

Listing 17-4. launchSettings for Blazor.Wasm.OpenIdConnect

```
{
  "iisSettings": {
    "windowsAuthentication": false,
    "anonymousAuthentication": true,
    "iisExpress": {
      "applicationUrl": "http://localhost:38381",
      "sslPort": 44357
    }
  },
  "profiles": {
    "Blazor.Wasm.OpenIdConnect": {
      "commandName": "Project",
```

```
      "dotnetRunMessages": true,
      "launchBrowser": true,
      "inspectUri": "{wsProtocol}://{url.hostname}:{url.port}/_framework/
      debug/ws-proxy?browser={browserInspectUri}",
      "applicationUrl": "https://localhost:5003;http://localhost:5002",
      "environmentVariables": {
        "ASPNETCORE_ENVIRONMENT": "Development"
      }
    },
    "IIS Express": {
      "commandName": "IISExpress",
      "launchBrowser": true,
      "inspectUri": "{wsProtocol}://{url.hostname}:{url.port}/_framework/
      debug/ws-proxy?browser={browserInspectUri}",
      "environmentVariables": {
        "ASPNETCORE_ENVIRONMENT": "Development"
      }
    }
  }
}
```

Now we are ready to register this Blazor WASM application in our identity provider.

Registering the Client Application

Add a new client called BlazorWasm to the Config class in the IdentityProvider project as shown in Listing 17-5. Here, we specify the client's name and Id, we choose the Authorization Code flow with PKCE, and we pass it the redirectUris for our client application. Finally, we also list the required scopes. Since we first will implement authentication, we only need the OpenId and Profile scopes. Optionally, you can also enable client consent, but I left this out for practicality.

Listing 17-5. Registering the Blazor WASM Client

```
new Client
{
  ClientName = "BlazorWasm",
  ClientId = "BlazorWasm",
  AllowedGrantTypes = GrantTypes.Code,
  RequirePkce = true,
  RequireClientSecret = false,
  RedirectUris = new List<string>{
    "https://localhost:5003/authentication/login-callback"
  },
  PostLogoutRedirectUris = new List<string> {
    "https://localhost:5003/authentication/logout-callback"
  },
  AllowedCorsOrigins = {
    "https://localhost:5003"
  },
  AllowedScopes = {
    IdentityServerConstants.StandardScopes.OpenId,
    IdentityServerConstants.StandardScopes.Profile,
  }
  // RequireConsent = true
}
```

Implementing Authentication

In the Blazor Server application, we hard-coded all the options for OpenId Connect; here, we will use configuration. Look for appsettings.json in the wwwroot and replace it as in Listing 17-6. Here, we specify the identity provider's URL in the Authority property, and we set the remaining properties to the same values as in Listing 17-5.

Listing 17-6. The Application Settings

```
{
  "oidc": {
    "Authority": "https://localhost:5011/",
    "ClientId": "BlazorWasm",
    "ResponseType": "code",
    "DefaultScopes": [
      "openid",
      "profile"
    ],
    "PostLogoutRedirectUri": "authentication/logout-callback",
    "RedirectUri": "authentication/login-callback"
  }
}
```

Open the Blazor.Wasm.OpenIdConnect project's Startup class and replace the configuration section name as in Listing 17-7. This will read all options from configuration.

Listing 17-7. Binding to the OIDC Configuration

```
builder.Configuration.Bind("oidc", options.ProviderOptions);
```

Now we are ready to test our solution. Start the IdentityProvider project and then your Blazor WASM application. After a little while, your browser should show the Blazor application as shown in Figure 17-3 with a **Log in** link in the top right corner.

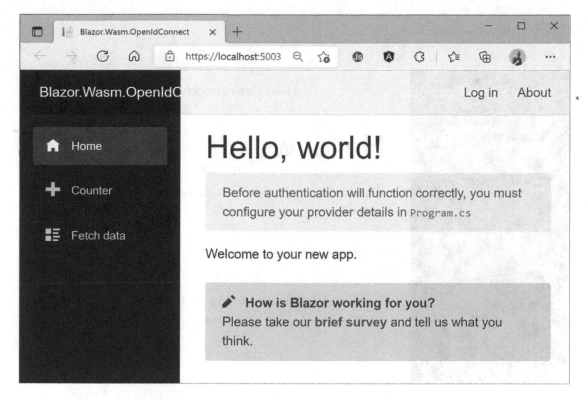

Figure 17-3. *The Blazor Application Before Logging In*

Click the Log in link and then complete the login procedure with a registered user, for example, **peter@u2u.be** and password **u2u-secret**. After this, the Blazor application will display the user's name as in Figure 17-4.

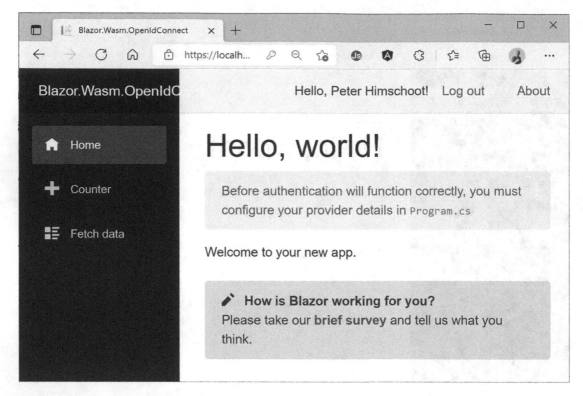

Figure 17-4. *The Blazor Application After Logging In*

Customizing the Login Experience

There are still a couple of things we can do. Let us first remove the alert in Listing 17-8 from the Index component warning us about the need to configure our provider details. Since authentication works, we don't need this anymore.

Listing 17-8. Remove the Provider Details Alert

```
<div class="alert alert-warning" role="alert">
  Before authentication will function correctly, you must configure your
provider details in <code>Program.cs</code>
</div>
```

Next, we can customize the RemoteAuthenticatorView. This has a series of RenderFragment properties that allow you to display a UI during the process of logging in and out. Listing 17-9 shows a couple of simple examples.

Listing 17-9. Customizing the Login and Logout Process

```
@page "/authentication/{action}"
@using Microsoft.AspNetCore.Components.WebAssembly.Authentication
<RemoteAuthenticatorView Action="@Action">
  <LoggingIn>
    <p>Logging in...</p>
  </LoggingIn>
  <LogInFailed>
    <p>Login failed.</p>
  </LogInFailed>
  <LogOutSucceeded>
    <p>You have successfully logged out.</p>
  </LogOutSucceeded>
</RemoteAuthenticatorView>

@code {
  [Parameter] public string Action { get; set; }
}
```

Congratulations! You have just completed the process of authentication with Blazor WASM. Here, most of the code was generated by the application's template, so this was not a lot of work!

Accessing a Protected API

Time to implement the Fetch data link. Currently, this uses some sample data, and of course, we want to access this data from the WeatherService API just like in the previous chapter.

Fetching Data from the WeatherService API

Start by installing the Microsoft.Extensions.Http package. Add a new folder called Services to the Blazor.Wasm.OpenIdConnect project, and inside it, add a new WeatherForecastService class as in Listing 17-10. Just like with Blazor Server, this uses an IHttpClientFactory instance to create the configured HttpClient.

Listing 17-10. The WeatherService Class

```
using System;
using System.Net.Http;
using System.Net.Http.Json;
using System.Threading.Tasks;
using static Blazor.Wasm.OpenIdConnect.Pages.FetchData;

namespace Blazor.Wasm.OpenIdConnect.Services
{
  public class WeatherForecastService
  {
    private readonly IHttpClientFactory httpClientFactory;

    public WeatherForecastService(
      IHttpClientFactory httpClientFactory)
      => this.httpClientFactory = httpClientFactory;

    public async ValueTask<WeatherForecast[]>
      GetForecastAsync(DateTime startDate)
    {
      HttpClient httpClient =
        this.httpClientFactory
            .CreateClient(nameof(WeatherForecastService));
      WeatherForecast[] result =
        await httpClient
          .GetFromJsonAsync<WeatherForecast[]>("weatherforecast");
      return result;
    }
  }
}
```

Now we are ready to configure dependency injection, so add Listing 17-11 to the client project's `Startup.ConfigureServices` method.

Listing 17-11. Configuring Dependency Injection

```
builder.Services
  .AddHttpClient<WeatherForecastService>(
    client =>
      client.BaseAddress = new Uri("https://localhost:5005")
  );
builder.Services.AddSingleton<WeatherForecastService>();
```

Append Listing 17-12 to your _Imports.razor.

Listing 17-12. Adding the Services Namespace

```
@using Blazor.Wasm.OpenIdConnect.Services
```

Update the FetchData component as in Listing 17-13 to use the
WeatherForecastService.

Listing 17-13. The FetchData Component Using the WeatherForecastService

```
@page "/fetchdata"
@inject WeatherForecastService weatherService

...

@code {
  private WeatherForecast[] forecasts;

  protected override async Task OnInitializedAsync()
  {
    forecasts =
      await weatherService.GetForecastAsync(DateTime.Now);
  }

  public class WeatherForecast
  {
    ...
  }
}
```

First, let us see if all of this works by first removing the `Authorize` attribute from the `WeatherForecastController.Get` method. Run the IdentityProvider, WeatherService, and Blazor.Wasm.OpenIdConnect projects. Click the Fetch data link, and you should get the forecasts from the WeatherService. Nice!

Using the AuthorizationMessageHandler

Add the `Authorize` attribute again, now without a policy like in Listing 17-14. Later, we will enable the policy.

Listing 17-14. Protecting the WeatherService API

```
[HttpGet]
[Authorize()]
// [Authorize(Policy = Policies.FromBelgium)]
public IEnumerable<WeatherForecast> Get()
```

However, clicking the Fetch data link will not work! We need to retrieve an access token and pass it using a Bearer header to the WeatherService API which requires the u2uApi scope. So first we need to tell IdentityService4 to grant access to this scope by adding it to the list of `AllowedScopes` as in Listing 17-15.

Listing 17-15. Adding the Scope to the Client Configuration

```
AllowedScopes = {
  IdentityServerConstants.StandardScopes.OpenId,
  IdentityServerConstants.StandardScopes.Profile,
  "u2uApi",
}
```

We should also add this to the client configuration as in Listing 17-16.

Listing 17-16. Requesting the u2uApi Scope in Configuration

```
{
  "oidc": {
    "Authority": "https://localhost:5011/",
    "ClientId": "BlazorWasm",
    "ResponseType": "code",
```

```
    "DefaultScopes": [
      "openid",
      "profile",
      "u2uApi"
    ],
    "PostLogoutRedirectUri": "authentication/logout-callback",
    "RedirectUri": "authentication/login-callback"
  }
}
```

When accessing the API, we will need to attach the proper access token. For this, we need to use the AuthorizationMessageHandler. With an HttpMessageHandler, you can configure the request, so here we retrieve the AuthorizationMessageHandler and make it attach the access token for the u2uApi scope. Update dependency injection by adding an HttpMessageHandler as in Listing 17-17 which will do just that. We do need to pass the base URI to which access tokens need to be attached by setting the authorizedUrls property.

Listing 17-17. Adding the AuthorizationMessageHandler

```
builder.Services
  .AddHttpClient<WeatherForecastService>(
    client
    => client.BaseAddress = new Uri("https://localhost:5005")
  )
  .AddHttpMessageHandler(handlerConfig =>
  {
    AuthorizationMessageHandler handler =
    handlerConfig.GetService<AuthorizationMessageHandler>()
    .ConfigureHandler(
        authorizedUrls: new[] { "https://localhost:5005" },
        scopes: new[] { "u2uApi" }
      );
    return handler;
  });
```

Run your solution again. Now you should be able to access the WeatherService API. Whohoo!

Adding Client-Side Authorization

Should the user be able to click the Fetch data link when they're not authorized? Of course, not. First, we should protect the FetchData component. Add the Microsoft.AspNetCore.Authorization namespace to your _Imports.razor file as in Listing 17-18.

Listing 17-18. Using Microsoft.AspNetCore.Authorization

```
@using Microsoft.AspNetCore.Authorization
```

Now apply the Authorize attribute to the FetchData component as in Listing 17-19.

Listing 17-19. Protecting the FetchData Component

```
@page "/fetchdata"
@inject WeatherForecastService weatherService
@attribute [Authorize]
```

Any unauthorized user will now be redirected to the login page when they click the Fetch data link in the navigation menu. I do think it is better to hide the link using the AuthorizeView in the NavMenu component as in Listing 17-20.

Listing 17-20. Hiding the Fetch data Link

```
<div class="@NavMenuCssClass" @onclick="ToggleNavMenu">
  <nav class="flex-column">
    <div class="nav-item px-3">
      <NavLink class="nav-link" href="" Match="NavLinkMatch.All">
        <span class="oi oi-home"
              aria-hidden="true"></span> Home
      </NavLink>
    </div>
    <div class="nav-item px-3">
      <NavLink class="nav-link" href="counter">
        <span class="oi oi-plus"
              aria-hidden="true"></span> Counter
      </NavLink>
    </div>
```

```
<AuthorizeView>
  <Authorized>
    <div class="nav-item px-3">
      <NavLink class="nav-link" href="fetchdata">
        <span class="oi oi-list-rich"
              aria-hidden="true"></span> Fetch data
      </NavLink>
    </div>
  </Authorized>
</AuthorizeView>
    </nav>
</div>
```

Run the solution again. When you're not logged in, the Fetch data link should be hidden, and then when you log in, it will show.

Again, congratulations are in order. You added support for calling a protected API. The next thing we will do is to use roles to protect our API even further.

Using Role-Based Security

Time to add some role-based access control. We can assign role claims to users and then use a role to give certain users access to components and resources, and others will be denied access although they have been authenticated. Here, we will add a component to review the user's claims, and then we will use the user's role to protect it.

Creating the Claims Component

Let us start by adding a route to view the user's claims. Add Listing 17-21 to the _Imports. razor file. This will give us access to the Claim type.

Listing 17-21. Using System.Security.Claims

```
@using System.Security.Claims
```

Now add a new Blazor component called Claims and modify it to match Listing 17-22. Here, we inject the AuthenticationStateProvider which allows us to access the AuthenticationState. In the OnInitializedAsync method, we call the

GetAuthenticationStateAsync method and use it to fill the UserName and UserClaims properties (just like in the previous chapter).

Listing 17-22. Listing the User's Claims

```
@page "/claims"

@inject AuthenticationStateProvider AuthenticationStateProvider

@attribute [Authorize]

<h3>Claims</h3>

<h2>Hi @UserName</h2>

@foreach(var claim in UserClaims)
{
  <p>@claim.Type - @claim.Value</p>
}
@code {
  private IEnumerable<Claim> UserClaims { get; set; }
  private string UserName { get; set; } = "Unknown";

  protected override async Task OnInitializedAsync()
  {
    AuthenticationState authState =
      await AuthenticationStateProvider.GetAuthenticationStateAsync();

    if (authState is not null)
    {
      UserName = authState.User.Identity.Name;
      UserClaims = authState.User.Claims;
    }
  }
}
```

Now add a new navigation link to the NavMenu component as in Listing 17-23. We only give access to users that have been authenticated, so we wrap this inside an AuthorizeView we added before to protect the Fetch data link.

Listing 17-23. Adding the Claims Link to the NavMenu

```
<AuthorizeView>
  <Authorized>
    <div class="nav-item px-3">
      <NavLink class="nav-link" href="fetchdata">
        <span class="oi oi-list-rich"
              aria-hidden="true"></span> Fetch data
      </NavLink>
    </div>
    <div class="nav-item px-3">
      <NavLink class="nav-link" href="claims">
        <span class="oi oi-list-rich"
              aria-hidden="true"></span> Claims
      </NavLink>
    </div>
  </Authorized>
</AuthorizeView>
```

Run your solution (IdentityProvider, WeatherServices, and Blazor.Wasm. OpenIdConnect). After logging in with peter@u2u.be, you should see the user's claims as in Figure 17-5.

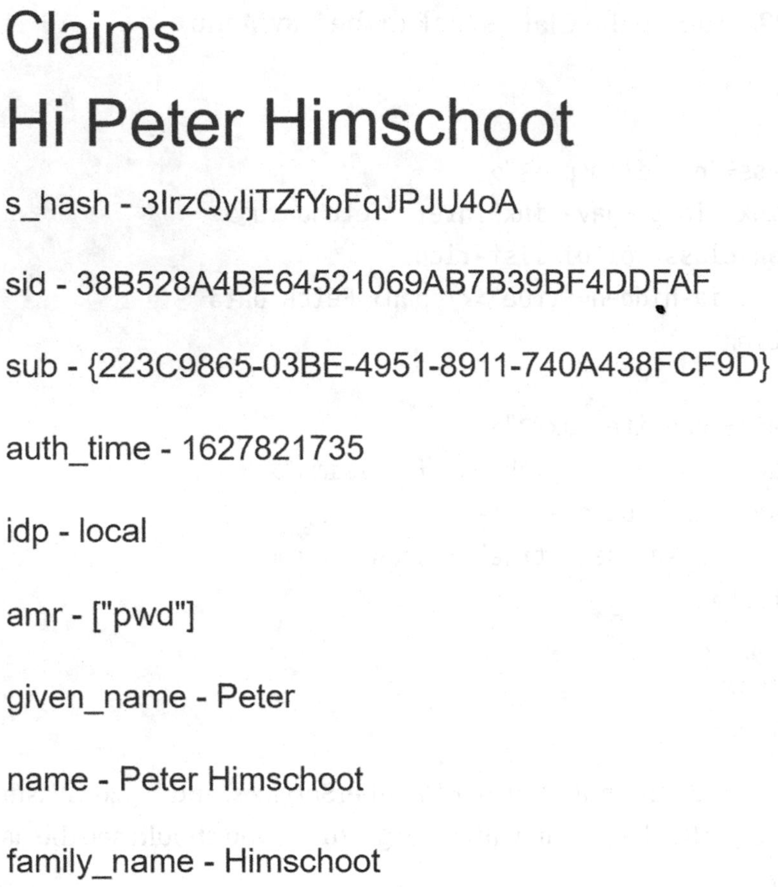

Claims

Hi Peter Himschoot

s_hash - 3IrzQyIjTZfYpFqJPJU4oA

sid - 38B528A4BE64521069AB7B39BF4DDFAF

sub - {223C9865-03BE-4951-8911-740A438FCF9D}

auth_time - 1627821735

idp - local

amr - ["pwd"]

given_name - Peter

name - Peter Himschoot

family_name - Himschoot

Figure 17-5. *The User's Claims*

Hmm. No roles claim. Let us fix this.

Enabling RBAC

Let us first look at the IdentityProvider project's `Config.GetClients` method. As you can see, this client does not have the roles scope in the `AllowedScopes` property. Add it as in Listing 17-24.

Listing 17-24. Adding the Roles Scopes to the Client

```
new Client
{
  ClientName = "BlazorWasm",
  ...
```

```
AllowedScopes = {
  IdentityServerConstants.StandardScopes.OpenId,
  IdentityServerConstants.StandardScopes.Profile,
  "u2uApi",
  "roles",
}
// RequireConsent = true
}
```

Our client should also require the roles scope, so update the appsettings.json from the Blazor.Wasm.OpenIdConnect project as in Listing 17-25.

Listing 17-25. Updating the appsettings.json File

```
{
  "oidc": {
    "Authority": "https://localhost:5011/",
    "ClientId": "BlazorWasm",
    "ResponseType": "code",
    "DefaultScopes": [
      "openid",
      "profile",
      "u2uApi",
      "roles"
    ],
    "PostLogoutRedirectUri": "authentication/logout-callback",
    "RedirectUri": "authentication/login-callback"
  }
}
```

Run again. Now you should see the role claim (if not, try logging out and then log in again since the claims are stored in a cookie and you need to refresh that cookie).

Viewing a user's claims should only be possible for people who have sufficient rights to do so, so let us protect the Claims route so only users with an admin role can see it. This is quite simple: update the Authorize attribute to include the admin role as in Listing 17-26.

Listing 17-26. Requiring the Admin Role

```
@attribute [Authorize(Roles = "admin")]
```

Run again. However, you will not be allowed to access the Claims component as shown in Figure 17-6. Why?

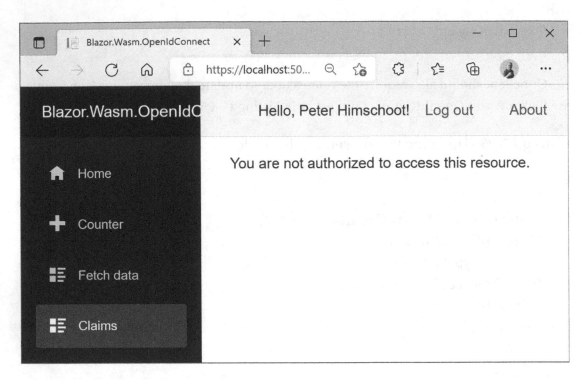

Figure 17-6. *Unauthorized User*

Promoting the Role Claim

Which claim represents the user's role? Using claims is very flexible, so you could use any claim. That is why we need to tell the OIDC middleware which claim represents the role, so in the Blazor project, we need to set the userOptions.RoleClaim property as in Listing 17-27.

Listing 17-27. Specifying the Role Claim

```
builder.Services.AddOidcAuthentication(options =>
{
  builder.Configuration.Bind("oidc", options.ProviderOptions);
```

```
// Explain which claim contains the roles of the user
options.UserOptions.RoleClaim = "role";
});
```

Run again. Log in with peter@u2u.be who has the admin role. You should be able to see the Claims route. Log in again with student@u2u.be, and you will see the unauthorized message. Maybe we should hide the Claims link when the user is not an admin? Update the NavMenu component by wrapping the claims NavLink with a <AuthorizeView Roles="admin"> as in Listing 17-28 which should take care of that.

Listing 17-28. Using AuthorizeView with Roles

```
<div class="@NavMenuCssClass" @onclick="ToggleNavMenu">
  <nav class="flex-column">
    <div class="nav-item px-3">
      <NavLink class="nav-link" href="" Match="NavLinkMatch.All">
        <span class="oi oi-home"
              aria-hidden="true"></span> Home
      </NavLink>
    </div>
    <div class="nav-item px-3">
      <NavLink class="nav-link" href="counter">
        <span class="oi oi-plus"
              aria-hidden="true"></span> Counter
      </NavLink>
    </div>
    <AuthorizeView>
      <Authorized>
        <div class="nav-item px-3">
          <NavLink class="nav-link" href="fetchdata">
            <span class="oi oi-list-rich"
                  aria-hidden="true"></span> Fetch data
          </NavLink>
        </div>
      </Authorized>
    </AuthorizeView>
    <AuthorizeView Roles="admin">
```

```
    <Authorized>
      <div class="nav-item px-3">
        <NavLink class="nav-link" href="claims">
          <span class="oi oi-list-rich"
                aria-hidden="true"></span> Claims
        </NavLink>
      </div>
    </Authorized>
  </AuthorizeView>
</nav>
</div>
```

Using Policy-Based Access Control

Let us change our mind a little and decide that forecasts can only be seen by users with the country claim set to Belgium. For this, we will reuse the FromBelgium policy we created in the previous chapter. First, we need to enable the country scope in both the identity provider project and the Blazor project.

Updating Scopes

Update the GetClients method in the IdentityProvider project by adding an additional scope to the AllowedScopes property as in Listing 17-29.

Listing 17-29. Adding the Country Scope to the Identity Provider

```
AllowedScopes = {
  IdentityServerConstants.StandardScopes.OpenId,
  IdentityServerConstants.StandardScopes.Profile,
  "u2uApi",
  "roles",
  "country"
}
```

Update the Blazor project's appsettings.json as in Listing 17-30.

Listing 17-30. Adding the Country Scope to the Blazor Client.

```
{
  "oidc": {
    "Authority": "https://localhost:5011/",
    "ClientId": "BlazorWasm",
    "ResponseType": "code",
    "DefaultScopes": [
      "openid",
      "profile",
      "u2uApi",
      "roles",
      "country"
    ],
    "PostLogoutRedirectUri": "authentication/logout-callback",
    "RedirectUri": "authentication/login-callback",

  }
}
```

If you like, you can run the solution again to verify that you got the country claim.

Adding Policies

Time to add the FromBelgium policy to your Blazor WASM project. Add the
Blazor.Shared.OpenIdConnect project as a project reference to the Blazor.Wasm.
OpenIdConnect project. Then add Listing 17-31 to the end of Program.Main, but before
await builder.Build().RunAsync();. This will enable the FromBelgium policy in our
client project.

Listing 17-31. Enabling Policy Authorization

```
builder.Services.AddAuthorizationCore(options =>
{
  options.AddPolicy(Policies.FromBelgium,
                    Policies.FromBelgiumPolicy());
});
```

Now enable this policy in the WeatherService API. We did most of the work in the previous chapter, so we only need to protect the WeatherForecastController.Get method using the FromBelgium policy as in Listing 17-32.

Listing 17-32. Using a Policy to Protect an API

```
[Authorize(Policy = Policies.FromBelgium)]
public IEnumerable<WeatherForecast> Get()
```

Run your project and log in with peter@u2u.be. You should be able to access the forecasts because this user has the country claim with value Belgium. Now try again with user student@u2u.be whose country claim has a different value. You will get an error. You can review this error by opening the browser's debugger, and on the console tab, just like in Figure 17-7, you should see status code 403 (Forbidden).

```
⊗ ▶ crit:                                           blazor.webassembly.js:1
   Microsoft.AspNetCore.Components.WebAssembly.Rendering.WebAssemblyRenderer[100]
        Unhandled exception rendering component: Response status code does not
   indicate success: 403 (Forbidden).
   System.Net.Http.HttpRequestException: Response status code does not indicate
   success: 403 (Forbidden).
      at System.Net.Http.HttpResponseMessage.EnsureSuccessStatusCode() in
   System.Net.Http.dll:token 0x6000246+0x8
      at System.Net.Http.Json.HttpClientJsonExtensions.
```

Figure 17-7. *Accessing the API with the Wrong Claims*

Again, we can prevent users from accessing this resource by hiding the Fetch data link in the NavMenu as in Listing 17-33.

Listing 17-33. Hiding the NavLink

```
<AuthorizeView Policy="FromBelgium">
  <Authorized>
    <div class="nav-item px-3">
      <NavLink class="nav-link" href="fetchdata">
        <span class="oi oi-list-rich"
              aria-hidden="true"></span> Fetch data
      </NavLink>
    </div>
  </Authorized>
</AuthorizeView>
```

Summary

In this chapter, we used OpenId Connect to protect a Blazor WebAssembly project. We configured our identity provider for this application and then went on to use authentication. Then we used the `AuthorizationMessageHandler` to attach an access token so we can invoke a protected API. We also used role-based access control and policy-based access control to protect some of our components and resources.

Index

A

Access tokens, 584
AccountOptions class, 576
Actions, 435
AddCookie method, 564
AddLineSegment method, 462
AddOpenIdConnect method, 598
AddSegments method, 461
AddSigningCredentials method, 557
AddSingleton, 206
AddTransient, 207
Ahead-Of-Time (AOT), 535
AngleSharp Diffing library, 345
AnimalSelected method, 187, 189
AnimalSelector component, 190
AppFeature class, 439
ASP.NET application, 568
ASP.NET Core, 233
    PizzasController, 236
    service, 233
    URI, 236
ASP.NET Core MVC, 51
Asynchronous communication, 268
Asynchronous JavaScript and XML (Ajax), 2
Asynchronous methods, 133, 134
Asynchronous re-renders, 343–345
async pattern, 397
Authentication, 547
AuthenticationStateProvider class, 564
Authorization, 547
Authorization Code flow, 605

AuthorizationMessageHandler, 619
AuthorizeView, 620
AuthorizeView templated component, 572
Azure Data Studio, 251

B

Blazor, 51
    browser's memory/circuit, 422
    browser storage, 433
    definition, 421
    local storage, 422–426
    Razor effects, 443–448
    Redux, 434
    server, 426–429, 431
    URL, 432
Blazor application
    hosted application
        deployment models, 536
        Microsoft Azure, 537, 539, 540, 542, 543
        publishing application, 545, 546
        publish profile, 543, 545
    WebAssembly
        base tag, 532, 533
        creating website, 523
        fixing GitHub 404s, 534
        GitHub, 521, 522
        Jekyll, disabling, 533, 534
        simple site, GitHub, 524
        site, 535
        WASM project, 525–529, 531

Blazor bootstrap process, 27

Blazor.Communication.Client project, 264

Blazor.Communication.Shared
    project, 263

Blazor components, 99, 408

  add item, VS, 101, 102

  Alert component, 103

    @ChildContent, 103, 104

    @if, 102

    Index.razor, 104

    <div> element, 102

    RenderFragment, 103

    ToggleAlert method, 104, 105

    VS IntelliSense, 103, 104

  @code, 99

  ComponentBase class, 99

  extensions, 102

  index page, 100

  simple alert, 101

  SurveyPrompt, 100, 101

Blazor error boundaries, 165, 167

Blazor project

  client project

    App component, 29, 30

    div tag, 28

    Index component, 30

    index.html, 28

    <script> element, 28

    main method, 29

  Counter screen, 22

  create project, 18, 19

  dotnet CLI, 17, 18

  Fetch data screen, 22, 23

  home page, 20, 21

  Index component, 21

  layout components, 30, 31

  prerequisites, 13

  run, VSC, 20

  server project

    ASPNETCORE_ENVIRONMENT, 25

    Configure section, 25

    launchSettings.json file, 25, 26

    Middleware, 25

    Program.cs., 24, 25

    UseDeveloperExceptionPage
      Middleware, 25

  shared project, 27

  SPA, 21

  SurveyPrompt, 21

  templates, 16, 17

  VS, 13, 14

  VSC, 15

Blazor routing

  base tag, 368, 369

  hamburger button, 363

  navigation, 366, 368

  NavLink component, 363, 364

  NavMenu component, 361, 362

  Router installation, 360, 361

  Route template, 364–366

  Toggle button, 363

Blazor Server

  benefits/drawbacks, 11, 12

  render tree, 10

  runtime model, 10, 11

Blazor Server application, 489, 562, 611

  API, 615

  login, 614

Blazor Server component, 609

Blazor Server experiment, 213, 214

BlazorWasm, 610

Blazor WebAssembly, 10, 52, 211, 212,
    506, 607

Bootstrap, 103

Bootstrap 4, 70

Browser, 1

Bugs
  coding, 290
  fixing, 289
  integration, 291
  post release, 292
  requirements, 290
  testing, 291
bUnit tests
  Blazor components, 303
  cascading parameters, 325, 327
  component interaction
    Act phase, 310
    Assert phase, 310
    Counter component, 308
    library, 309
    MouseTracker component, 309
    MouseTrackerShould
      class, 309–311
  Counter component, 304
  CounterShould class, 304, 305
  definition, 303
  Find method, 307
  MarkupMatches method, 306, 307
  passing parameters
    compiler, 313
    IntelliSense, 313
    message, 314
    nameof to Pass Property Names,
      314, 315
    string-based programming, 314
    Theory to Test Different Cases,
      313, 314
    TwoWayCounter component,
      311, 312
    TwoWayCounterShould test class,
      312, 313
  razor
    ChildContent, 341, 342

  _Imports.razor file, 339
  MarkupMatches method, 339
  passing parameters, 340, 341
  RCounterShould component, 339
  requirements, 339
  RTemplatedListShould
    component, 342
  writing tests, 339, 340
RenderFragment
  AddChildContent multiple
    times, 319
  Add<ListItem, string>, 325
  Alert component, 317
  AlertShould class, 317, 318
  ChildContent, 318, 319
  Enumerable.Repeat method, 322
  ItemContent parameter, 322, 323
  lambda function, 325
  ListItem component, 324
  RenderFragment<TItem>, 324, 325
  RenderItemsCorrectly method, 324
  TemplatedList component, 320, 321
  TemplatedListShould class, 321, 322
  TwoWayCounter, 319
RenderParagraphCorrectly
    WithInitialZero
    method, 307
semantic comparison, 306, 307
test output, 305–308
two-way data binding/events
  FluentAssertions, 315
  Increment property, 316
  SetParametersAndRender
    method, 316
  testing, 315, 316
and xUnit, 305
ByteString.CopyFrom method, 473

C

Caller property, 459
CascadingAuthentication
    State component, 567
Cascading Properties
    changes, 145
    CustomerEntry component, 145,
        147, 148
    customer parameter, 147, 148
    EditContext property, 147
    EditContext.NotifyField
        Changed method, 146
    InputWatcher class, 146, 147
    two-way data binding, 148
Cascading values and parameters
    ambiguities, 122
    CascadingParameter attribute, 121
    CascadingValue component, 120
    CounterData class, 119, 122
    GrandChild component, 121, 122
    GrandMother component, 120, 121
    INotifyPropertyChanged, 122
C# generics, 159
Changing detection
    add button, 67, 68
    Auto Increment, 68
    Blazor runtime, 69
    currentCount, 68
    discards, 68
    lambda function, 68
    re-render, 68
    StateHasChanged method, 68, 69
    .NET Timer, 69
Child component, 118
Circuit, 208
Claims based security, 547
ClaimsPrincipal instance, 551

Code challenge method, 606
Code First, 239
Code-first migration, 239, 246
Command Line Interface (CLI), 16
Component library, 168
    add components, 169, 170
    create, 168, 169
    refer, 170
    static resources, 172
    using, 170, 172
ComponentMetaData class, 187
Component under test, 305
ConfigurationExtensions class, 487
Configure method, 234, 474
ConfigureServices method, 242, 243, 429,
        459, 489, 503, 554, 564, 589, 592,
        598, 601
ConsoleOrderService class, 286
Content negotiation, 230
Context argument, 157
Context parameter, 157
CORS middleware, 587
CounterLocalStorage component, 424
Cross-Origin Requests, 428
CRUD operations, 229
CultureController class, 502
CultureInfo class, 486
CultureInfo instances, 484
CurrentCount property, 392
CurrentCulture property, 486

D

Database, 197
Database-First, 239
Data binding, 51
    one-way (*see* One-way data binding)
    two-way (*see* Two-way data binding)

Data Transfer Objects (DTO), 70
Debugging client-side Blazor
  VS
    IncrementCount method, 32, 33
    launchSettings.json File, 32
    Locals debugger window, 33
  VSC
    breakepoint, 34, 35
    inspecting variables, 35, 36
    JavaScript Preview Debugger, 34
    WASM Debugging Extension, 34
DeleteClaims method, 579
Dependency injection, 197, 399
  adding, 201
  constructor, 202
  property, 203
Dependency Inversion, 197, 198, 201
  configure, 204
  using, 199
Document Object Model (DOM), 51,
    352, 389
Don't Repeat Yourself (DRY), 300, 319
Dotnet-ef tool, 246, 247
DotNet.invokeMethod, 396
DotNet.invokeMethodAsync function,
    396, 419
DotNetObjectRef, 396, 397
drawLine method, 455
Dumb and Smart Components, 382
DynamicComponent component, 182, 187
Dynamic page, 351

E

EcmaScript, 2
Eich, B., 351
ElementReference, 393
Entities, 239

Entity Framework Core (EF), 238
  code-first migration, 246, 247, 249
  database connection, 244
  generate database, 250–252
Event handling
  arguments, 57
  data binding, 57
  IncrementCount() method, 57
Extension methods, 270

F

Factory, 375
Fake implementations
  dependencies
    fake objects, 330, 331
    FetchData component, 328, 329
    FetchDataShould class, 329
    output, 330
    runtime, 329
  mock
    Assert phase, 333
    definition, 333
    dummies, 333
    FetchData component, 334
    FetchDataShould class, 335
    ILogger, 334, 335
    IWeatherService, 336
    MOQ, 336, 338
    testing, 333, 334
    UseWeatherService, 336
  stubs
    definition, 331
    FetchData component, 332, 333
    IWeatherService, 331, 332
    MOQ, 337
    testing, 331, 332
    UseWeatherService, 332

FetchData component, 155, 161, 264,
    266, 334
FetchDataResultAction, 446
FindFirst method, 551
Flux, 435
Fluxor
    adding action, 441
    Blazor, 438–440
    creating store, 437
    definition, 436
    implementing reducer, 441–443
FocusAsync method, 402
ForAddress method, 477
ForecastGrpcService, 475
Forecasts property, 445
Framework-dependent deployment, 536
FromDateTime method, 473
FromRoute/FromBody attribute, 428

G

Generic type, 153
GetAllSegments method, 458, 461
GetAsync method, 433
GetAuthenticationStateAsync
    method, 622
GetClients method, 556, 587
getContext method, 455
GetForecastAsync method, 475, 592
getForecasts method, 469, 470, 472,
    473, 475
GetFromJsonAsync method, 269, 270
GetIdentityResources method, 556,
    578, 581
GetLocalizationOptions method, 488
GetMeasurementsPage method, 181
GetMenu method, 276
GetPizzas method, 237, 254, 256

GetRequiredService method, 215
GetUsers method, 555
Git, 521
GitHub, 146, 521
Globalization, 484, 506
Global scope, 389
Google Maps, 2
Grid templated component, 155
gRPC, 465
    client project
        enabling client, 477
        ForecastGrpcService, 475, 477
        packages, 475
        updating FetchData
            component, 478
    definition, 465
    IDL, 466
    pros/cons, 465, 466
    protocol buffers, 466
    proto files, network interchange
        installing, 467, 468
        service contract, 469–471
    REST, 479–481
    server implementation, 472–475

H

HandleAsync method, 447
HardCodedMenuService class, 221, 275
HasConversion<string>() method, 241
Hello World, 292
Hot reload, 36
    NET CLI, 36, 37
    VS, 37
HttpClient class, 266, 269
HttpClientJsonExtensions class, 270
HTTP headers, 228, 230
HTTP Status Codes, 229

hubConnection's SendSegments
method, 462
Hybrid flow, 551, 552
Hypertext Transfer Protocol (HTTP),
227, 228

I

IAsyncDisposable interface, 463
Identity provider, 548, 553
access token, 591, 592
adding clients, 556
adding login, 558
API, 587, 588
JWT, 589
IdentityServer4, 553, 557
IDisposable, 133
IIS, 24
IJSInProcessRuntime, 390
IJSRuntime instance, 390, 404
Image property, 473
IncrementCounter method, 431, 442, 443
Init method, 404
InitSegments method, 459, 461
@inject, 203
InsertOrder method, 285
InsertPizza method, 255
Integrated development environments
(IDE), 13
Integration tests, 293
Interface Definition Language (IDL), 466
Internationalization, 483
Internet Information Services (IIS), 536
Inversion-of-Control Container
(IoCC), 202
InvokeAsync<T> method, 390, 404
invokeMethodAsync function, 397, 419
IPrincipal interface, 551

IsLoading property, 445, 446
Isolation frameworks, 336
ItemList component, 508

J

JavaScript, 351, 389
C#
glue functions, 389
Interop, 390–392
.NET IJSRuntime, 390
passing reference, 393–395
Interop, local storage service,
398, 400–402
modules, 403–405
.NET methods, calling, 395–398
JavaScript Object Notation (JSON),
230, 231
jQuery, 51
JSInterop Blazor application, 403
JSInvokable attribute, 395, 419
JSON serialization, 273, 281, 389, 395
JsonSerializerOptions, 273
JSON Web Token (JWT), 549
JSRuntime, 398, 401
Just-In-Time (JIT), 3

K

Kestrel, 24

L

Lambda Functions, 58
Language picker, 500, 501, 505
adding users, 512
MainLayout, 516, 517
markup, 514

Layout components, 352
   configuration
      App.razor, 355, 356
      ErrorLayout, 355, 357
      ErrorLayout.razor.css, 356
      RouteView, 355
   LayoutComponentBase, 352
   MainLayout, 354
   MainLayout.razor, 353
   setting
      _Imports.razor, 358
      @layout, 357, 358
      MainLayoutRight, 357
      reverse, 357, 358
Lazy loading
   assembly
      App.razor, 372, 373
      BlazorWebAssemblyLazyLoad, 371
      dependency injection, 373
      loading, 372
      Navigating UI, 373, 374
      OnNavigate method, 372
      OnNavigateAsync, 372
      runtime error, 372
   dependencies
      FetchData component, 374, 376
      IWeatherServiceFactory, 375–377
      OnNavigate method, 374, 375
      WeatherService class, 375
   libraries, 369–371
Life Cycle Hooks
   asynchronous methods, 133, 134
   cleanup, 133
   IDisposable, 133
   LifeCycle component
      Blazor runtime, 126
      code, 123
      FetchData component, 128
      @implements syntax, 125
      Index component, 127
      markup, 125
      OnParametersSet method, 126, 127
      output, 126
      process, 127
      SetParametersAsync method,
         126, 127
      ShouldRender method, 128
   LifeCycle component
      code, 124, 125
   OnAfterRender method, 132
   OnAfterRenderAsync method, 132
   OnInitialized, 129, 130
   OnInitializedAsync, 129, 130
   OnParametersSet, 130, 131
   OnParametersSetAsync, 130, 131
   SetParametersAsync method, 128, 129
   ShouldRender method, 131, 132
Lifetime dependency, 209
ListView2 component, 164
Loading UI, 278
Locale, 483
Localization, 483
Localized version
   first resource file, 494, 495
   resource lookup, 498, 499
   SurveyPrompt, 496, 497
localizer.GetString method, 493
localStorage service, 405
LocalStorage service, 389, 400
<base/> element, 368

M

MapBox, 409
MapControllers method, 235
Mars Climate Orbiter, 290

MenuService service, 276
MenuService Class, 275, 284
MicrosoftBlazorBook, 522
Microsoft.Extensions.Localization
        namespace, 492
Mock, 333
Mono, 7, 8
MOQ, 336
MSSQLLocalDB database server, 245
Multi-platform App UI (MAUI), 7
MVVM, 105

N

Navigate, 366
NavigationManager, 367
navigationManager.ToAbsoluteUri
        method, 461
NavLink, 363
NavLinkMatch.All, 364
NavLinkMatch.Prefix, 364
NavMenu, 361
Nested layouts
    _Imports.razer, 359
    Index component, 360
    NestedLayout.razor, 359
    style, 359
.NET methods, 13, 485
NonVirtualMeasurements component,
        175, 176
NuGet package, 168, 437
Nullable reference types
    C#
        flag, 45
        Nullable Compiler Option, 44
        project file, 44, 45
        reference, 45, 46
    constructor, 46, 47

libraries, 49
.NET, 43
nullable name, 47
null-forgiving operator, 47, 48
null pointer, 43
person class, 46
Nullable value types, 44
Null forgiving operator, 47

O

Object interaction tests, 334
Object-Relational Mapper, 238
OnAfterRender, 132, 394
OnAfterRenderAsync method,132, 394,
        397, 402, 457
One-way data binding, 53
    attribute binding, 55, 56
    conditional attributes, 56
    Counter page, 54
    Counter.razor, 53
    @currentCount razor, 54
OnInitialiazedAsync, 401
OnInitialized method, 444, 501
OnInitialized, 129, 130
OnInitializedAsync method, 129, 130, 268,
        392, 410, 431, 433, 456, 621
OnModelCreating method, 241, 283
OnParametersSet, 130, 131
OnParametersSetAsync, 130, 131
OpenId method, 556
OpenId Connect, 547, 551
    access tokens, 584
    API, 583
    app component, 567
    Blazor server, 563
    claims, 577
    configure, 564

OpenId Connect (*cont.*)
    id token, 571
    index component, 566
    URI, 568
    URL, 570
    user consent, 561, 562
OrderService class, 286
Outlook Web Access (OWA), 2
Outlook Web Application, 352
Output caching, 351
OwningComponentBase class, 215

P, Q

Parent-child communication
    Blazor runtime, 109
    ComponentBase, 107
    Dismissible, 107
    EventCallback<T>
        InvokeAsync method, 116
        ShowAlert property, 116, 117
        ShowChanged, 115
        Timer component, 116
    StateHasChanged method, 109, 110
    Timer class, 108
    Timer component, 108, 109
    ToggleAlert method, 109, 110
    Two-way data binding
        Alert, 114
        Dismissible class, 111, 112
        Dismissible Show property, 112
        Index page, 110, 111
        messages, 111
        properties, 111
        ShowAlert property, 110
        ShowChanged delegate
          property, 112
        updating UI, 113

Passing parameters in the route, 364
Persistence ignorance, 238
Pig-Wig syntax, 163
PizzaController class, 253
PizzaItem component, 191, 507
PizzaList component, 518
Pizza microservice, 253, 254
    POST, 260
    testing, 257, 258
PizzaPlace
    anchor, 380, 381
    CurrentPizza property, 379
    dependency injection, 378, 379
    dumb component, 382
    Index component, 383, 384
    navigation, 377
    PizzaInfo class, 386
    PizzaInfo component, 385
    PizzaInformation, 382
    PizzaItem component, 382
    PizzaList component, 382
    ShowPizzaInformation, 381, 383
    smart component, 382
    state class, 377
    state singleton instance, 378
PizzaPlace application, 191, 259, 277, 513
    leaflet library, 407
    map component, 409–411, 413
    map JavaScript library, 406
    map provider, register, 409
    map Razor library, 408, 409
    markers, 413, 414, 416–418
PizzaPlace.Client project, 286
PizzaPlace component, 507
PizzaPlaceDbContext class, 241, 282
PizzaPlace into components
    CustomerEntry component
        code, 142

Index component, 144, 145
    markup, 142, 143
disable the Submit button, 148–151
menu, 134
PizzaItem component
    code, 135
    Index component, 135, 136
    parameters, 136
PizzaList component
    Index.razor, 138
    markup, 137
    PizzaItem component, 138
    PizzaList.razor, 136, 137
ShoppingBasket Component
    code, 138, 139
    Index, 141
    markup, 140, 141
    vs. PizzaList component, 141
    tuples, 141
PizzaPlace.Server project, 234
PizzaPlace single-page application
    AddToBasket method
        Add method, 80
        breakpoint, 81
        debugger, 81
        lambda function, 80
        @onclick event handler, 80
        ordering Pizza, 79
        PizzaPlace's menu, 81
    AddToBasket method
        ordering Pizza, 79
    Basket class, 73
    converting values, 78, 79
    Customer class, 72, 73
    customer information
        adding elements, 86, 87
        enter details, 88
        PlaceOrder method, 87, 88

debugging
    DebuggingExtensions class, 88, 89
    showing state, 89
    State change, 89
Menu Class, 72
open-iconic, 70
Pizza Class, 71
PizzaPlace project, 69, 70
Shared project, 74
shopping basket
    current order, 86
    displaying, 81, 82
    GetPizza method, 83
    RemoveAt method, 84
    RemoveFromBasket method, 83, 84
    LINQ Select method, 83
    State class, 85
    tuples, 83
Spiciness Class, 71
State class, 74
UI options class, 73, 74
user interface (UI)
    HTML, 76, 77
    iteration, 77
    menu, 75
    PizzaPlace menu, 76
    using statement, 76
Policy Based Access Control (PBAC),
    595, 596
    adding policies, 629, 630
    update scopes, 628
PostAsJsonAsync extension method, 272
PostLogoutRedirectUris property, 575
POST method, 232
ProductList component, 198, 200
Proof Key for Code Exchange (PKCE),
    605, 606
Protocol Buffers, 466

pure function, 436
PutAsJsonAsync extension method, 272
PUT method, 229

R

Razor
  @code section, 52
  definition, 51
  SurveyPrompt.razor, 52
  Title property, 52
Razor page, 574
Razor Template, 160
Real-time applications, 449
RedirectToLogin component, 567
ReduceFetchDataAction
    method, 446
Redux pattern
  actions, 435
  application, 434, 435
  definition, 434
  reducers, 436
  views, 436
@ref attribute, 394
@ref, 118
Regular expressions, 347
Release To Manufacture (RTM), 12
Remote Procedure Calls (RPC), 465
RenderFragment, 155, 160
RenderFragment<TItem>, 160
Render tree, 9
repeated keyword, 470
Representational State Transfer
    (REST), 227
Role-based access control, 621
  claims, 621
  RBAC, 624, 625
  role claim, 626, 627

Role based access control (RBAC),
    580, 581
Route constraints, 365, 366
Route templates, 360

S

Same-origin policy, 429
Scoped dependency, 208
Scoped lifetime, 217
Scopes, 555
Self-contained deployment, 536
Semantic comparison, 306
  customization
    ignore casing/using, 348
    ignore elements, 346
    razor tests, 346, 347
    regular expression, 347
    simple Card component, 347, 348
    unit test, 348
  strings to compare markup, 346
SendSegments method, 459
Server bootstrap process, 41, 42
Service object, 197
Services, 197, 218, 398
  IMenuService, 219, 221, 222
  ordering pizzas, 223, 224
set/get/delete glue functions, 392
SetAsync method, 433
SetParametersAsync, 128, 129
ShoppingBasket component, 193, 510
ShouldRender, 131, 132
SignalR, 449
  browsers, 450
  client
    cleaning hub connection, 463, 464
    implementation, 461, 462
    notifying hub, 462

definition, 449
hub
    BoardHub class, 458, 459
    configuring server, 459, 460
    methods, 458
    WhiteBoard application, 450–452
        action, 457
        mouse handling logic, 453, 454
        painting segment, 455–457
Single-page applications (SPA), 1, 21,
    351, 352
Single Responsibility Principle, 99
Singleton, 206, 399
Singleton lifetime, 217
Singleton Pattern, 378
Slow network, 267
SQLite connection, 239, 244
SQL Server, 239
Stack-based virtual machine, 5
Startup's Configure method, 460
State, 377
Stateful programming, 421
StateHasChanged, 109, 110, 114, 128
StateManagementWASM application, 422
State verification tests, 332
Static page, 351
StoreInitializer component, 439
Stub, 331
Subject under test (SUT), 295
SubResource Integrity Checking, 408
Success property, 433
Swagger, 385, 586

T

Task.FromResult method, 473
Templated components, 153, 361
Tight-coupling, 198

TItem, 159
Token, 547
Transient, 207
Transient lifetime, 217
Transpiling, 3
Triple A of unit testing, 295
Tuples, 81, 83
Two-way data binding
    add increment, 60
    @bind:event syntax, 62
    binding to events, 61
    @bind syntax, 61
    both directions, 61
    event propagation, 64
        event handlers, 64, 65
        mousemove event, 65
        stopping, 65, 66
    formatting dates, 66
    IncrementCount method, 59, 60
    preventing default actions, 62, 63
@typeparam, 153

U

Unit testing, 197
    automatic/repeatable, 292
    Blazor components
        bUnit, 294
        xUnit, 293, 294
    consistency, 292
    life cycle, development, 292
    run/review
        .NET Core Test Explorer
            extension, 297
        result, 298
        setting, 298
        Test Explorer, 296–298
        test fails, 297

Unit testing (*cont.*)
    VSC, 298
  sanity, 301–303
  slow resources, 292
  test methods, 295, 296
  test pass, 299, 300
  theories, 300
Universal Resource Identifier (URI), 228
UpdateCounter method, 396, 397
UseCors method, 429
UseRequestLocalization method, 490
UseRouting and UseEndpoints
    methods, 429
@using statement, 509
@using WhiteBoard.Client statement, 450

V

Validation, 90
  add annotations, 90
  CSS rules, 96
  CSS styling, 96
  DataAnnotationsValidator
      component, 92
  EditForm, 91
  errors, 94, 95
  feedback
    customized, 97
    invalid class, 96
    modified class, 96
    valid class, 95
    validation-message class, 96
  InputText, 91
  System.ComponentModel.
      Annotations, 90
  ValidationMessage, 93, 94
  ValidationSummary component, 95
Value property, 433, 440

View and View Model
  DismissibleAlert component
    code, 106
    markup, 105, 106
    partial class, 106
  partial class, 105
Virtualization
  add paging, 178, 179
  display rows, 173, 174
  Virtualize component, 177
Virtualize component, 177
VirtualMeasurements component, 181
Visual Studio Code, 168
Visual Studio Code (VSC), 15
Visual Studio (VS), 14

W

Wars
  first browser, 2
  second browser, 3
WASM bootstrap process
  browser's developer tools, 38
  browser's storage, 38, 39
  download size, 40, 41
  index.html File, 37, 38
  .NET runtime, 40
  network log, 39, 40
  Network tab, 40
WeatherForecast class, 264
WeatherForecastController class, 261, 262
WeatherForecastController.Get
    method, 618
WeatherForecastService, 617
Web applications, 24
WebAssembly (WASM), 52
  Blazor
    DOM generation process, 9, 10

IncrementCount method, 9
razor file, 8, 9
render tree, 9
browsers, 6, 7
compilers, 5
definition, 5
execution process, 4
Google Earth, 4, 5
Mono, 7, 8
Windows 2000, 5, 6

WebSockets, 449
Window, 389
Windows Communication Foundation
    (WFC), 466
Windows Presentation Foundation
    (WPF), 122

X, Y, Z

xUnit, 293, 305

Printed in the United States
by Baker & Taylor Publisher Services